m a t t   k i n d t          t y l e r   j e n k i n s

G R A S S  K I N G S ™

# DISCARD

v o l u m e   o n e

BOOM!
STUDIOS

**BOOM! STUDIOS**

**GRASS KINGS Volume One, July 2019.**
Published by BOOM! Studios, a division of
Boom Entertainment, Inc. Grass Kings is ™ &
© 2019 Matt Kindt & Tyler Jenkins. Originally
published in single magazine form as GRASS
KINGS No. 1-6. ™ & © 2017 Matt Kindt & Tyler Jenkins. All rights reserved.
BOOM! Studios™ and the BOOM! Studios logo are trademarks of Boom
Entertainment, Inc., registered in various countries and categories. All characters,
events, and institutions depicted herein are fictional. Any similarity between any
of the names, characters, persons, events, and/or institutions in this publication
to actual names, characters, and persons, whether living or dead, events, and/or
institutions is unintended and purely coincidental. BOOM! Studios does not read
or accept unsolicited submissions of ideas, stories, or artwork.

BOOM! Studios, 5670 Wilshire Boulevard, Suite 400, Los Angeles, CA,
90036-5679. Printed in China. First Printing.

ISBN: 978-1-68415-379-4, eISBN: 978-1-64144-362-3

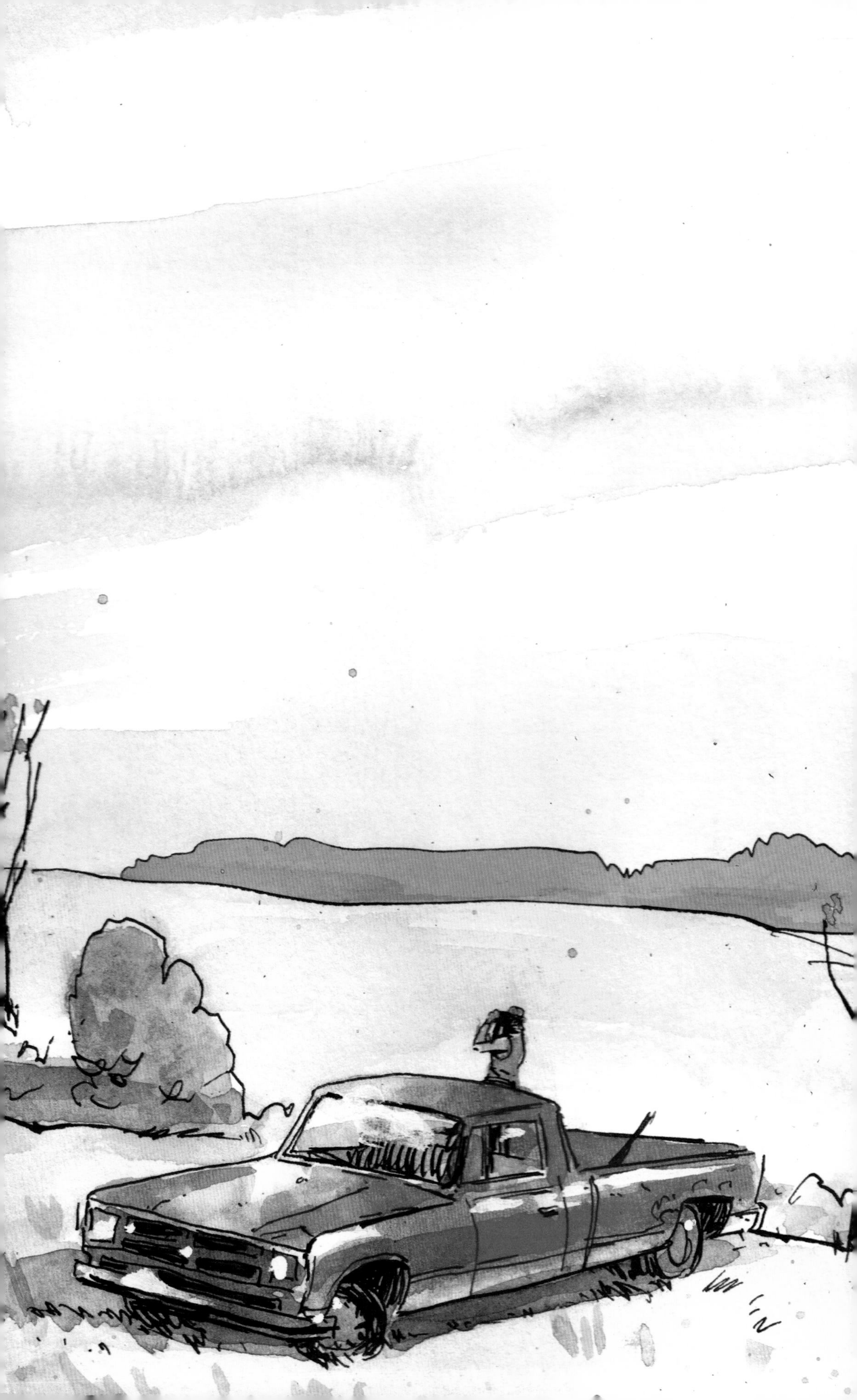

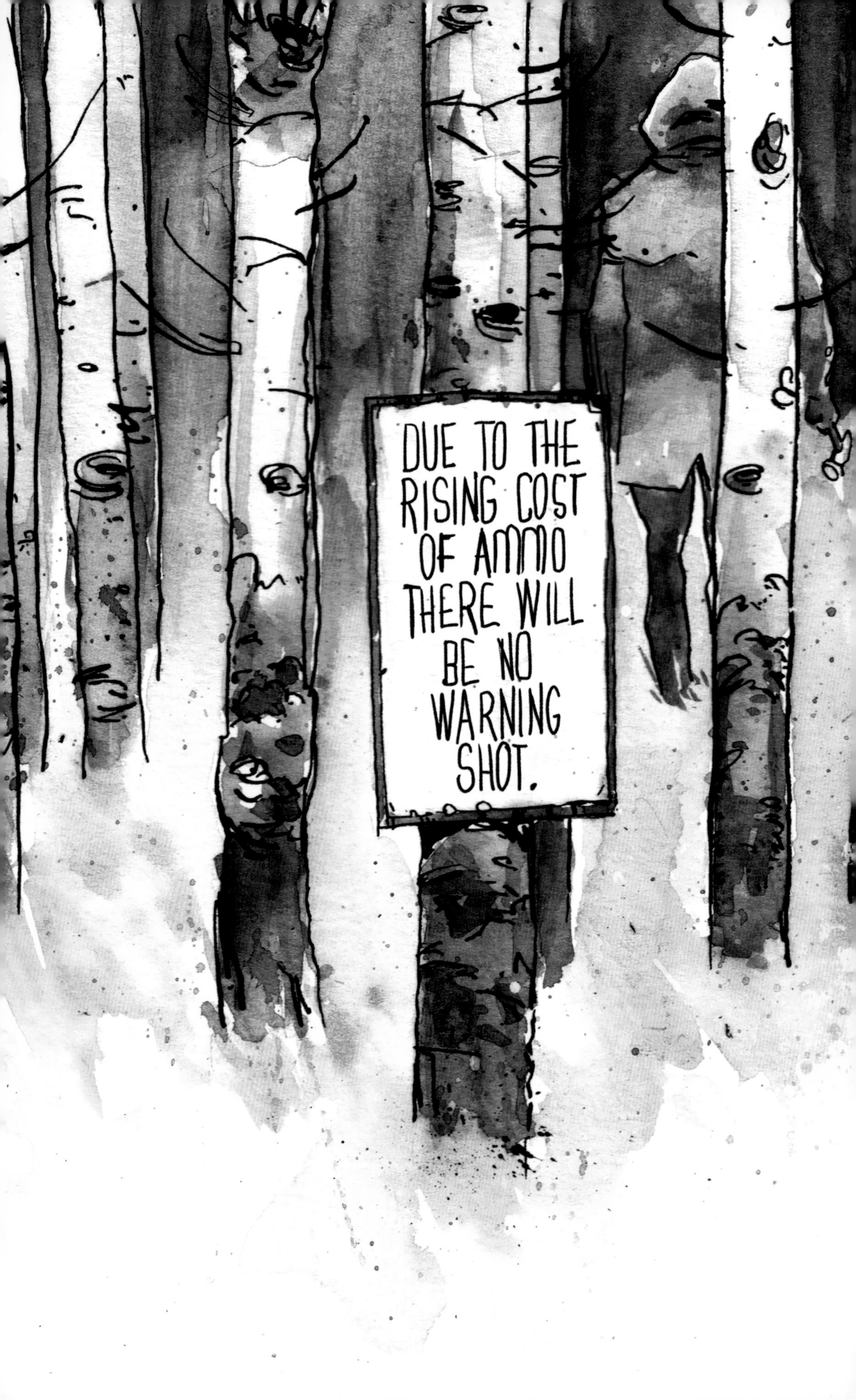
DUE TO THE RISING COST OF AMMO THERE WILL BE NO WARNING SHOT.

# G R A S S ♔ K I N G S ™

created by **matt kindt + tyler jenkins**

written by **matt kindt**
illustrated by **tyler jenkins**
lettered by **jim campbell**
cover by **tyler jenkins**

designers **scott newman + chelsea roberts**
editors **jasmine amiri + eric harburn**

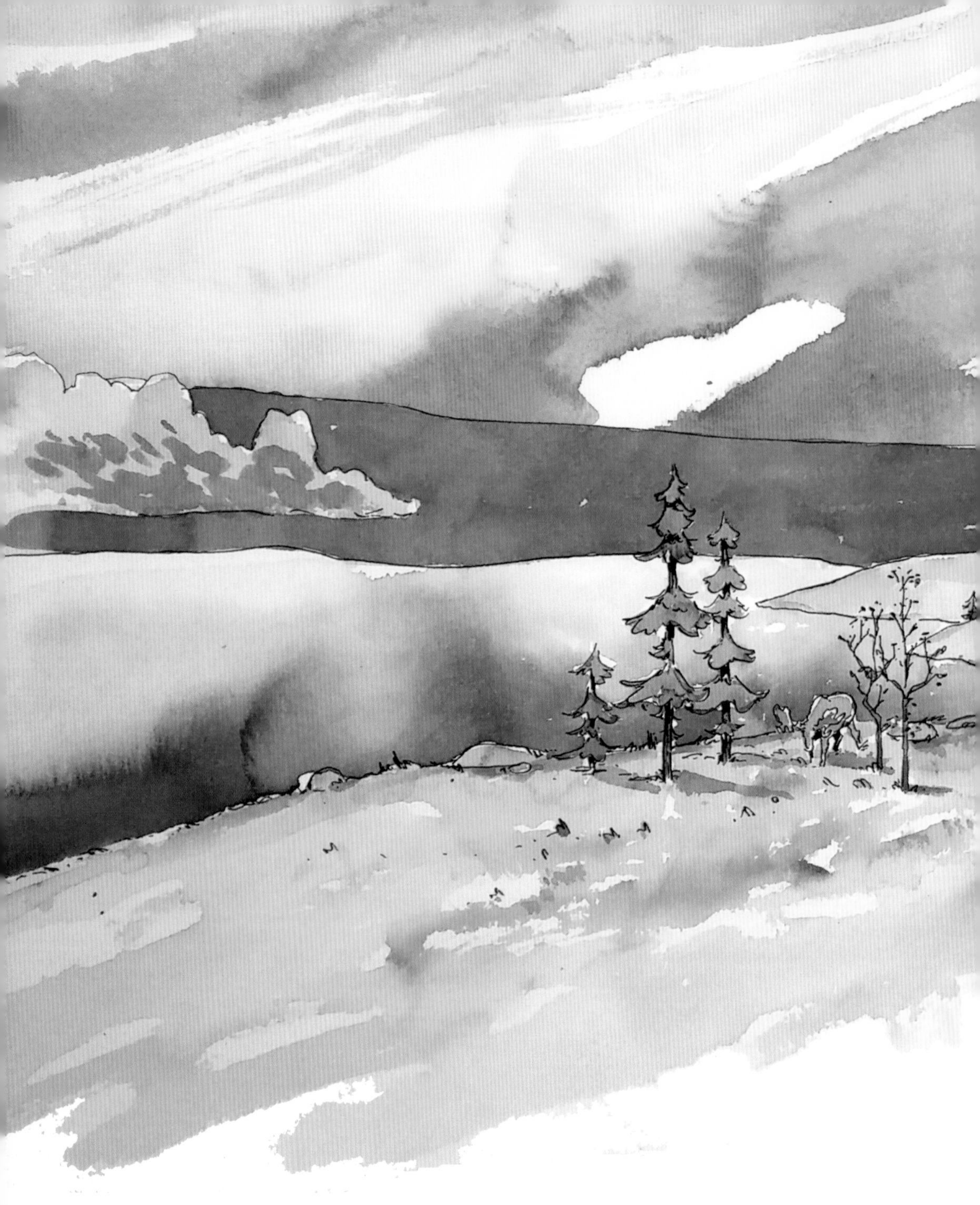

# chapter one

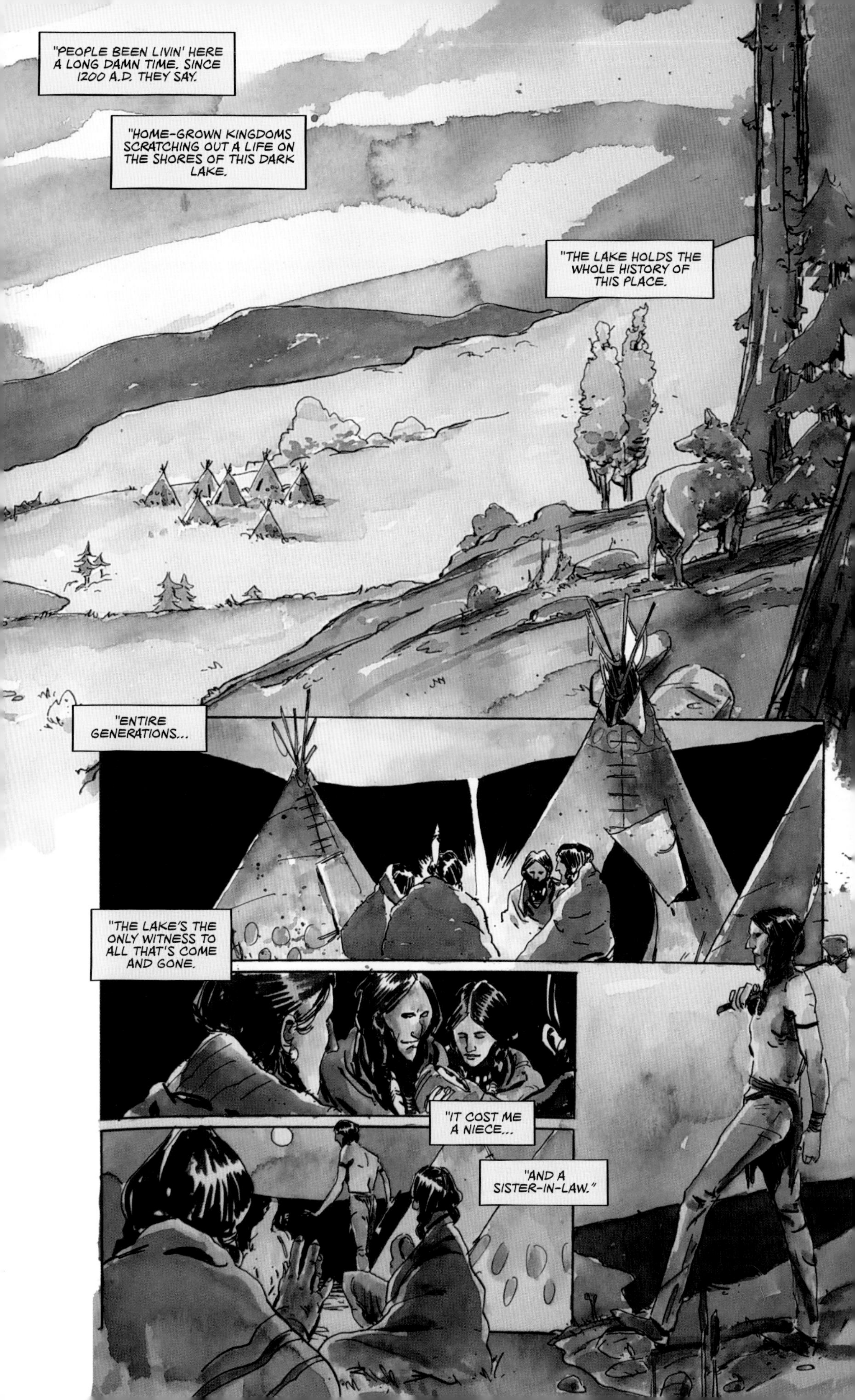
"PEOPLE BEEN LIVIN' HERE A LONG DAMN TIME. SINCE 1200 A.D. THEY SAY.
"HOME-GROWN KINGDOMS SCRATCHING OUT A LIFE ON THE SHORES OF THIS DARK LAKE.
"THE LAKE HOLDS THE WHOLE HISTORY OF THIS PLACE.
"ENTIRE GENERATIONS...
"THE LAKE'S THE ONLY WITNESS TO ALL THAT'S COME AND GONE.
"IT COST ME A NIECE...
"AND A SISTER-IN-LAW."

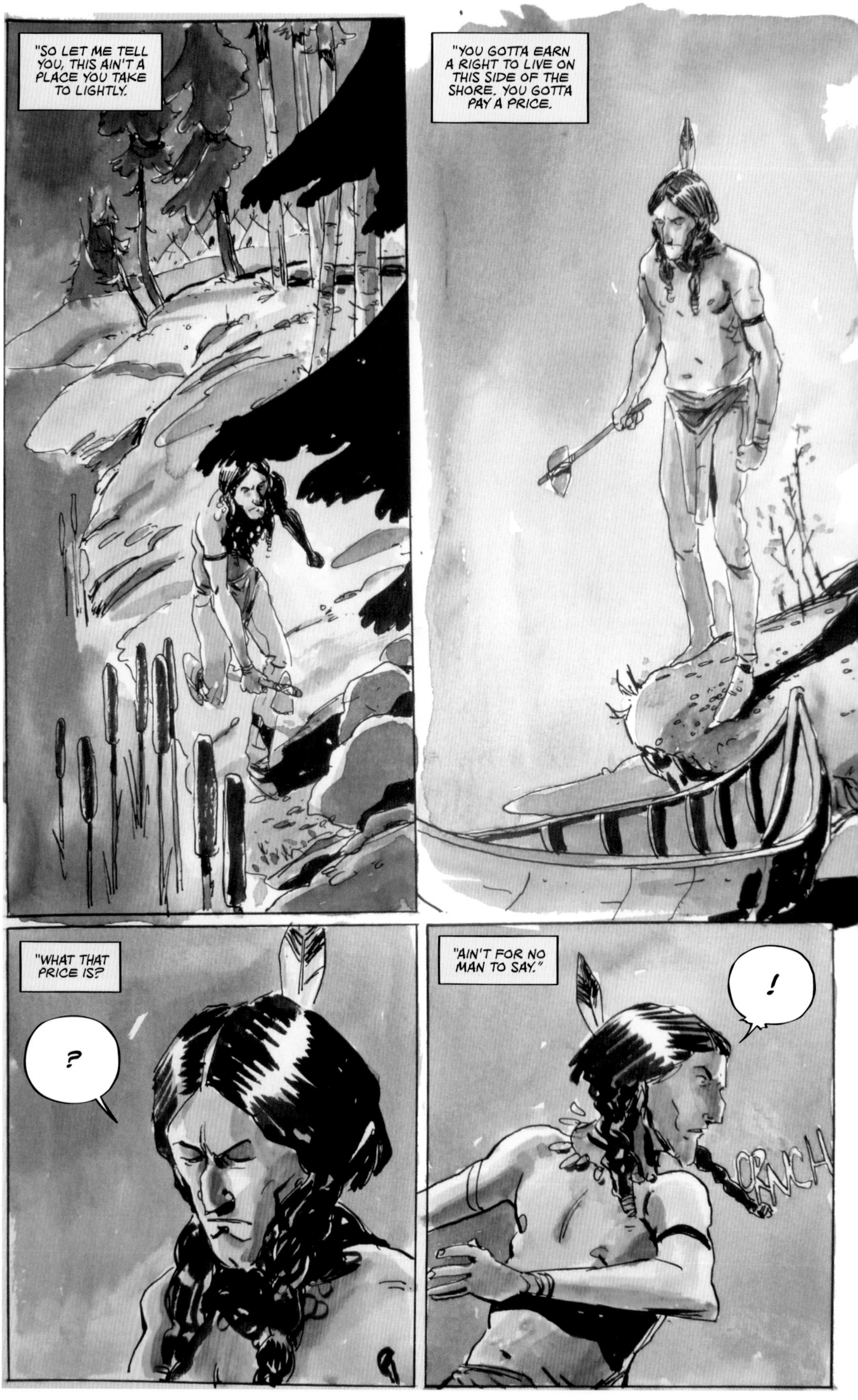
"SO LET ME TELL YOU, THIS AIN'T A PLACE YOU TAKE TO LIGHTLY.
"YOU GOTTA EARN A RIGHT TO LIVE ON THIS SIDE OF THE SHORE. YOU GOTTA PAY A PRICE.
"WHAT THAT PRICE IS?
?
"AIN'T FOR NO MAN TO SAY."
!
CRNCH

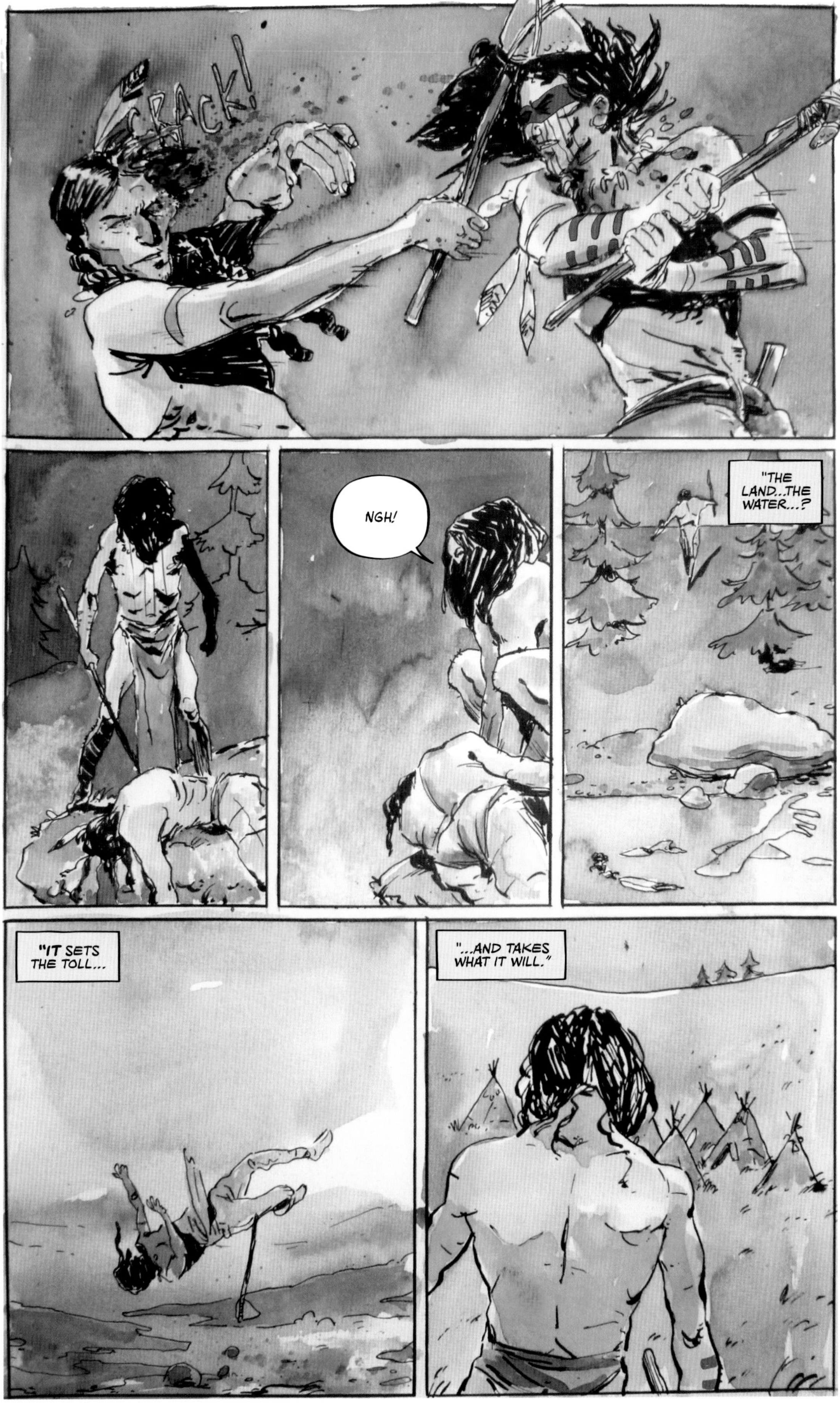
CRACK!
NGH!
"THE LAND..THE WATER...?
"IT SETS THE TOLL...
"...AND TAKES WHAT IT WILL."

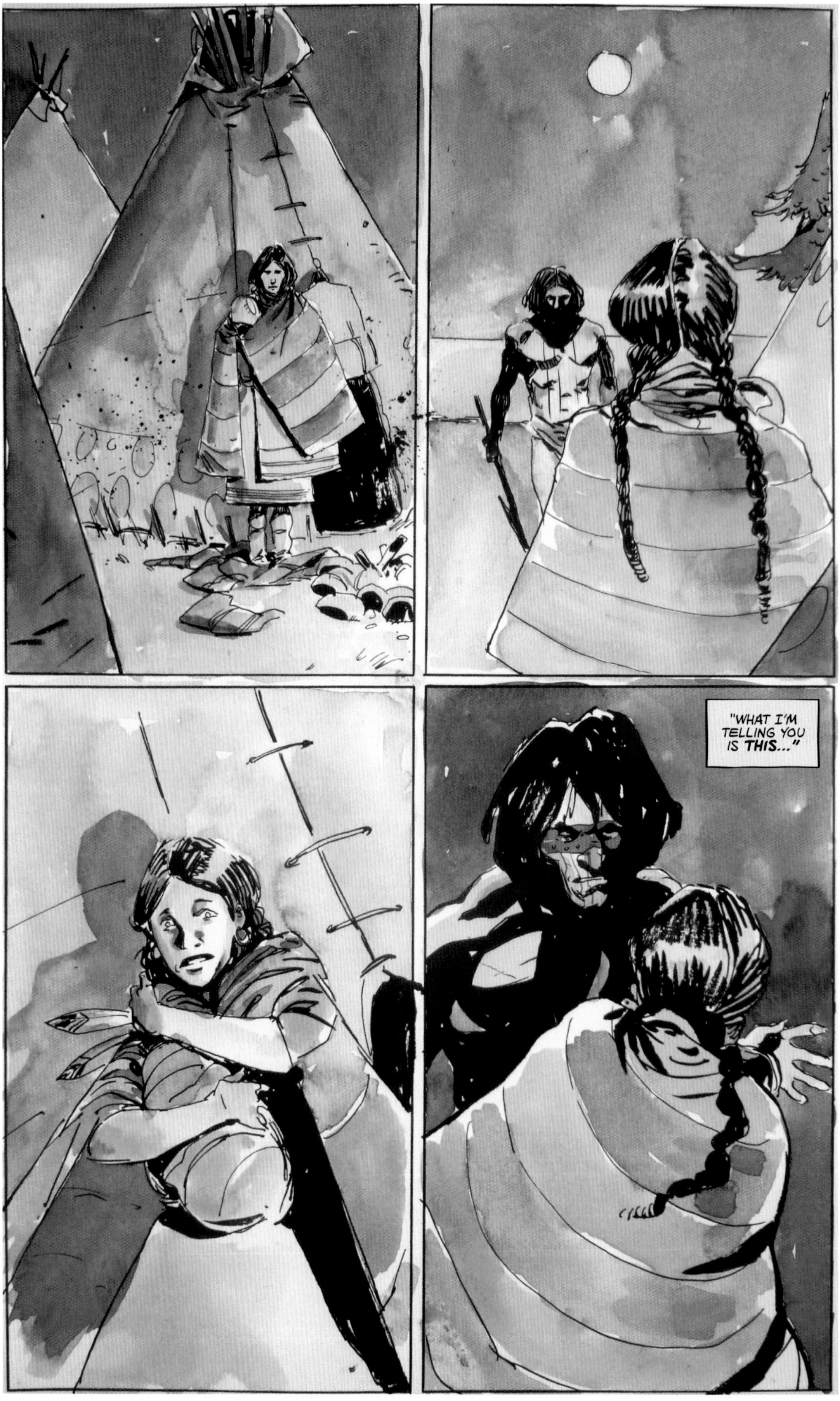
"WHAT I'M TELLING YOU IS THIS..."

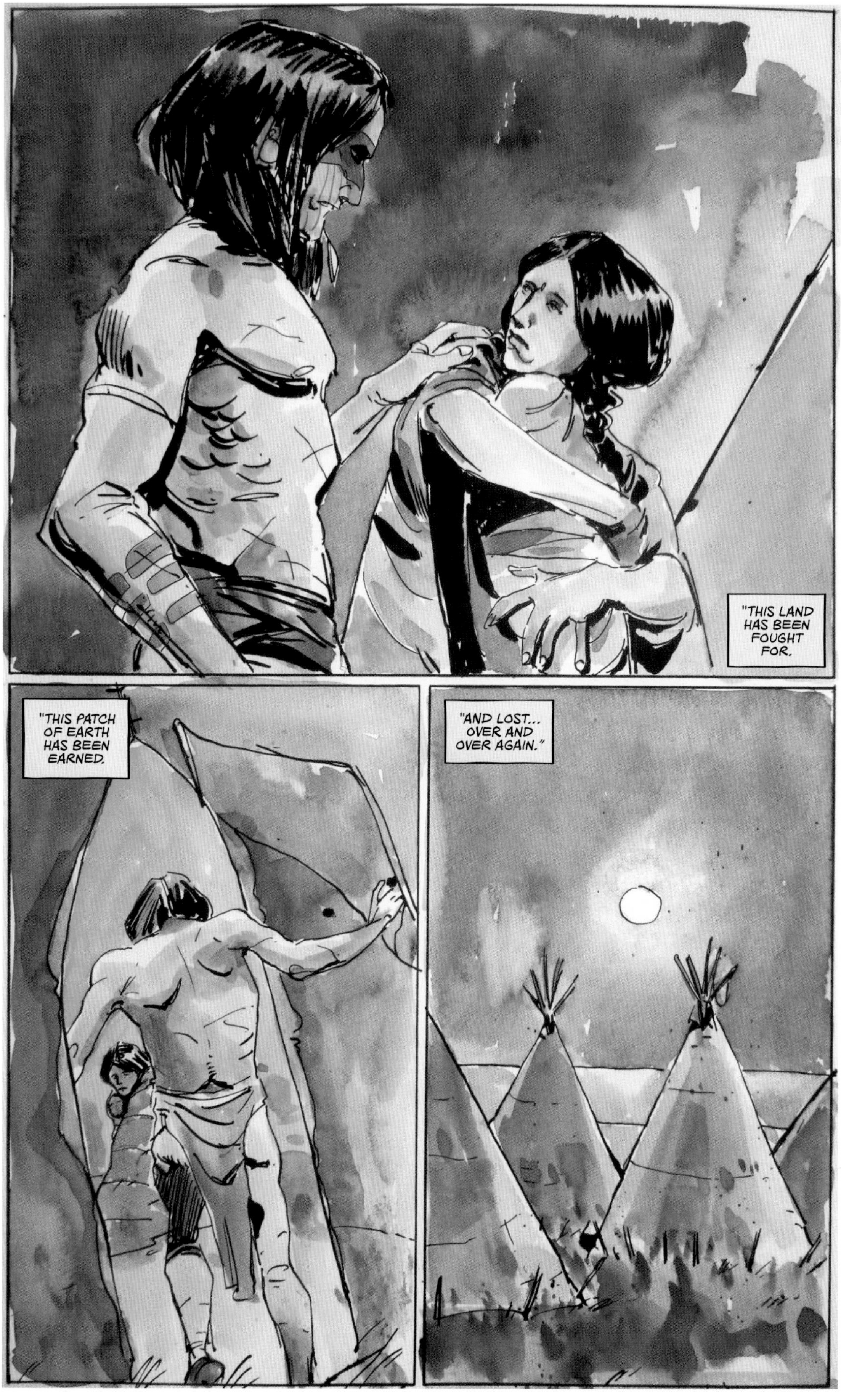
"THIS LAND HAS BEEN FOUGHT FOR.
"THIS PATCH OF EARTH HAS BEEN EARNED.
"AND LOST... OVER AND OVER AGAIN."

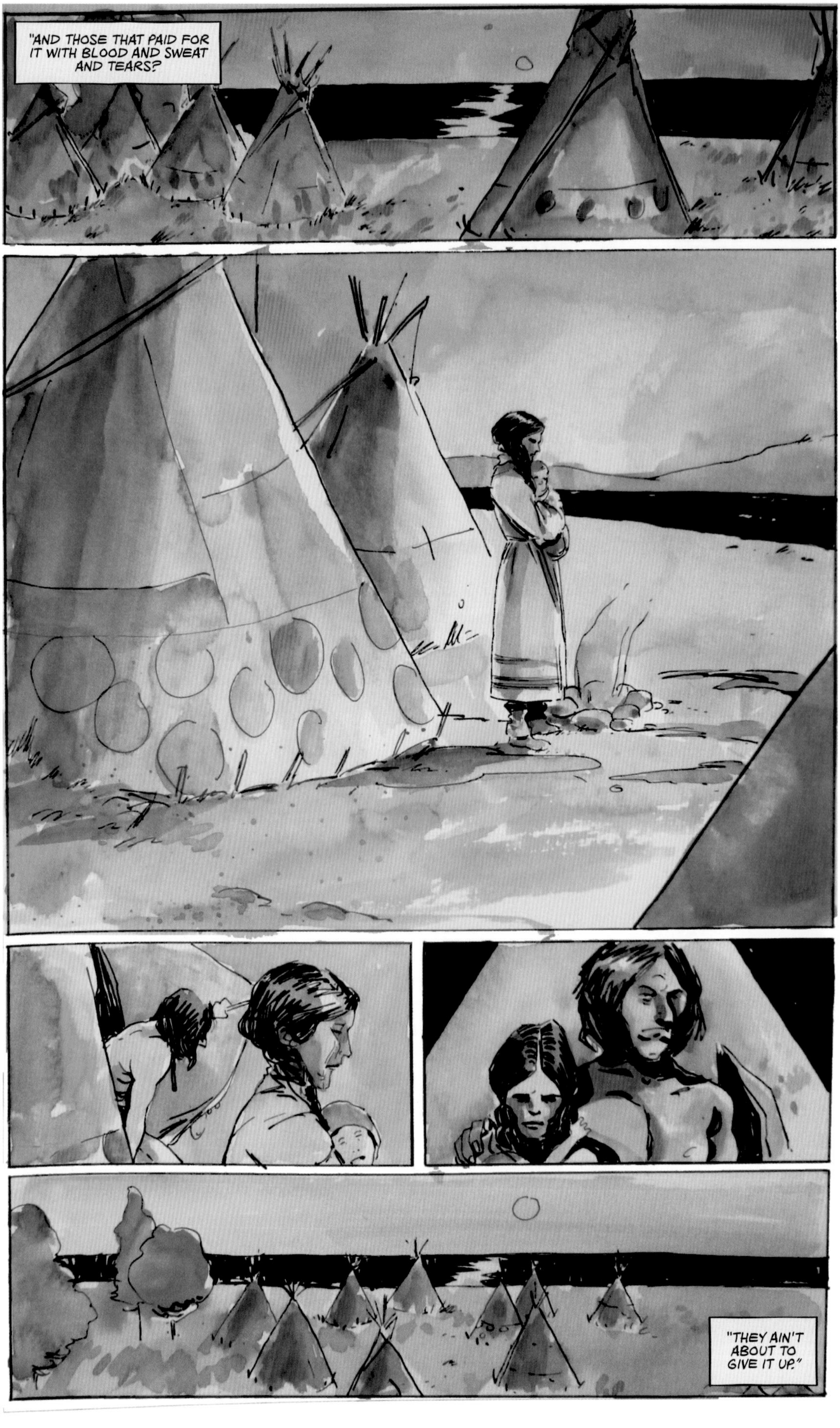
"AND THOSE THAT PAID FOR IT WITH BLOOD AND SWEAT AND TEARS?
"THEY AIN'T ABOUT TO GIVE IT UP."

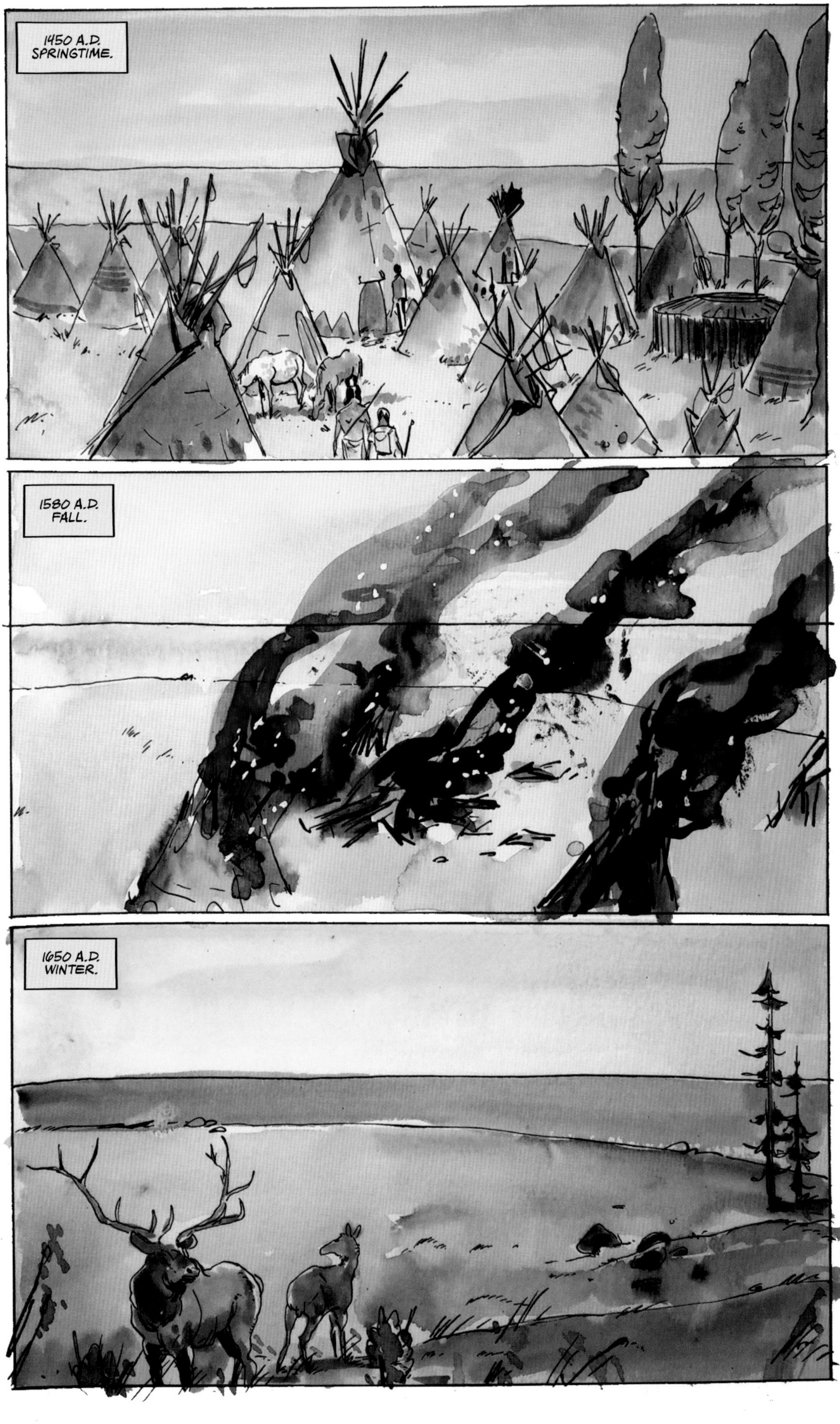
1450 A.D.
SPRINGTIME.
1580 A.D.
FALL.
1650 A.D.
WINTER.

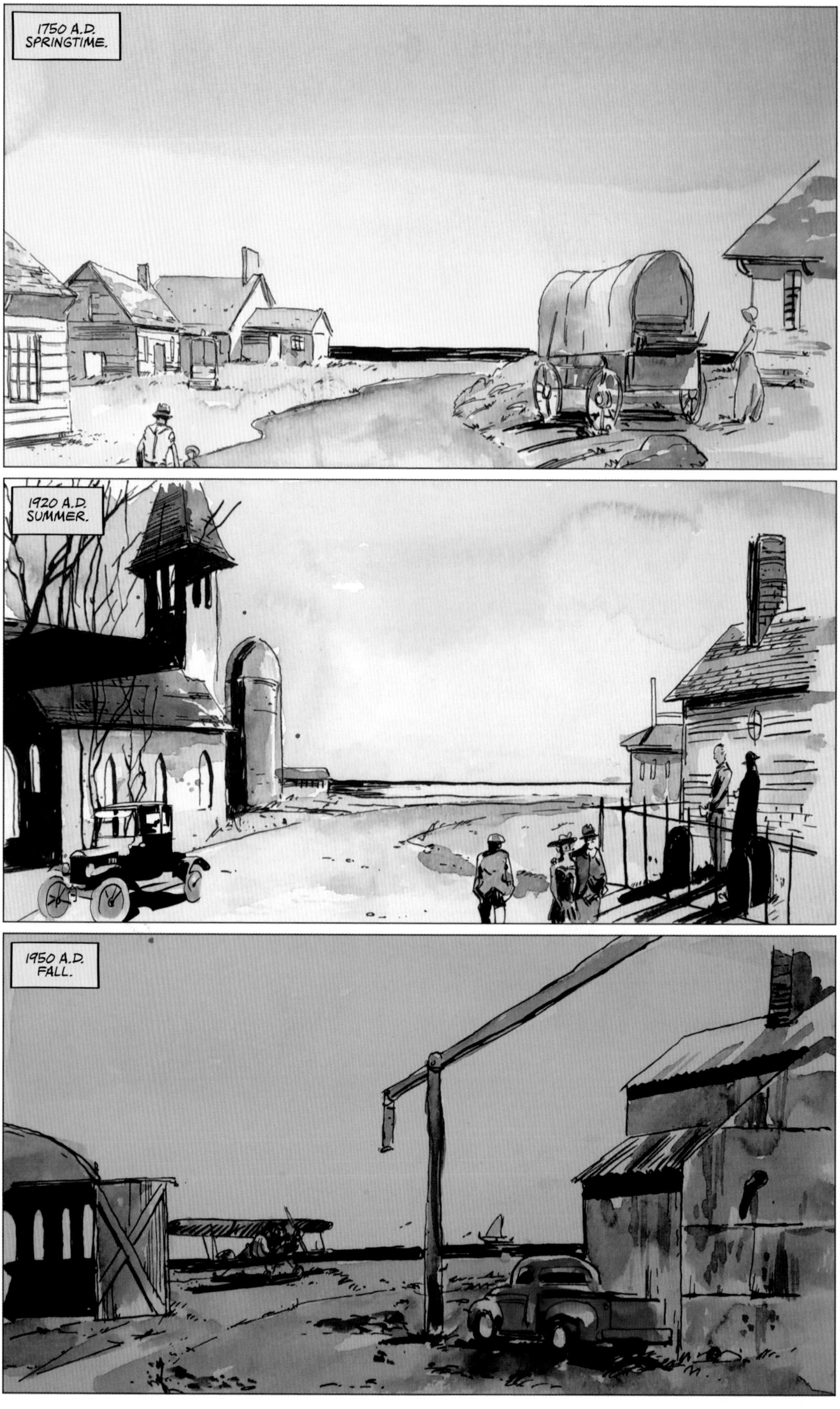
1750 A.D.
SPRINGTIME.
1920 A.D.
SUMMER.
1950 A.D.
FALL.

NOW.

TO MAKE A LONG STORY SHORT. YOU WERE CAUGHT POKING AROUND ON **OUR** LAND AND YOU AIN'T WELCOME.

WE GOT RULES HERE. YOU DON'T STEP ON OUR LAND WITHOUT US SAYIN' YOU CAN.

HA HA! YOU'RE SO FULL OF CRAP.

YOU'RE A BUNCH OF SQUATTERS. SHERIFF IN CARGILL SAYS YER ON THIS LAND ILLEGALLY. AIN'T NO LAW SAYS YOU GOT A RIGHT TO THIS PLACE.

SON...YOU ARE LUCKY I WAS THE ONE FOUND YOU AND NOT MY BROTHER. ROBERT WOULD NOT'A BEEN HALF AS UNDERSTANDING AS I'M ABOUT TO BE.

OUR SHERIFF SAYS YOU AIN'T A REAL LAWMAN. THAT YOU USED TO BE BUT NOW YOU'RE JUST PRETENDIN', TAKIN' ORDERS FROM YOUR LITTLE BROTHER, **ROBERT.** HE THINKS HE'S SOME KINDA **KING.**

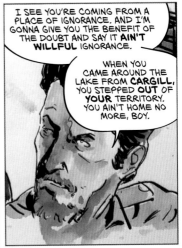

I SEE YOU'RE COMING FROM A PLACE OF IGNORANCE. AND I'M GONNA GIVE YOU THE BENEFIT OF THE DOUBT AND SAY IT **AIN'T WILLFUL** IGNORANCE.

WHEN YOU CAME AROUND THE LAKE FROM **CARGILL,** YOU STEPPED **OUT** OF **YOUR** TERRITORY. YOU AIN'T HOME NO MORE, BOY.

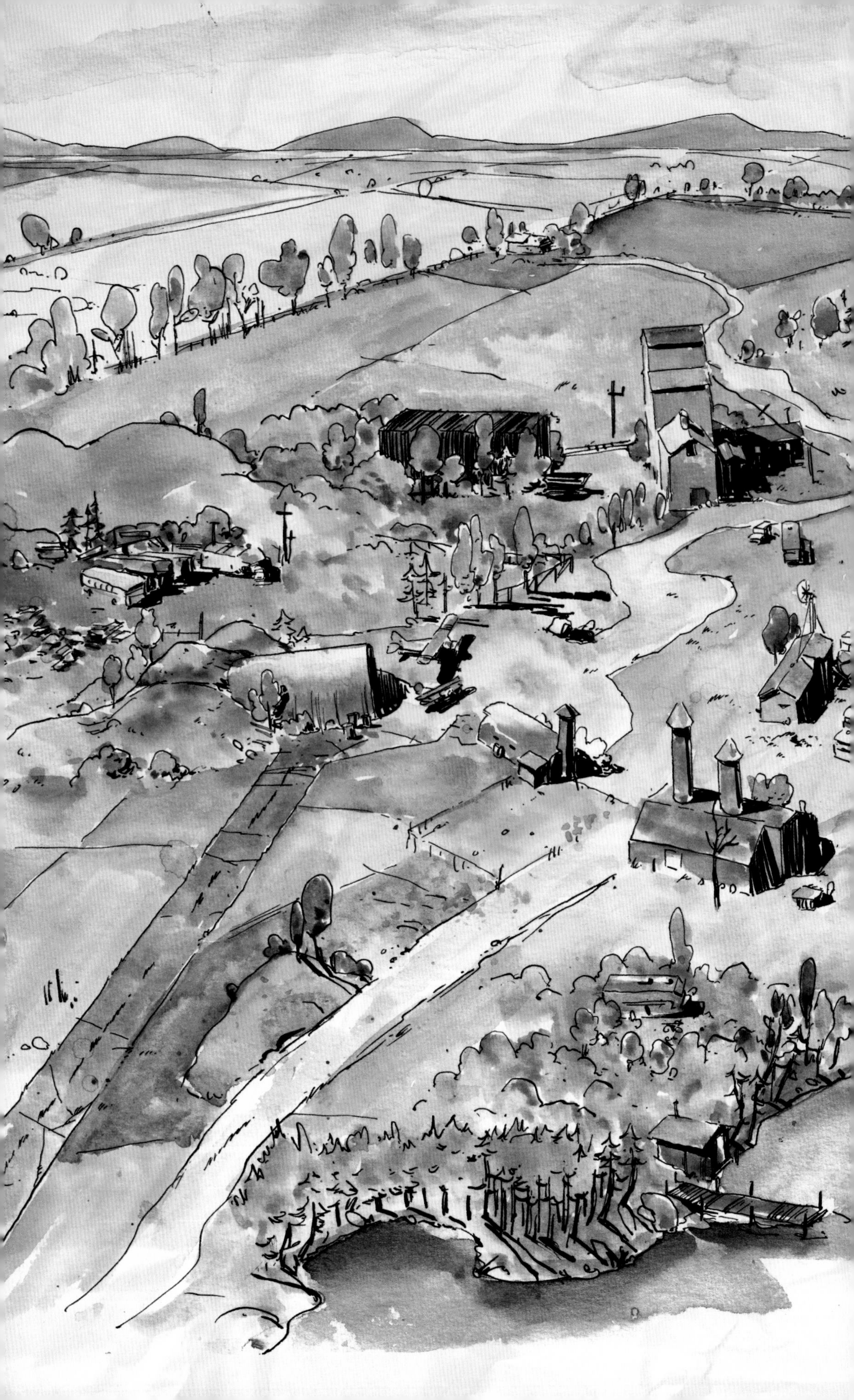

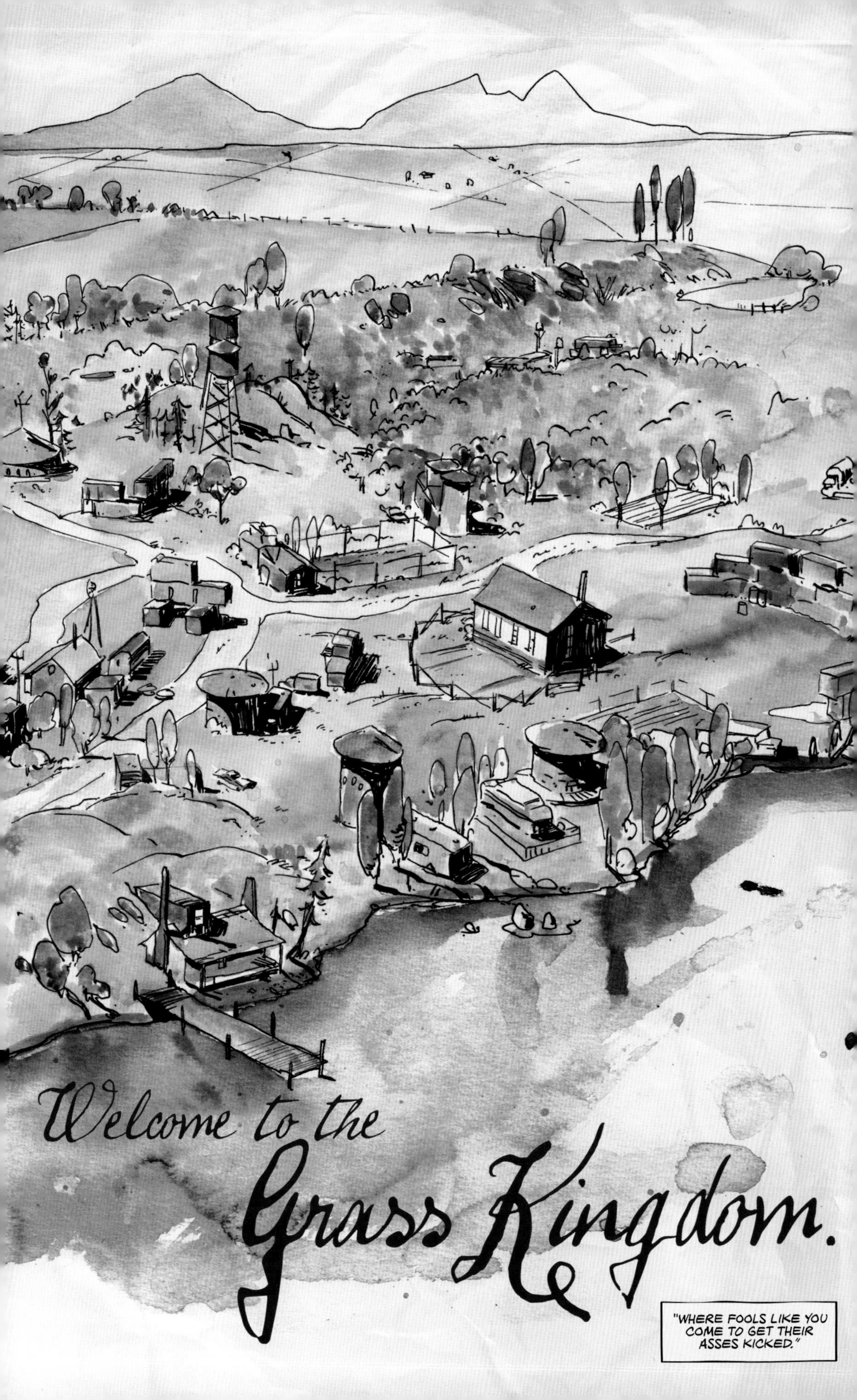
Welcome to the
Grass Kingdom.
"WHERE FOOLS LIKE YOU COME TO GET THEIR ASSES KICKED."

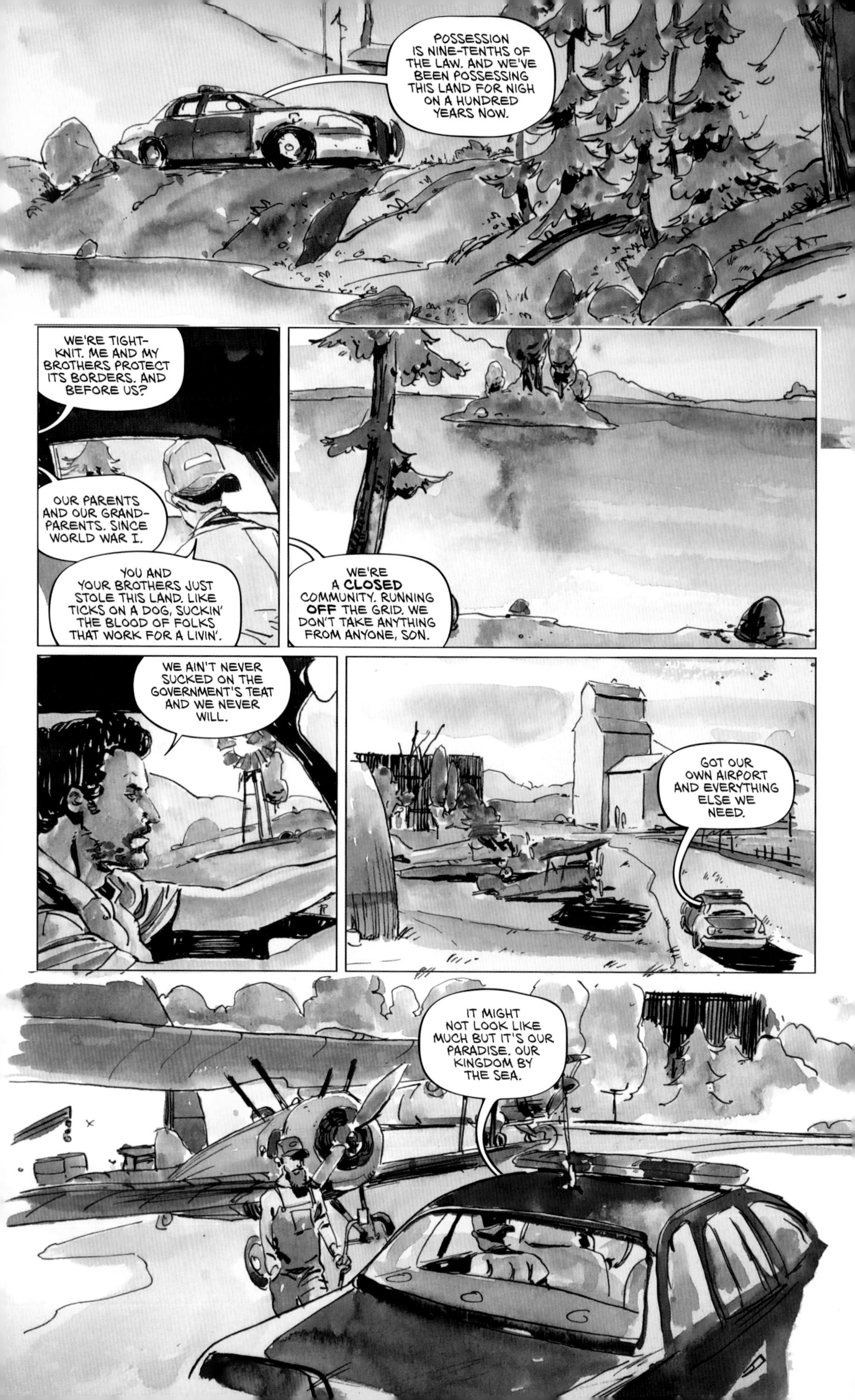

POSSESSION IS NINE-TENTHS OF THE LAW. AND WE'VE BEEN POSSESSING THIS LAND FOR NIGH ON A HUNDRED YEARS NOW.
WE'RE TIGHT-KNIT. ME AND MY BROTHERS PROTECT ITS BORDERS. AND BEFORE US?
OUR PARENTS AND OUR GRAND-PARENTS. SINCE WORLD WAR I.
YOU AND YOUR BROTHERS JUST STOLE THIS LAND. LIKE TICKS ON A DOG, SUCKIN' THE BLOOD OF FOLKS THAT WORK FOR A LIVIN'.
WE'RE A **CLOSED** COMMUNITY. RUNNING **OFF** THE GRID. WE DON'T TAKE ANYTHING FROM ANYONE, SON.
WE AIN'T NEVER SUCKED ON THE GOVERNMENT'S TEAT AND WE NEVER WILL.
GOT OUR OWN AIRPORT AND EVERYTHING ELSE WE NEED.
IT MIGHT NOT LOOK LIKE MUCH BUT IT'S OUR PARADISE. OUR KINGDOM BY THE SEA.

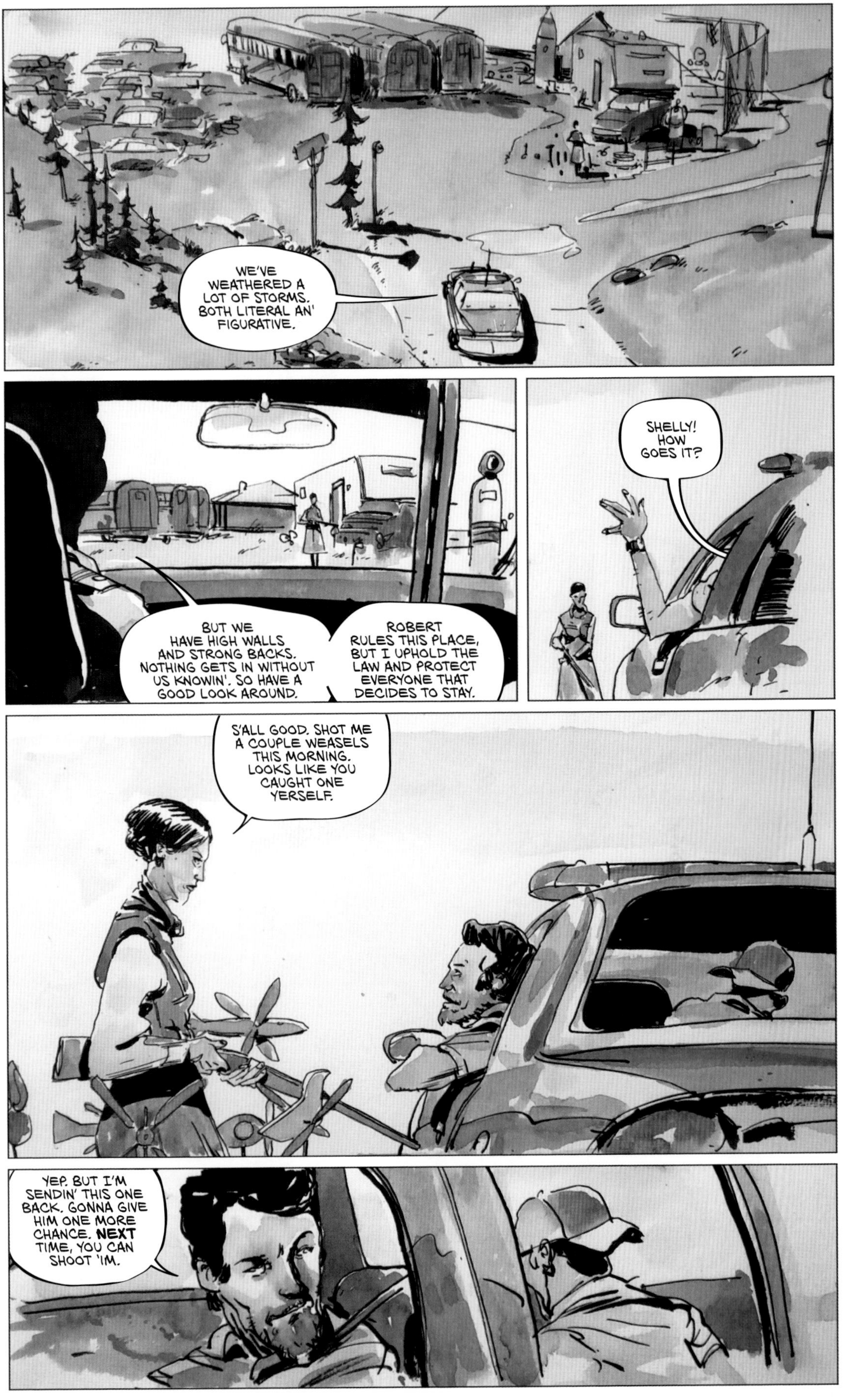

WE'VE WEATHERED A LOT OF STORMS. BOTH LITERAL AN' FIGURATIVE.
BUT WE HAVE HIGH WALLS AND STRONG BACKS. NOTHING GETS IN WITHOUT US KNOWIN'. SO HAVE A GOOD LOOK AROUND.
ROBERT RULES THIS PLACE, BUT I UPHOLD THE LAW AND PROTECT EVERYONE THAT DECIDES TO STAY.
SHELLY! HOW GOES IT?
S'ALL GOOD. SHOT ME A COUPLE WEASELS THIS MORNING. LOOKS LIKE YOU CAUGHT ONE YERSELF.
YEP. BUT I'M SENDIN' THIS ONE BACK. GONNA GIVE HIM ONE MORE CHANCE. **NEXT** TIME, YOU CAN SHOOT 'IM.

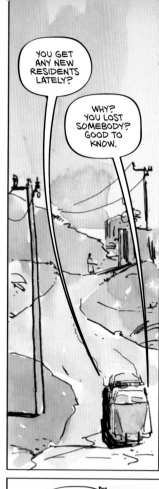

YOU GET ANY NEW RESIDENTS LATELY?

WHY? YOU LOST SOMEBODY? GOOD TO KNOW.

I SEE YOU DOWN THERE, BRUCE. YOU GOT COMPANY?

ARCHIE? HOW GOES IT?

ALL CLEAR. YOU FIND THAT SNAKE THAT SNUCK IN THIS MORNING?

YEP. GIVIN' HIM A RIDE AS WE SPEAK.

WELL, LET HIM KNOW, NEXT TIME I SEE HIM THROUGH MY SCOPE I'M GONNA DROP HIM. ALSO--YOU MIGHT WANNA CHECK ON YOUR BROTHER. ROBERT'S BEEN DRINKIN' AND SMASHIN' THINGS UP AGAIN.

WILL DO, ARCHIE. YOU NEED ANYTHING?

ALL GOOD. TELL PINBALL TO RUN ME UP SOME MORE WATER WHEN HE GETS A CHANCE.

WILL DO.

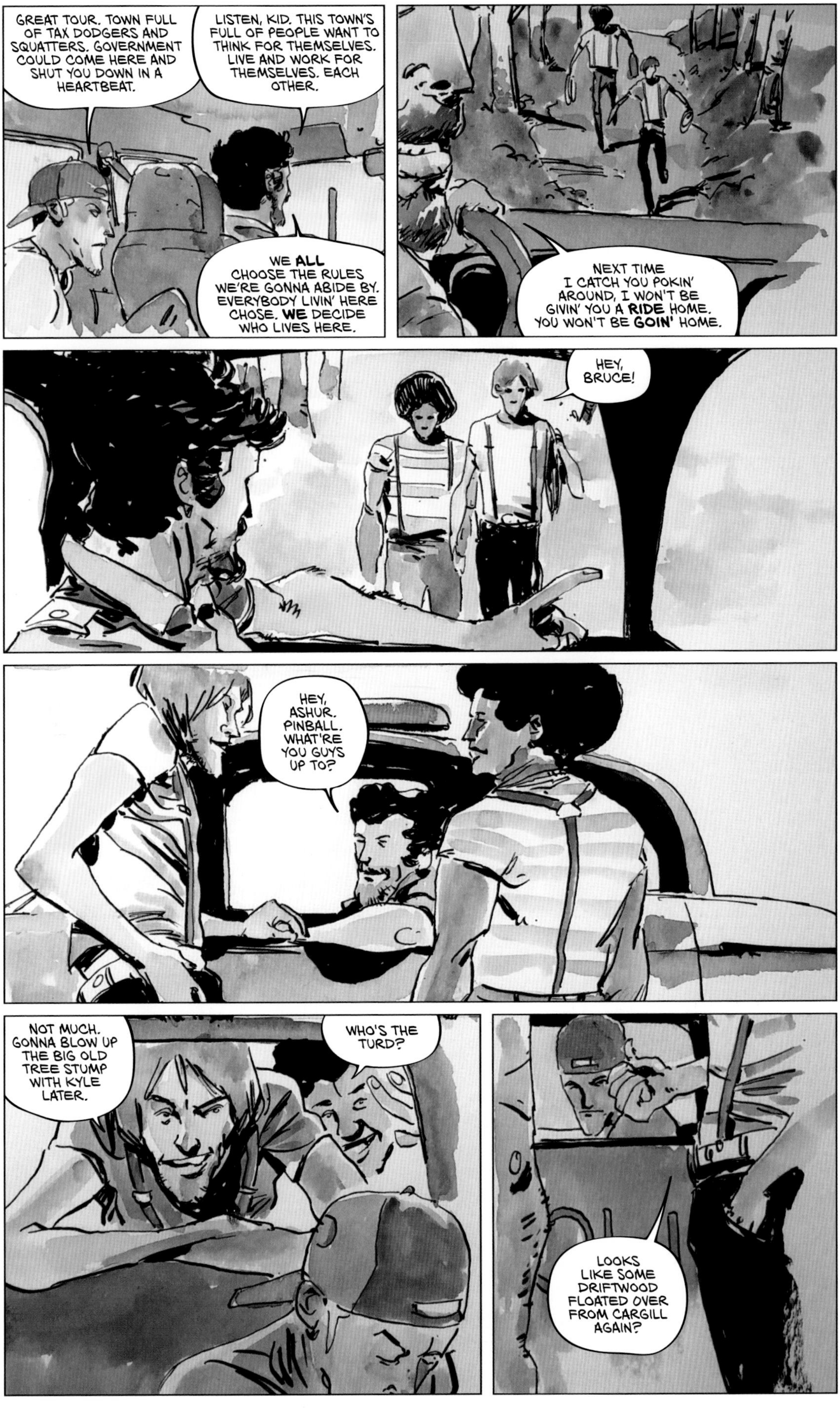
GREAT TOUR. TOWN FULL OF TAX DODGERS AND SQUATTERS. GOVERNMENT COULD COME HERE AND SHUT YOU DOWN IN A HEARTBEAT.
LISTEN, KID. THIS TOWN'S FULL OF PEOPLE WANT TO THINK FOR THEMSELVES. LIVE AND WORK FOR THEMSELVES. EACH OTHER.
WE ALL CHOOSE THE RULES WE'RE GONNA ABIDE BY. EVERYBODY LIVIN' HERE CHOSE. WE DECIDE WHO LIVES HERE.
NEXT TIME I CATCH YOU POKIN' AROUND, I WON'T BE GIVIN' YOU A RIDE HOME. YOU WON'T BE GOIN' HOME.
HEY, BRUCE!
HEY, ASHUR. PINBALL. WHAT'RE YOU GUYS UP TO?
NOT MUCH. GONNA BLOW UP THE BIG OLD TREE STUMP WITH KYLE LATER.
WHO'S THE TURD?
LOOKS LIKE SOME DRIFTWOOD FLOATED OVER FROM CARGILL AGAIN?

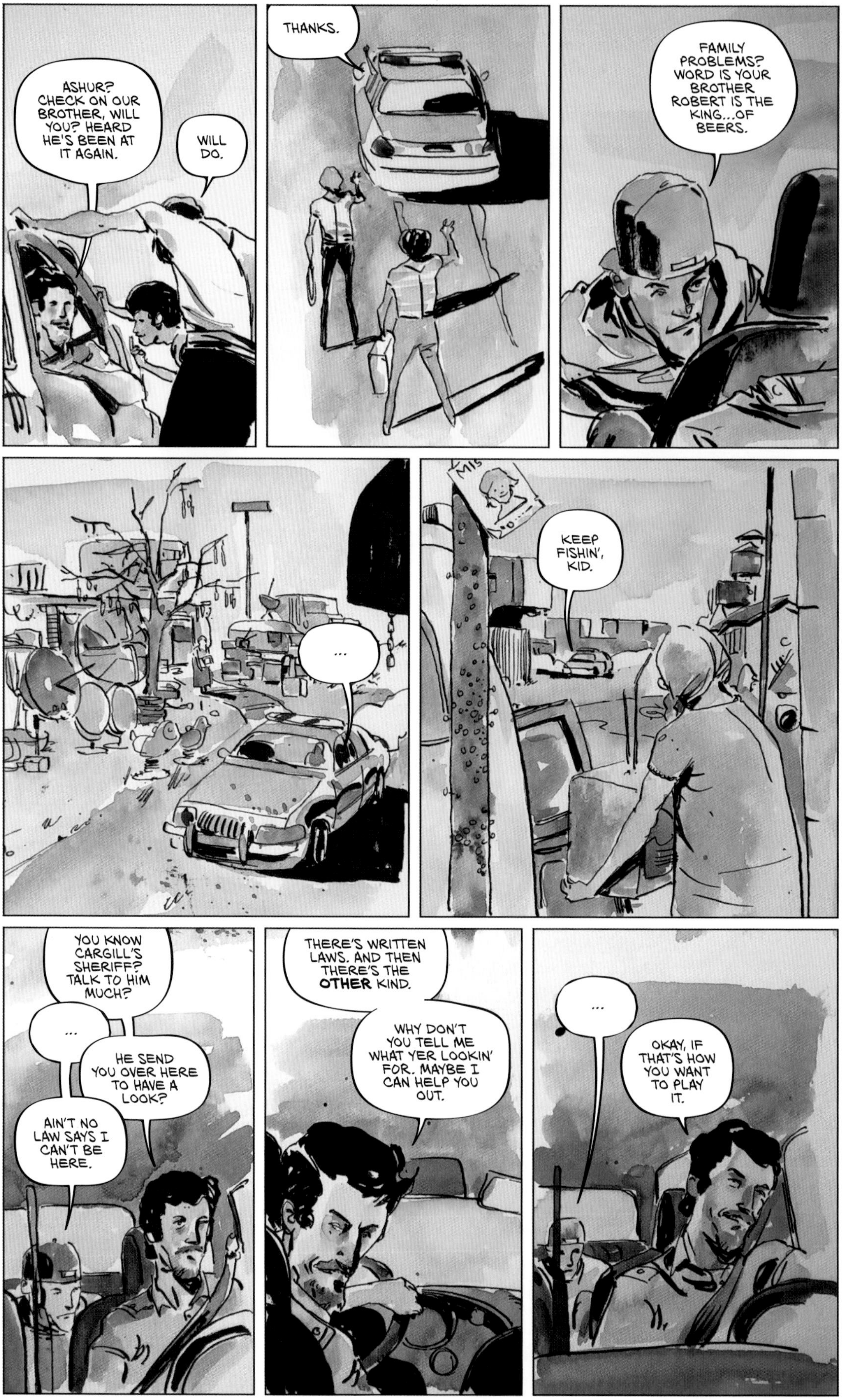
ASHUR? CHECK ON OUR BROTHER, WILL YOU? HEARD HE'S BEEN AT IT AGAIN.
WILL DO.
THANKS.
FAMILY PROBLEMS? WORD IS YOUR BROTHER ROBERT IS THE KING...OF BEERS.
...
KEEP FISHIN', KID.
YOU KNOW CARGILL'S SHERIFF? TALK TO HIM MUCH?
...
HE SEND YOU OVER HERE TO HAVE A LOOK?
AIN'T NO LAW SAYS I CAN'T BE HERE.
THERE'S WRITTEN LAWS. AND THEN THERE'S THE OTHER KIND.
WHY DON'T YOU TELL ME WHAT YER LOOKIN' FOR. MAYBE I CAN HELP YOU OUT.
...
OKAY, IF THAT'S HOW YOU WANT TO PLAY IT.

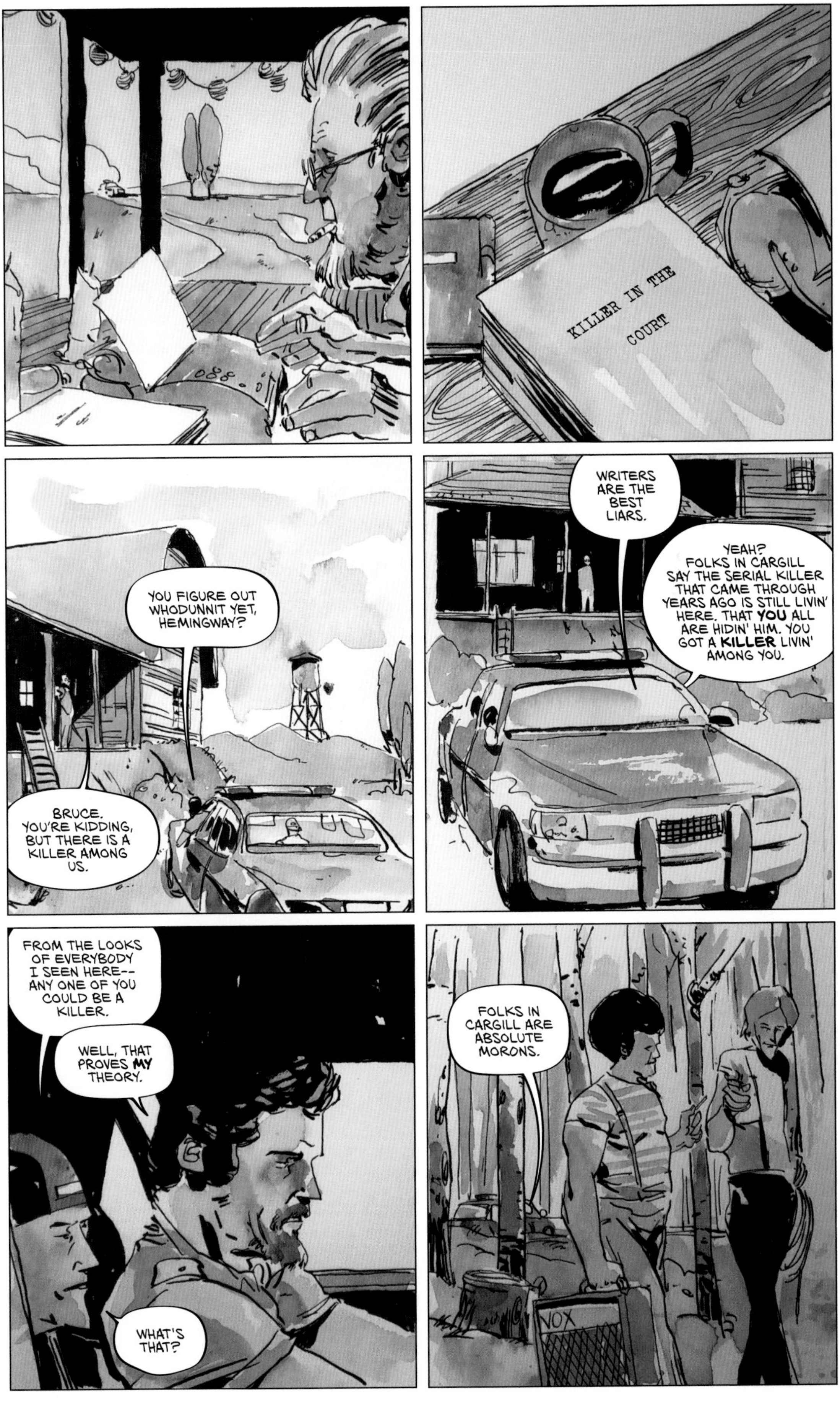
KILLER IN THE
COURT
YOU FIGURE OUT WHODUNNIT YET, HEMINGWAY?
BRUCE. YOU'RE KIDDING, BUT THERE IS A KILLER AMONG US.
WRITERS ARE THE BEST LIARS.
YEAH? FOLKS IN CARGILL SAY THE SERIAL KILLER THAT CAME THROUGH YEARS AGO IS STILL LIVIN' HERE. THAT **YOU** ALL ARE HIDIN' HIM. YOU GOT A **KILLER** LIVIN' AMONG YOU.
FROM THE LOOKS OF EVERYBODY I SEEN HERE-- ANY ONE OF YOU COULD BE A KILLER.
WELL, THAT PROVES **MY** THEORY.
WHAT'S THAT?
FOLKS IN CARGILL ARE ABSOLUTE MORONS.
VOX

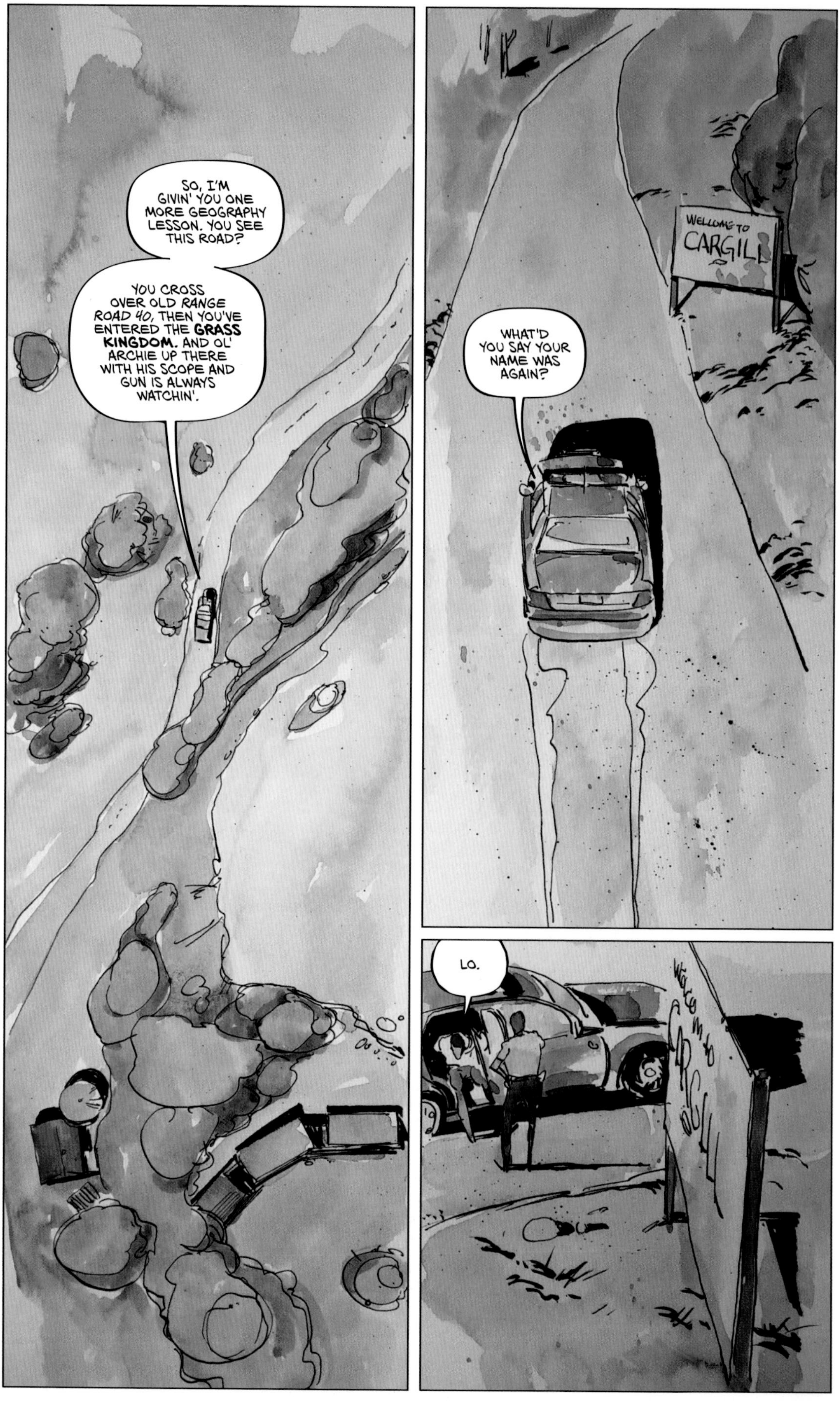
SO, I'M GIVIN' YOU ONE MORE GEOGRAPHY LESSON. YOU SEE THIS ROAD?
YOU CROSS OVER OLD *RANGE ROAD 40*, THEN YOU'VE ENTERED THE **GRASS KINGDOM.** AND OL' ARCHIE UP THERE WITH HIS SCOPE AND GUN IS ALWAYS WATCHIN'.
WELCOME TO CARGILL
WHAT'D YOU SAY YOUR NAME WAS AGAIN?
LO.

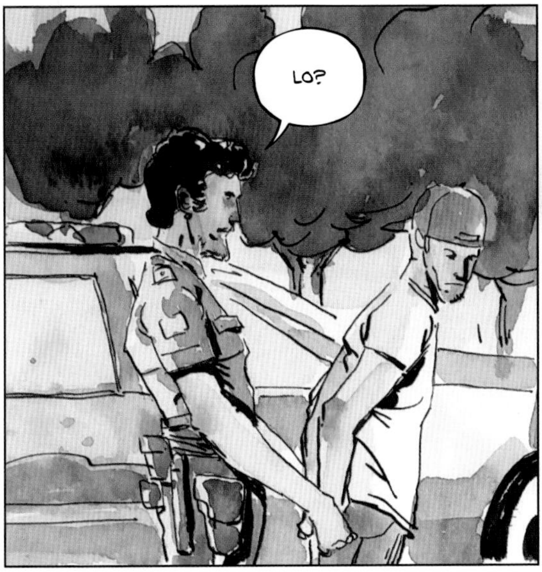
LO?

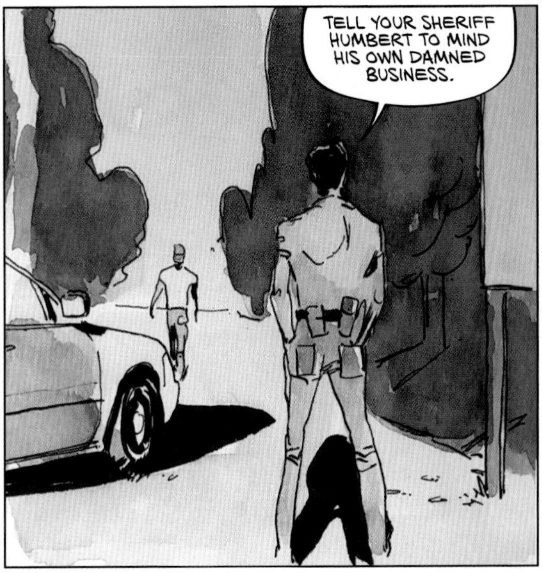
TELL YOUR SHERIFF HUMBERT TO MIND HIS OWN DAMNED BUSINESS.

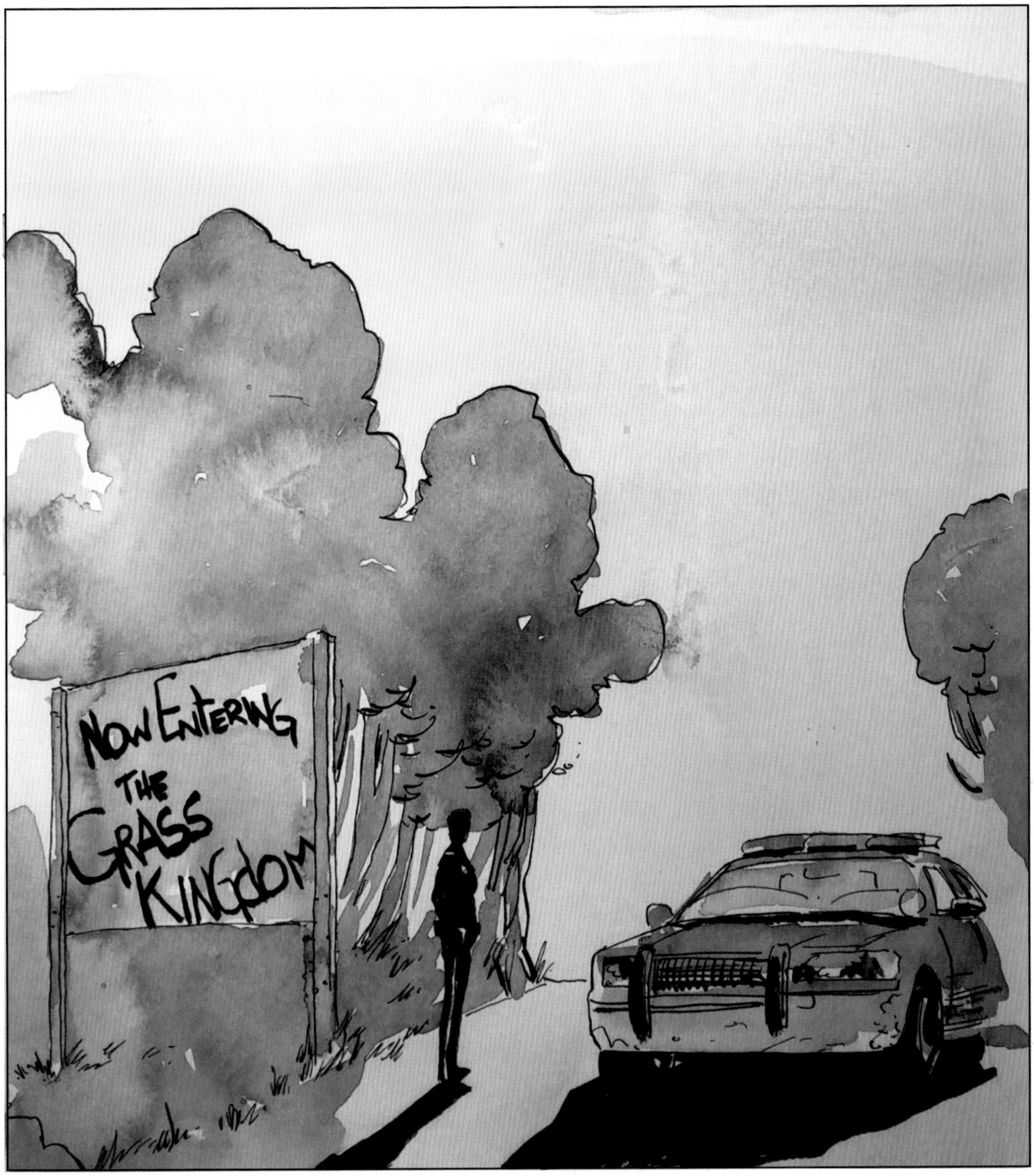
NOW ENTERING THE GRASS KINGDOM

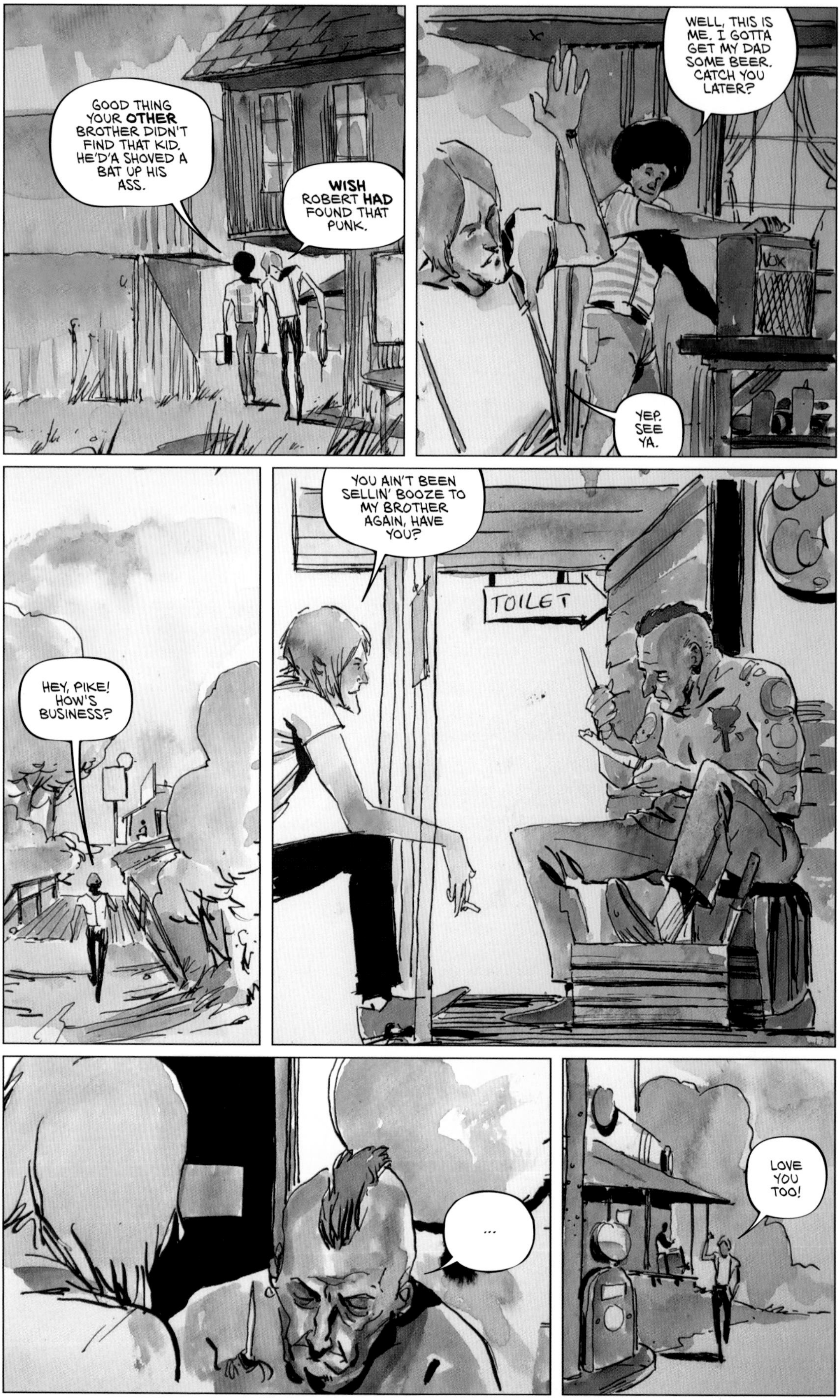
GOOD THING YOUR **OTHER** BROTHER DIDN'T FIND THAT KID. HE'D'A SHOVED A BAT UP HIS ASS.
**WISH** ROBERT **HAD** FOUND THAT PUNK.
WELL, THIS IS ME. I GOTTA GET MY DAD SOME BEER. CATCH YOU LATER?
YEP. SEE YA.
HEY, PIKE! HOW'S BUSINESS?
YOU AIN'T BEEN SELLIN' BOOZE TO MY BROTHER AGAIN, HAVE YOU?
TOILET
...
LOVE YOU TOO!

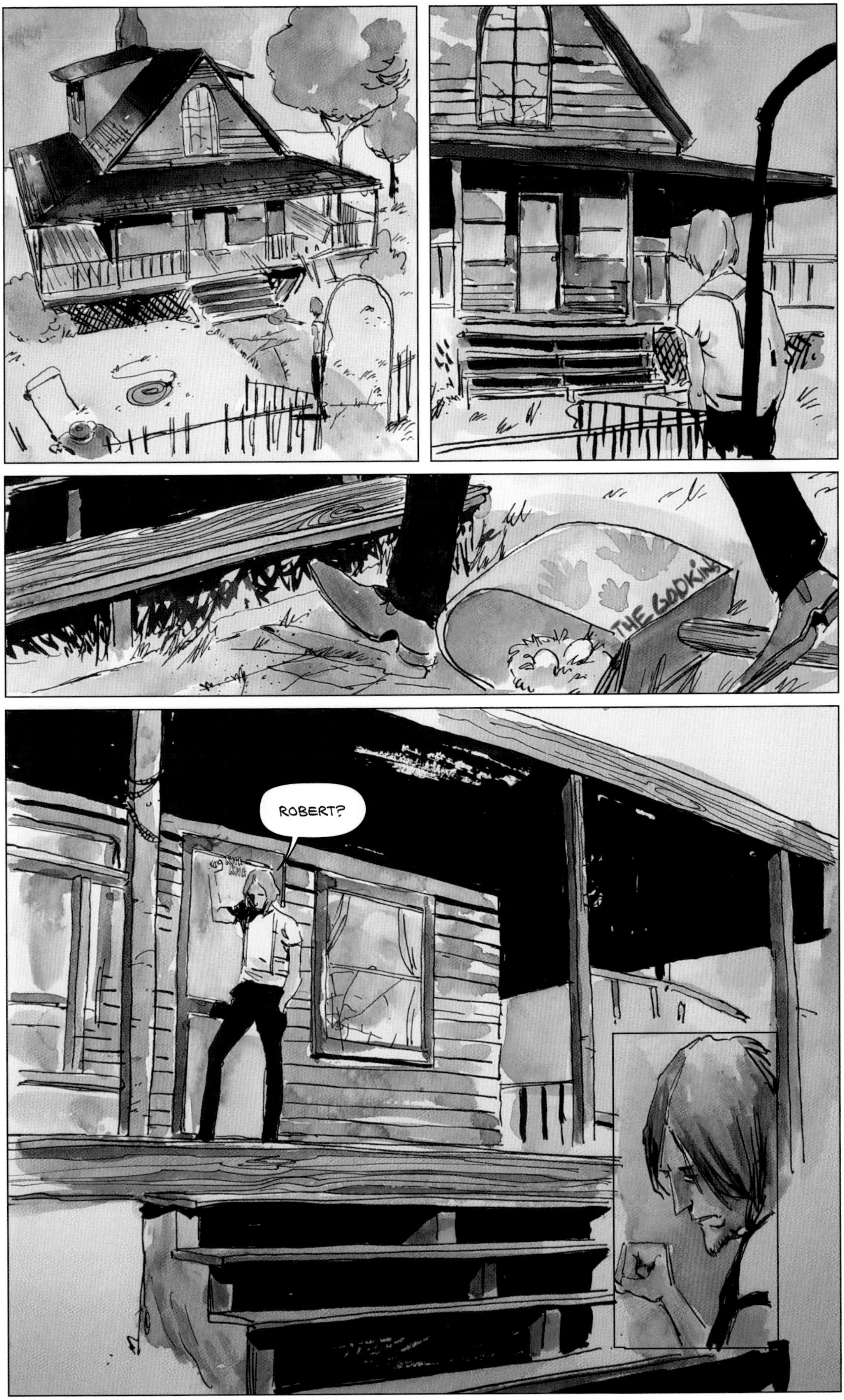
THE GODKinG
ROBERT?

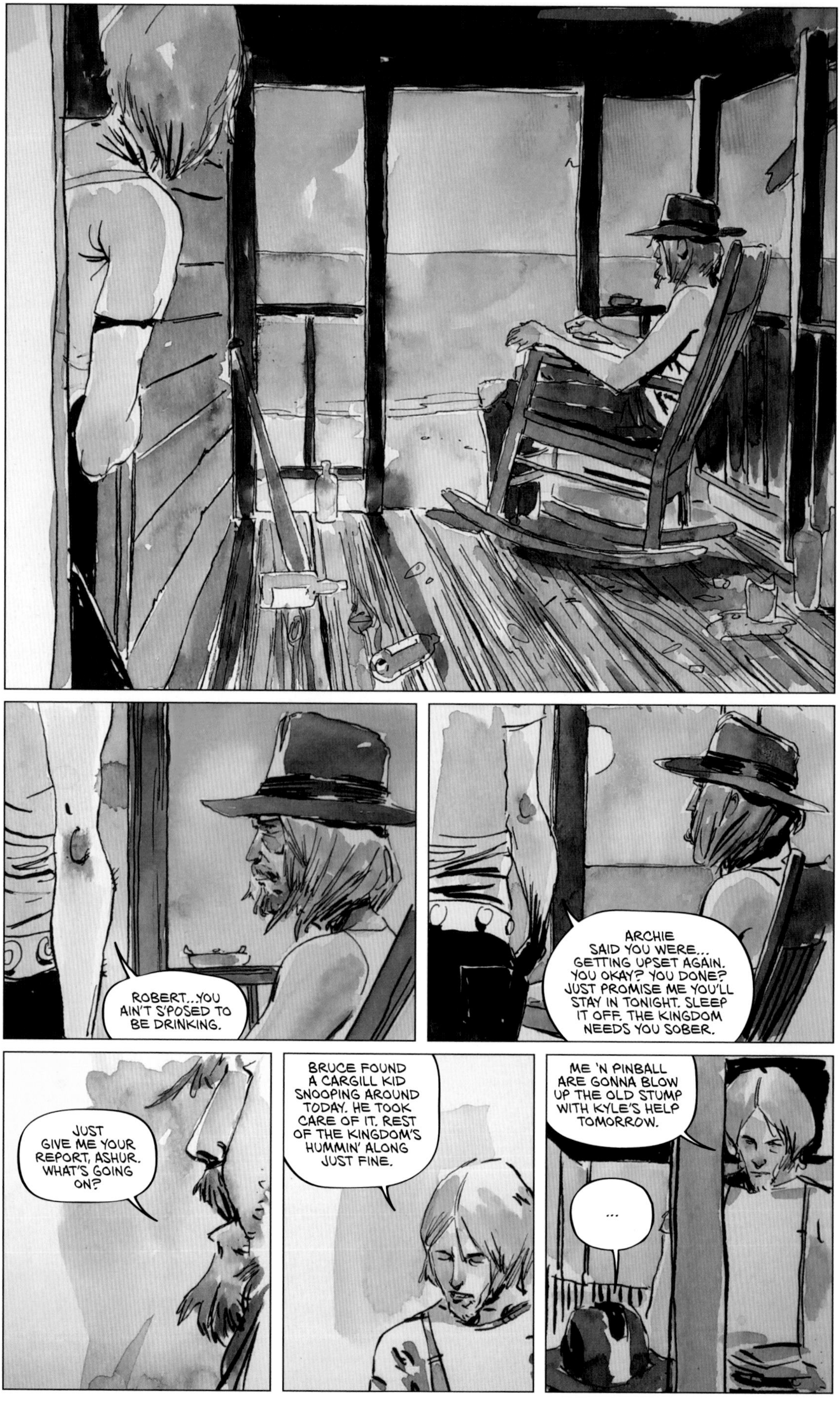
ROBERT...YOU AIN'T S'POSED TO BE DRINKING.
ARCHIE SAID YOU WERE... GETTING UPSET AGAIN. YOU OKAY? YOU DONE? JUST PROMISE ME YOU'LL STAY IN TONIGHT. SLEEP IT OFF. THE KINGDOM NEEDS YOU SOBER.
JUST GIVE ME YOUR REPORT, ASHUR. WHAT'S GOING ON?
BRUCE FOUND A CARGILL KID SNOOPING AROUND TODAY. HE TOOK CARE OF IT. REST OF THE KINGDOM'S HUMMIN' ALONG JUST FINE.
ME 'N PINBALL ARE GONNA BLOW UP THE OLD STUMP WITH KYLE'S HELP TOMORROW.
...

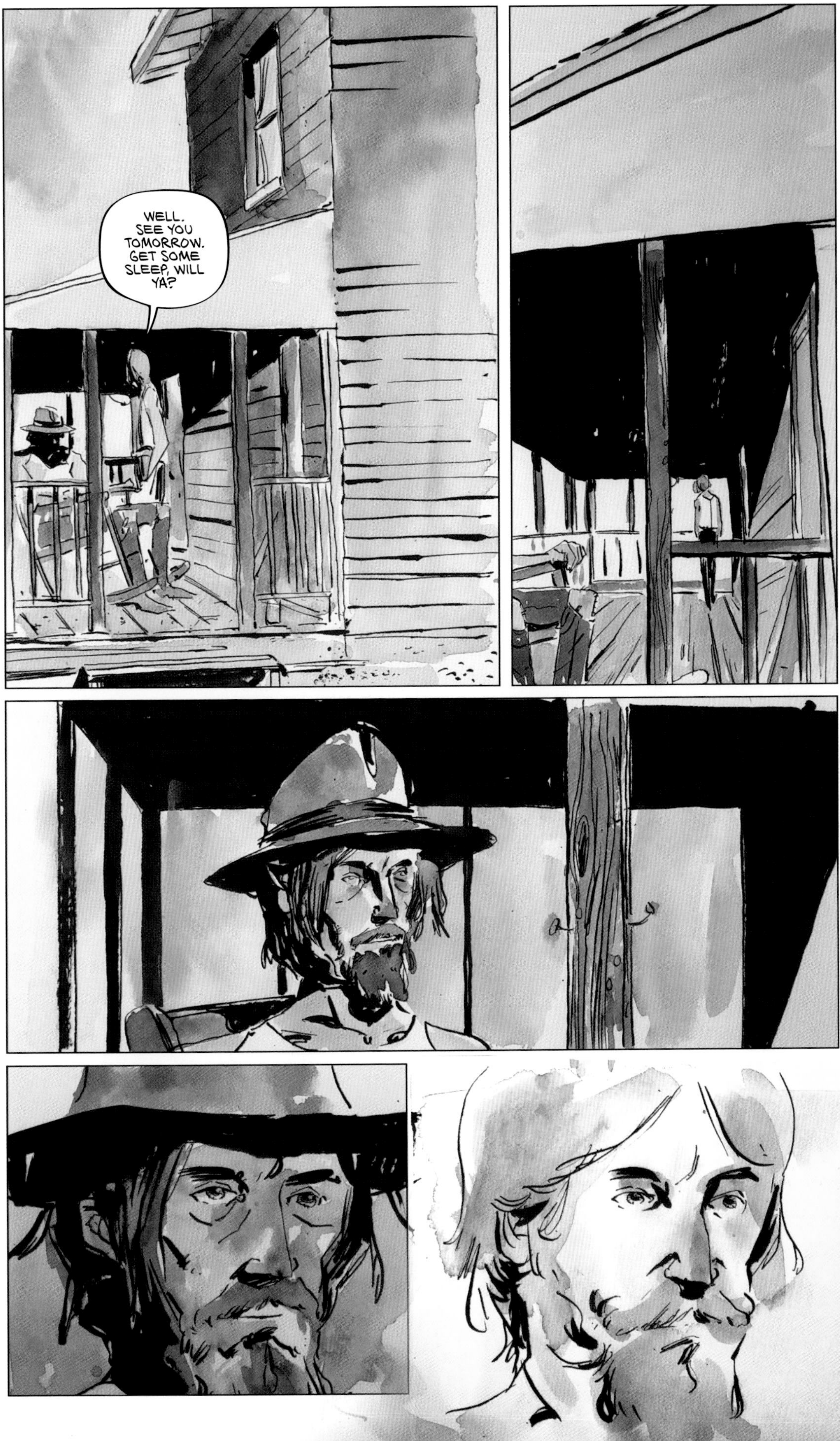
WELL. SEE YOU TOMORROW. GET SOME SLEEP, WILL YA?

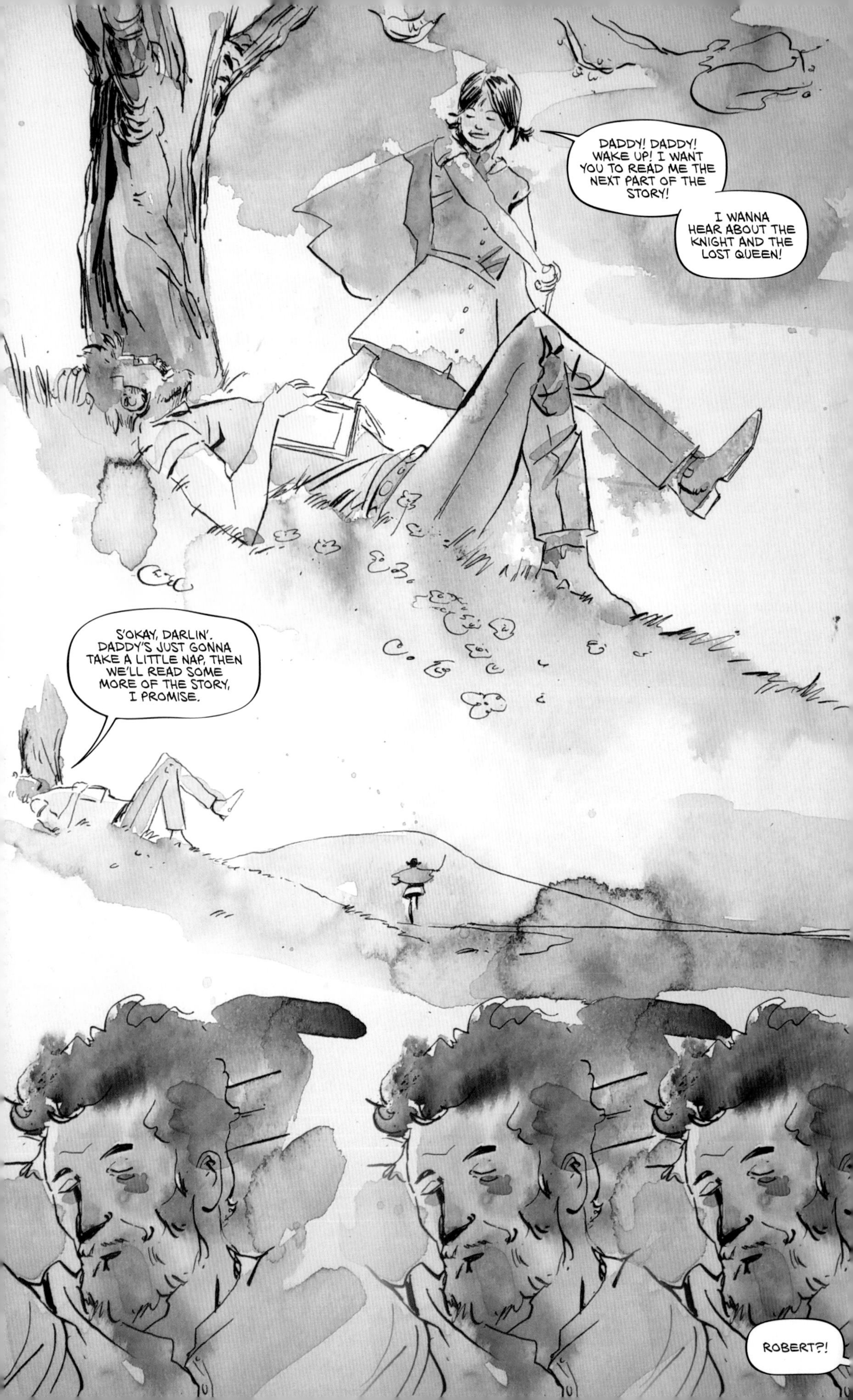
DADDY! DADDY! WAKE UP! I WANT YOU TO READ ME THE NEXT PART OF THE STORY!
I WANNA HEAR ABOUT THE KNIGHT AND THE LOST QUEEN!
S'OKAY, DARLIN'. DADDY'S JUST GONNA TAKE A LITTLE NAP, THEN WE'LL READ SOME MORE OF THE STORY, I PROMISE.
ROBERT?!

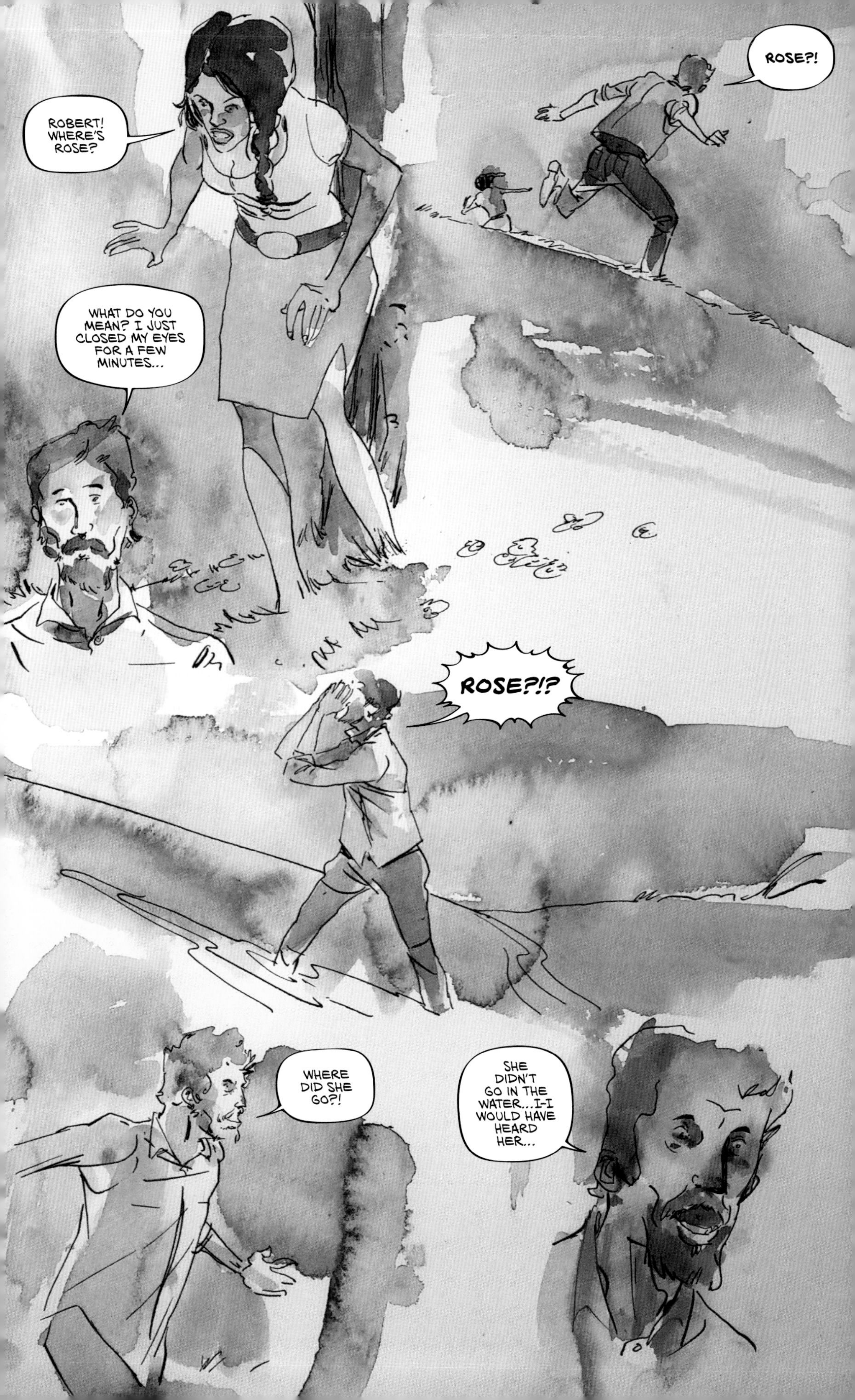
ROBERT! WHERE'S ROSE?
ROSE?!
WHAT DO YOU MEAN? I JUST CLOSED MY EYES FOR A FEW MINUTES...
ROSE?!?
WHERE DID SHE GO?!
SHE DIDN'T GO IN THE WATER...I-I WOULD HAVE HEARD HER...

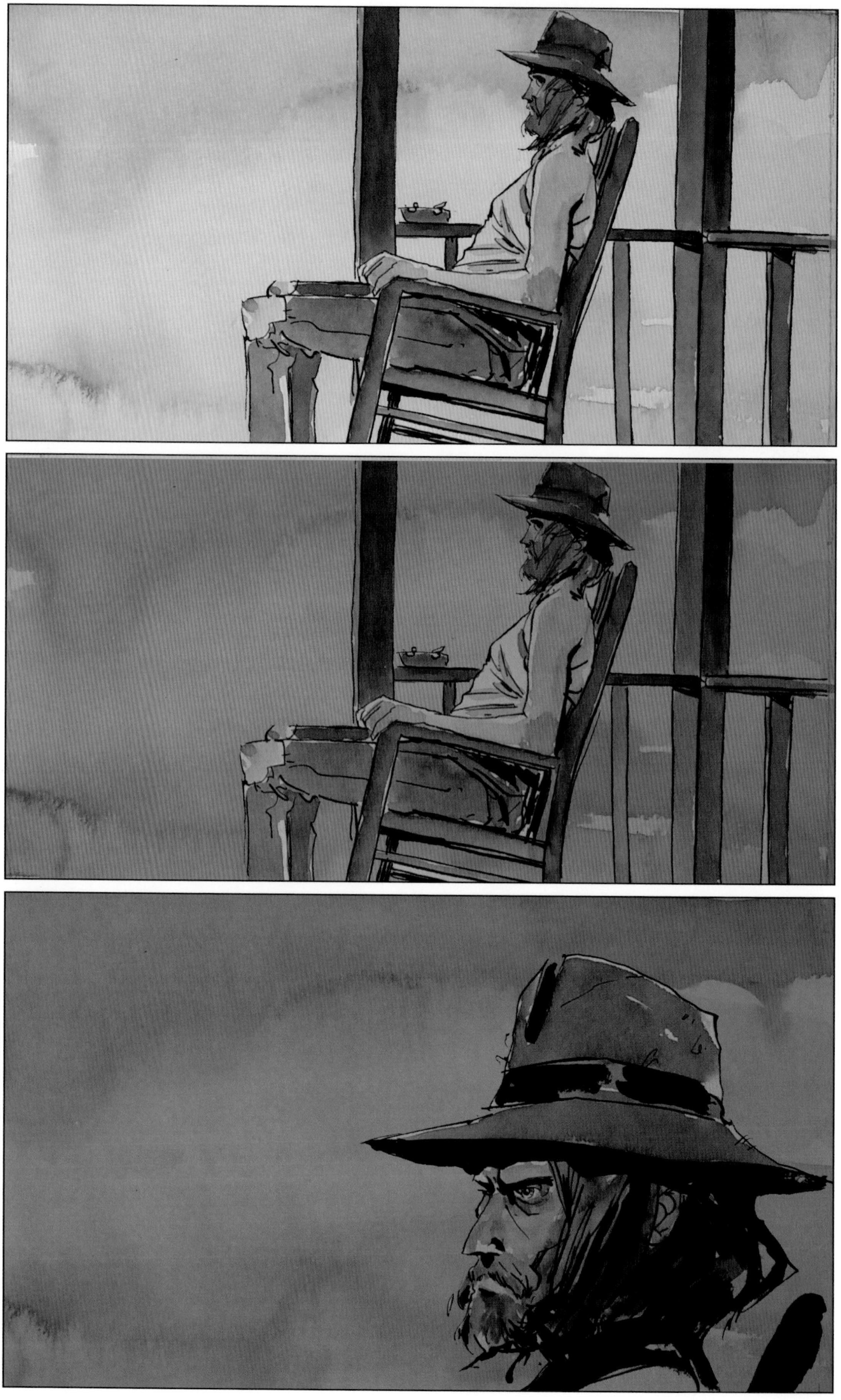

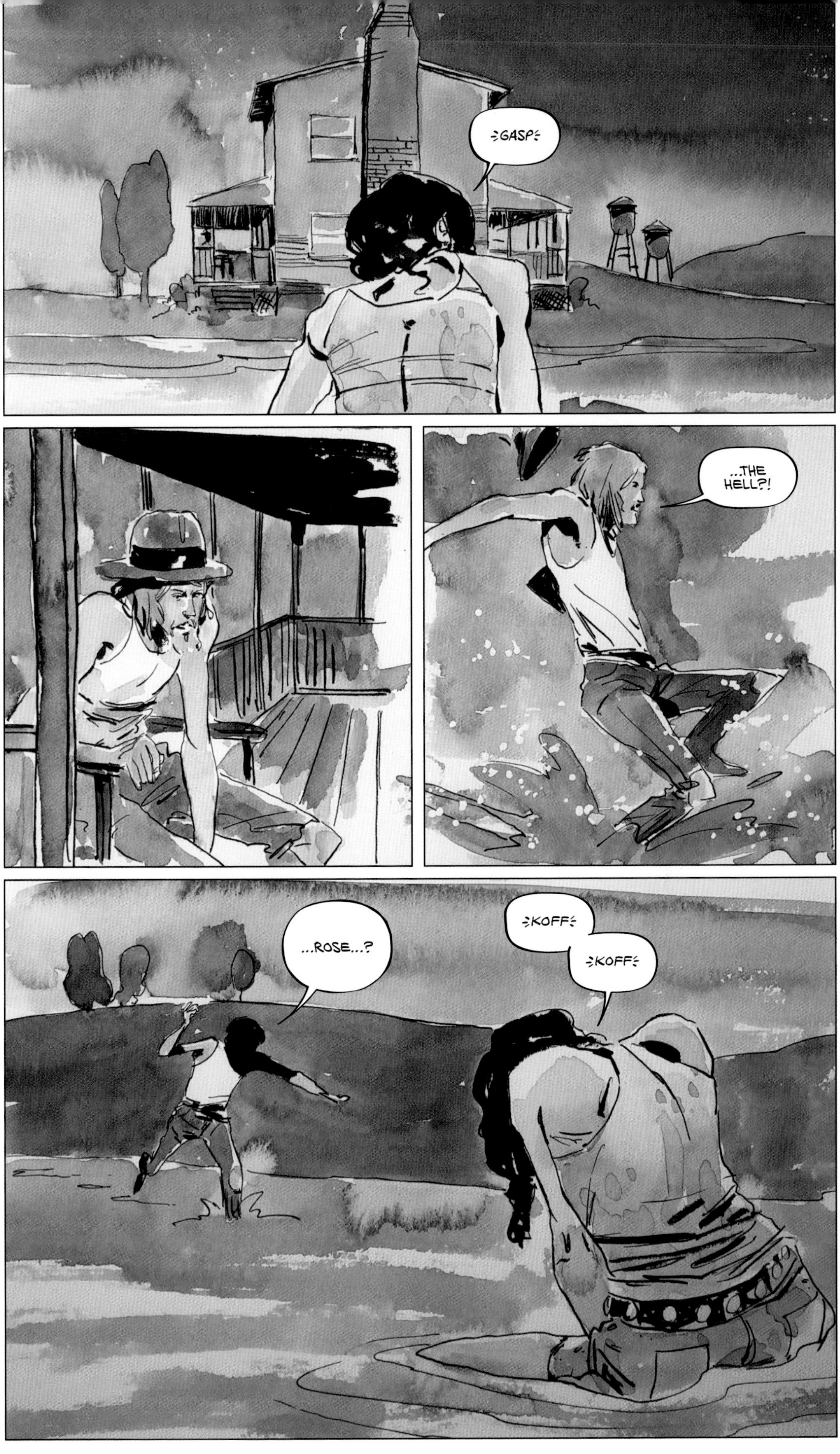
GASP
...THE HELL?!
...ROSE...?
KOFF
KOFF

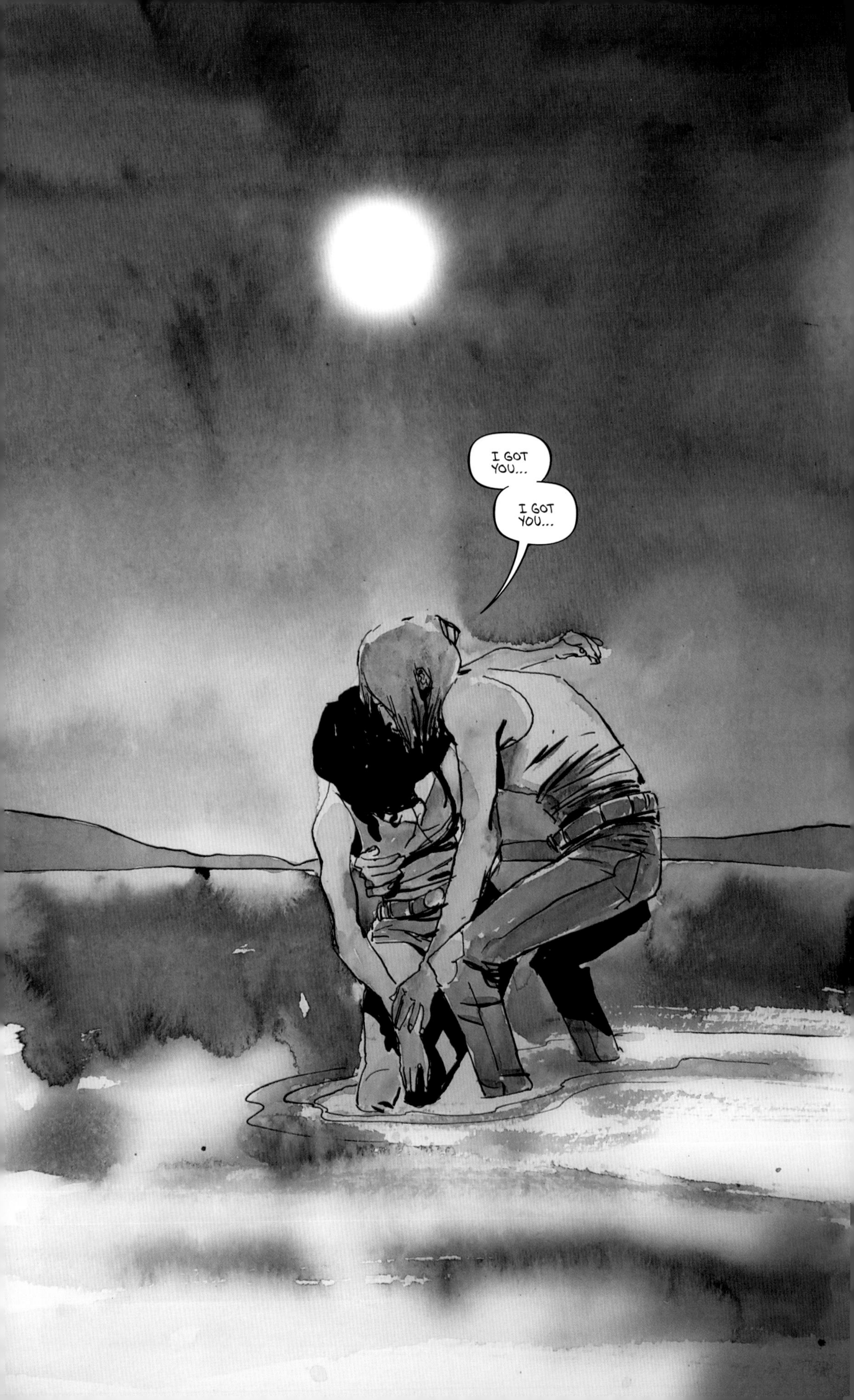
I GOT YOU...
I GOT YOU...

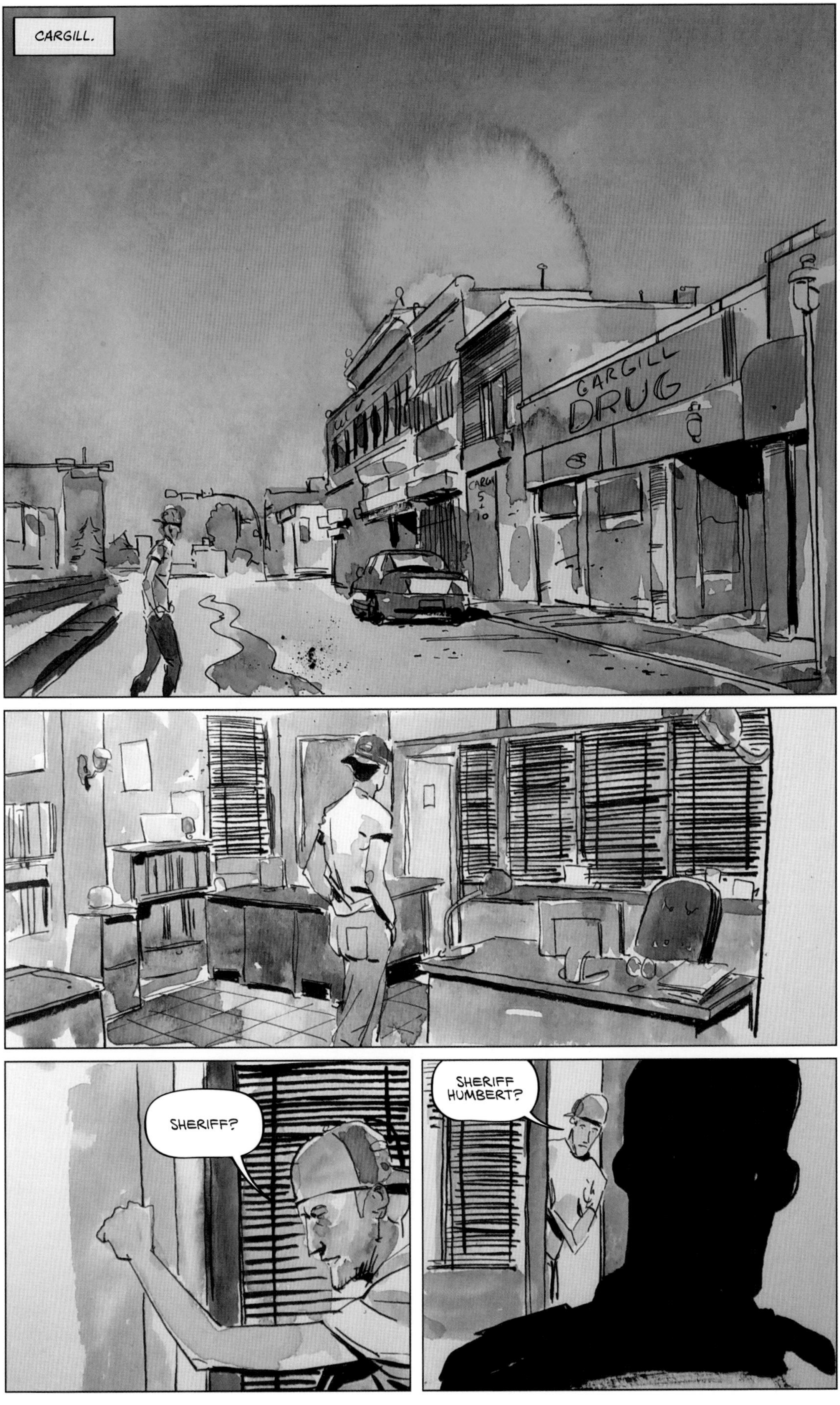
CARGILL.
CARGILL DRUG
SHERIFF?
SHERIFF HUMBERT?

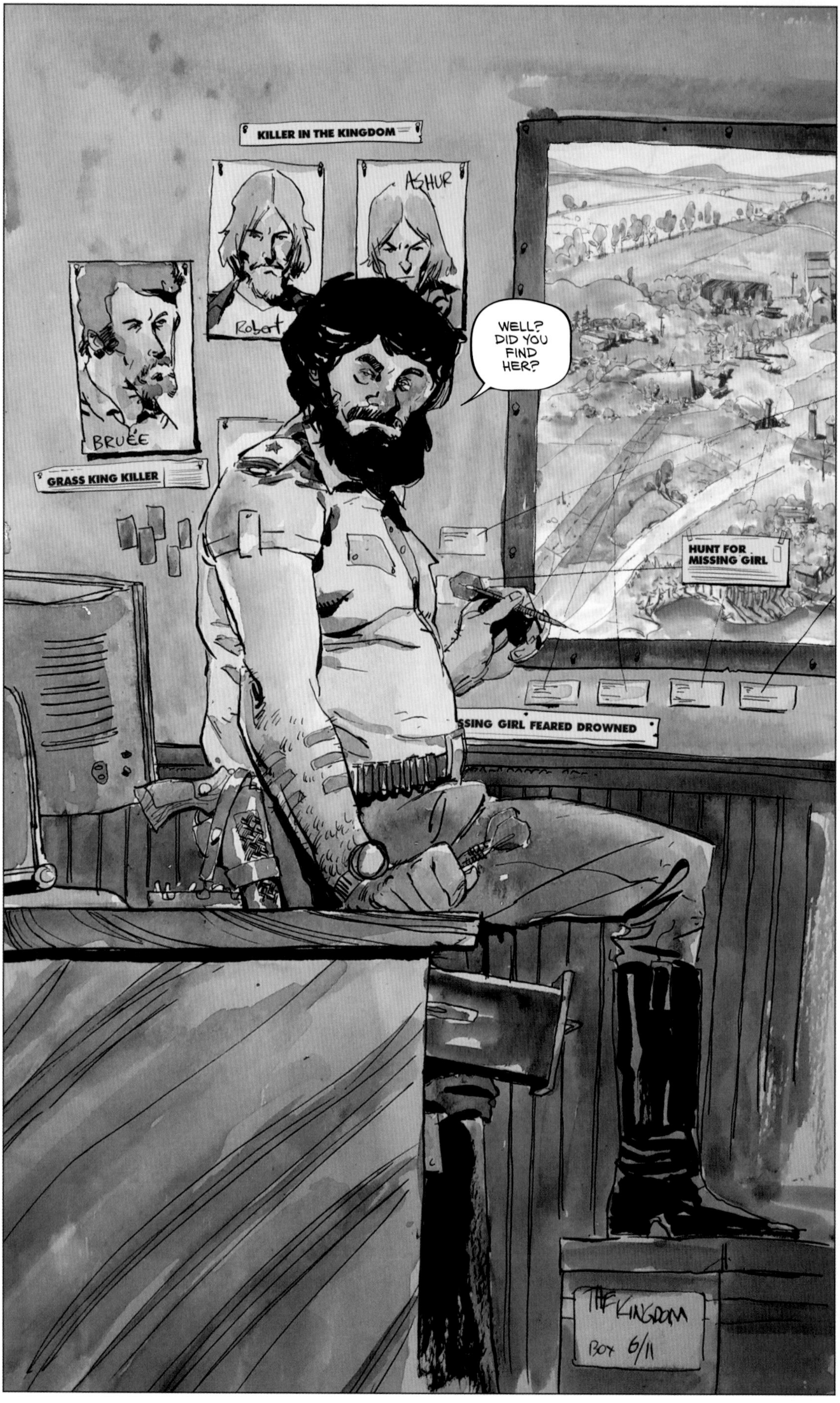

KILLER IN THE KINGDOM
ASHUR
Robert
BRUCE
GRASS KING KILLER
WELL? DID YOU FIND HER?
HUNT FOR MISSING GIRL
SSING GIRL FEARED DROWNED
THE KINGDOM
Box 6/11

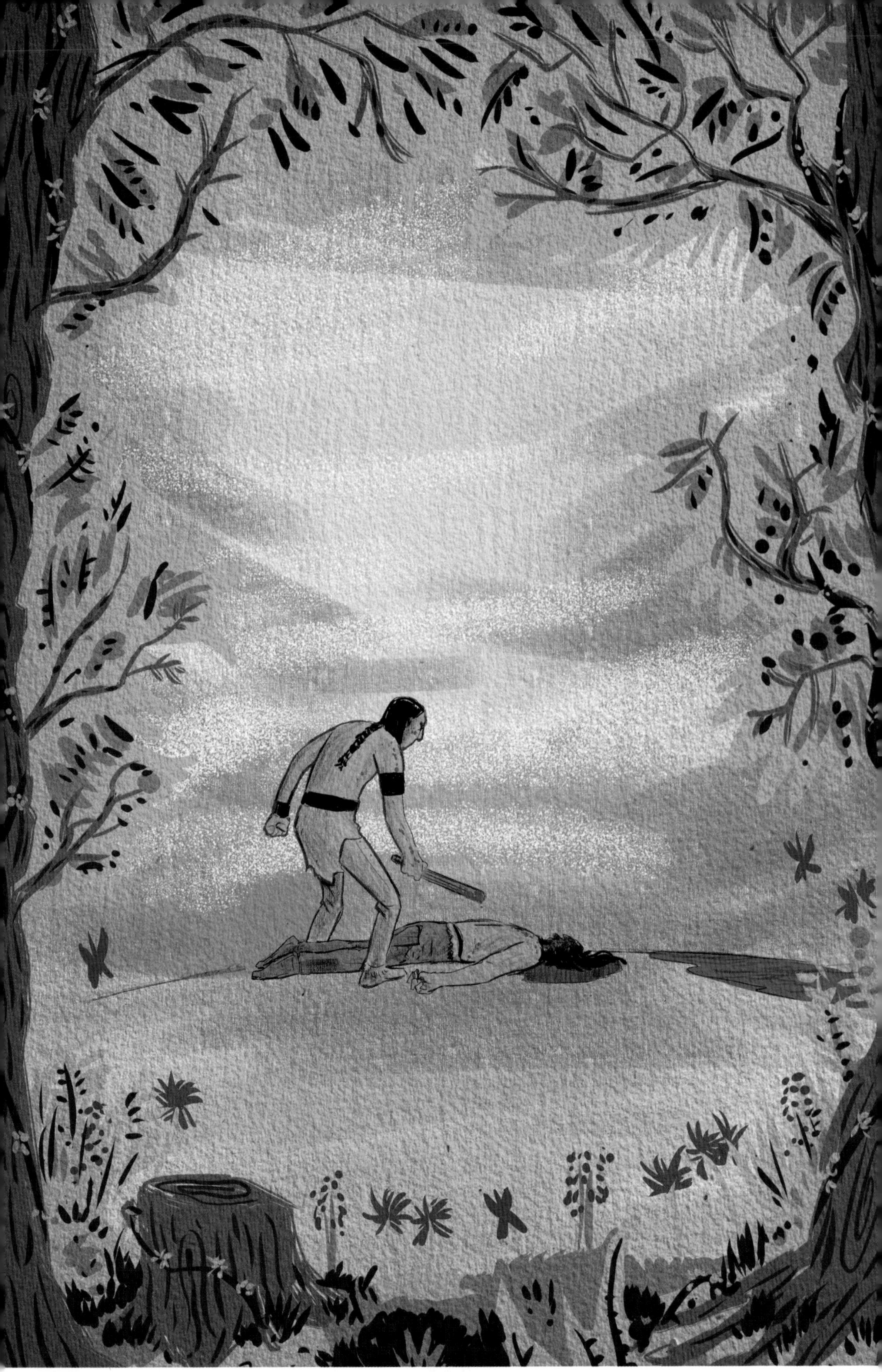

issue #1 cover by matt kindt

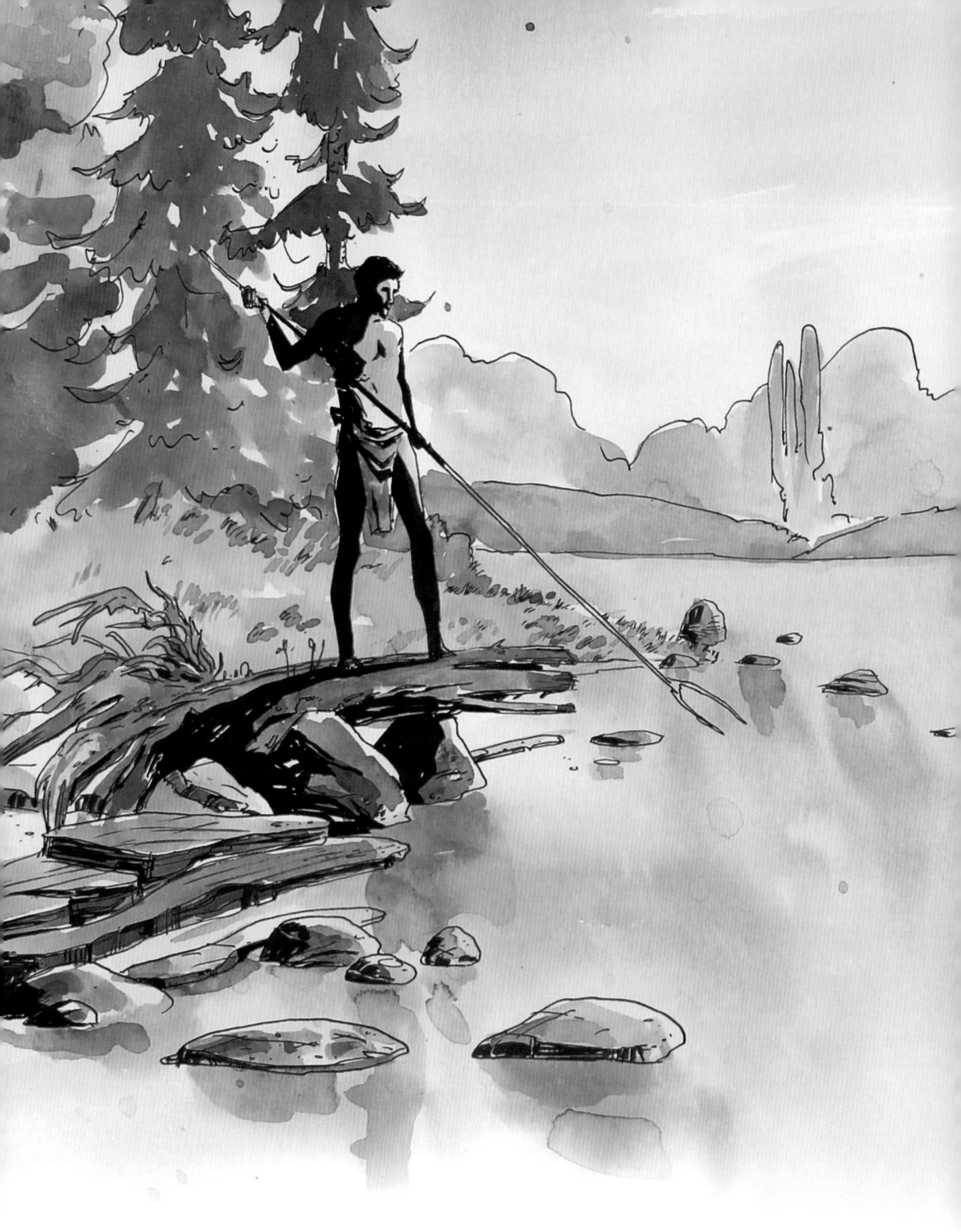

# c h a p t e r   t w o

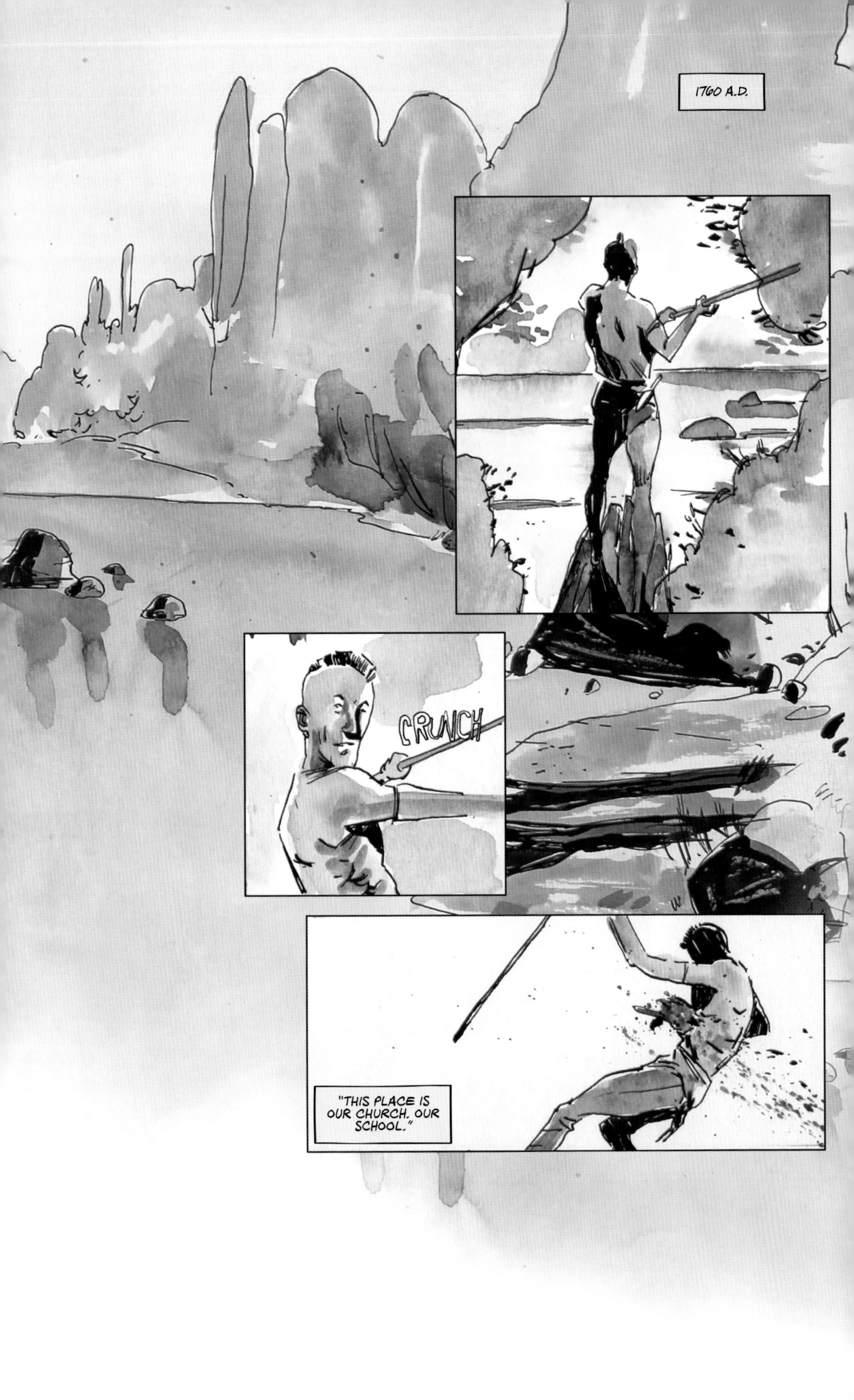
1760 A.D.
CRUNCH
"THIS PLACE IS OUR CHURCH, OUR SCHOOL."

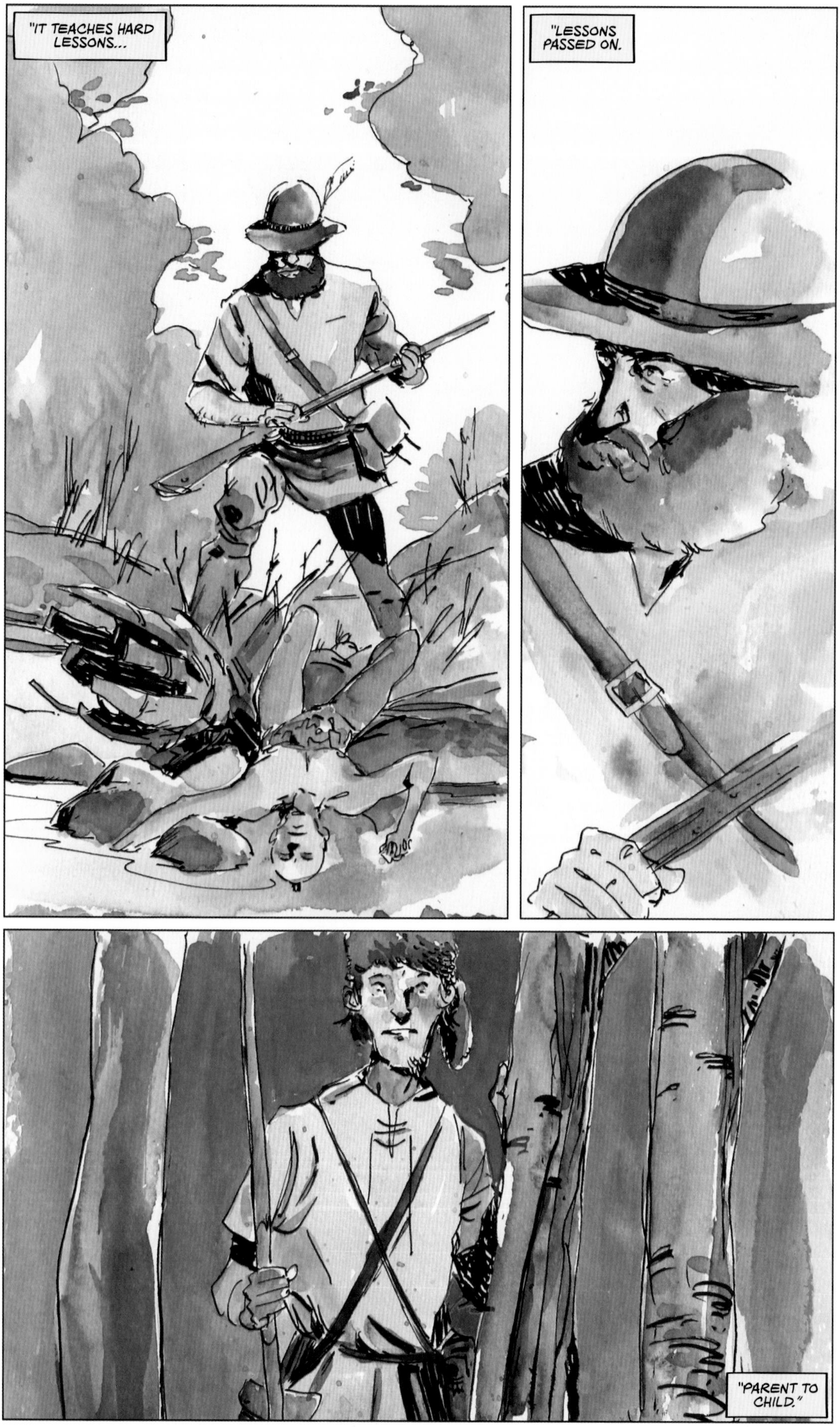
"IT TEACHES HARD LESSONS...
"LESSONS PASSED ON.
"PARENT TO CHILD."

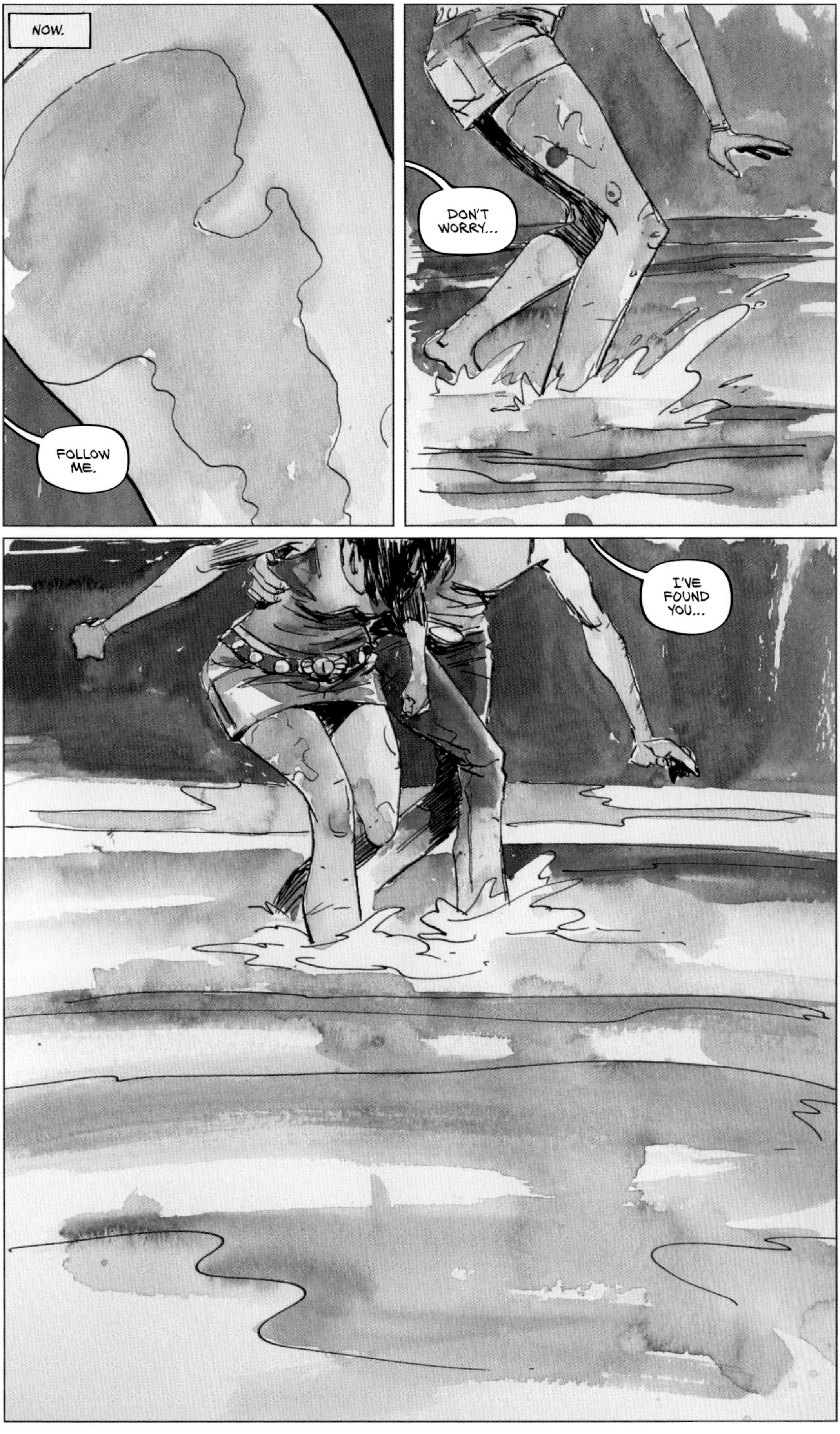
NOW.
FOLLOW ME.
DON'T WORRY...
I'VE FOUND YOU...

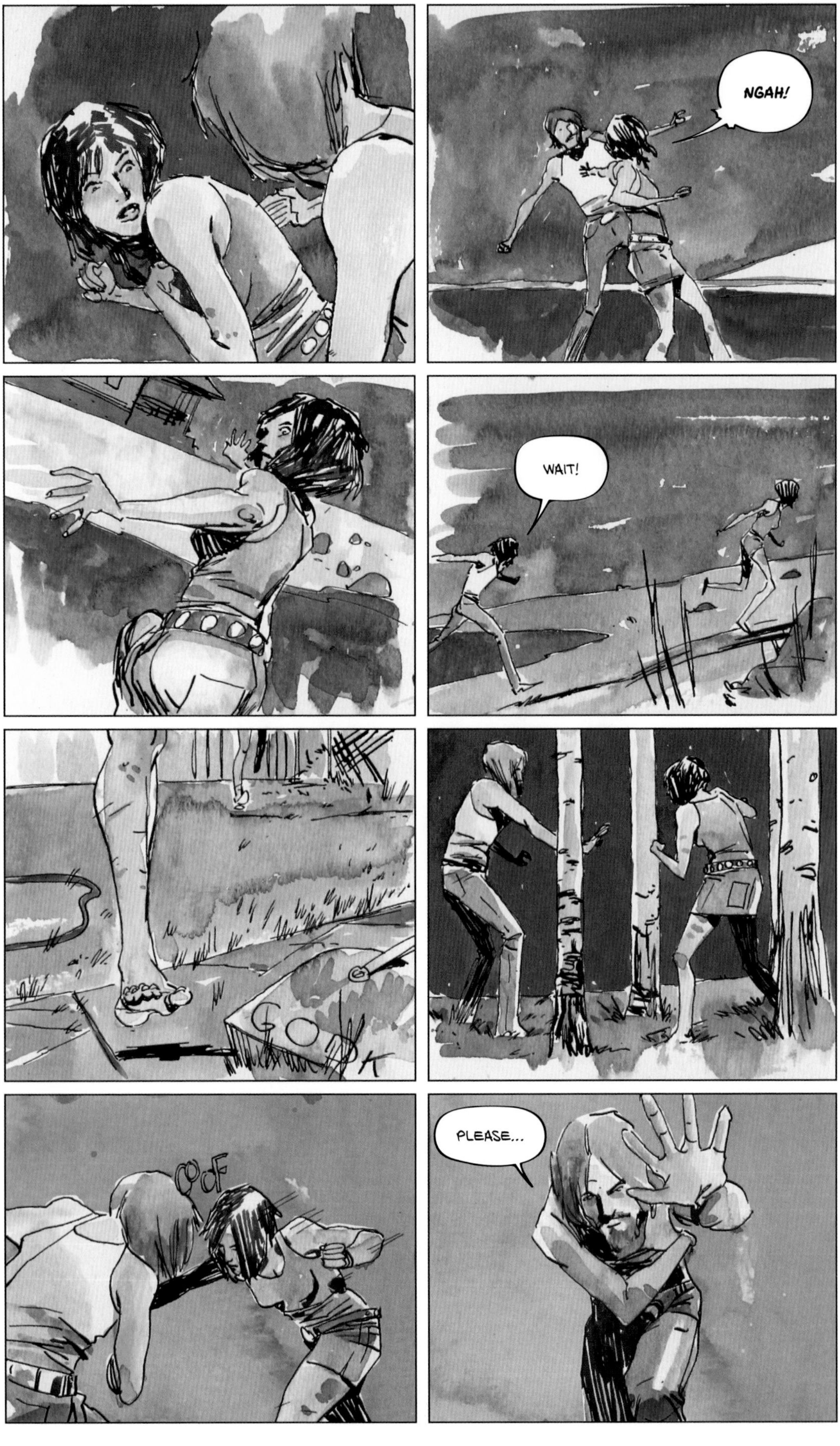
NGAH!
WAIT!
OOF
PLEASE...

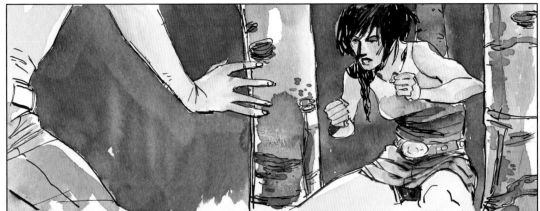

...NO...

...NNH...

GET YOU BACK HOME... GET YOU WARM.

YOU'RE GOING TO BE OKAY.

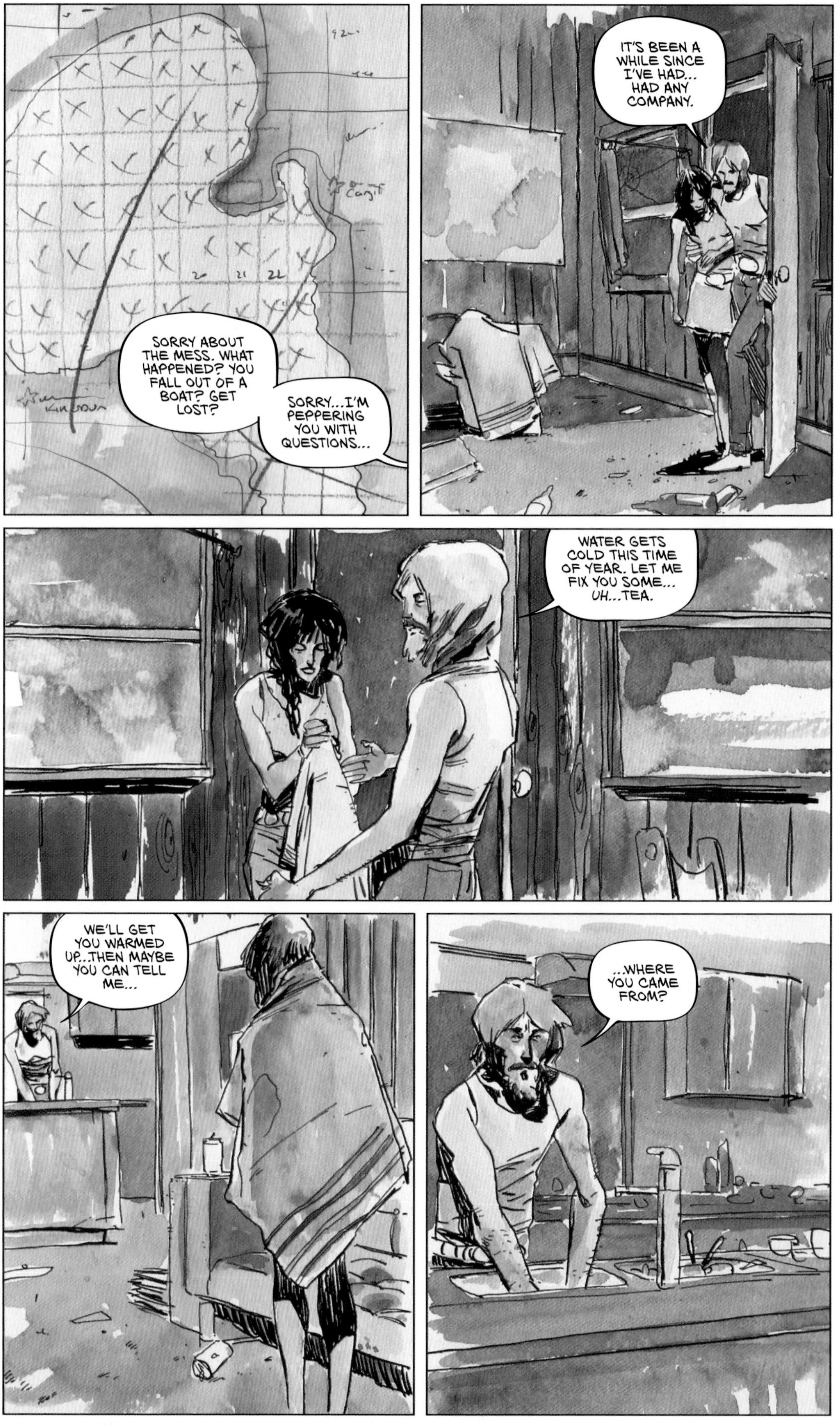
SORRY ABOUT THE MESS. WHAT HAPPENED? YOU FALL OUT OF A BOAT? GET LOST?
SORRY...I'M PEPPERING YOU WITH QUESTIONS...
IT'S BEEN A WHILE SINCE I'VE HAD... HAD ANY COMPANY.
WATER GETS COLD THIS TIME OF YEAR. LET ME FIX YOU SOME... UH...TEA.
WE'LL GET YOU WARMED UP..THEN MAYBE YOU CAN TELL ME...
...WHERE YOU CAME FROM?

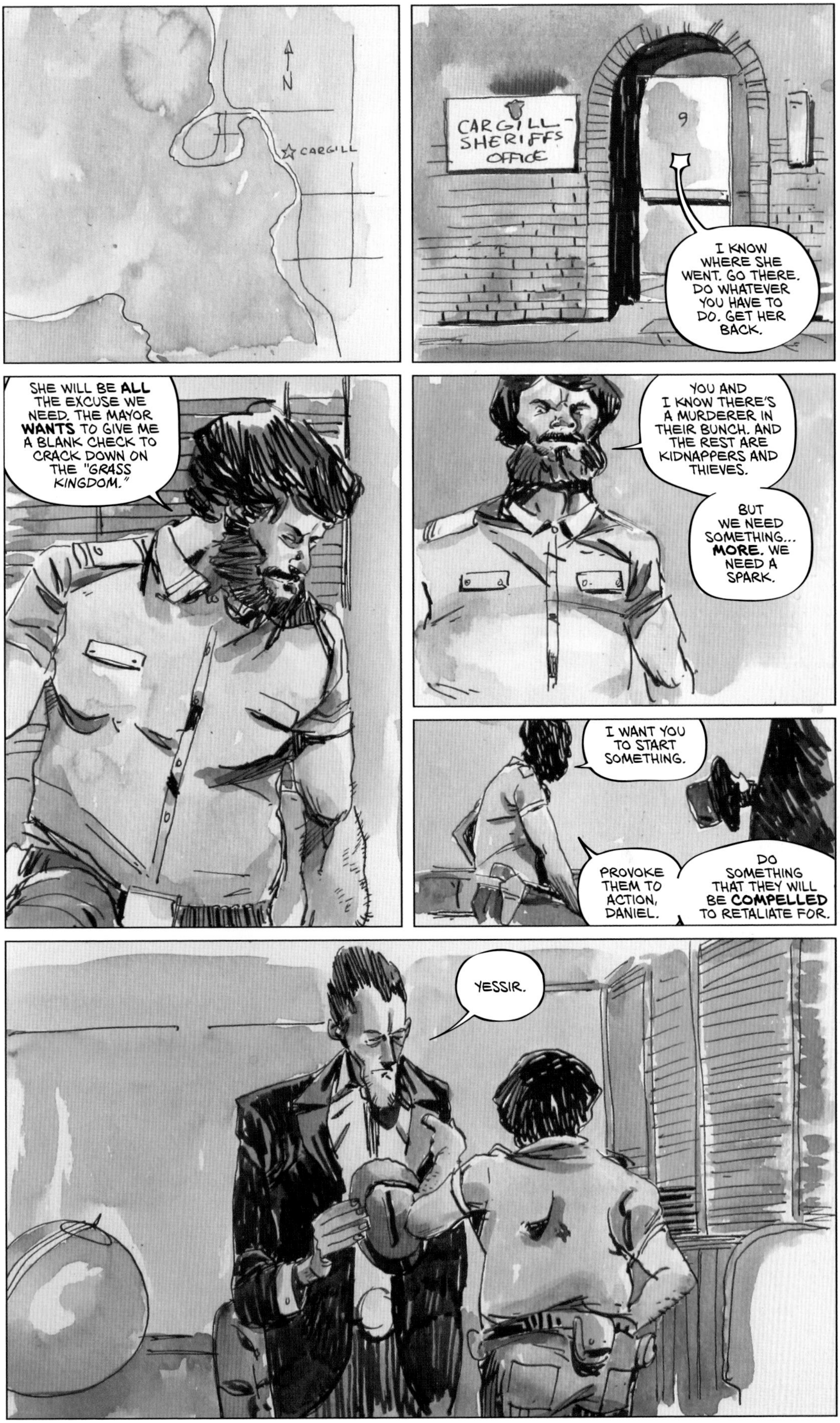
N
CARGILL
CARGILL SHERIFFS OFFICE
9
I KNOW WHERE SHE WENT. GO THERE. DO WHATEVER YOU HAVE TO DO. GET HER BACK.
SHE WILL BE **ALL** THE EXCUSE WE NEED. THE MAYOR **WANTS** TO GIVE ME A BLANK CHECK TO CRACK DOWN ON THE "GRASS KINGDOM."
YOU AND I KNOW THERE'S A MURDERER IN THEIR BUNCH. AND THE REST ARE KIDNAPPERS AND THIEVES.
BUT WE NEED SOMETHING... **MORE.** WE NEED A SPARK.
I WANT YOU TO START SOMETHING.
PROVOKE THEM TO ACTION, DANIEL.
DO SOMETHING THAT THEY WILL BE **COMPELLED** TO RETALIATE FOR.
YESSIR.

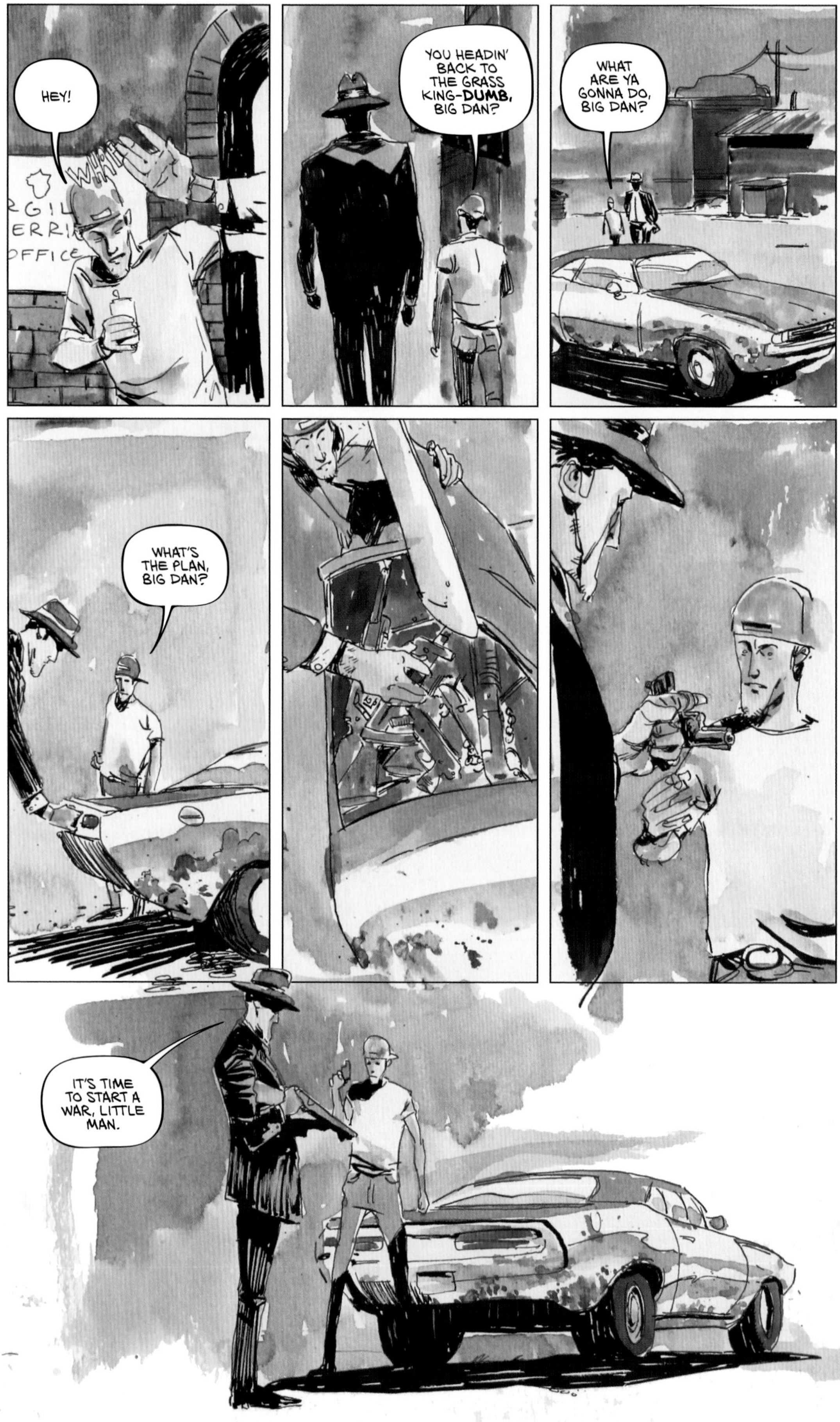
HEY!
YOU HEADIN' BACK TO THE GRASS KING-**DUMB,** BIG DAN?
WHAT ARE YA GONNA DO, BIG DAN?
WHAT'S THE PLAN, BIG DAN?
IT'S TIME TO START A WAR, LITTLE MAN.

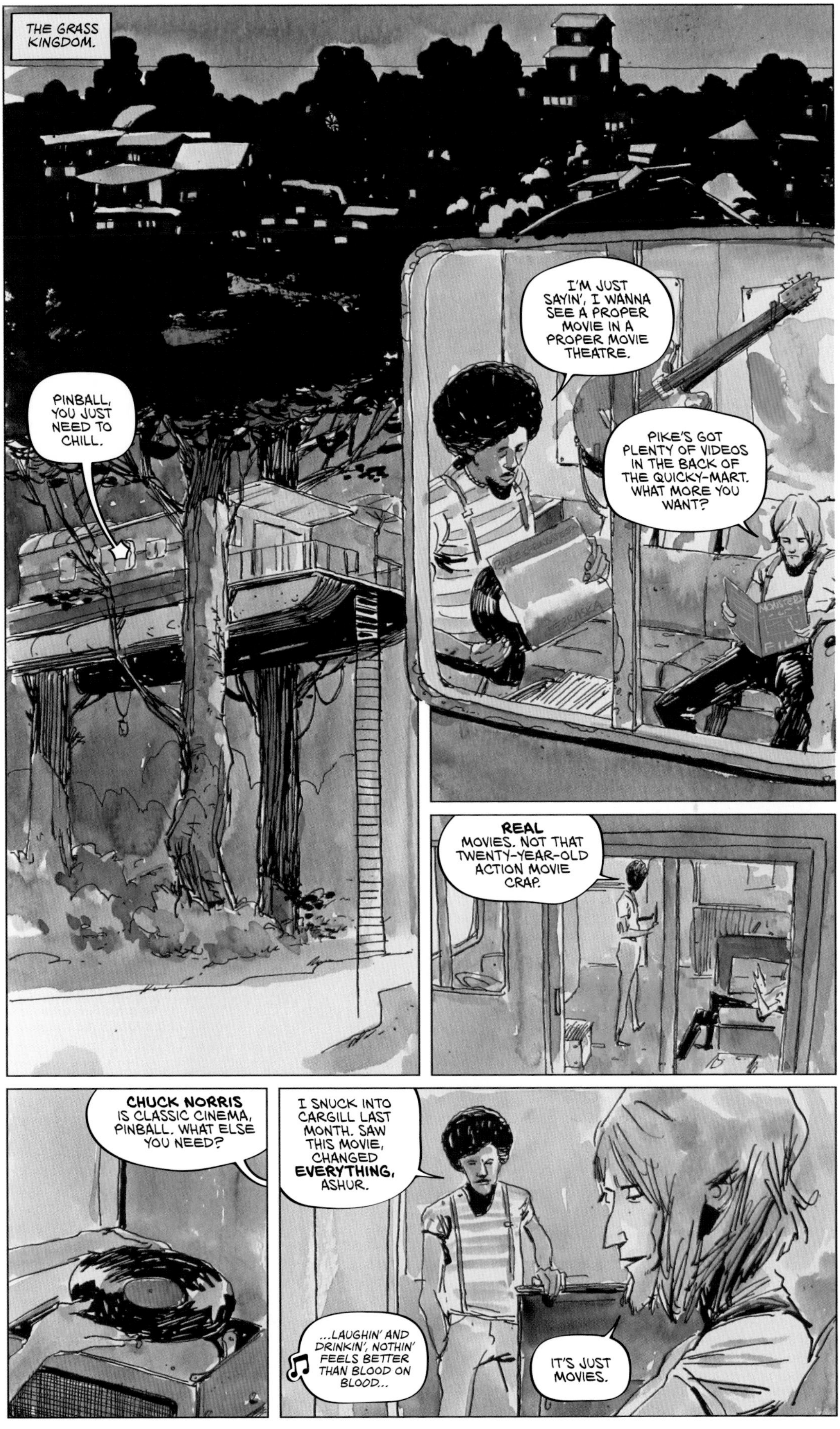
THE GRASS KINGDOM.
I'M JUST SAYIN', I WANNA SEE A PROPER MOVIE IN A PROPER MOVIE THEATRE.
PINBALL, YOU JUST NEED TO CHILL.
PIKE'S GOT PLENTY OF VIDEOS IN THE BACK OF THE QUICKY-MART. WHAT MORE YOU WANT?
REAL MOVIES. NOT THAT TWENTY-YEAR-OLD ACTION MOVIE CRAP.
CHUCK NORRIS IS CLASSIC CINEMA, PINBALL. WHAT ELSE YOU NEED?
I SNUCK INTO CARGILL LAST MONTH. SAW THIS MOVIE, CHANGED EVERYTHING, ASHUR.
...LAUGHIN' AND DRINKIN', NOTHIN' FEELS BETTER THAN BLOOD ON BLOOD...
IT'S JUST MOVIES.

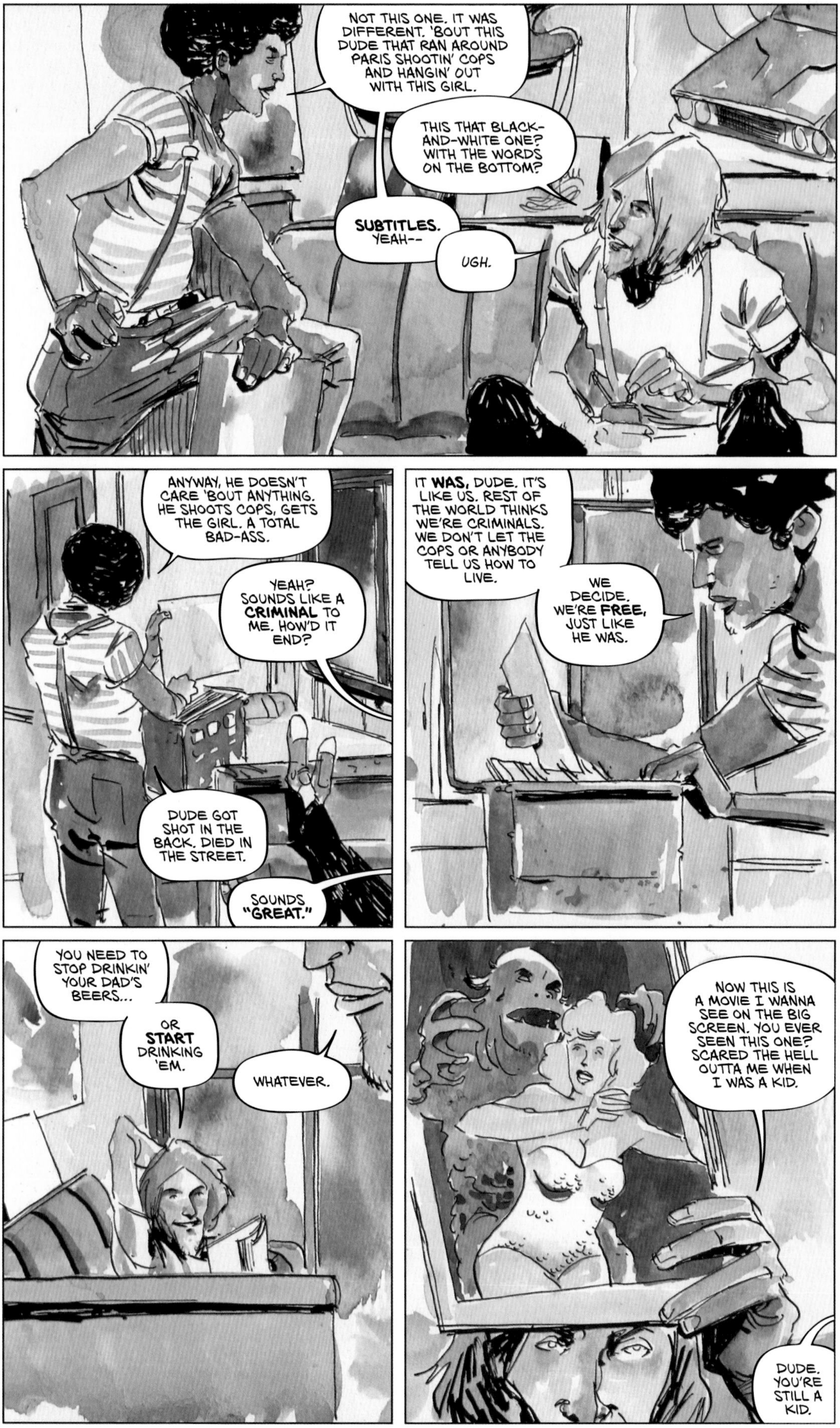
NOT THIS ONE. IT WAS DIFFERENT. 'BOUT THIS DUDE THAT RAN AROUND PARIS SHOOTIN' COPS AND HANGIN' OUT WITH THIS GIRL.
THIS THAT BLACK-AND-WHITE ONE? WITH THE WORDS ON THE BOTTOM?
**SUBTITLES.** YEAH--
UGH.
ANYWAY, HE DOESN'T CARE 'BOUT ANYTHING. HE SHOOTS COPS, GETS THE GIRL. A TOTAL BAD-ASS.
YEAH? SOUNDS LIKE A **CRIMINAL** TO ME. HOW'D IT END?
DUDE GOT SHOT IN THE BACK. DIED IN THE STREET.
SOUNDS **"GREAT."**
IT **WAS,** DUDE. IT'S LIKE US. REST OF THE WORLD THINKS WE'RE CRIMINALS. WE DON'T LET THE COPS OR ANYBODY TELL US HOW TO LIVE.
WE DECIDE. WE'RE **FREE,** JUST LIKE HE WAS.
YOU NEED TO STOP DRINKIN' YOUR DAD'S BEERS...
OR **START** DRINKING 'EM.
WHATEVER.
NOW THIS IS A MOVIE I WANNA SEE ON THE BIG SCREEN. YOU EVER SEEN THIS ONE? SCARED THE HELL OUTTA ME WHEN I WAS A KID.
DUDE. YOU'RE STILL A KID.

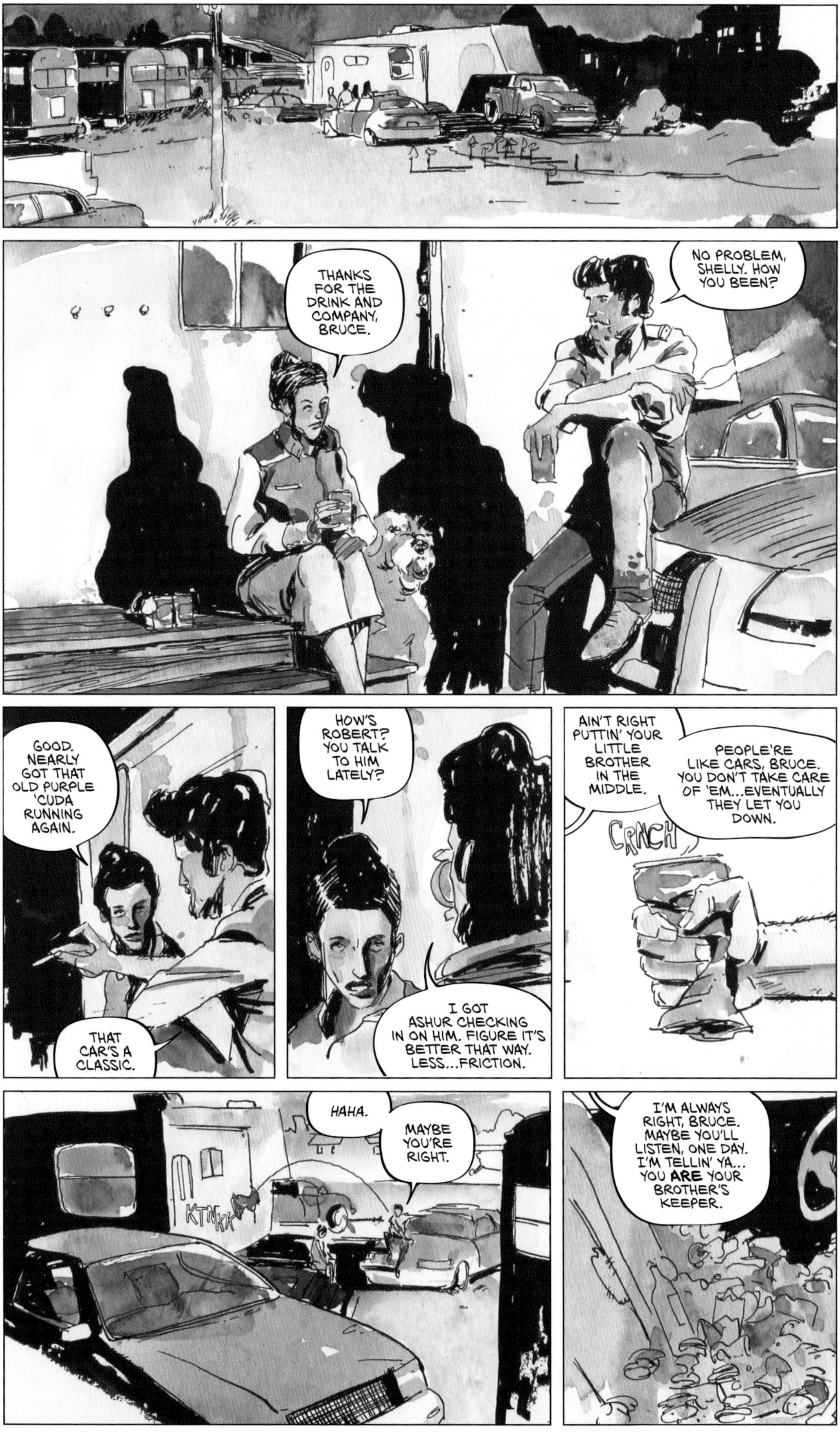
THANKS FOR THE DRINK AND COMPANY, BRUCE.
NO PROBLEM, SHELLY. HOW YOU BEEN?
GOOD. NEARLY GOT THAT OLD PURPLE 'CUDA RUNNING AGAIN.
THAT CAR'S A CLASSIC.
HOW'S ROBERT? YOU TALK TO HIM LATELY?
I GOT ASHUR CHECKING IN ON HIM. FIGURE IT'S BETTER THAT WAY. LESS...FRICTION.
AIN'T RIGHT PUTTIN' YOUR LITTLE BROTHER IN THE MIDDLE.
PEOPLE'RE LIKE CARS, BRUCE. YOU DON'T TAKE CARE OF 'EM...EVENTUALLY THEY LET YOU DOWN.
CRNCH
HAHA.
MAYBE YOU'RE RIGHT.
KTNKK
I'M ALWAYS RIGHT, BRUCE. MAYBE YOU'LL LISTEN, ONE DAY. I'M TELLIN' YA... YOU **ARE** YOUR BROTHER'S KEEPER.

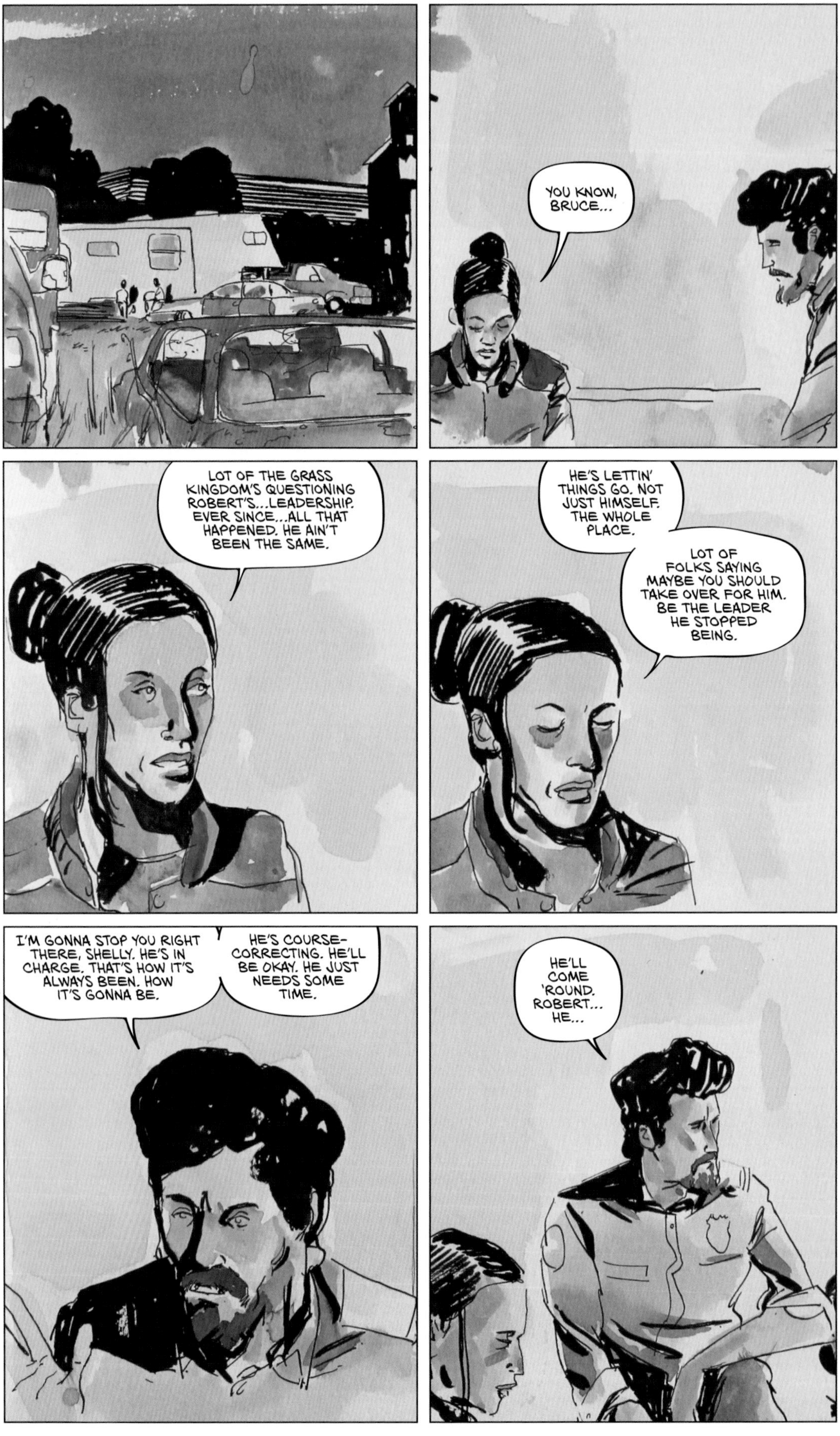
YOU KNOW, BRUCE...
LOT OF THE GRASS KINGDOM'S QUESTIONING ROBERT'S...LEADERSHIP. EVER SINCE...ALL THAT HAPPENED. HE AIN'T BEEN THE SAME.
HE'S LETTIN' THINGS GO. NOT JUST HIMSELF. THE WHOLE PLACE.
LOT OF FOLKS SAYING MAYBE YOU SHOULD TAKE OVER FOR HIM. BE THE LEADER HE STOPPED BEING.
I'M GONNA STOP YOU RIGHT THERE, SHELLY. HE'S IN CHARGE. THAT'S HOW IT'S ALWAYS BEEN. HOW IT'S GONNA BE.
HE'S COURSE-CORRECTING. HE'LL BE OKAY. HE JUST NEEDS SOME TIME.
HE'LL COME 'ROUND. ROBERT... HE...

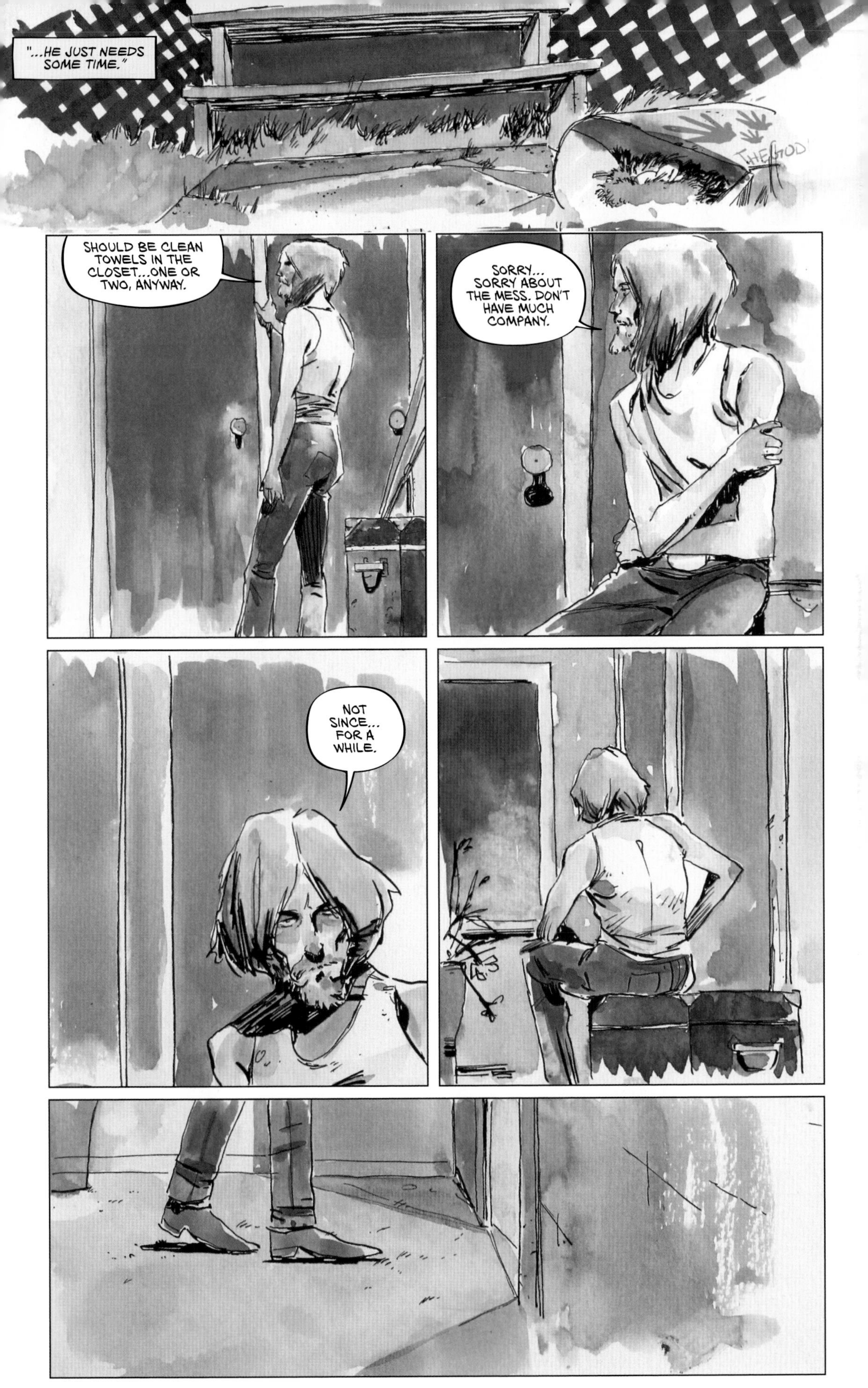
"...HE JUST NEEDS SOME TIME."
SHOULD BE CLEAN TOWELS IN THE CLOSET...ONE OR TWO, ANYWAY.
SORRY... SORRY ABOUT THE MESS. DON'T HAVE MUCH COMPANY.
NOT SINCE... FOR A WHILE.

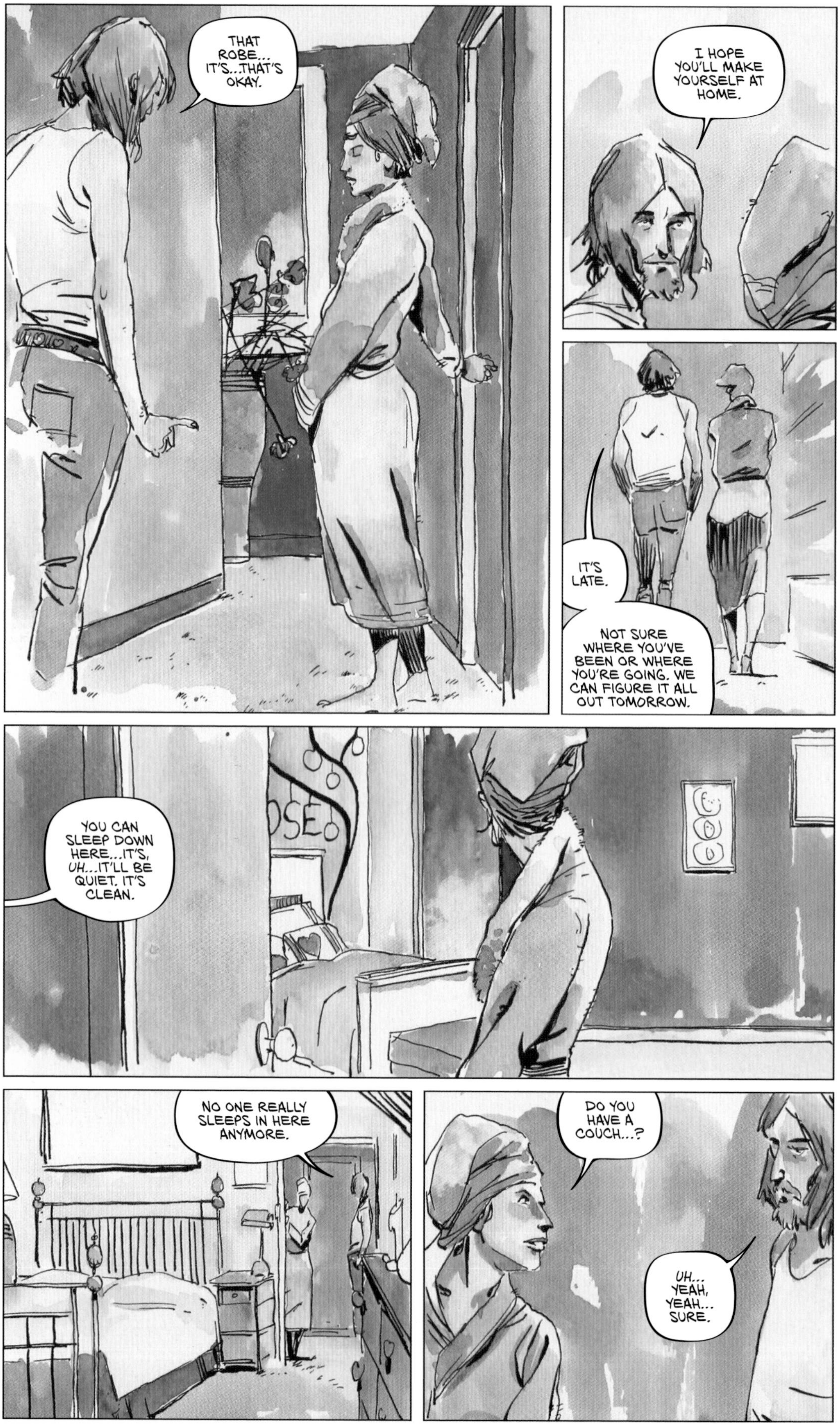
THAT ROBE... IT'S...THAT'S OKAY.
I HOPE YOU'LL MAKE YOURSELF AT HOME.
IT'S LATE.
NOT SURE WHERE YOU'VE BEEN OR WHERE YOU'RE GOING. WE CAN FIGURE IT ALL OUT TOMORROW.
YOU CAN SLEEP DOWN HERE...IT'S, UH...IT'LL BE QUIET. IT'S CLEAN.
NO ONE REALLY SLEEPS IN HERE ANYMORE.
DO YOU HAVE A COUCH...?
UH... YEAH, YEAH... SURE.

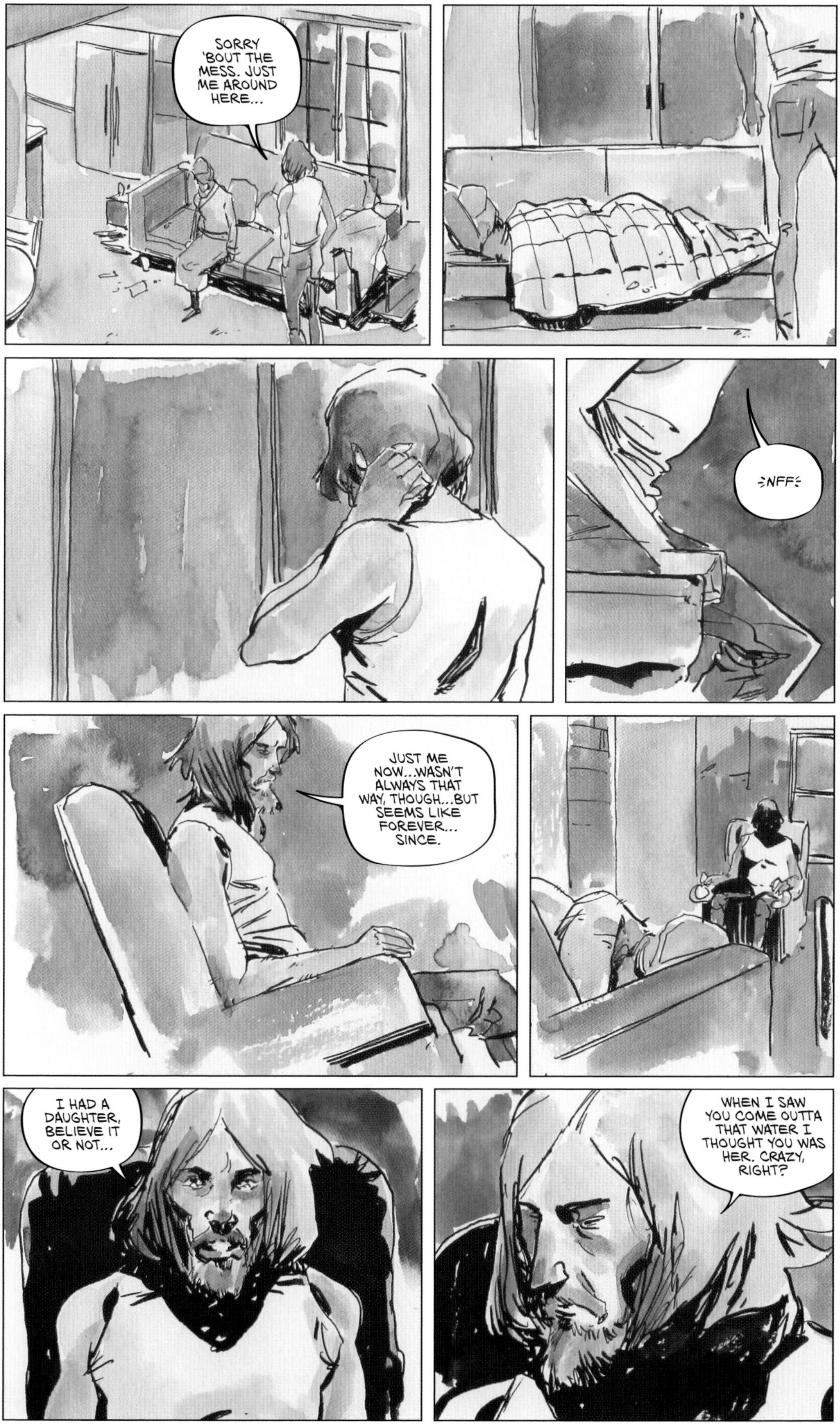
SORRY 'BOUT THE MESS. JUST ME AROUND HERE...
NFF
JUST ME NOW...WASN'T ALWAYS THAT WAY, THOUGH...BUT SEEMS LIKE FOREVER... SINCE.
I HAD A DAUGHTER, BELIEVE IT OR NOT...
WHEN I SAW YOU COME OUTTA THAT WATER I THOUGHT YOU WAS HER. CRAZY, RIGHT?

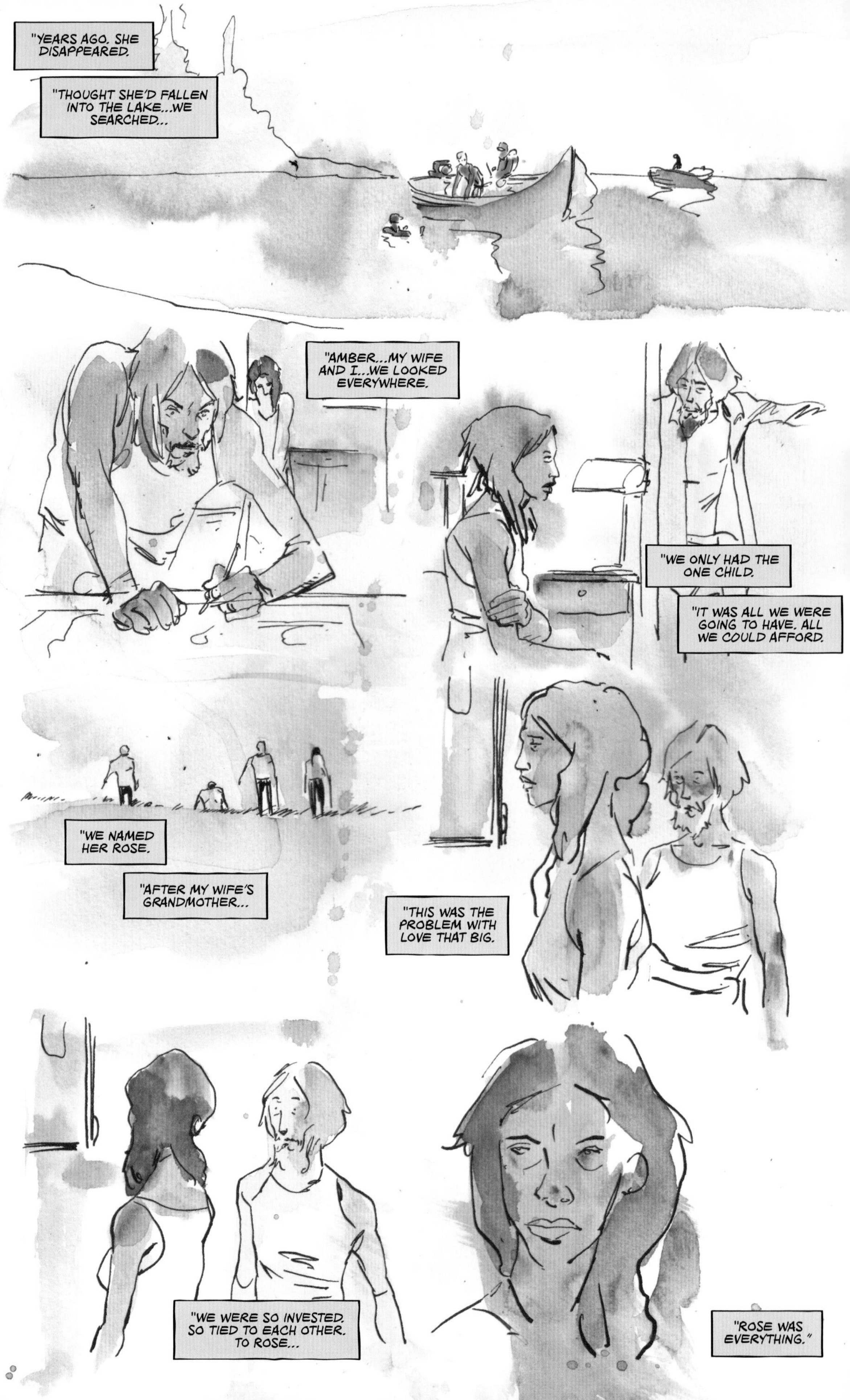
"YEARS AGO, SHE DISAPPEARED.
"THOUGHT SHE'D FALLEN INTO THE LAKE...WE SEARCHED...
"AMBER...MY WIFE AND I...WE LOOKED EVERYWHERE.
"WE ONLY HAD THE ONE CHILD.
"IT WAS ALL WE WERE GOING TO HAVE. ALL WE COULD AFFORD.
"WE NAMED HER ROSE.
"AFTER MY WIFE'S GRANDMOTHER...
"THIS WAS THE PROBLEM WITH LOVE THAT BIG.
"WE WERE SO INVESTED. SO TIED TO EACH OTHER. TO ROSE...
"ROSE WAS EVERYTHING."

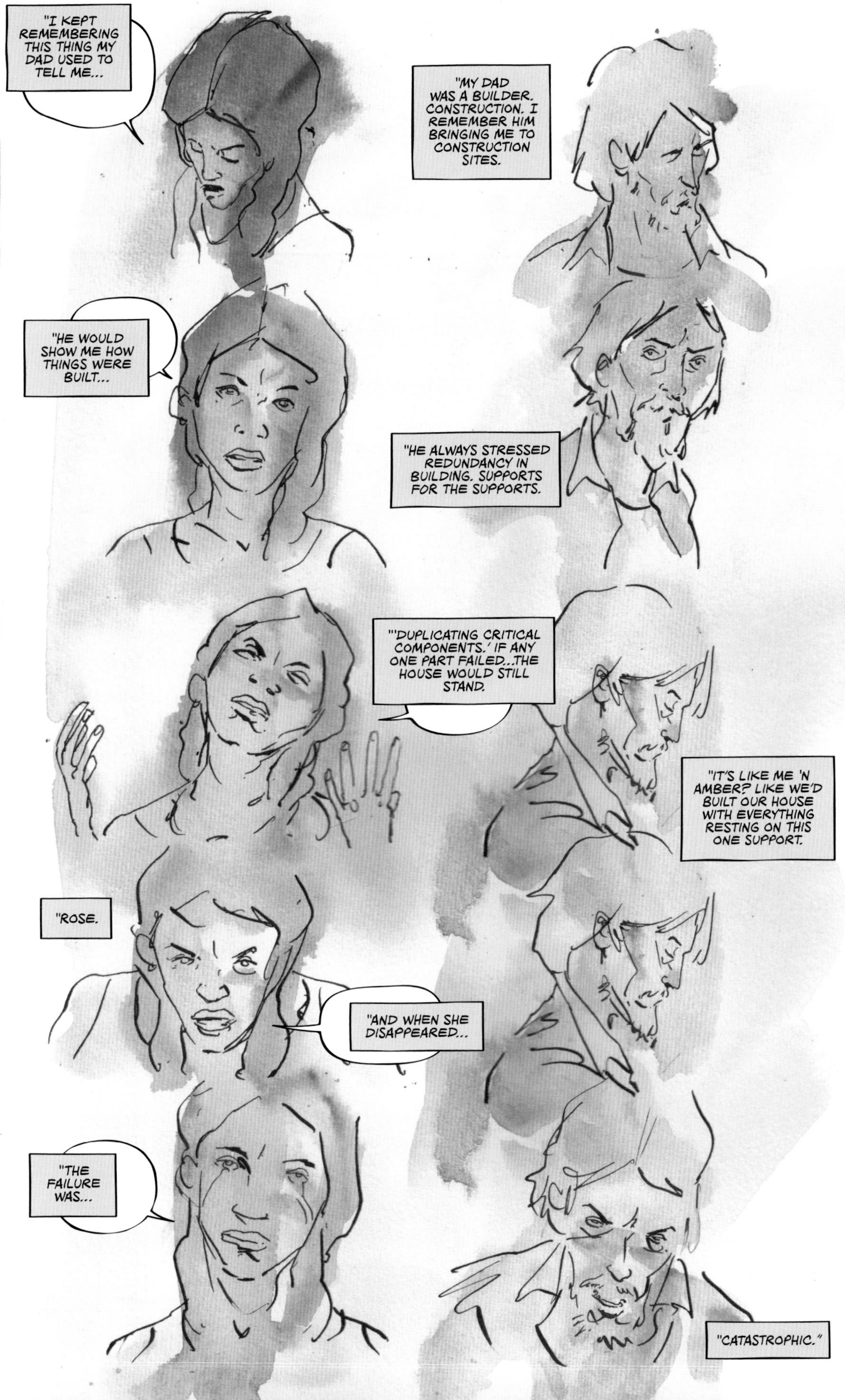
"I KEPT REMEMBERING THIS THING MY DAD USED TO TELL ME...
"MY DAD WAS A BUILDER. CONSTRUCTION. I REMEMBER HIM BRINGING ME TO CONSTRUCTION SITES.
"HE WOULD SHOW ME HOW THINGS WERE BUILT...
"HE ALWAYS STRESSED REDUNDANCY IN BUILDING. SUPPORTS FOR THE SUPPORTS.
"'DUPLICATING CRITICAL COMPONENTS.' IF ANY ONE PART FAILED...THE HOUSE WOULD STILL STAND.
"IT'S LIKE ME 'N AMBER? LIKE WE'D BUILT OUR HOUSE WITH EVERYTHING RESTING ON THIS ONE SUPPORT.
"ROSE.
"AND WHEN SHE DISAPPEARED...
"THE FAILURE WAS...
"CATASTROPHIC."

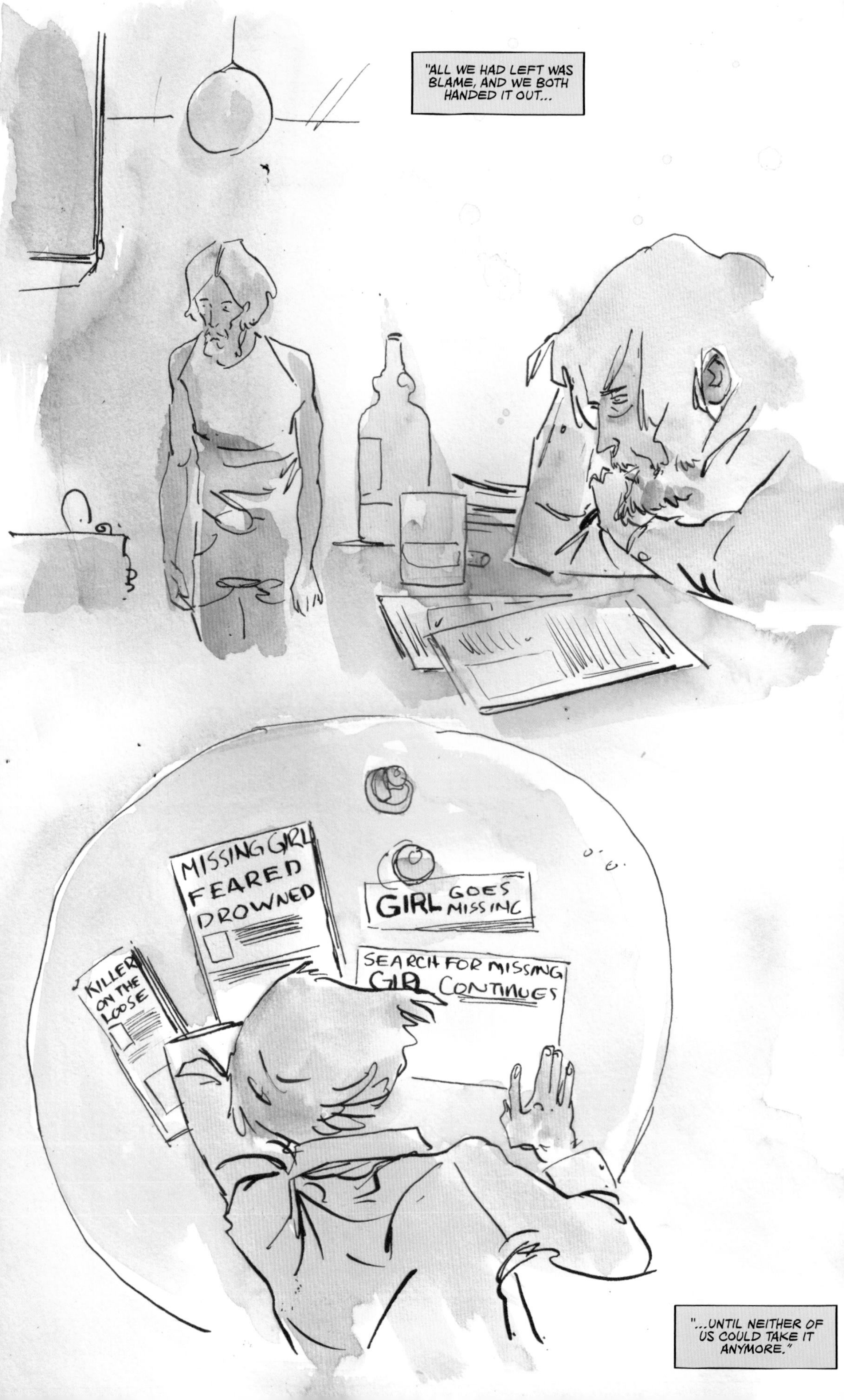
"ALL WE HAD LEFT WAS BLAME, AND WE BOTH HANDED IT OUT...
MISSING GIRL FEARED DROWNED
GIRL GOES MISSING
KILLER ON THE LOOSE
SEARCH FOR MISSING GIRL CONTINUES
"...UNTIL NEITHER OF US COULD TAKE IT ANYMORE."

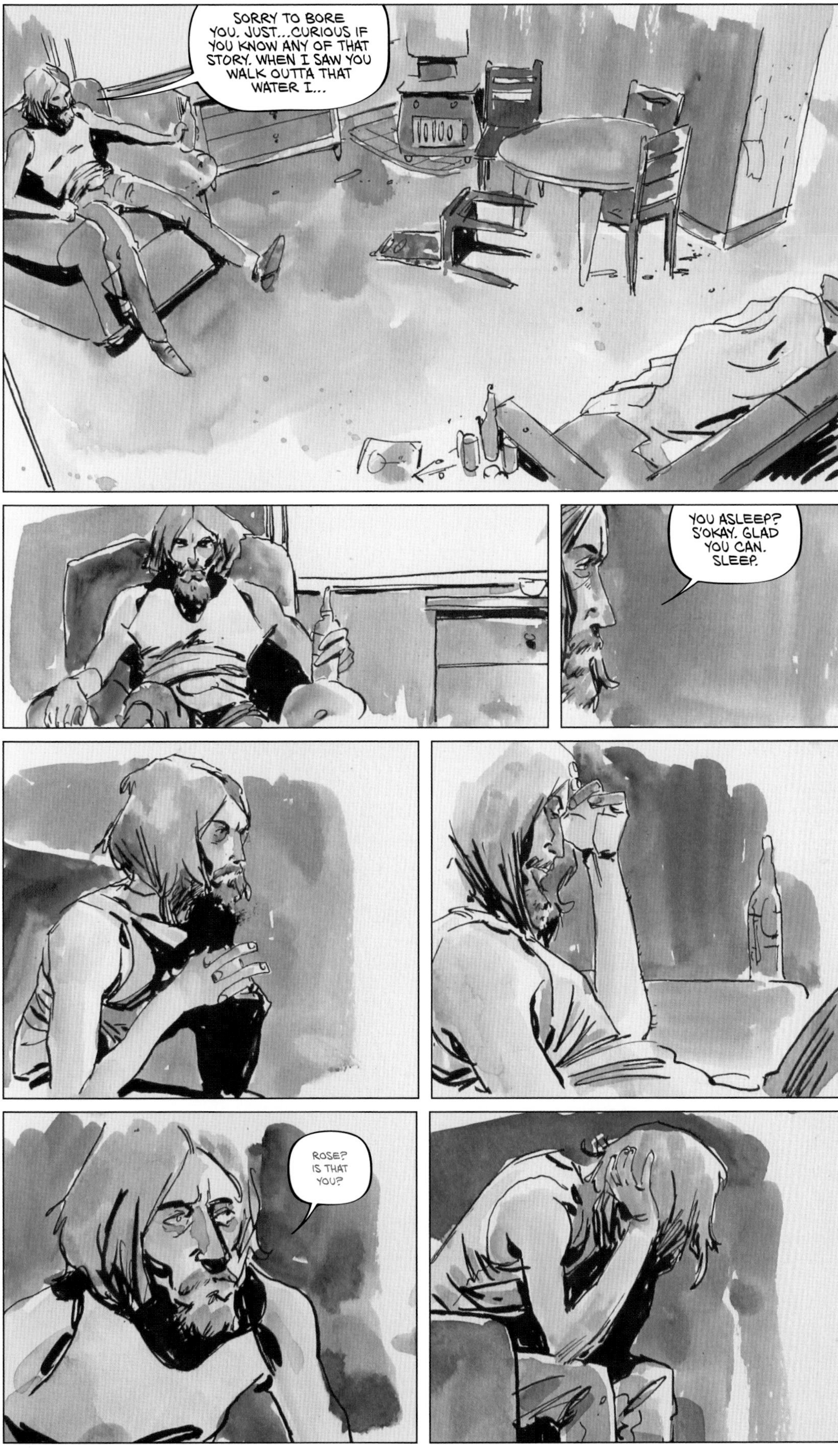
SORRY TO BORE YOU. JUST...CURIOUS IF YOU KNOW ANY OF THAT STORY. WHEN I SAW YOU WALK OUTTA THAT WATER I...
YOU ASLEEP? S'OKAY. GLAD YOU CAN. SLEEP.
ROSE? IS THAT YOU?

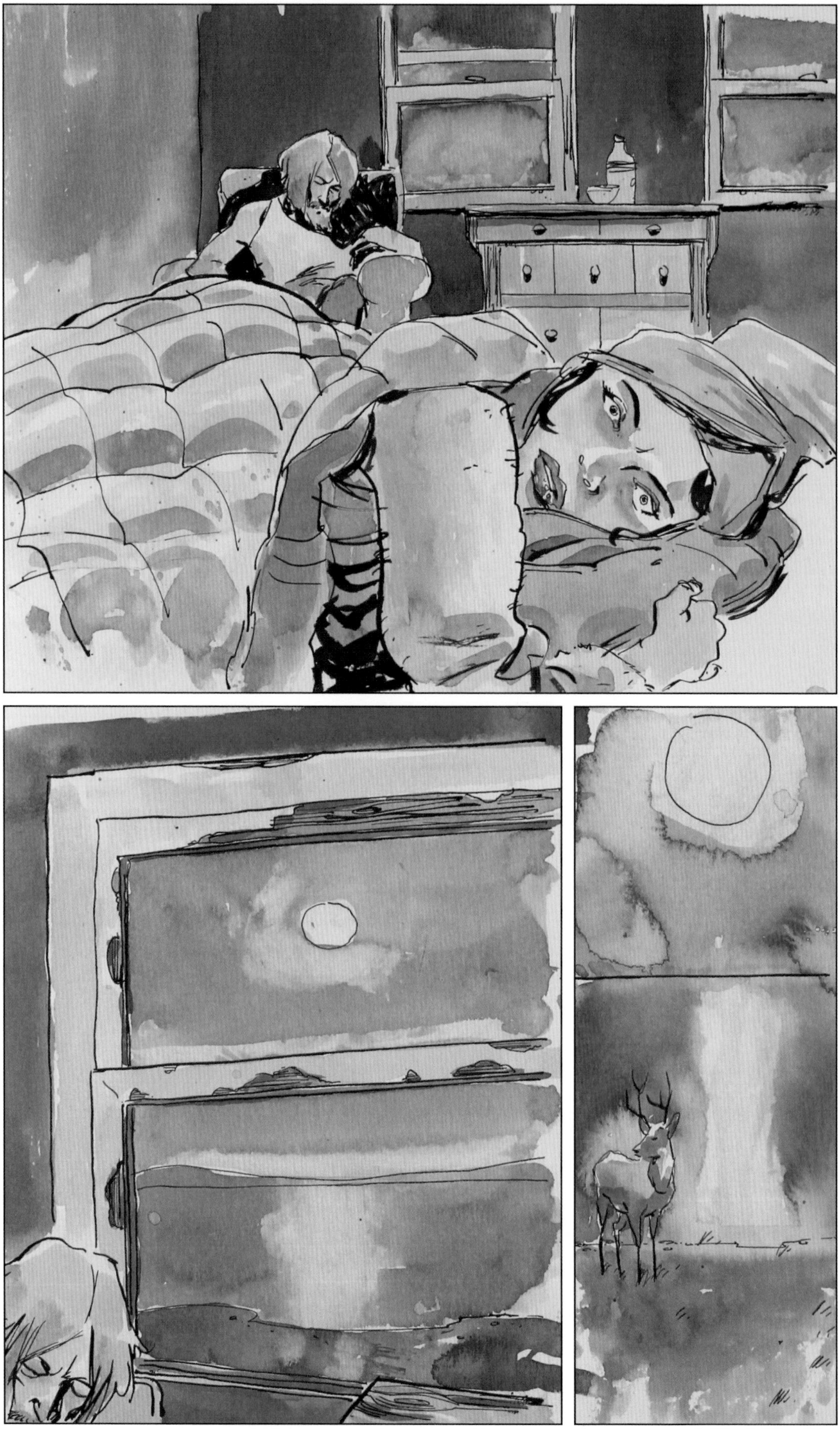

WE SHOULD MAKE OUR OWN MOVIE.

DUDE. YOU HAVE THE ATTENTION SPAN OF A GNAT. LAST WEEK YOU WERE READY TO STEAL A PLANE AND FLY CROSS-COUNTRY.

I'M STILL UP FOR THAT, TOO! WE COULD BE THE KEROUACS OF THE SKY!

SERIOUSLY. YOU DRINK WAY TOO MUCH SODA.

IT'S CALLED MOTIVATION. GET OFF YOUR ASS AND LOOK IT UP SOME TIME!

HA! SURE. GET BACK TO ME NEXT WEEK WHEN YOU HAVE ANOTHER CRAZY IDEA.

I'M WRITING A BOOK. FILLING IT WITH EVERY NUTTY SCHEME YOU'VE EVER HAD.

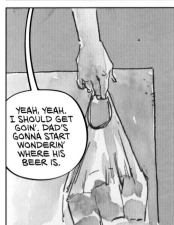

YEAH, YEAH. I SHOULD GET GOIN'. DAD'S GONNA START WONDERIN' WHERE HIS BEER IS.

CATCH YOU TOMORROW.

SEE YA.

HM?

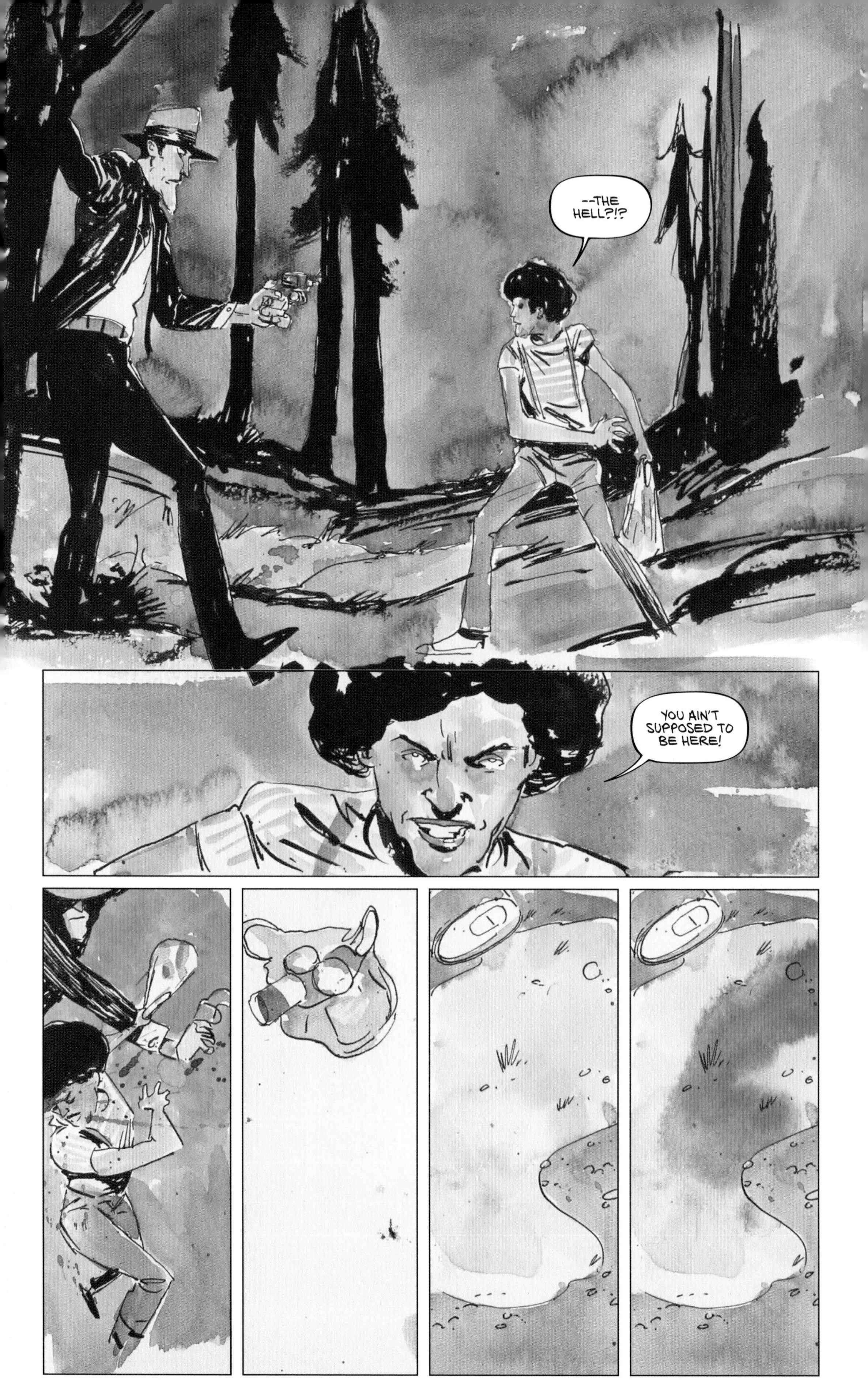
--THE HELL?!?
YOU AIN'T SUPPOSED TO BE HERE!

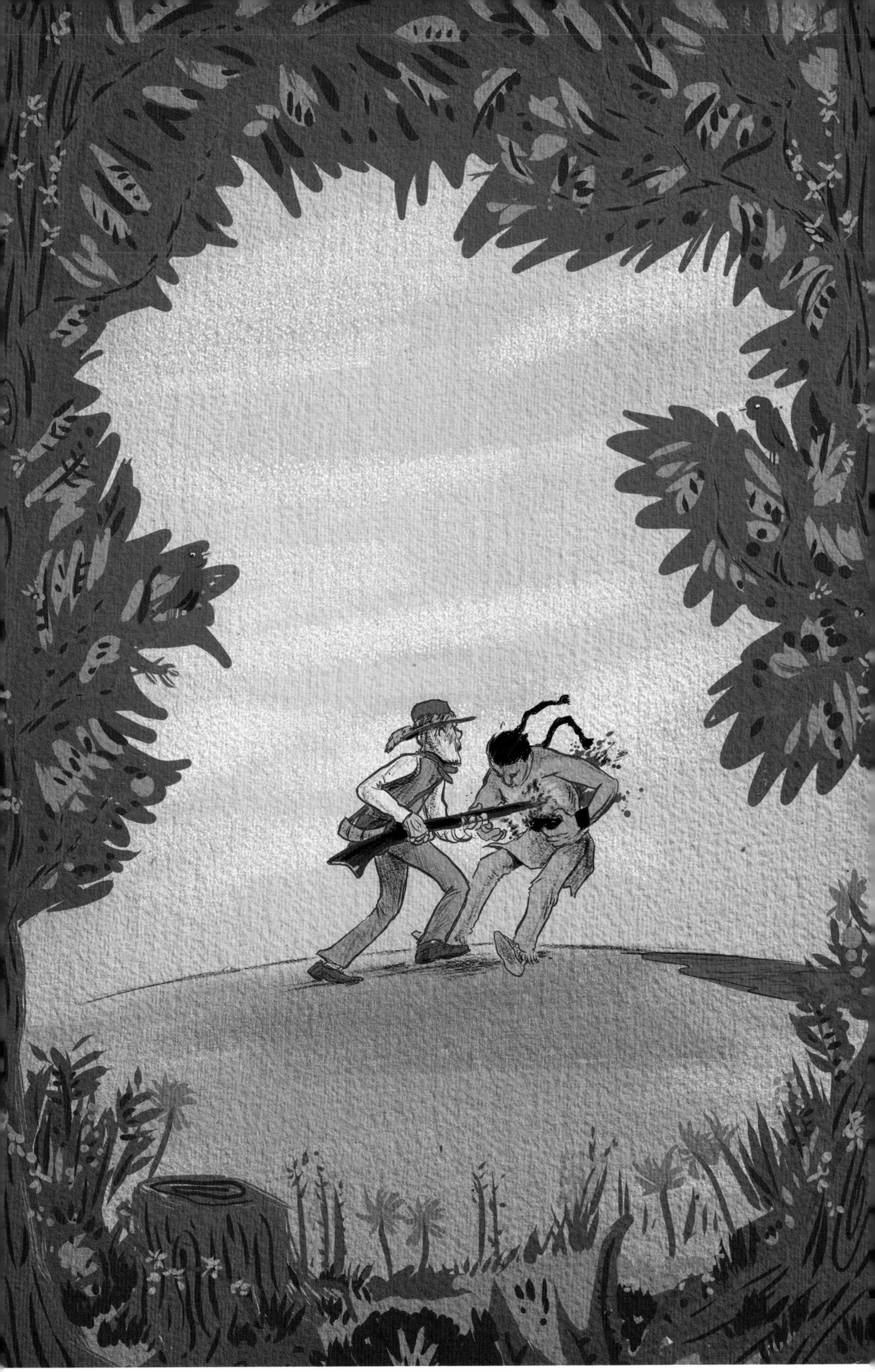

issue #2 cover by matt kindt

# chapter three

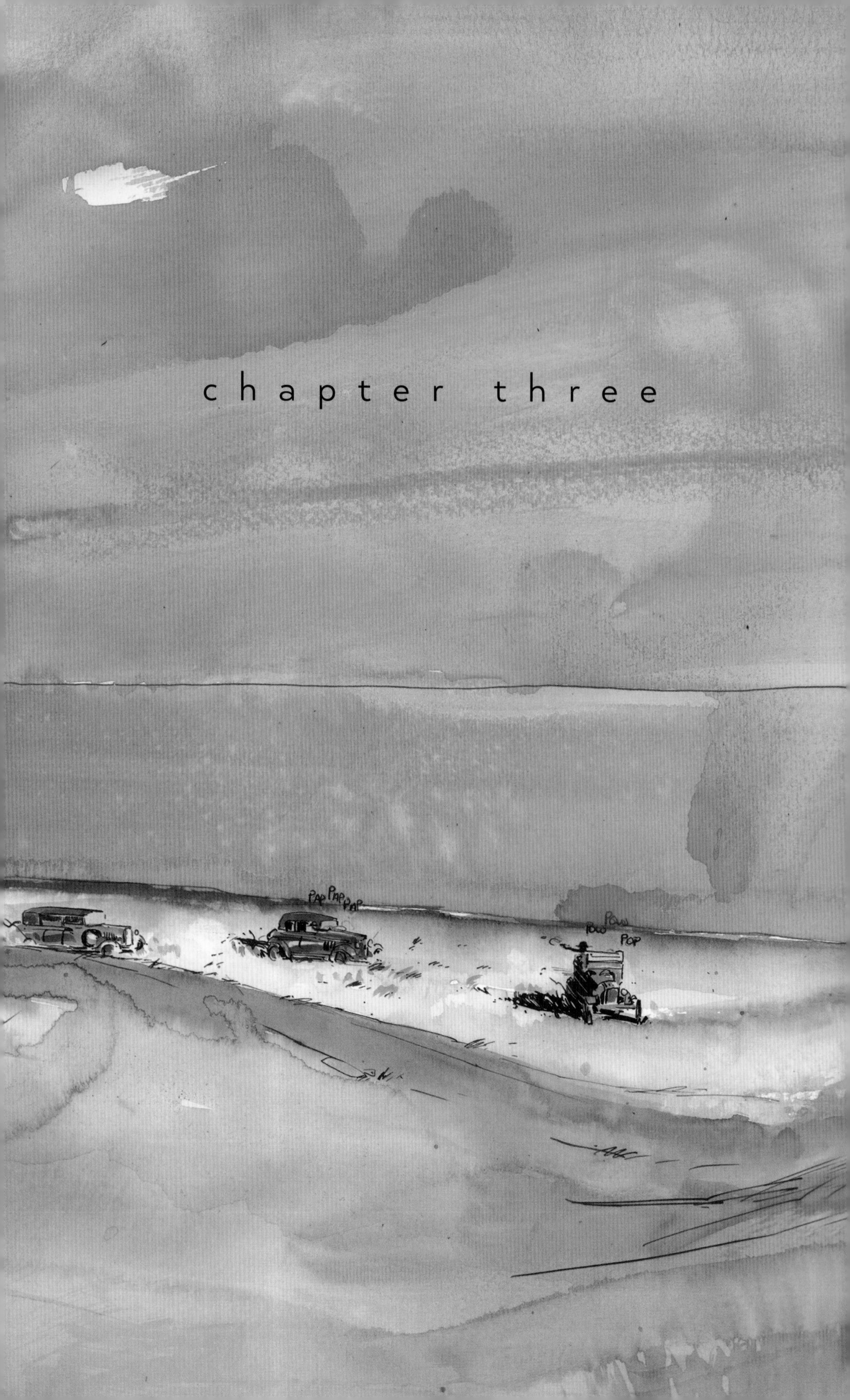
PAP PAP PAP
POW POW
POP

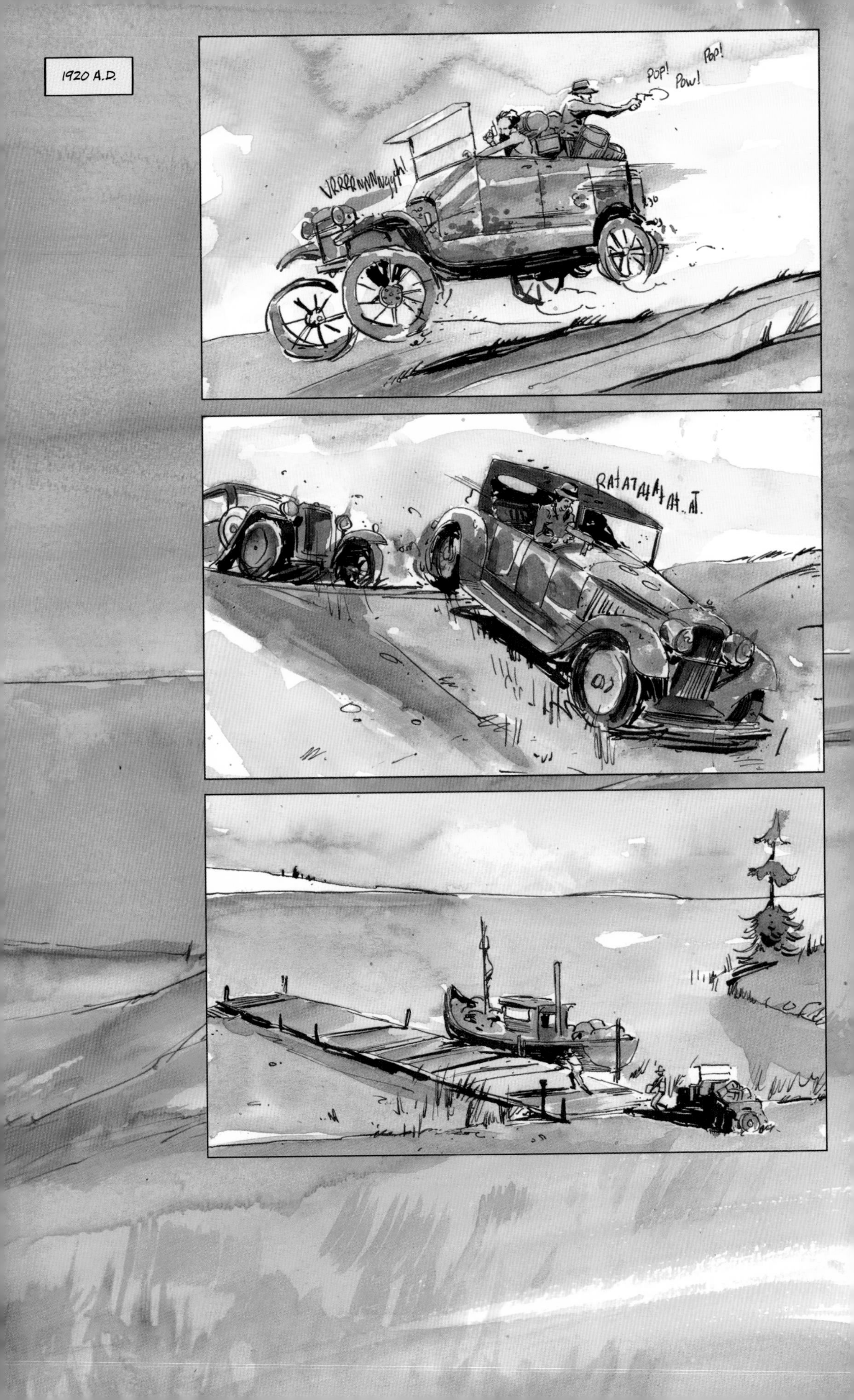
1920 A.D.
VRRRRNNNNgggh!
POP!
POW!
POP!
RATATATATAT..AT.

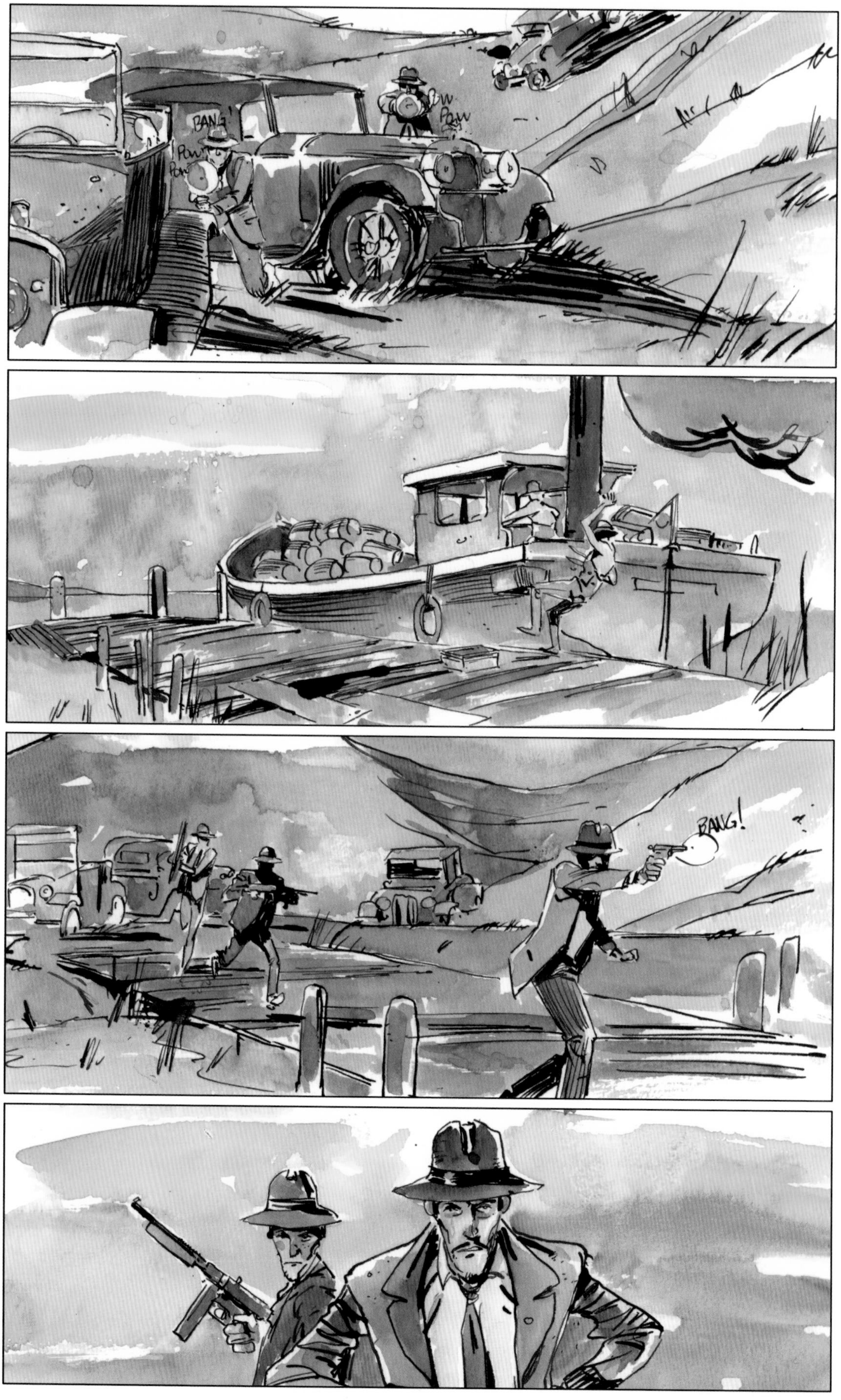
BANG!
Pow
Pow
Pow
Pow
BANG!

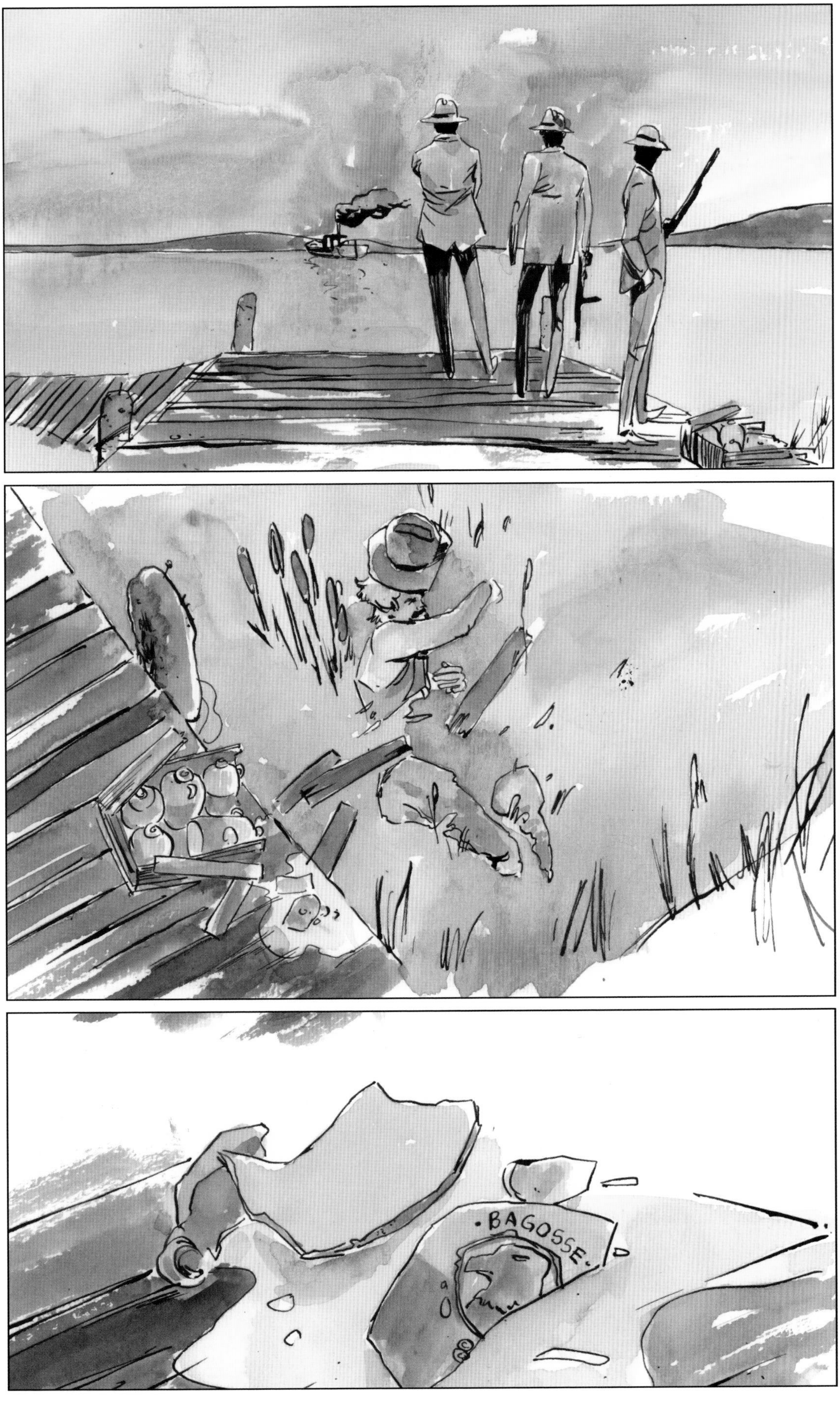

·BAGOSSE·

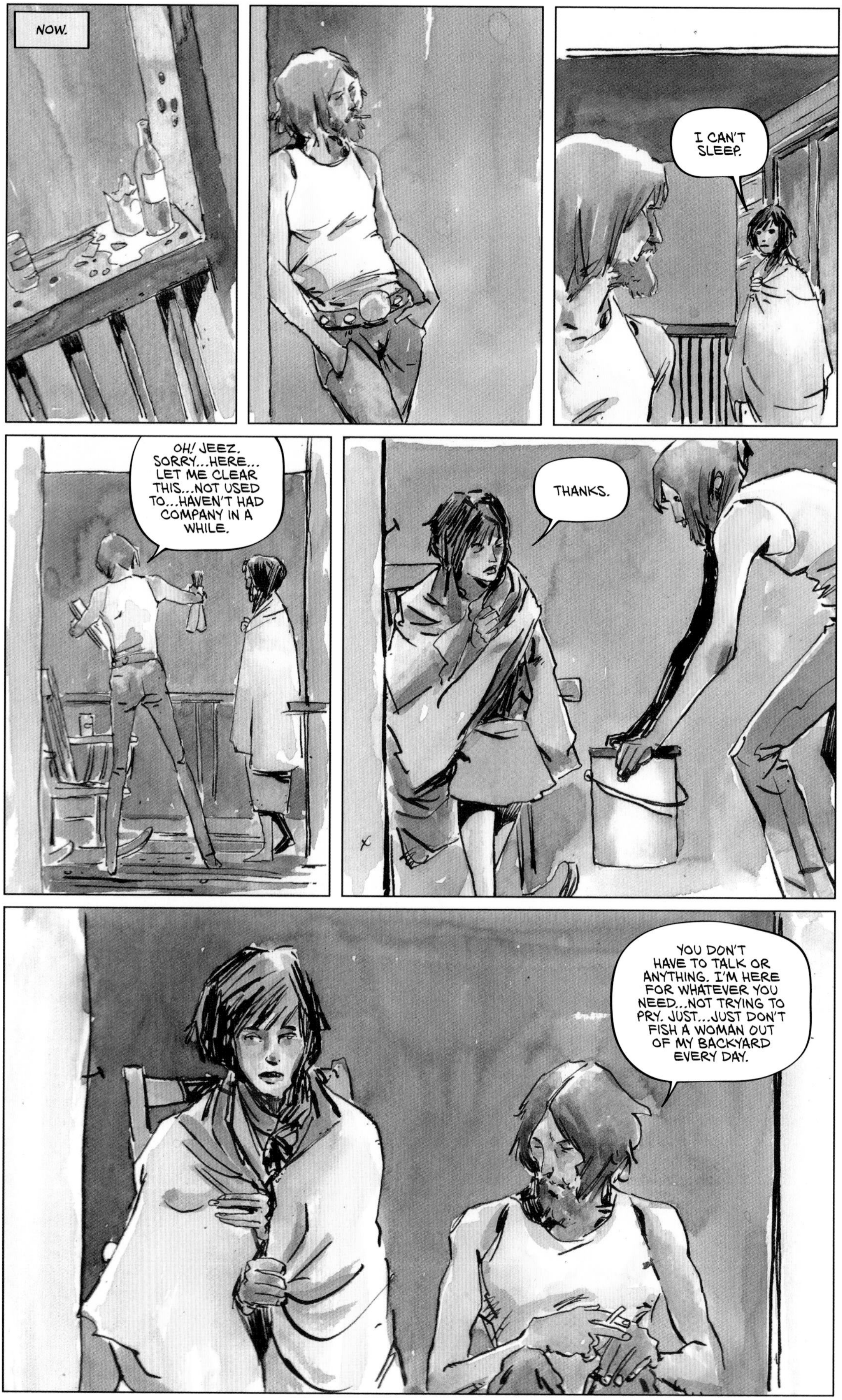
NOW.
I CAN'T SLEEP.
OH! JEEZ. SORRY...HERE... LET ME CLEAR THIS...NOT USED TO...HAVEN'T HAD COMPANY IN A WHILE.
THANKS.
YOU DON'T HAVE TO TALK OR ANYTHING. I'M HERE FOR WHATEVER YOU NEED...NOT TRYING TO PRY. JUST...JUST DON'T FISH A WOMAN OUT OF MY BACKYARD EVERY DAY.

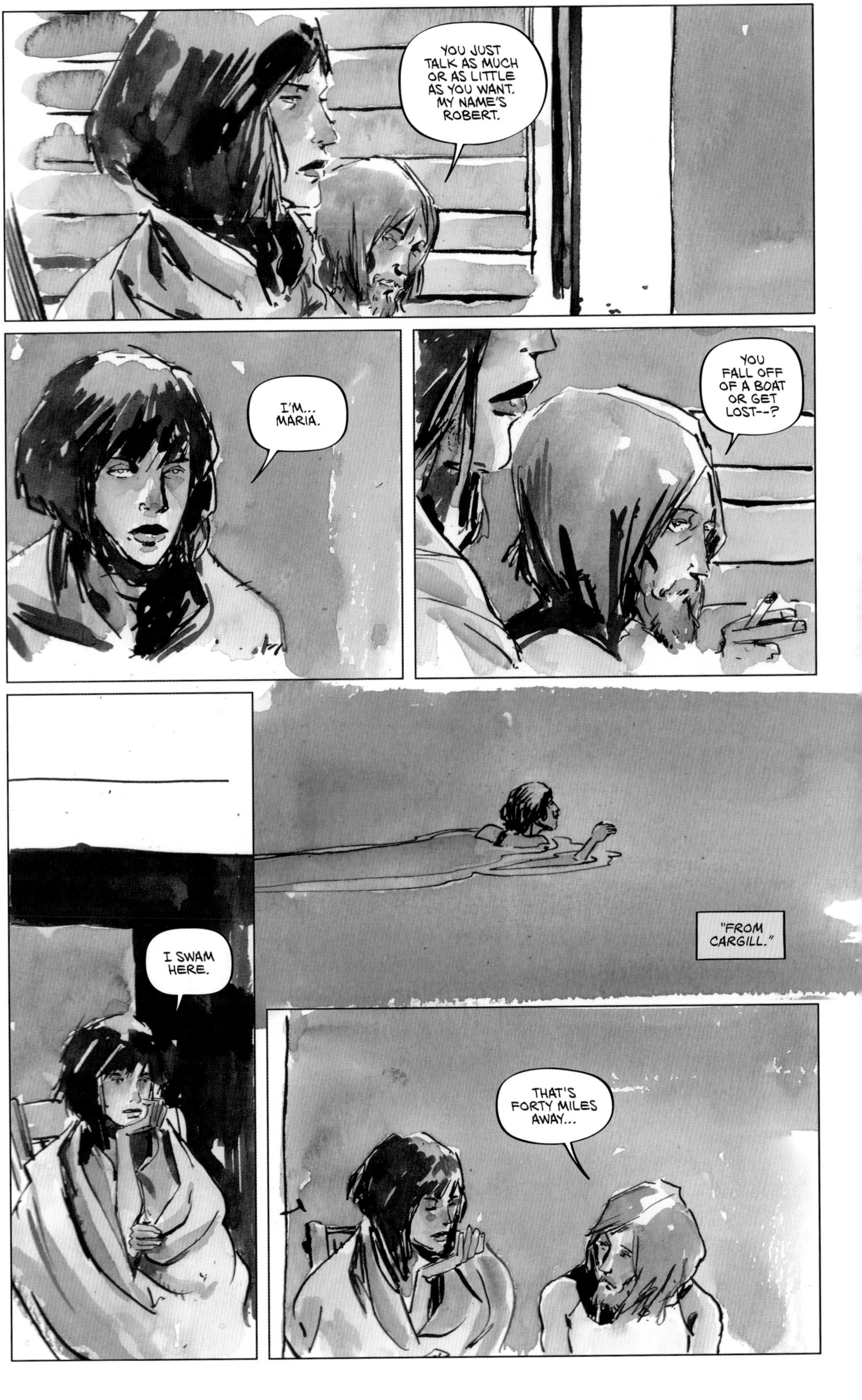
YOU JUST TALK AS MUCH OR AS LITTLE AS YOU WANT. MY NAME'S ROBERT.
I'M... MARIA.
YOU FALL OFF OF A BOAT OR GET LOST--?
I SWAM HERE.
"FROM CARGILL."
THAT'S FORTY MILES AWAY...

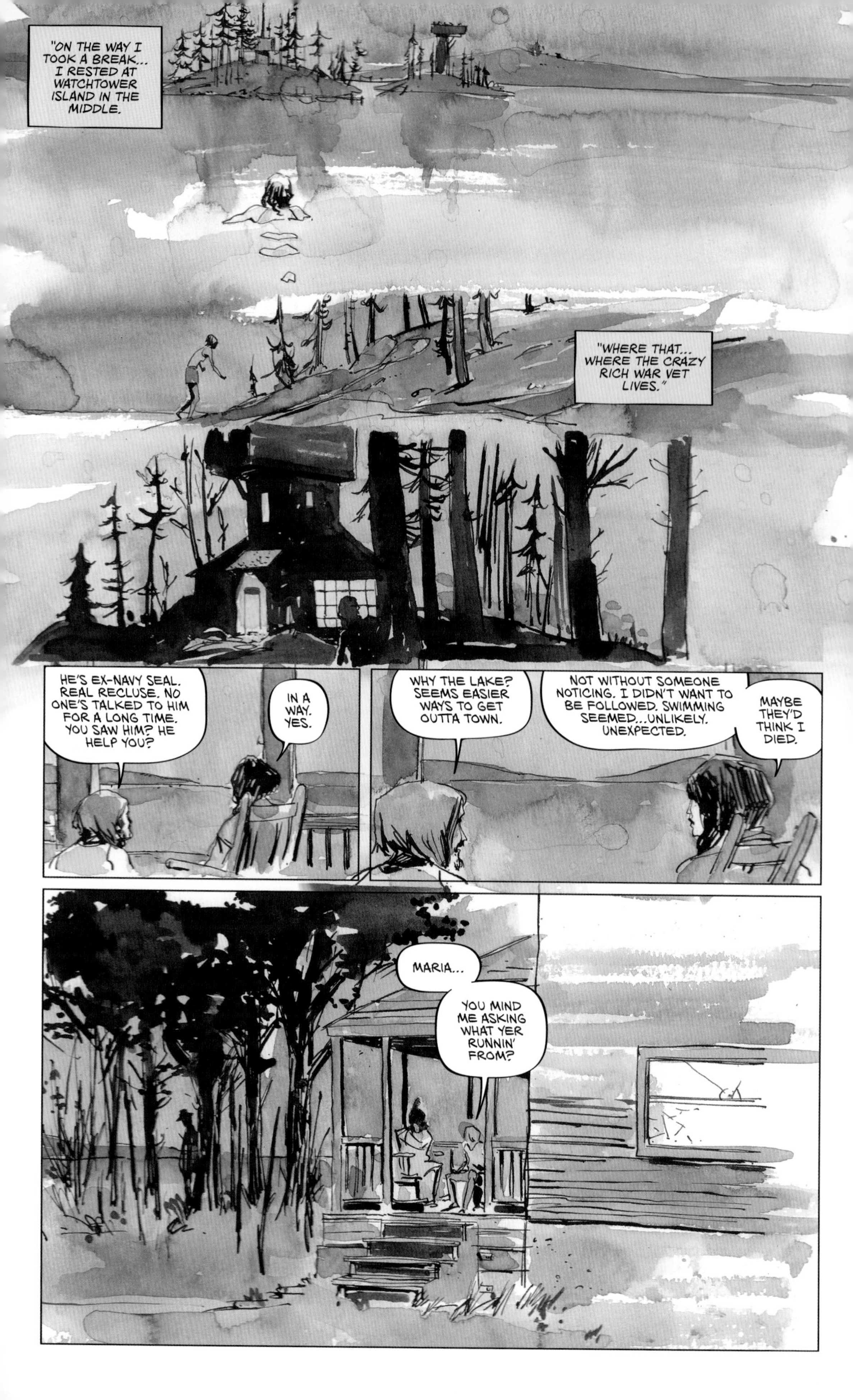
"ON THE WAY I TOOK A BREAK... I RESTED AT WATCHTOWER ISLAND IN THE MIDDLE.
"WHERE THAT... WHERE THE CRAZY RICH WAR VET LIVES."
HE'S EX-NAVY SEAL. REAL RECLUSE. NO ONE'S TALKED TO HIM FOR A LONG TIME. YOU SAW HIM? HE HELP YOU?
IN A WAY. YES.
WHY THE LAKE? SEEMS EASIER WAYS TO GET OUTTA TOWN.
NOT WITHOUT SOMEONE NOTICING. I DIDN'T WANT TO BE FOLLOWED. SWIMMING SEEMED...UNLIKELY. UNEXPECTED.
MAYBE THEY'D THINK I DIED.
MARIA...
YOU MIND ME ASKING WHAT YER RUNNIN' FROM?

WHO. WHO I'M RUNNING FROM. HUMBERT.

OH... OH.

YEAH. THE SHERIFF OF CARGILL.

I DON'T EXPECT HE'LL FIND ME HERE. NOT YET, ANYWAY.

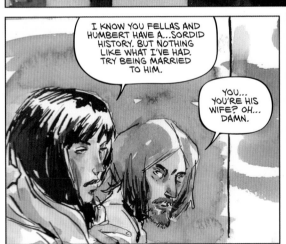

I KNOW YOU FELLAS AND HUMBERT HAVE A...SORDID HISTORY. BUT NOTHING LIKE WHAT I'VE HAD. TRY BEING MARRIED TO HIM.

YOU... YOU'RE HIS WIFE? OH... DAMN.

MARIA...HE FINDS YOU HERE, THERE'S GONNA BE A MESS OF TROUBLE.

I...I'M HUNGRY, BUT...I COULDN'T FIND ANYTHING INSIDE. MOSTLY... BEER.

CRAP. YEAH. SORRY ABOUT THAT. JUST... I'VE LET THINGS GO LATELY.

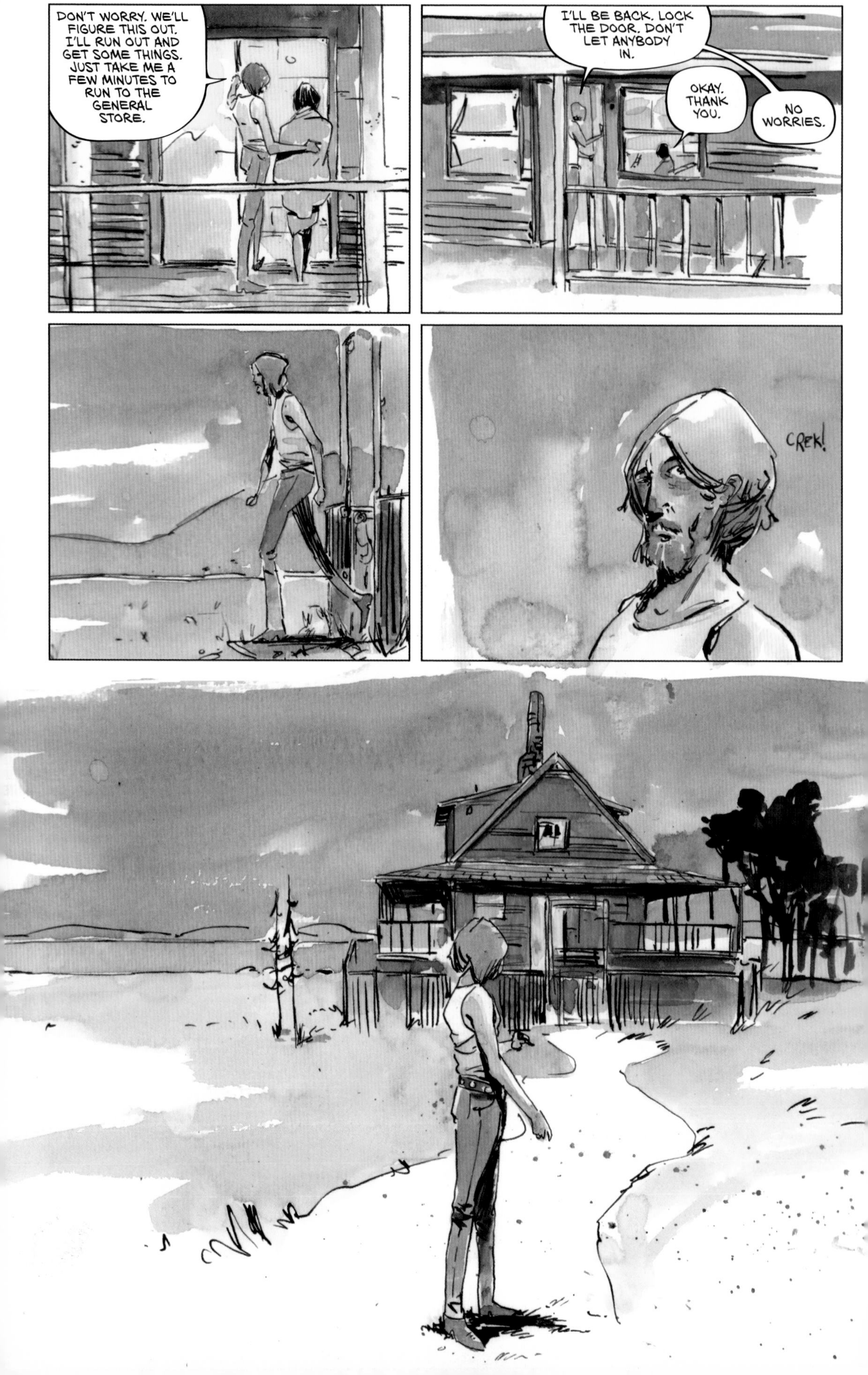
DON'T WORRY. WE'LL FIGURE THIS OUT. I'LL RUN OUT AND GET SOME THINGS. JUST TAKE ME A FEW MINUTES TO RUN TO THE GENERAL STORE.
I'LL BE BACK. LOCK THE DOOR. DON'T LET ANYBODY IN.
OKAY. THANK YOU.
NO WORRIES.
CREK!

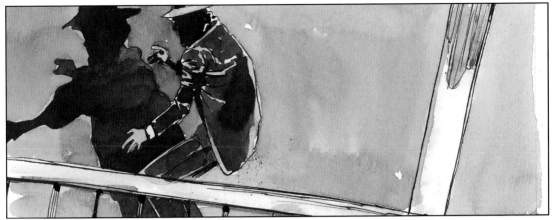

THAT AIN'T VERY NEIGHBORLY.

BIG DAN. I DON'T KNOW WHAT YER LOOKIN' FOR.

BUT HOPEFULLY IT'S AN ASS-KICKIN'.

ROBERT... HOW 'BOUT THAT. I'M SURPRISED YER SOBER ENOUGH TO STAND.

WON'T BE FOR LONG.

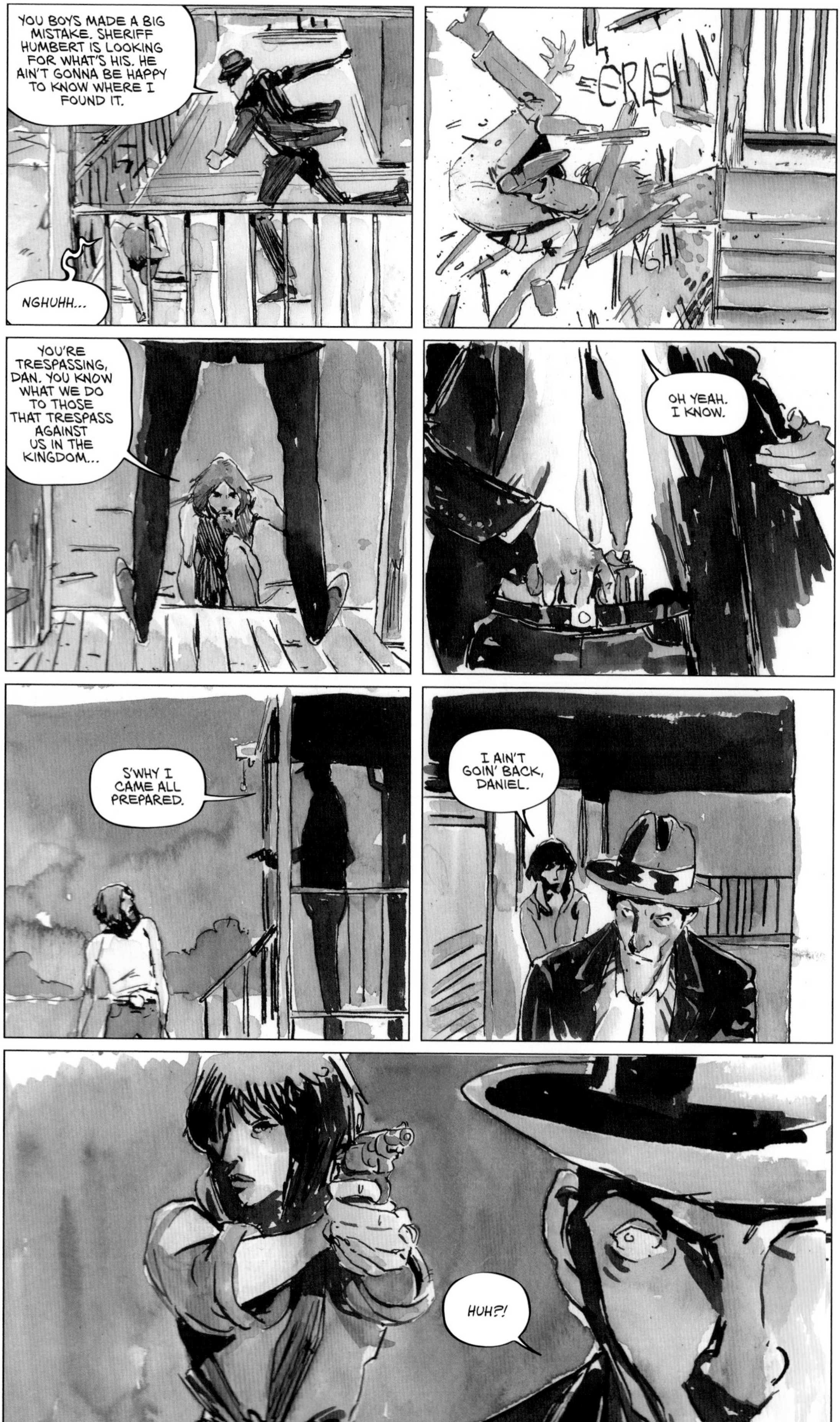
YOU BOYS MADE A BIG MISTAKE. SHERIFF HUMBERT IS LOOKING FOR WHAT'S HIS. HE AIN'T GONNA BE HAPPY TO KNOW WHERE I FOUND IT.
NGHUHH...
CRASH
NGH
YOU'RE TRESPASSING, DAN. YOU KNOW WHAT WE DO TO THOSE THAT TRESPASS AGAINST US IN THE KINGDOM...
OH YEAH. I KNOW.
S'WHY I CAME ALL PREPARED.
I AIN'T GOIN' BACK, DANIEL.
HUH?!

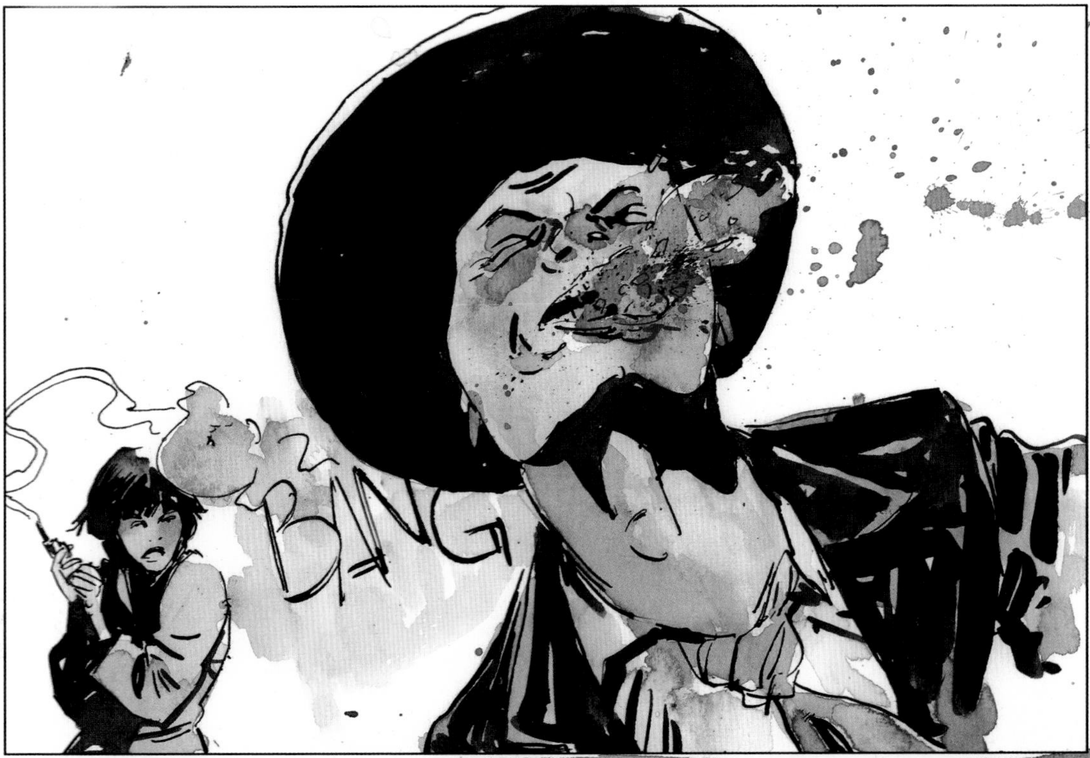
BANG

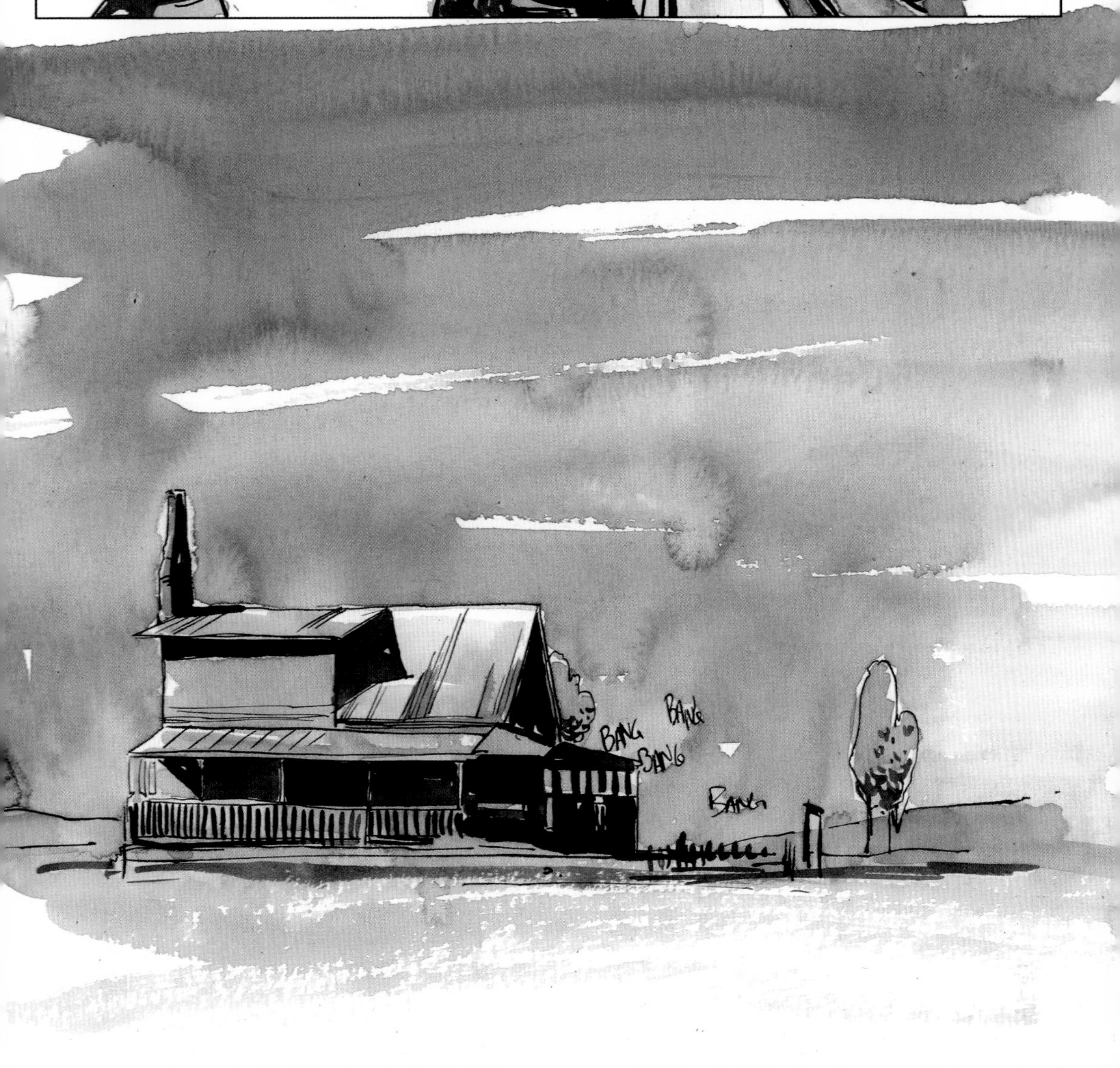
BANG
BANG
BANG
BANG

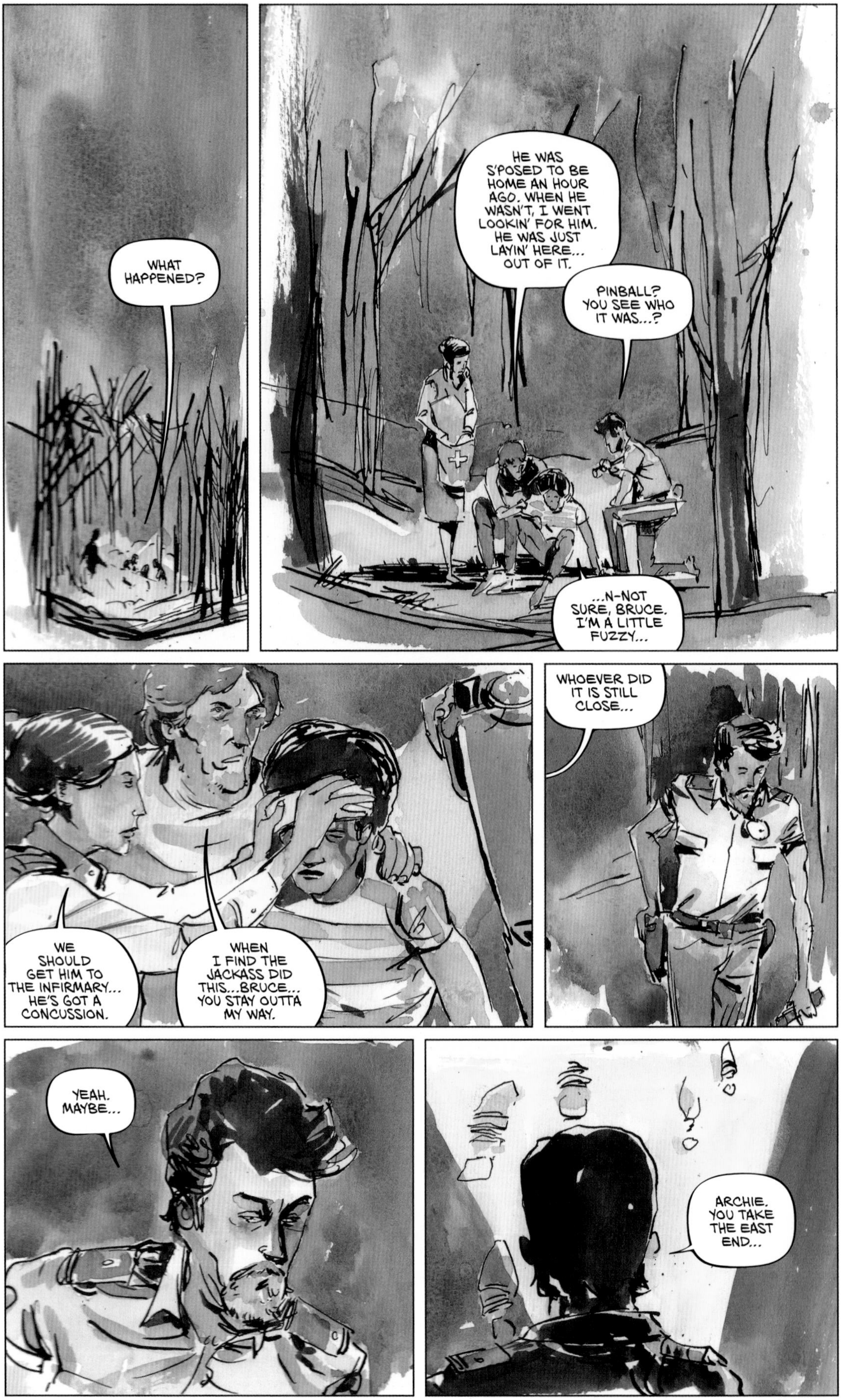
WHAT HAPPENED?
HE WAS S'POSED TO BE HOME AN HOUR AGO. WHEN HE WASN'T, I WENT LOOKIN' FOR HIM. HE WAS JUST LAYIN' HERE... OUT OF IT.
PINBALL? YOU SEE WHO IT WAS...?
...N-NOT SURE, BRUCE. I'M A LITTLE FUZZY...
WE SHOULD GET HIM TO THE INFIRMARY... HE'S GOT A CONCUSSION.
WHEN I FIND THE JACKASS DID THIS...BRUCE... YOU STAY OUTTA MY WAY.
WHOEVER DID IT IS STILL CLOSE...
YEAH. MAYBE...
ARCHIE. YOU TAKE THE EAST END...

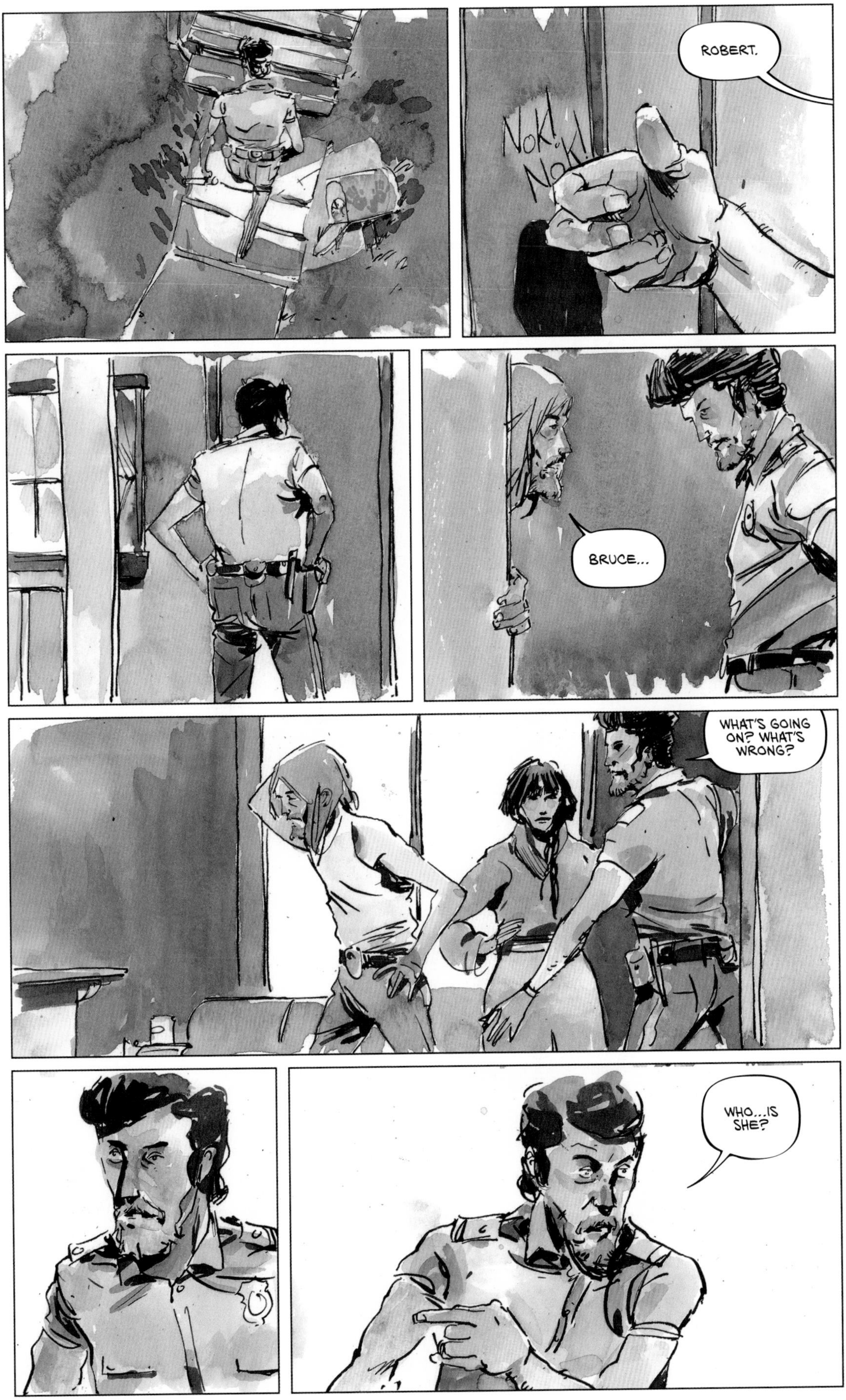
ROBERT.
NOK! NOK!
BRUCE...
WHAT'S GOING ON? WHAT'S WRONG?
WHO...IS SHE?

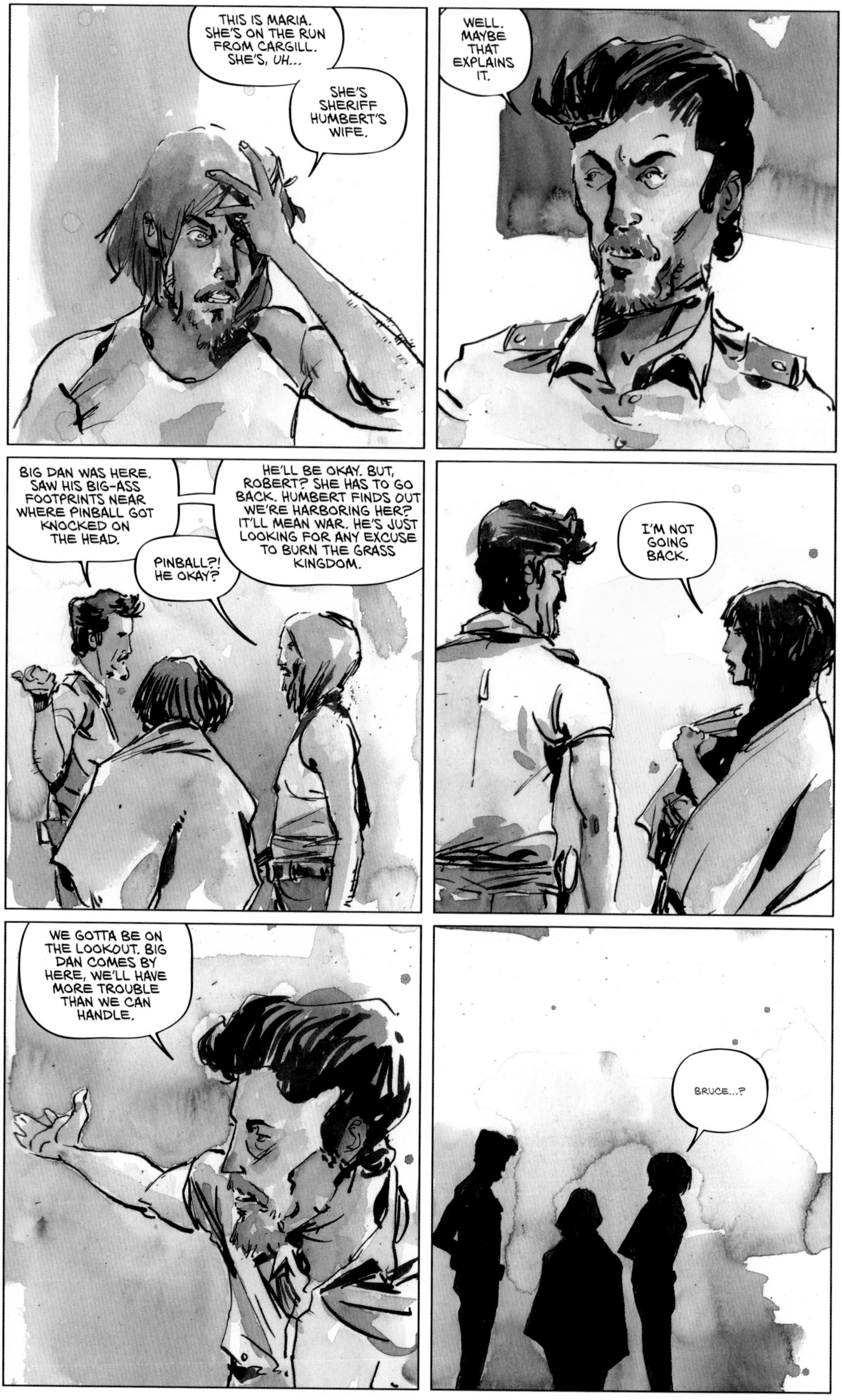
THIS IS MARIA. SHE'S ON THE RUN FROM CARGILL. SHE'S, UH...
SHE'S SHERIFF HUMBERT'S WIFE.
WELL. MAYBE THAT EXPLAINS IT.
BIG DAN WAS HERE. SAW HIS BIG-ASS FOOTPRINTS NEAR WHERE PINBALL GOT KNOCKED ON THE HEAD.
PINBALL?! HE OKAY?
HE'LL BE OKAY. BUT, ROBERT? SHE HAS TO GO BACK. HUMBERT FINDS OUT WE'RE HARBORING HER? IT'LL MEAN WAR. HE'S JUST LOOKING FOR ANY EXCUSE TO BURN THE GRASS KINGDOM.
I'M NOT GOING BACK.
WE GOTTA BE ON THE LOOKOUT. BIG DAN COMES BY HERE, WE'LL HAVE MORE TROUBLE THAN WE CAN HANDLE.
BRUCE...?

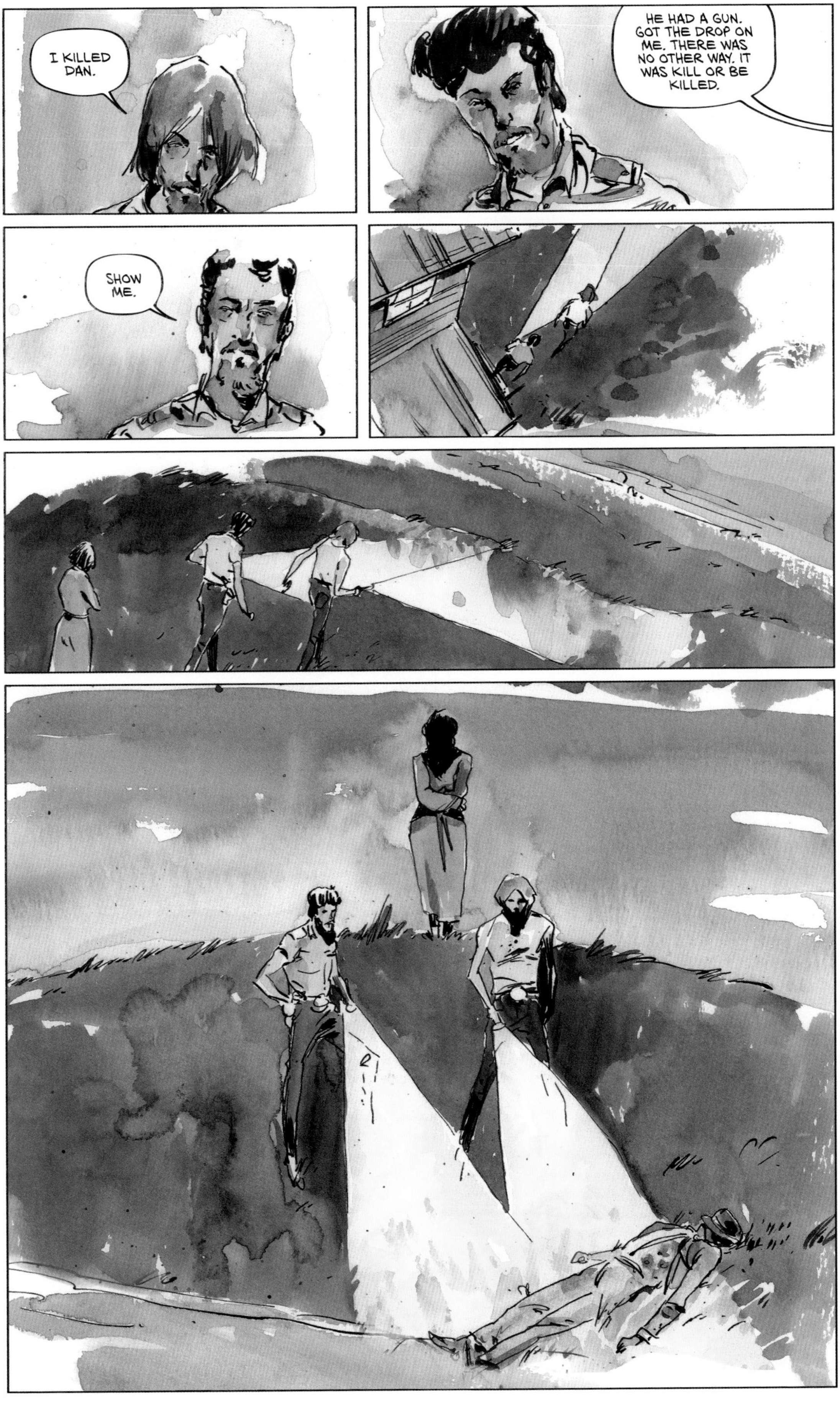
I KILLED DAN.
HE HAD A GUN. GOT THE DROP ON ME. THERE WAS NO OTHER WAY. IT WAS KILL OR BE KILLED.
SHOW ME.

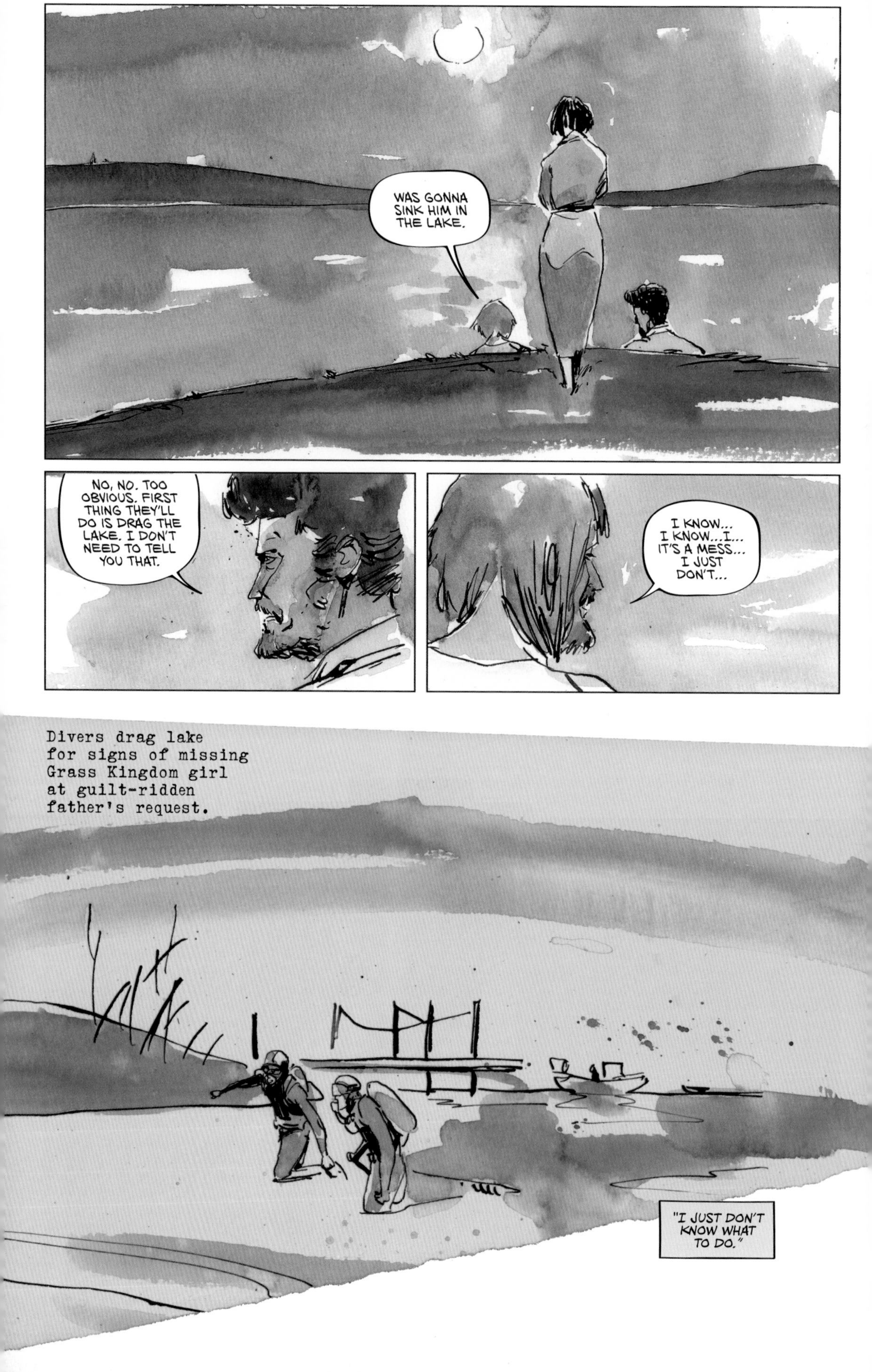
WAS GONNA SINK HIM IN THE LAKE.
NO, NO. TOO OBVIOUS. FIRST THING THEY'LL DO IS DRAG THE LAKE. I DON'T NEED TO TELL YOU THAT.
I KNOW... I KNOW...I... IT'S A MESS... I JUST DON'T...
Divers drag lake for signs of missing Grass Kingdom girl at guilt-ridden father's request.
"I JUST DON'T KNOW WHAT TO DO."

Father, in argument with mother, attempts to shift blame by pointing finger at recent bear attacks for possible cause of daughter's disappearance.

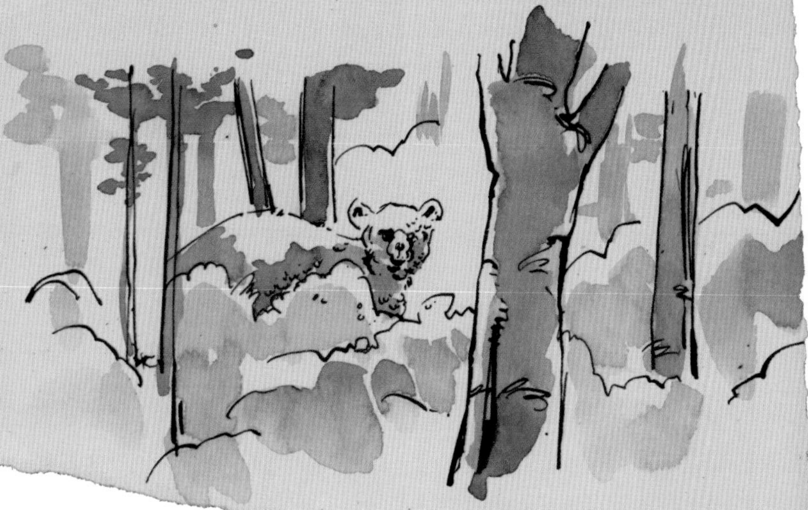

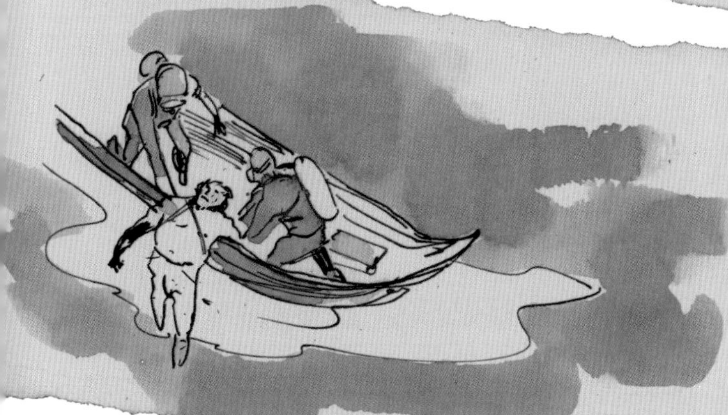

Wife leaves man over daughter's death. Meanwhile, he becomes obsessed with rumors of local serial killer. Convinced anyone or anything but his own neglect is to blame for daughter's disappearance.

Sheriff Humbert and his newly deputized son refuse government help--convinced they can solve recent rash of murders by themselves. Clash with grieving father over the facts. Sheriff and deputy remain skeptical of existence of a serial killer.

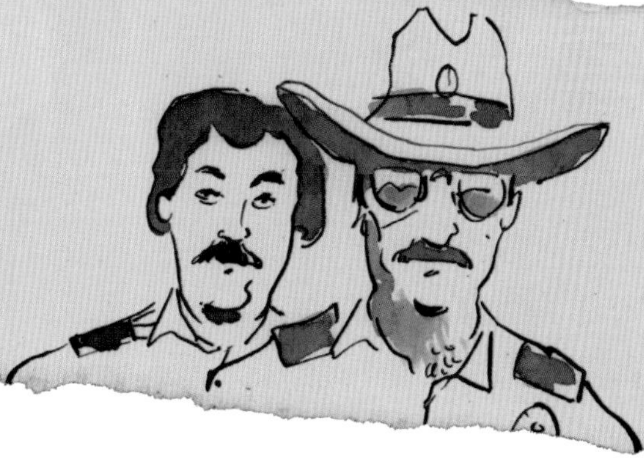

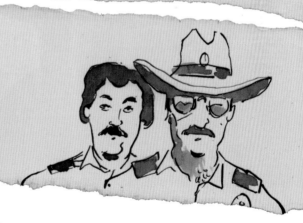

Dragging of lake reveals hundreds of unidentified remains...lending some credence to father's claims that daughter might have been a victim.

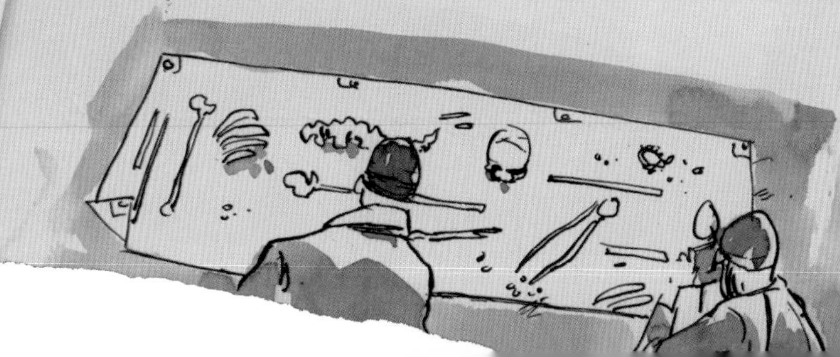

However, discovery is too late to save man's marriage.

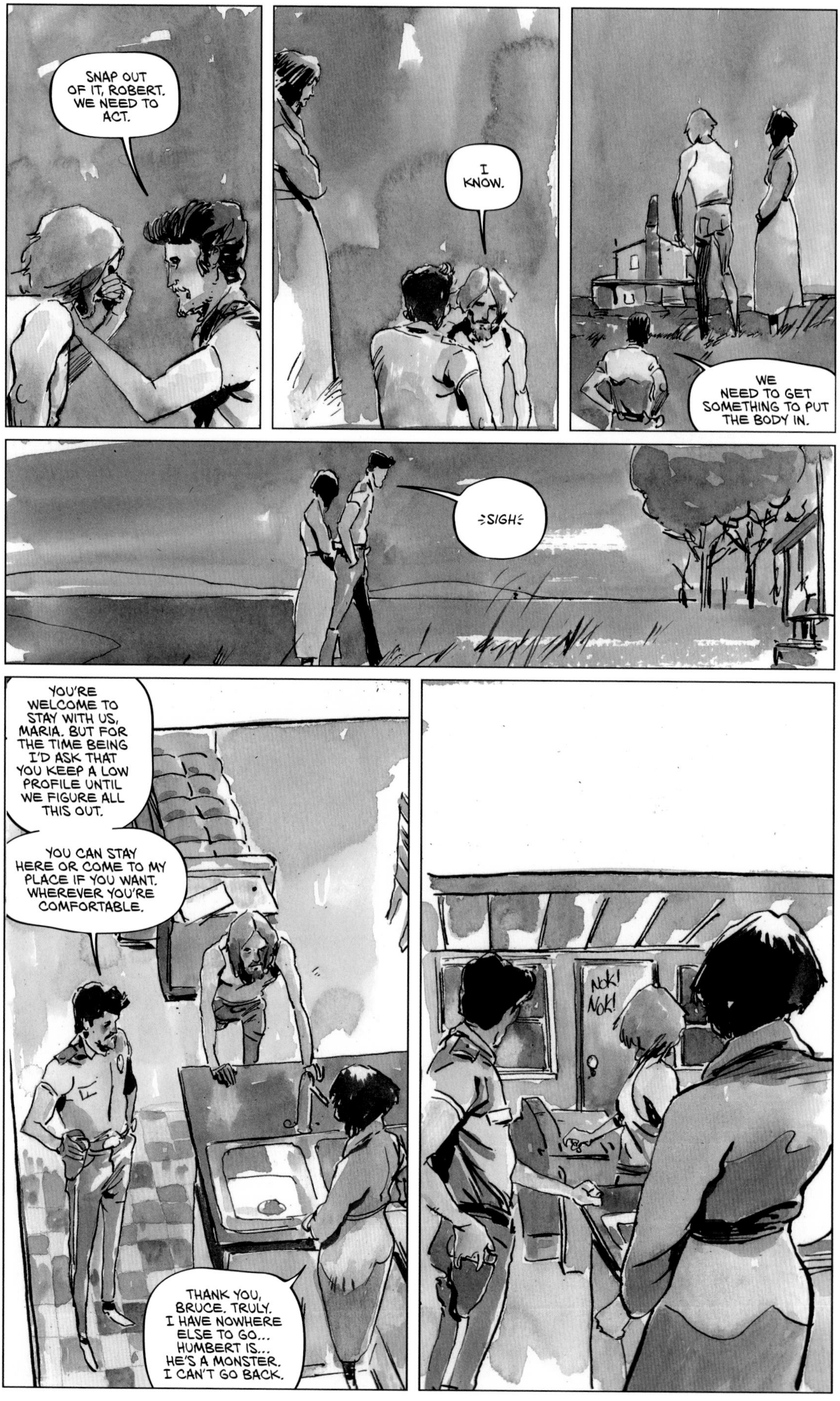
SNAP OUT OF IT, ROBERT. WE NEED TO ACT.
I KNOW.
WE NEED TO GET SOMETHING TO PUT THE BODY IN.
SIGH
YOU'RE WELCOME TO STAY WITH US, MARIA. BUT FOR THE TIME BEING I'D ASK THAT YOU KEEP A LOW PROFILE UNTIL WE FIGURE ALL THIS OUT.
YOU CAN STAY HERE OR COME TO MY PLACE IF YOU WANT. WHEREVER YOU'RE COMFORTABLE.
THANK YOU, BRUCE. TRULY. I HAVE NOWHERE ELSE TO GO... HUMBERT IS... HE'S A MONSTER. I CAN'T GO BACK.
NOK! NOK!

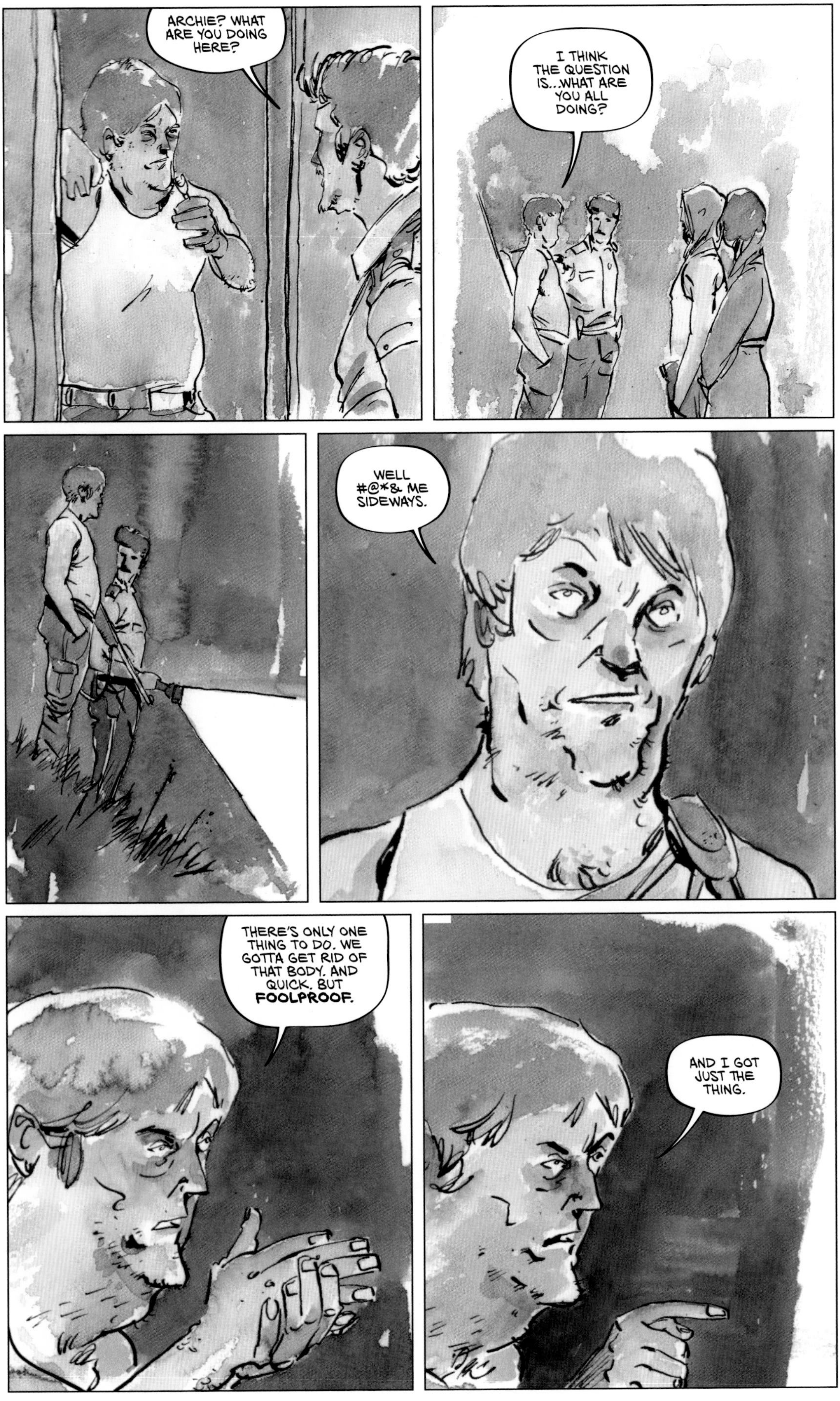
ARCHIE? WHAT ARE YOU DOING HERE?
I THINK THE QUESTION IS...WHAT ARE YOU ALL DOING?
WELL #@*& ME SIDEWAYS.
THERE'S ONLY ONE THING TO DO. WE GOTTA GET RID OF THAT BODY. AND QUICK. BUT **FOOLPROOF.**
AND I GOT JUST THE THING.

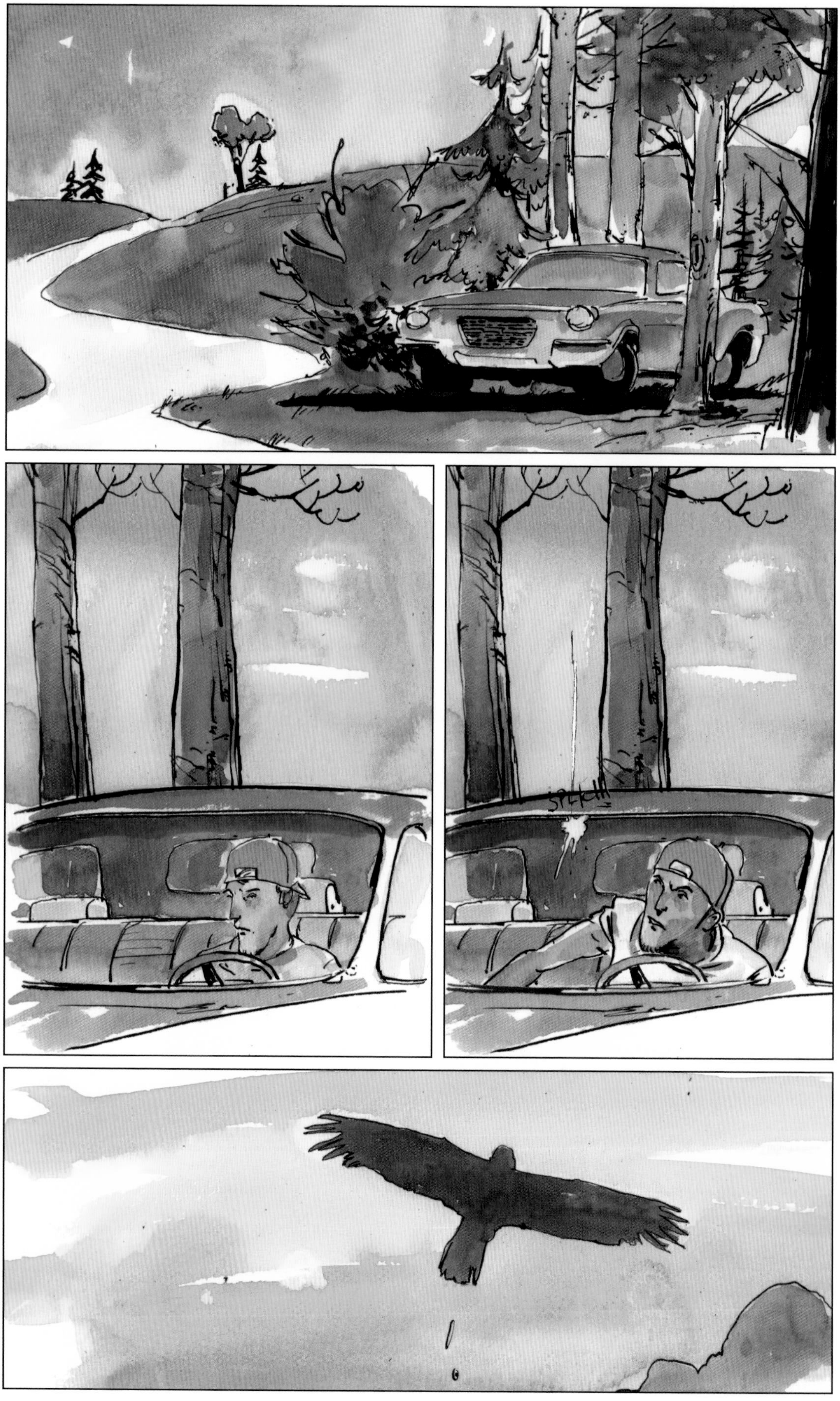

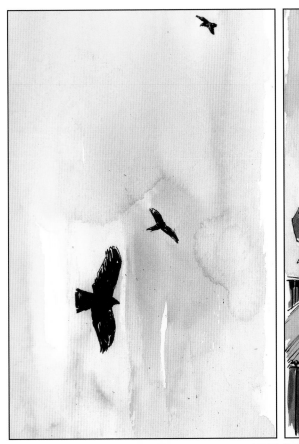

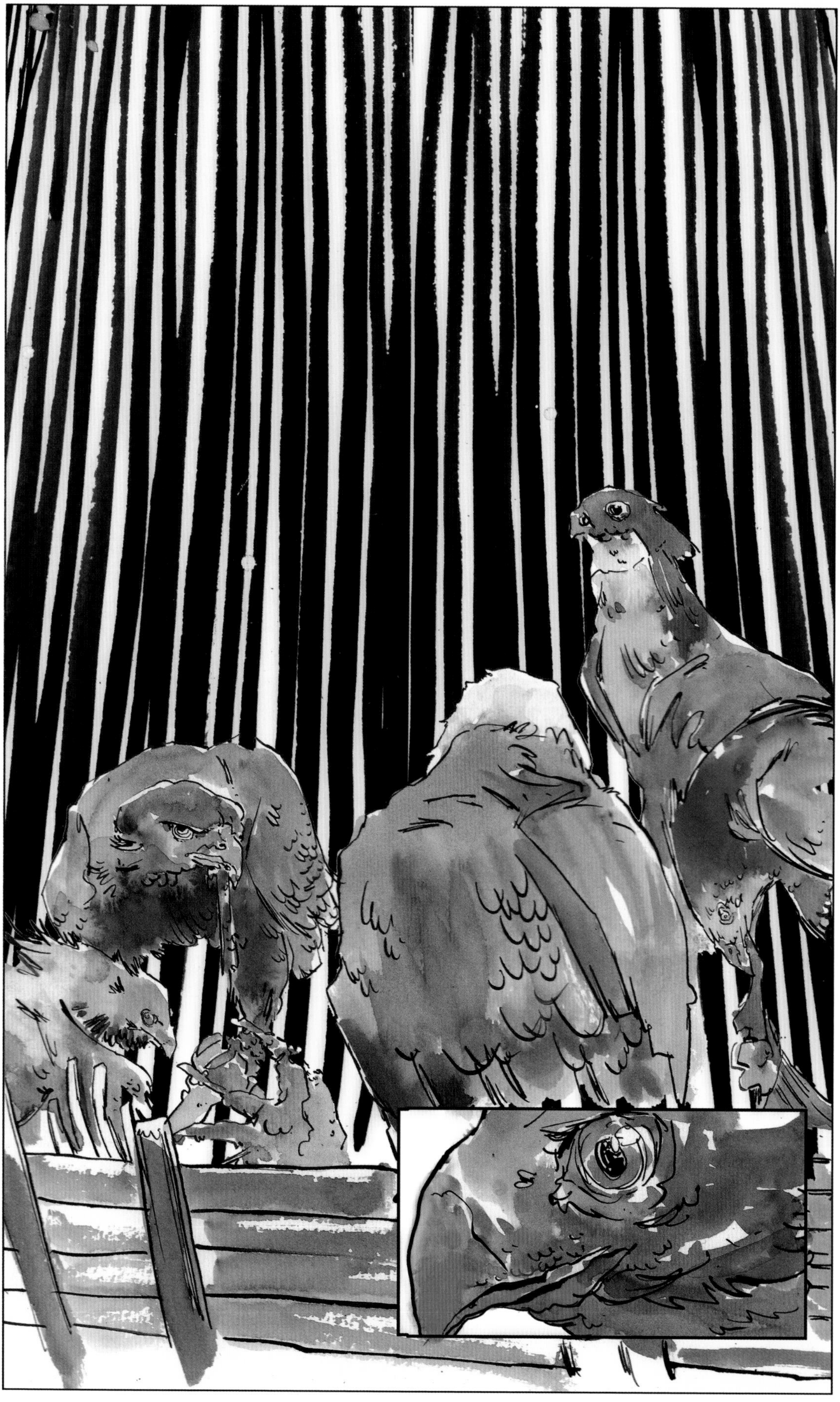

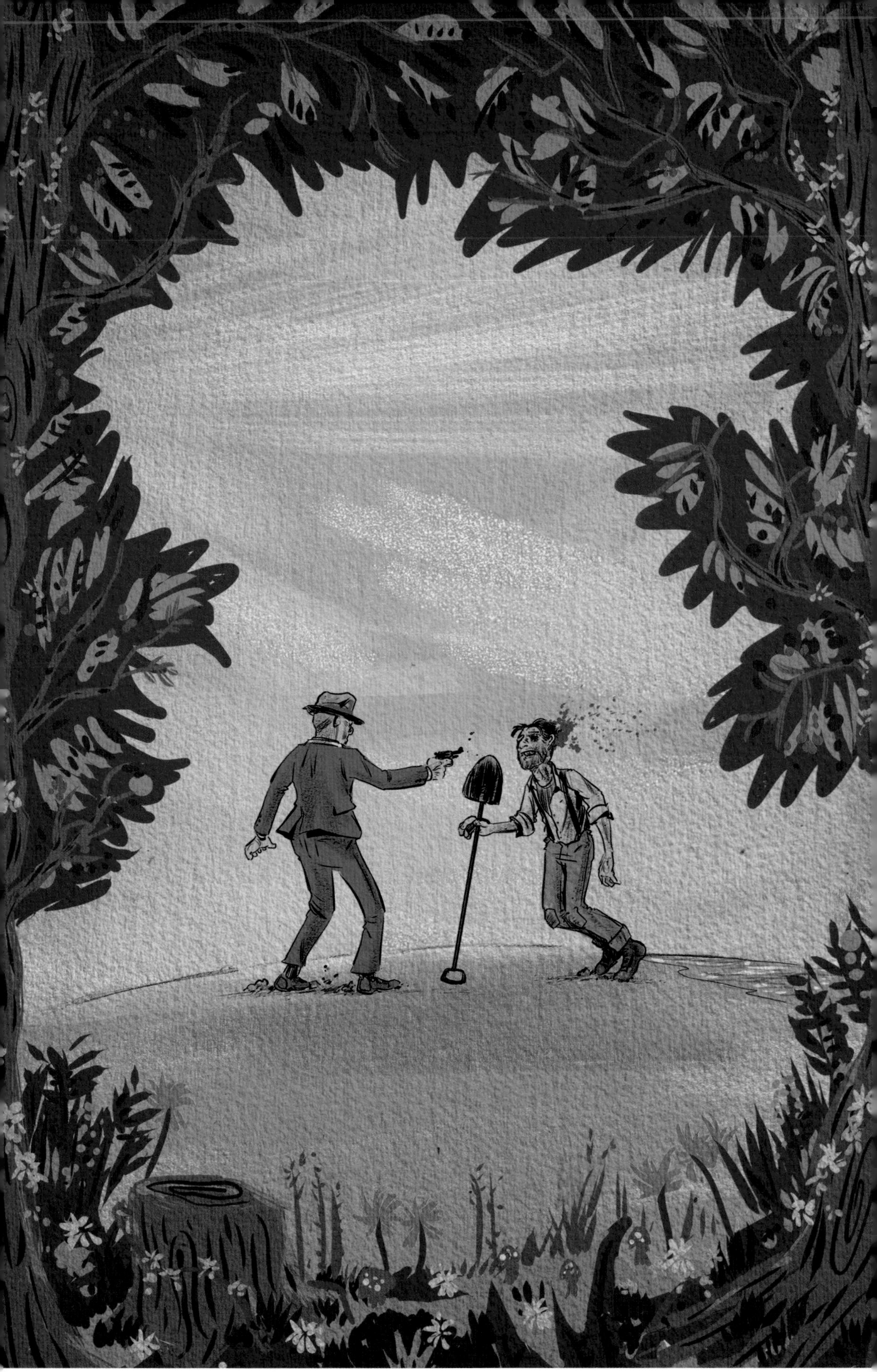

issue #3 cover by matt kindt

# chapter four

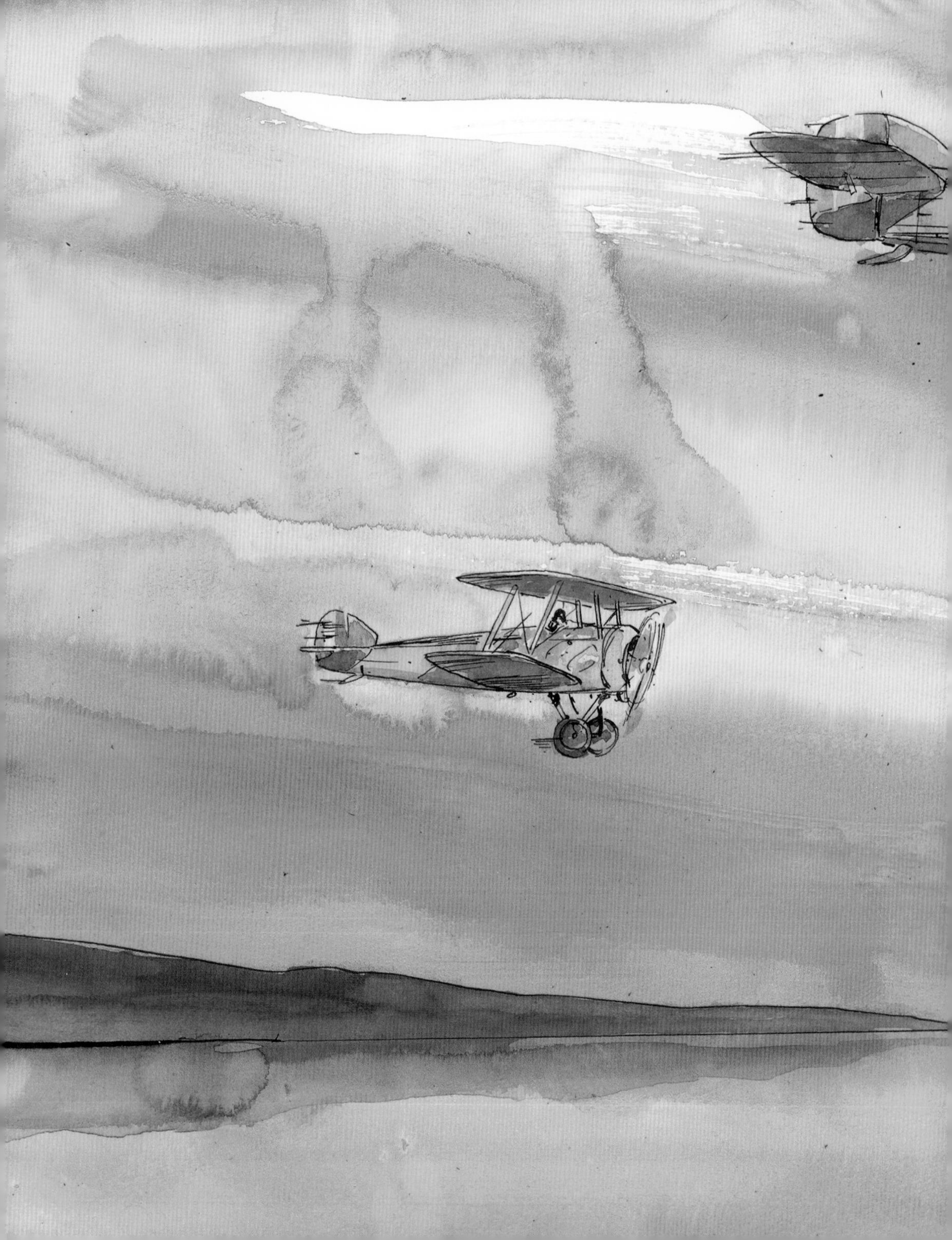

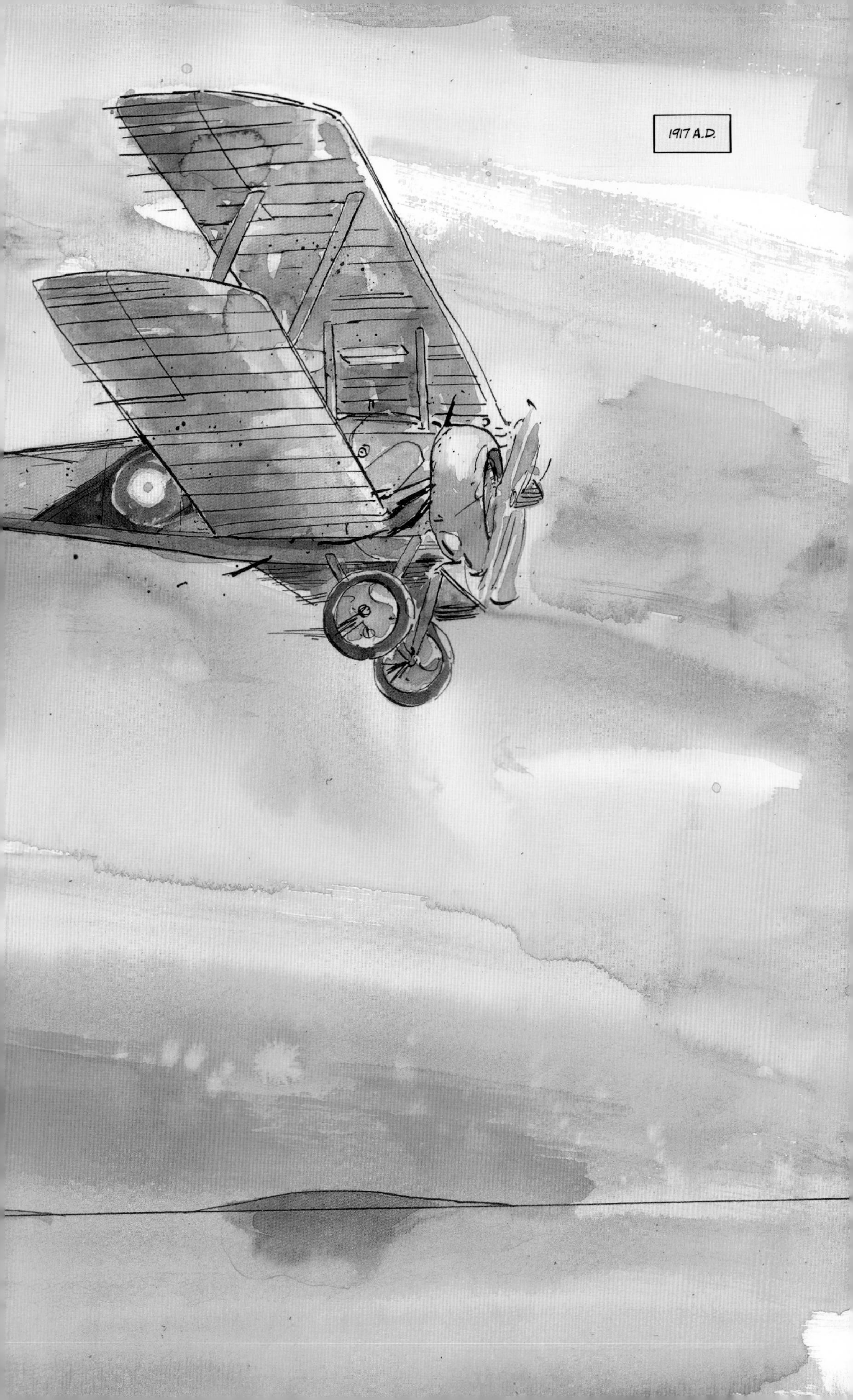
1917 A.D.

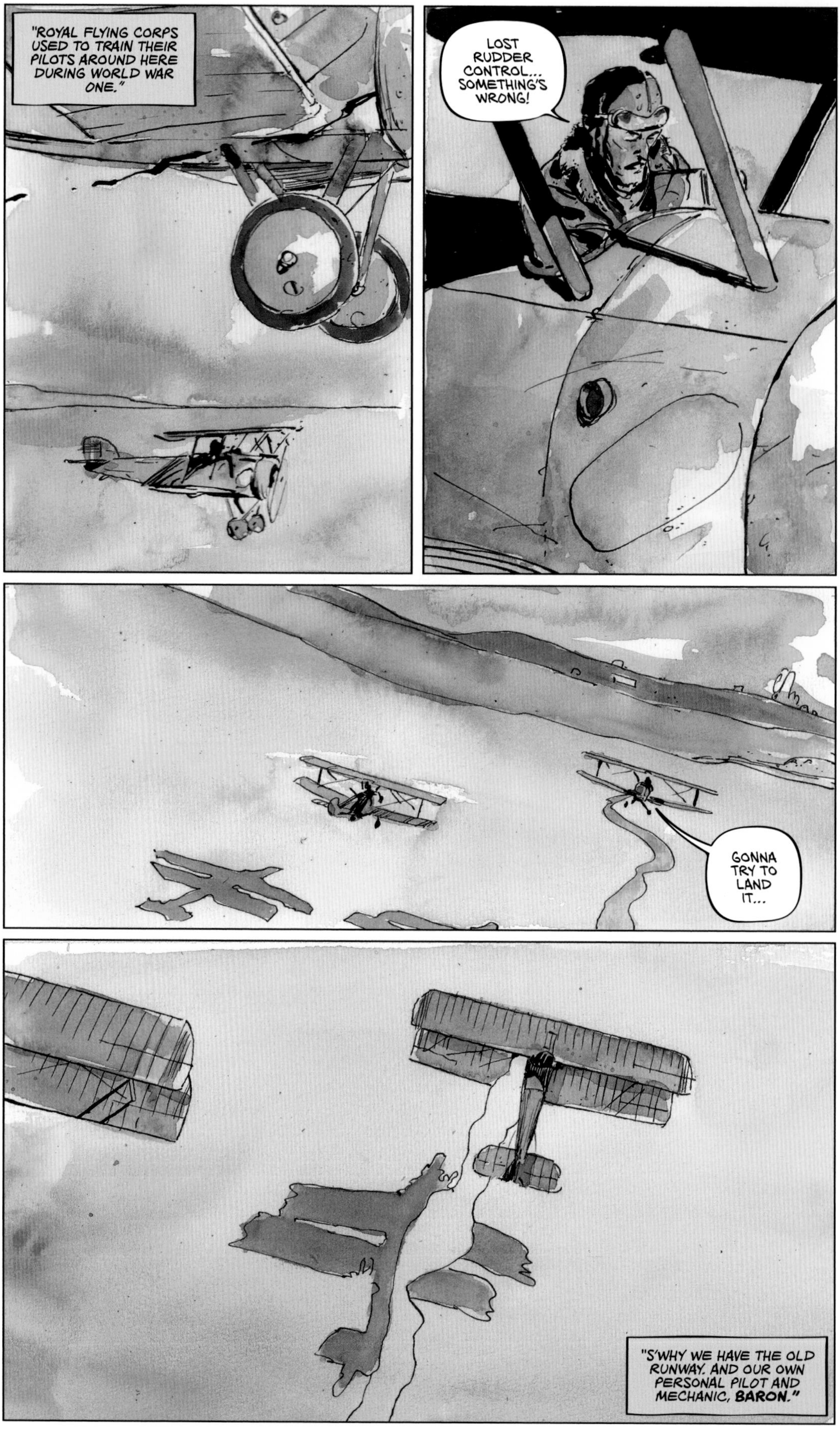
"ROYAL FLYING CORPS USED TO TRAIN THEIR PILOTS AROUND HERE DURING WORLD WAR ONE."
LOST RUDDER CONTROL... SOMETHING'S WRONG!
GONNA TRY TO LAND IT...
"S'WHY WE HAVE THE OLD RUNWAY. AND OUR OWN PERSONAL PILOT AND MECHANIC, **BARON**."

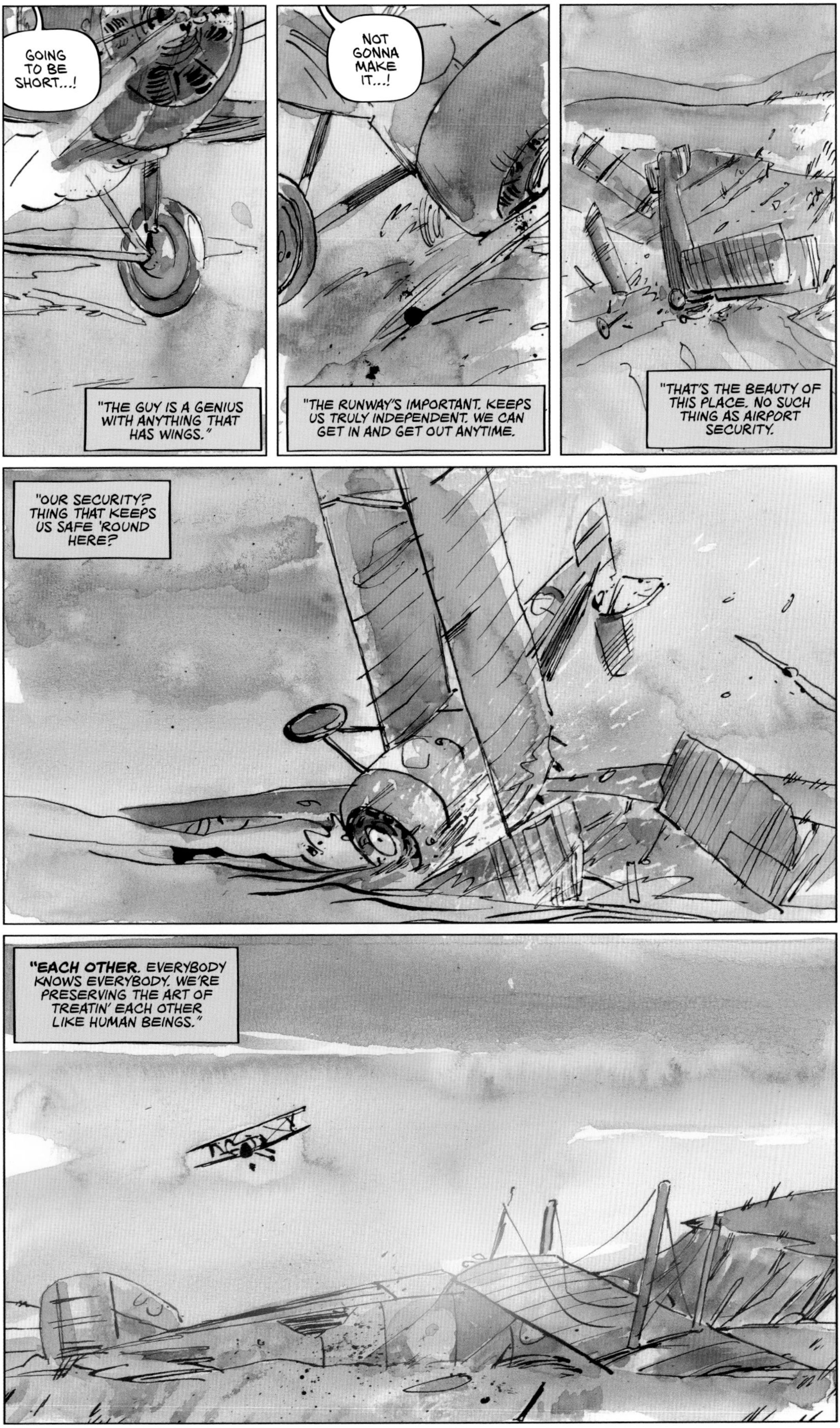
GOING TO BE SHORT...!
"THE GUY IS A GENIUS WITH ANYTHING THAT HAS WINGS."
NOT GONNA MAKE IT...!
"THE RUNWAY'S IMPORTANT. KEEPS US TRULY INDEPENDENT. WE CAN GET IN AND GET OUT ANYTIME.
"THAT'S THE BEAUTY OF THIS PLACE. NO SUCH THING AS AIRPORT SECURITY.
"OUR SECURITY? THING THAT KEEPS US SAFE 'ROUND HERE?
"**EACH OTHER**. EVERYBODY KNOWS EVERYBODY. WE'RE PRESERVING THE ART OF TREATIN' EACH OTHER LIKE HUMAN BEINGS."

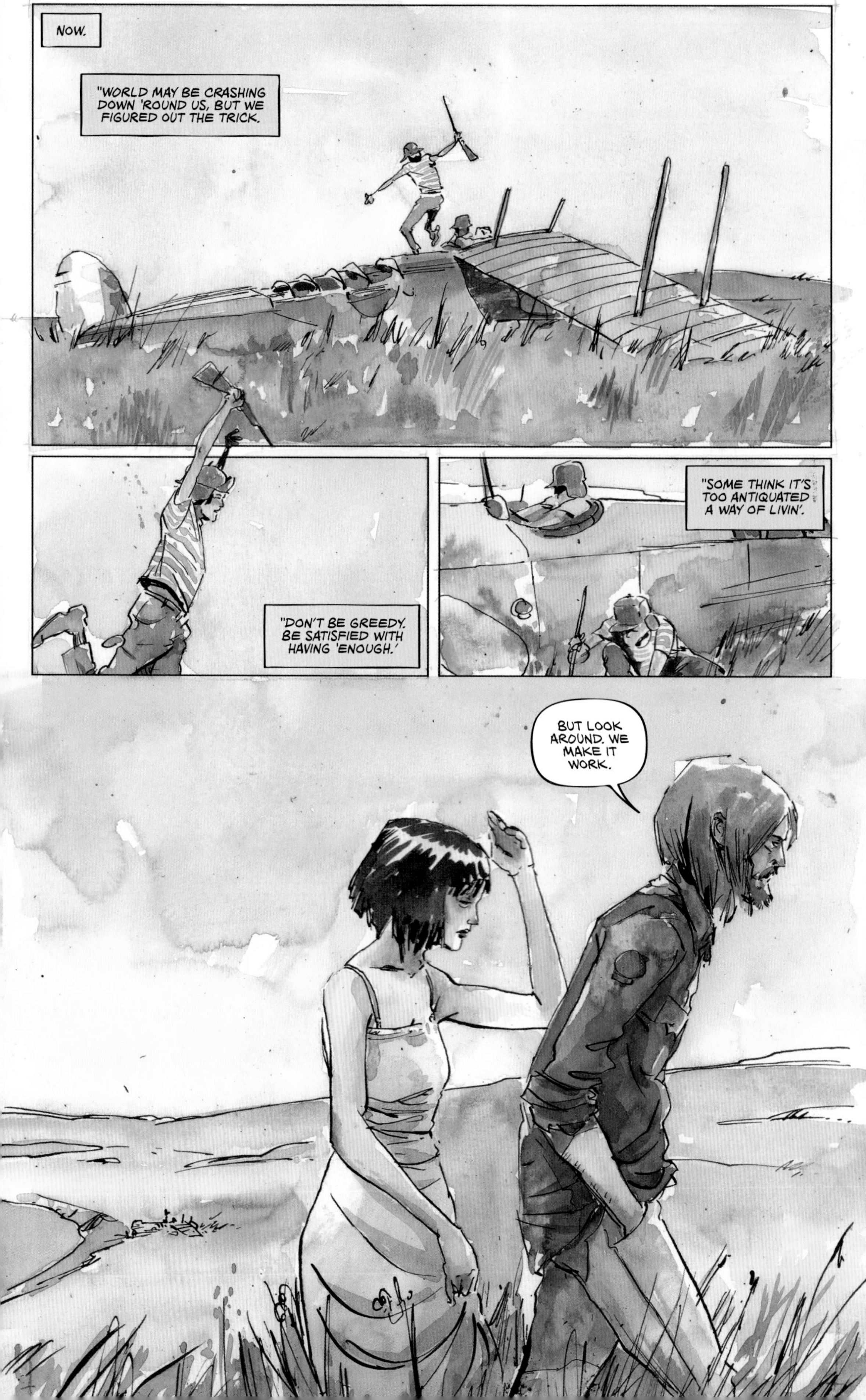
NOW.
"WORLD MAY BE CRASHING DOWN 'ROUND US, BUT WE FIGURED OUT THE TRICK.
"DON'T BE GREEDY. BE SATISFIED WITH HAVING 'ENOUGH.'
"SOME THINK IT'S TOO ANTIQUATED A WAY OF LIVIN'.
BUT LOOK AROUND. WE MAKE IT WORK.

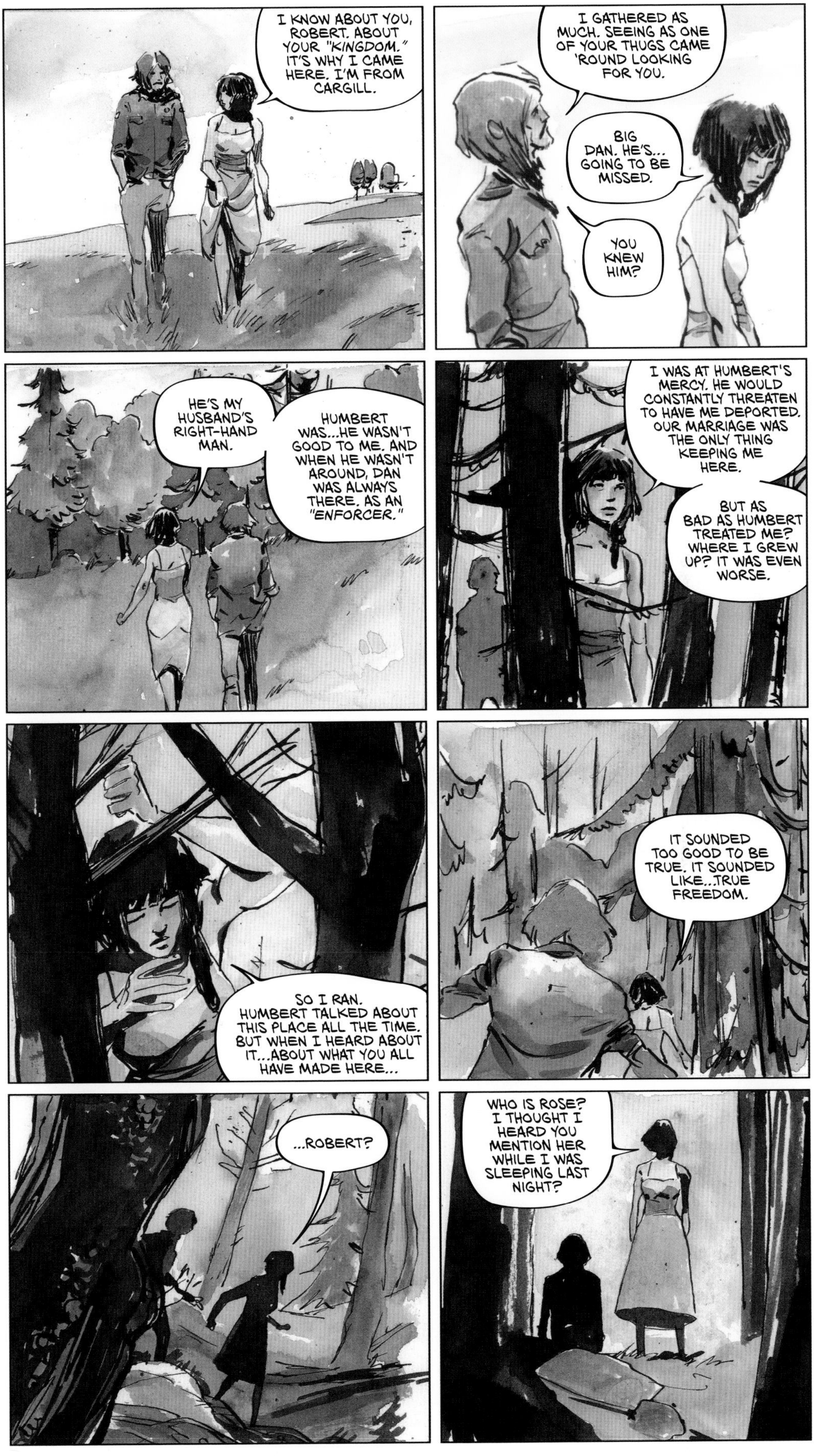
I KNOW ABOUT YOU, ROBERT. ABOUT YOUR "KINGDOM." IT'S WHY I CAME HERE. I'M FROM CARGILL.
I GATHERED AS MUCH. SEEING AS ONE OF YOUR THUGS CAME 'ROUND LOOKING FOR YOU.
BIG DAN. HE'S... GOING TO BE MISSED.
YOU KNEW HIM?
HE'S MY HUSBAND'S RIGHT-HAND MAN.
HUMBERT WAS...HE WASN'T GOOD TO ME. AND WHEN HE WASN'T AROUND, DAN WAS ALWAYS THERE. AS AN "ENFORCER."
I WAS AT HUMBERT'S MERCY. HE WOULD CONSTANTLY THREATEN TO HAVE ME DEPORTED. OUR MARRIAGE WAS THE ONLY THING KEEPING ME HERE.
BUT AS BAD AS HUMBERT TREATED ME? WHERE I GREW UP? IT WAS EVEN WORSE.
SO I RAN. HUMBERT TALKED ABOUT THIS PLACE ALL THE TIME. BUT WHEN I HEARD ABOUT IT...ABOUT WHAT YOU ALL HAVE MADE HERE...
IT SOUNDED TOO GOOD TO BE TRUE. IT SOUNDED LIKE...TRUE FREEDOM.
...ROBERT?
WHO IS ROSE? I THOUGHT I HEARD YOU MENTION HER WHILE I WAS SLEEPING LAST NIGHT?

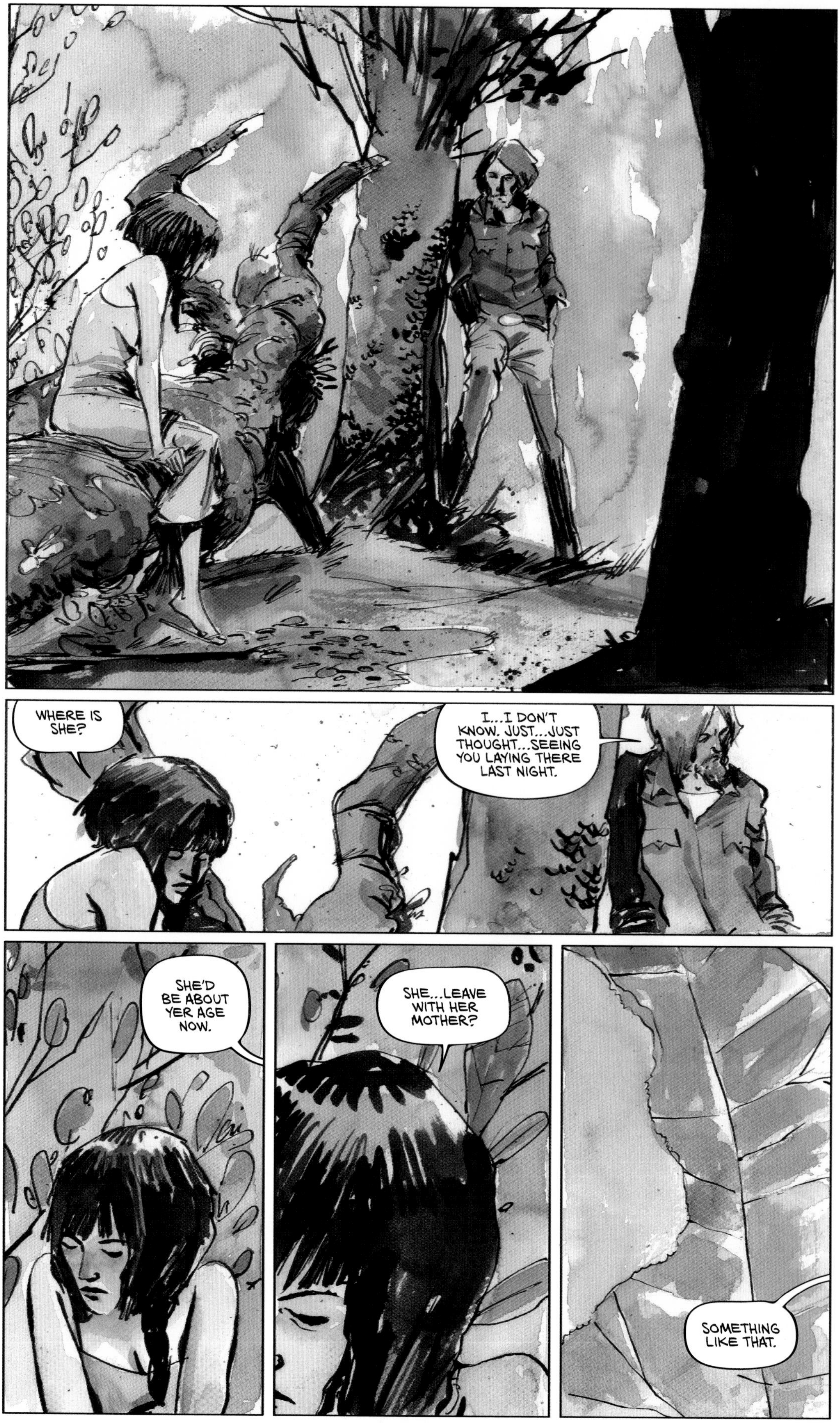
WHERE IS SHE?
I... I DON'T KNOW. JUST... JUST THOUGHT... SEEING YOU LAYING THERE LAST NIGHT.
SHE'D BE ABOUT YER AGE NOW.
SHE... LEAVE WITH HER MOTHER?
SOMETHING LIKE THAT.

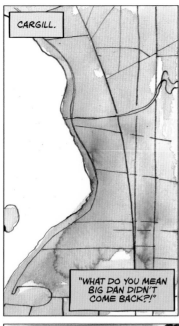

CARGILL.

"WHAT DO YOU MEAN BIG DAN DIDN'T COME BACK?!"

DAMMIT, LO! WHAT HAPPENED?!

CARGILL POLICE

I SENT BIG DAN OVER THERE TO FIND MARIA, AND YOU COME BACK ALONE NOT KNOWING ANYTHING! WHAT GOOD ARE YOU?

IT WAS D-DARK! AND BIG DAN TOLD ME TO STAY IN THE CAR. I DIDN'T SEE WHAT HAPPENED. HE JUST NEVER CAME BACK.

I HAD TO WALK ALL THE WAY BACK!

SOMETHING BAD HAPPENED TO BIG DAN, THOUGH, SHERIFF. I KNOW IT. DAN WOULDN'T'A JUST LEFT ME THERE. AND HIS CAR.

WELL, LO. GET READY. LOOKS LIKE WE STILL GOT BUSINESS...

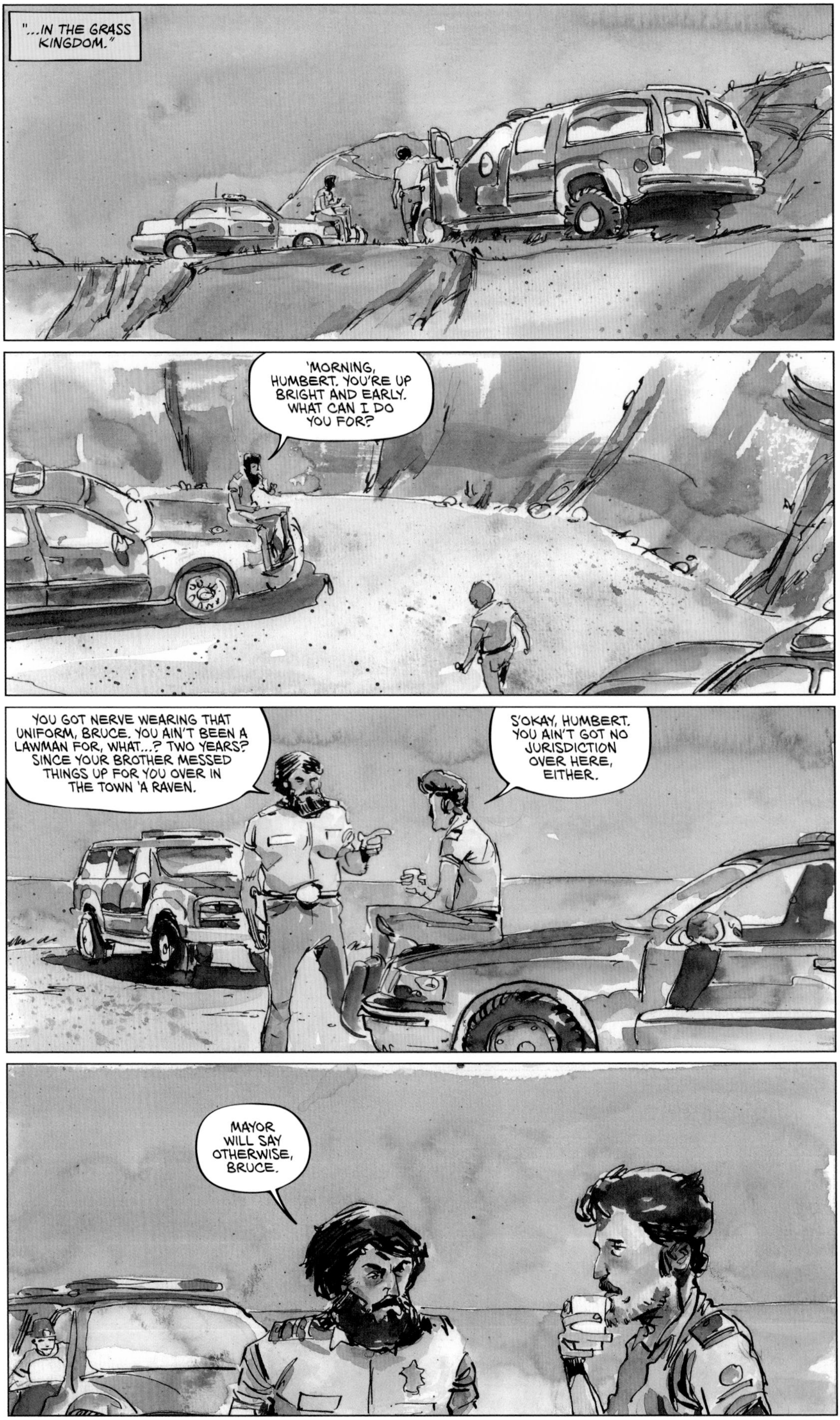
"...IN THE GRASS KINGDOM."
'MORNING, HUMBERT. YOU'RE UP BRIGHT AND EARLY. WHAT CAN I DO YOU FOR?
YOU GOT NERVE WEARING THAT UNIFORM, BRUCE. YOU AIN'T BEEN A LAWMAN FOR, WHAT...? TWO YEARS? SINCE YOUR BROTHER MESSED THINGS UP FOR YOU OVER IN THE TOWN 'A RAVEN.
S'OKAY, HUMBERT. YOU AIN'T GOT NO JURISDICTION OVER HERE, EITHER.
MAYOR WILL SAY OTHERWISE, BRUCE.

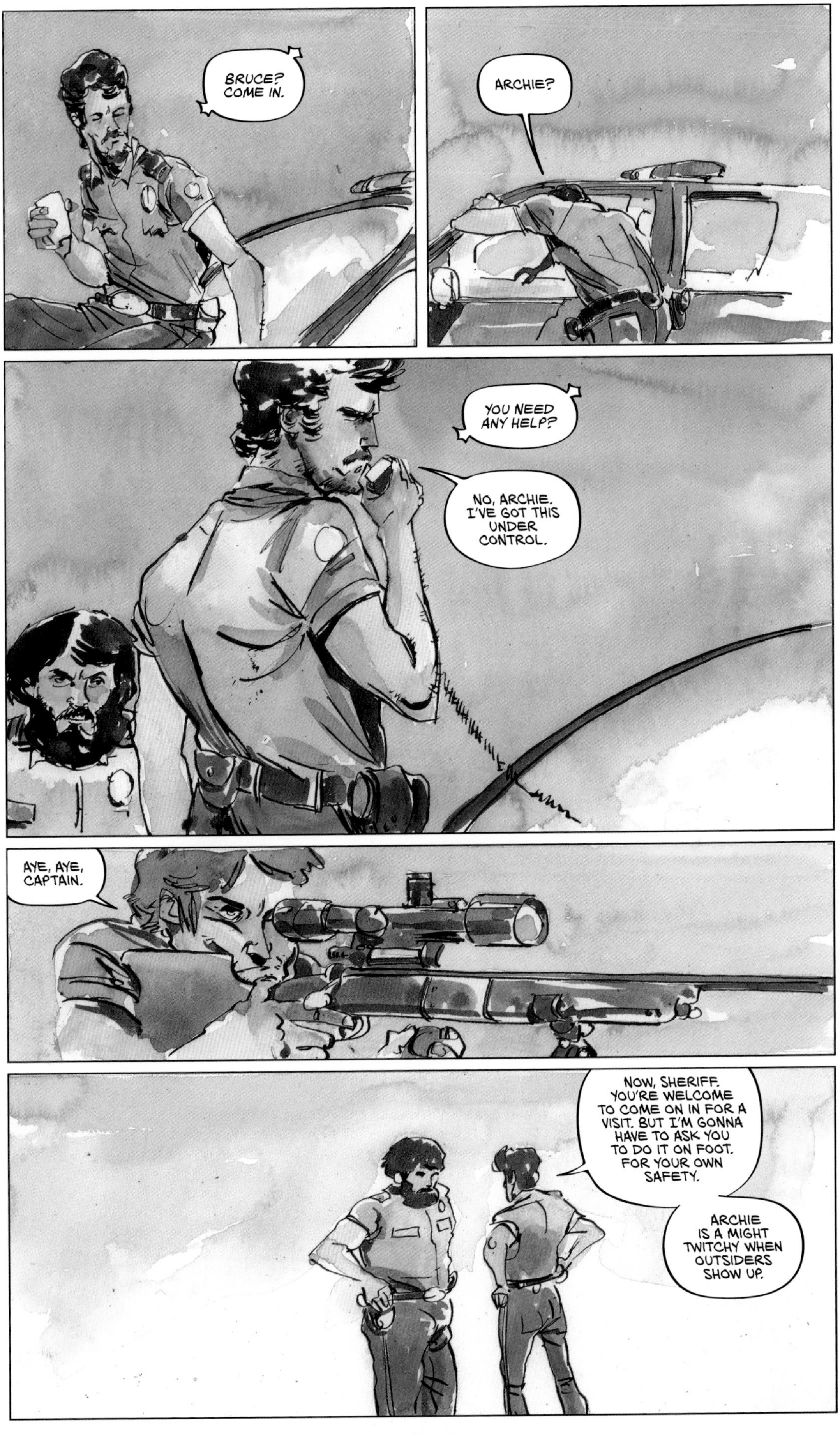
BRUCE? COME IN.
ARCHIE?
YOU NEED ANY HELP?
NO, ARCHIE. I'VE GOT THIS UNDER CONTROL.
AYE, AYE, CAPTAIN.
NOW, SHERIFF. YOU'RE WELCOME TO COME ON IN FOR A VISIT. BUT I'M GONNA HAVE TO ASK YOU TO DO IT ON FOOT. FOR YOUR OWN SAFETY.
ARCHIE IS A MIGHT TWITCHY WHEN OUTSIDERS SHOW UP.

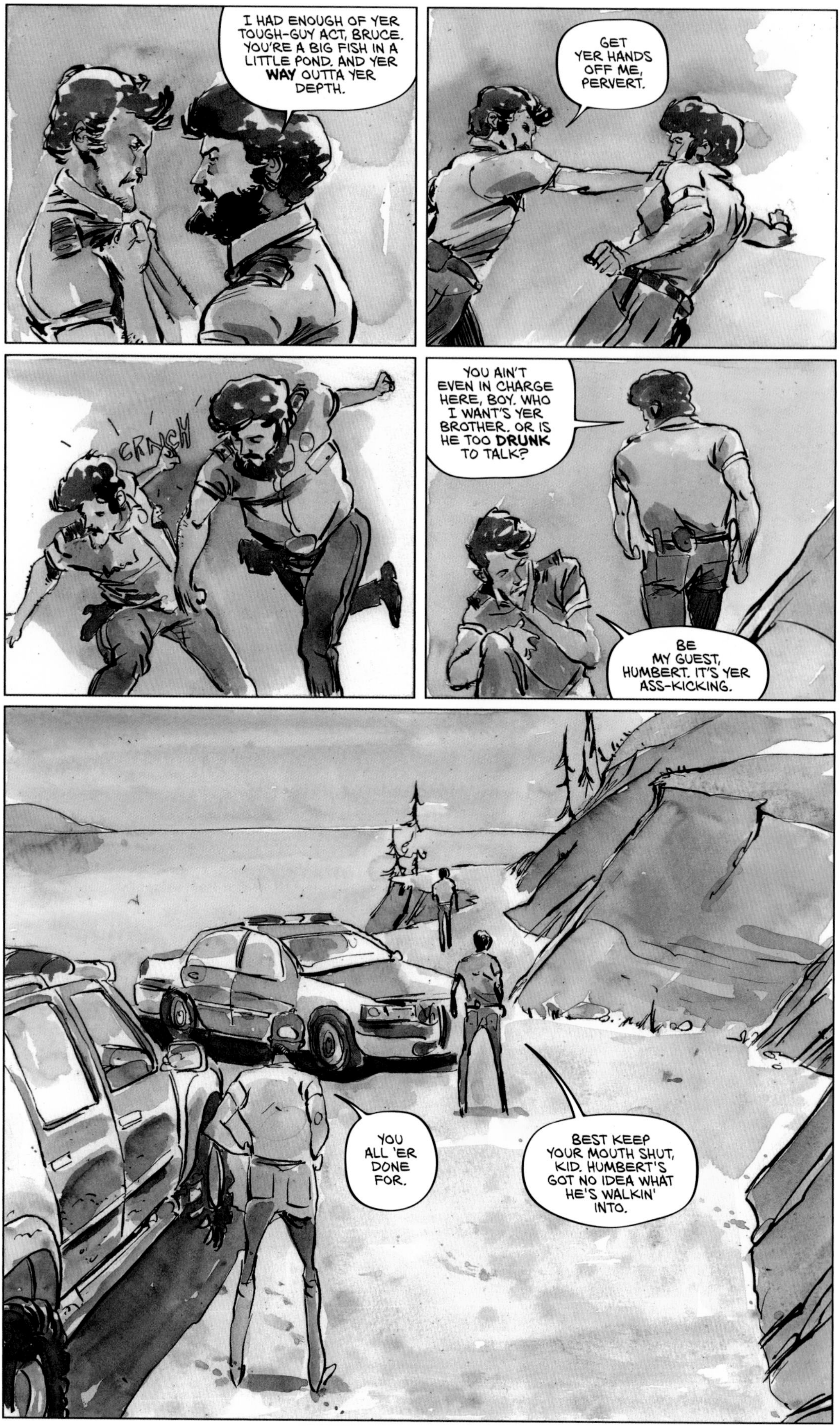
I HAD ENOUGH OF YER TOUGH-GUY ACT, BRUCE. YOU'RE A BIG FISH IN A LITTLE POND. AND YER **WAY** OUTTA YER DEPTH.
GET YER HANDS OFF ME, PERVERT.
CRNCH
YOU AIN'T EVEN IN CHARGE HERE, BOY. WHO I WANT'S YER BROTHER. OR IS HE TOO **DRUNK** TO TALK?
BE MY GUEST, HUMBERT. IT'S YER ASS-KICKING.
YOU ALL 'ER DONE FOR.
BEST KEEP YOUR MOUTH SHUT, KID. HUMBERT'S GOT NO IDEA WHAT HE'S WALKIN' INTO.

ROBERT? ROBERT! YOU SOBER?!

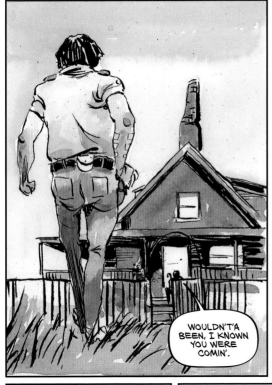

WOULDN'T'A BEEN, I KNOWN YOU WERE COMIN'.

GLAD TO SEE THE FEARLESS LEADER ISN'T PASSED OUT IN A DITCH SOMEWHERE.

YOUR GRASS KINGDOM TOOK ON A NEW MEMBER, I **KNOW** YOU KNOW ABOUT IT. WHERE IS SHE?

YOU ACTUALLY TRYING TO DO YOUR JOB, SHERIFF?

THAT'S SOMETHING NEW.

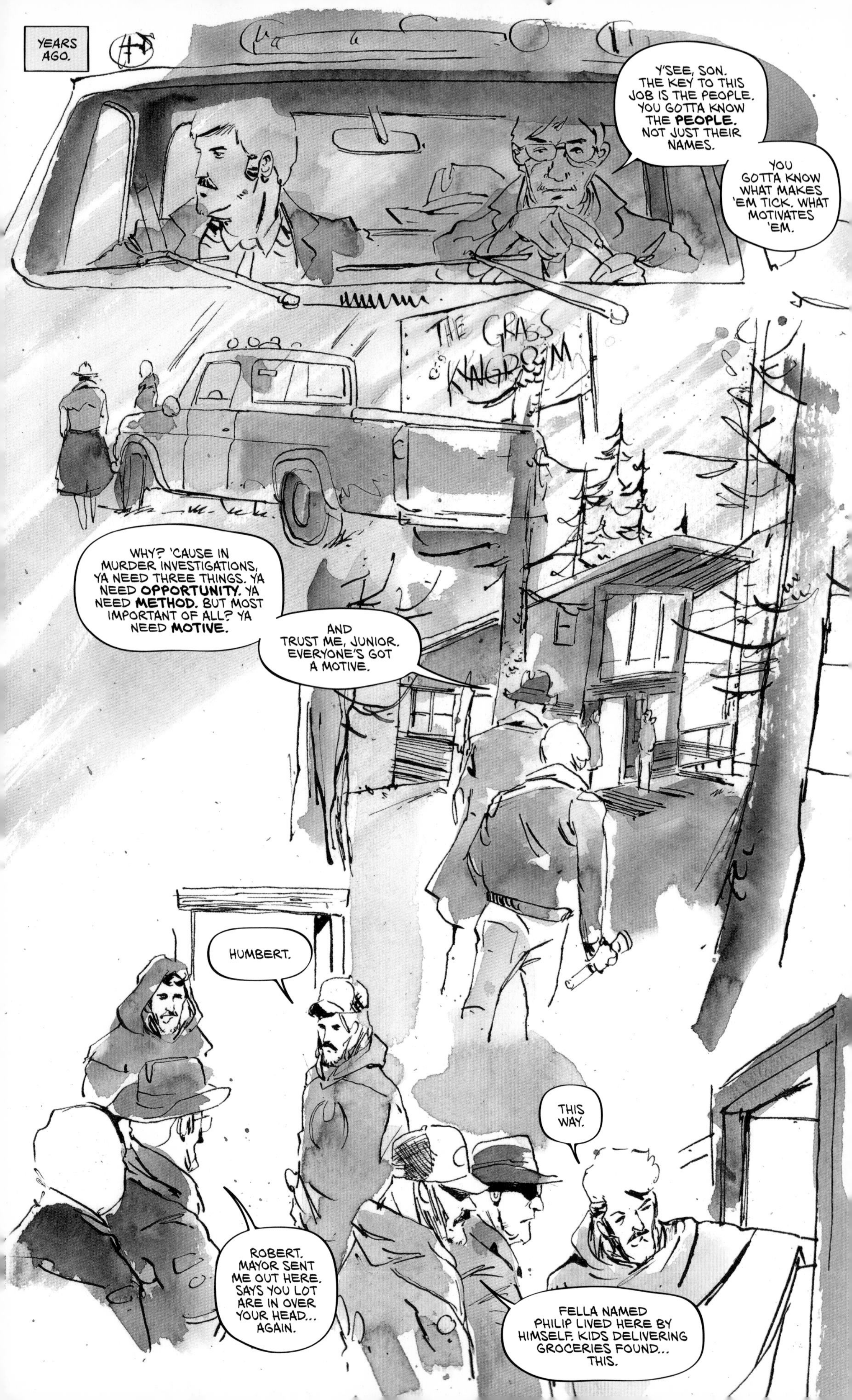
YEARS AGO.
Y'SEE, SON. THE KEY TO THIS JOB IS THE PEOPLE. YOU GOTTA KNOW THE **PEOPLE.** NOT JUST THEIR NAMES.
YOU GOTTA KNOW WHAT MAKES 'EM TICK. WHAT MOTIVATES 'EM.
THE GRASS KINGDOM
WHY? 'CAUSE IN MURDER INVESTIGATIONS, YA NEED THREE THINGS. YA NEED **OPPORTUNITY.** YA NEED **METHOD.** BUT MOST IMPORTANT OF ALL? YA NEED **MOTIVE.**
AND TRUST ME, JUNIOR. EVERYONE'S GOT A MOTIVE.
HUMBERT.
ROBERT. MAYOR SENT ME OUT HERE. SAYS YOU LOT ARE IN OVER YOUR HEAD... AGAIN.
THIS WAY.
FELLA NAMED PHILIP LIVED HERE BY HIMSELF. KIDS DELIVERING GROCERIES FOUND... THIS.

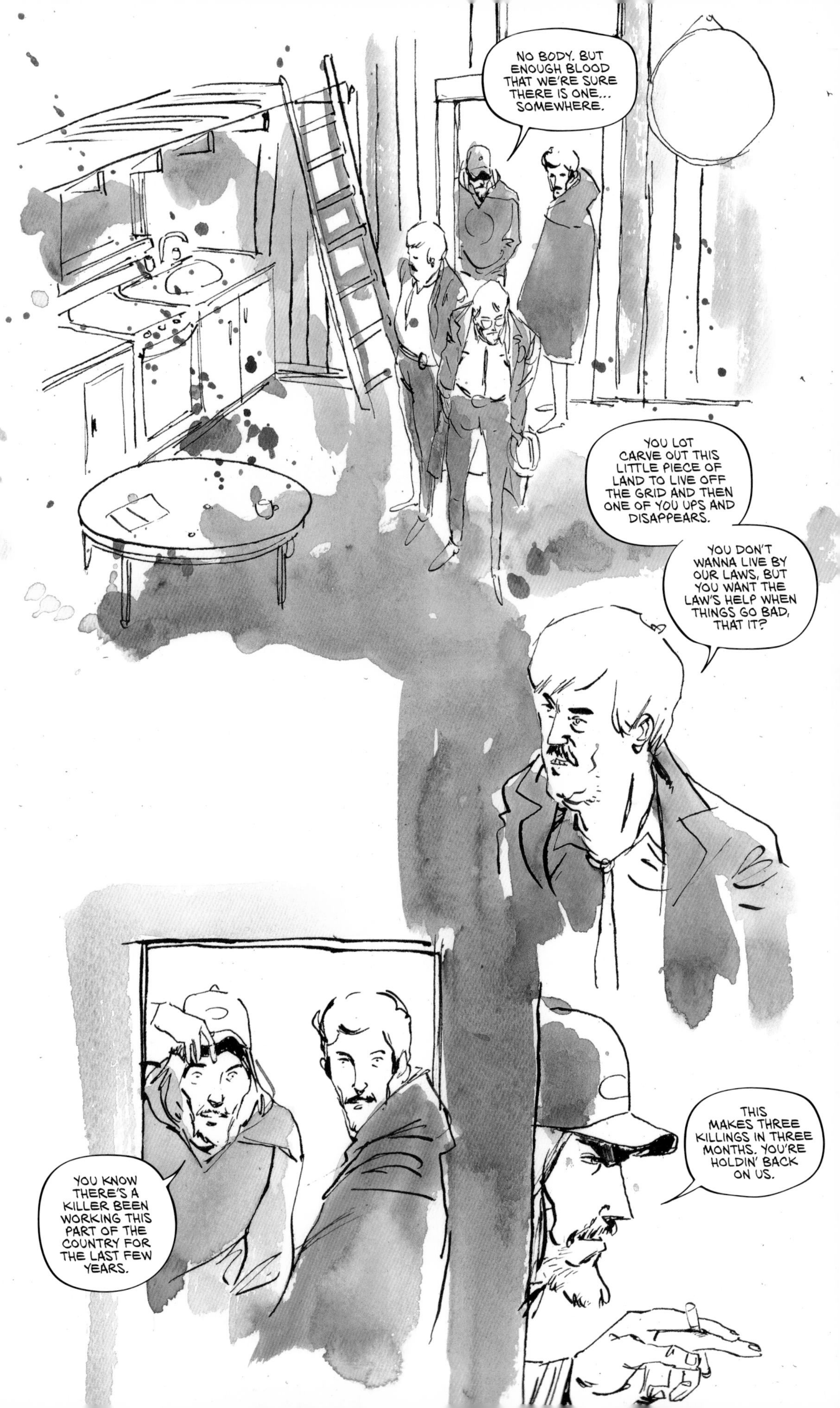
NO BODY. BUT ENOUGH BLOOD THAT WE'RE SURE THERE IS ONE... SOMEWHERE.
YOU LOT CARVE OUT THIS LITTLE PIECE OF LAND TO LIVE OFF THE GRID AND THEN ONE OF YOU UPS AND DISAPPEARS.
YOU DON'T WANNA LIVE BY OUR LAWS, BUT YOU WANT THE LAW'S HELP WHEN THINGS GO BAD, THAT IT?
THIS MAKES THREE KILLINGS IN THREE MONTHS. YOU'RE HOLDIN' BACK ON US.
YOU KNOW THERE'S A KILLER BEEN WORKING THIS PART OF THE COUNTRY FOR THE LAST FEW YEARS.

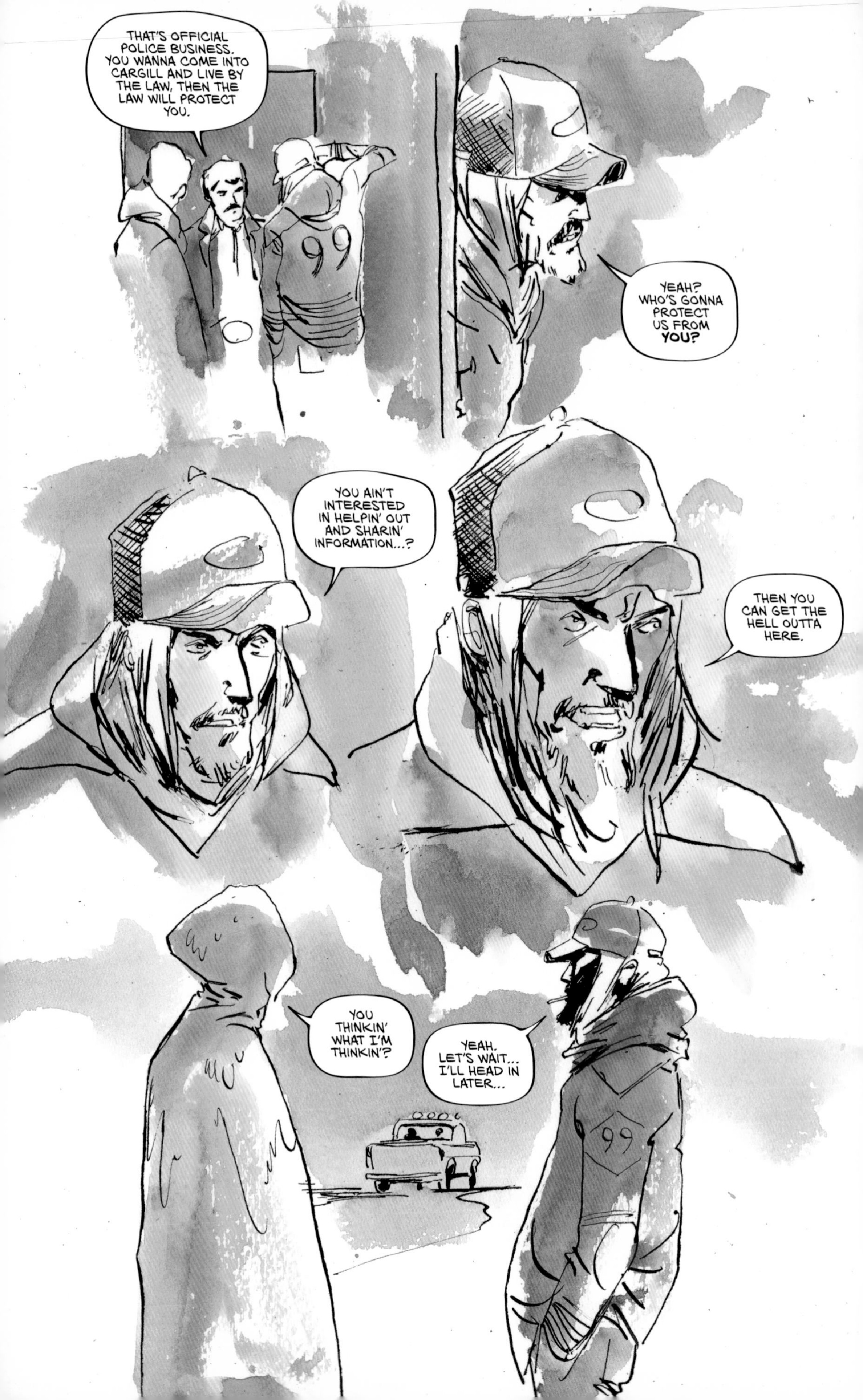
THAT'S OFFICIAL POLICE BUSINESS. YOU WANNA COME INTO CARGILL AND LIVE BY THE LAW, THEN THE LAW WILL PROTECT YOU.
YEAH? WHO'S GONNA PROTECT US FROM **YOU?**
YOU AIN'T INTERESTED IN HELPIN' OUT AND SHARIN' INFORMATION...?
THEN YOU CAN GET THE HELL OUTTA HERE.
YOU THINKIN' WHAT I'M THINKIN'?
YEAH. LET'S WAIT... I'LL HEAD IN LATER...

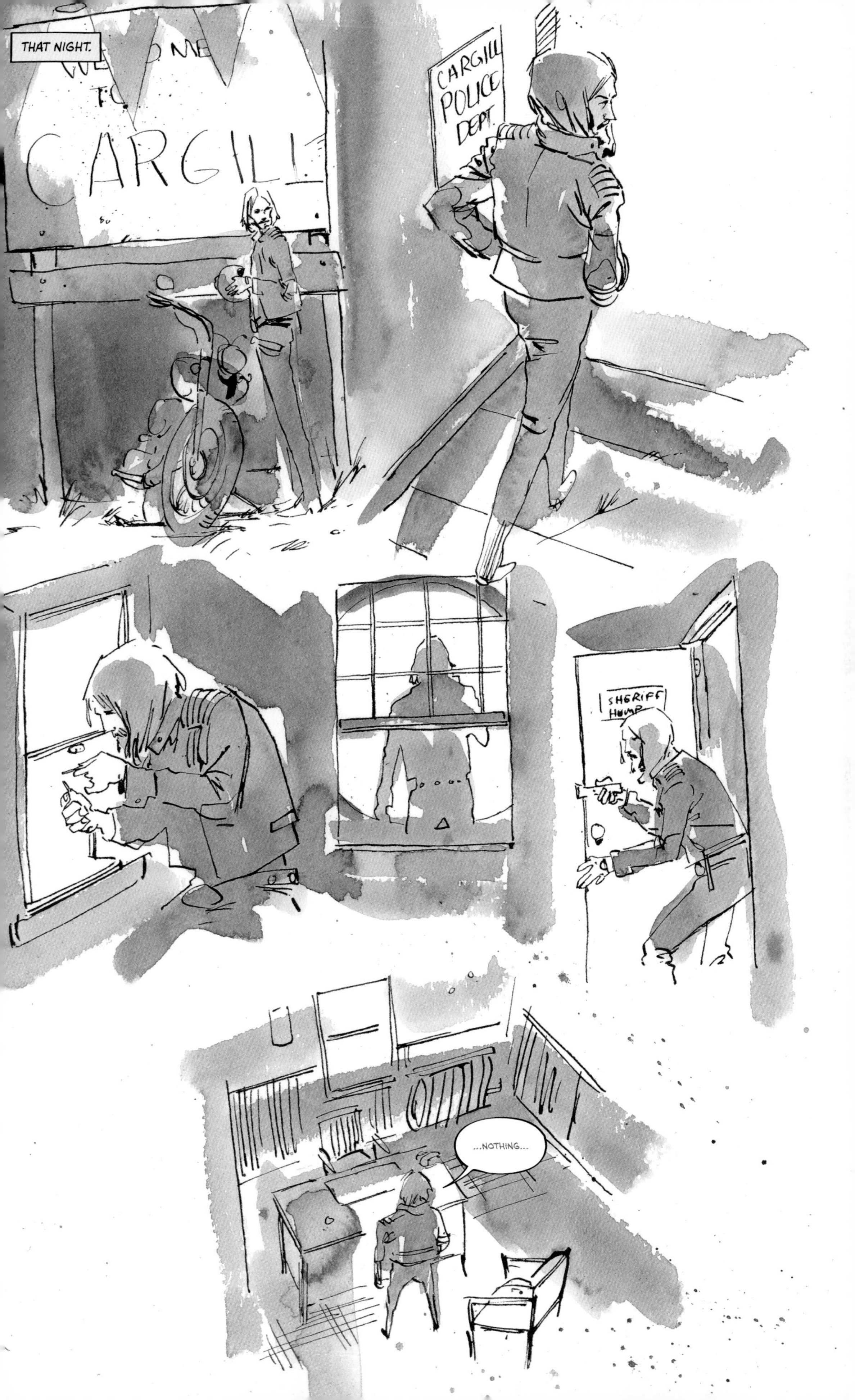
THAT NIGHT.
CARGILL
CARGILL POLICE DEPT.
SHERIFF
...NOTHING...

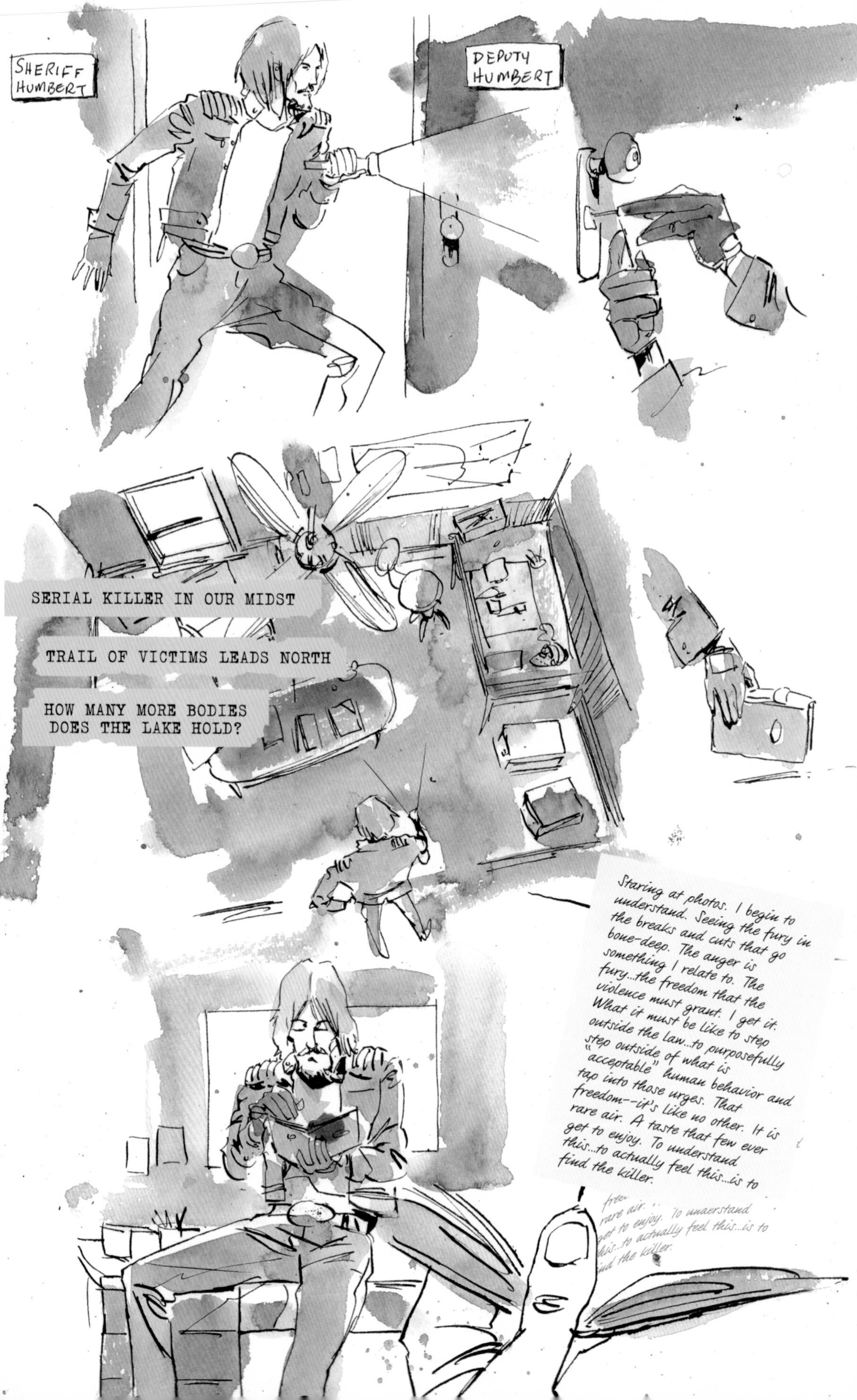
SHERIFF HUMBERT
DEPUTY HUMBERT
SERIAL KILLER IN OUR MIDST
TRAIL OF VICTIMS LEADS NORTH
HOW MANY MORE BODIES DOES THE LAKE HOLD?
Staring at photos. I begin to understand. Seeing the fury in the breaks and cuts that go bone-deep. The anger is something I relate to. The fury...the freedom that the violence must grant. I get it. What it must be like to step outside the law...to purposefully step outside of what is "acceptable" human behavior and tap into those urges. That freedom--it's like no other. It is rare air. A taste that few ever get to enjoy. To understand this...to actually feel this...is to find the killer.

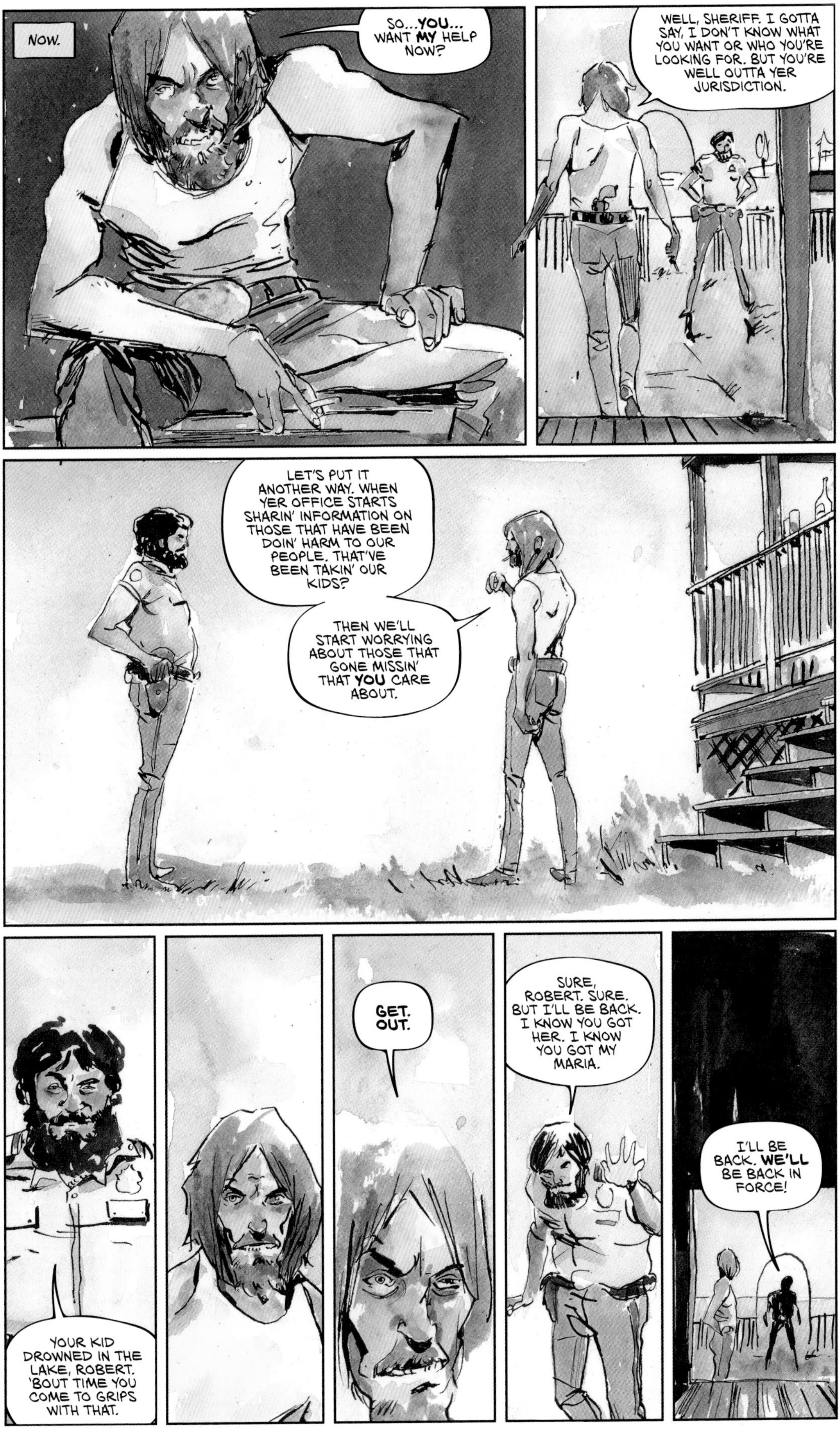
NOW.
SO...**YOU**... WANT **MY** HELP NOW?
WELL, SHERIFF. I GOTTA SAY, I DON'T KNOW WHAT YOU WANT OR WHO YOU'RE LOOKING FOR. BUT YOU'RE WELL OUTTA YER JURISDICTION.
LET'S PUT IT ANOTHER WAY. WHEN YER OFFICE STARTS SHARIN' INFORMATION ON THOSE THAT HAVE BEEN DOIN' HARM TO OUR PEOPLE. THAT'VE BEEN TAKIN' OUR KIDS?
THEN WE'LL START WORRYING ABOUT THOSE THAT GONE MISSIN' THAT **YOU** CARE ABOUT.
YOUR KID DROWNED IN THE LAKE, ROBERT. 'BOUT TIME YOU COME TO GRIPS WITH THAT.
**GET. OUT.**
SURE, ROBERT. SURE. BUT I'LL BE BACK. I KNOW YOU GOT HER. I KNOW YOU GOT MY MARIA.
I'LL BE BACK. **WE'LL** BE BACK IN FORCE!

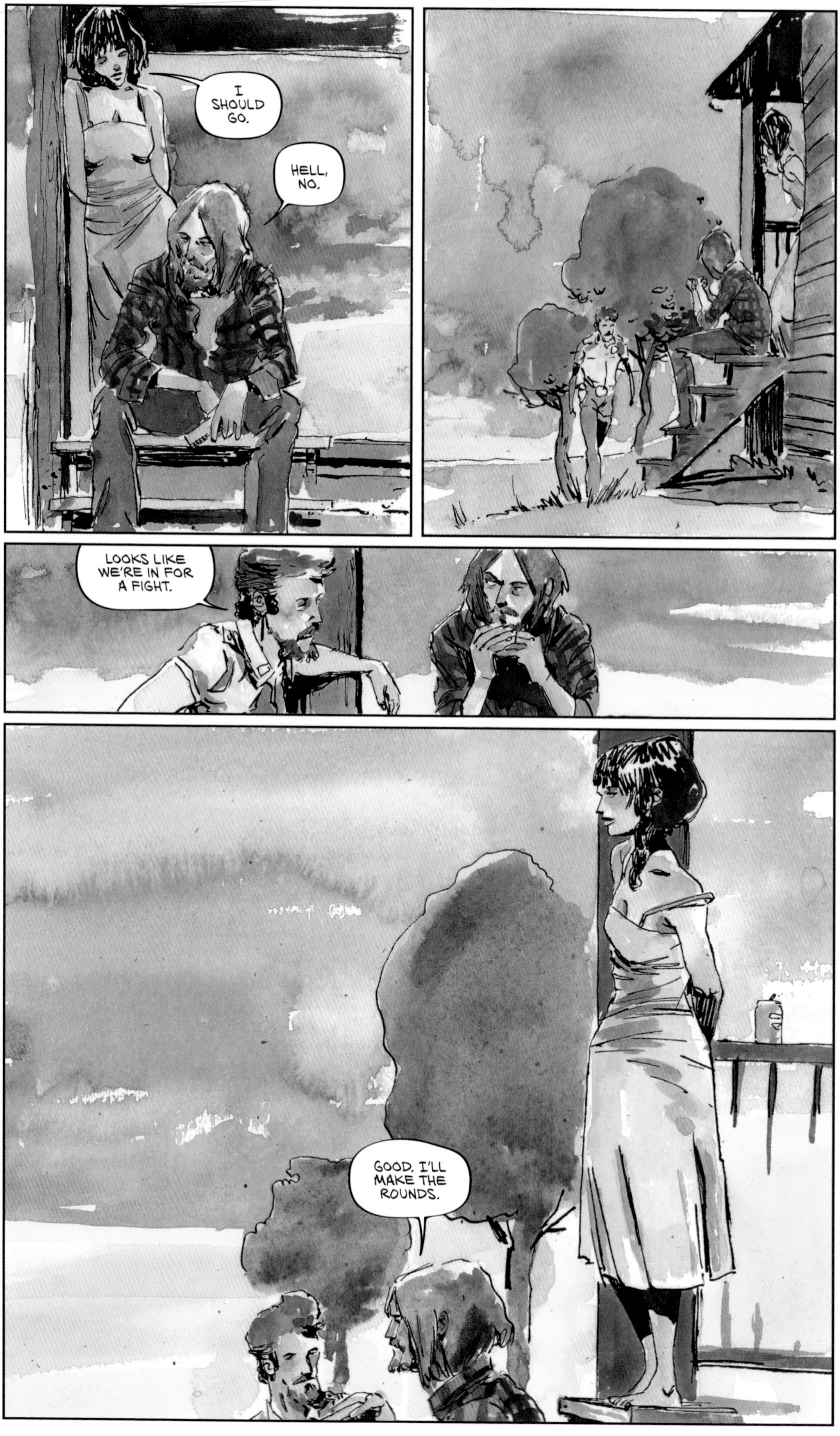
I SHOULD GO.
HELL, NO.
LOOKS LIKE WE'RE IN FOR A FIGHT.
GOOD. I'LL MAKE THE ROUNDS.

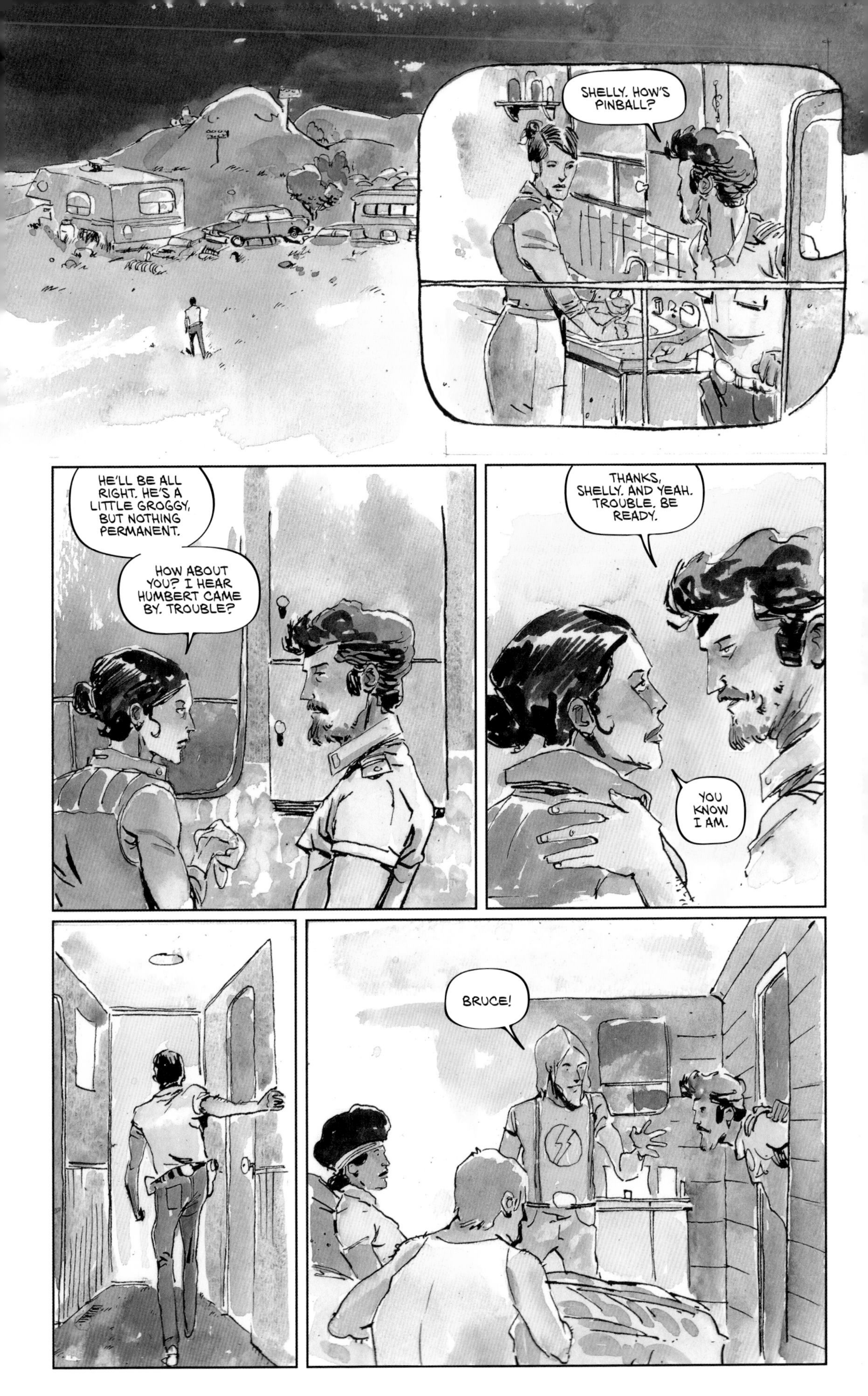
SHELLY. HOW'S PINBALL?
HE'LL BE ALL RIGHT. HE'S A LITTLE GROGGY, BUT NOTHING PERMANENT.
HOW ABOUT YOU? I HEAR HUMBERT CAME BY. TROUBLE?
THANKS, SHELLY. AND YEAH. TROUBLE. BE READY.
YOU KNOW I AM.
BRUCE!

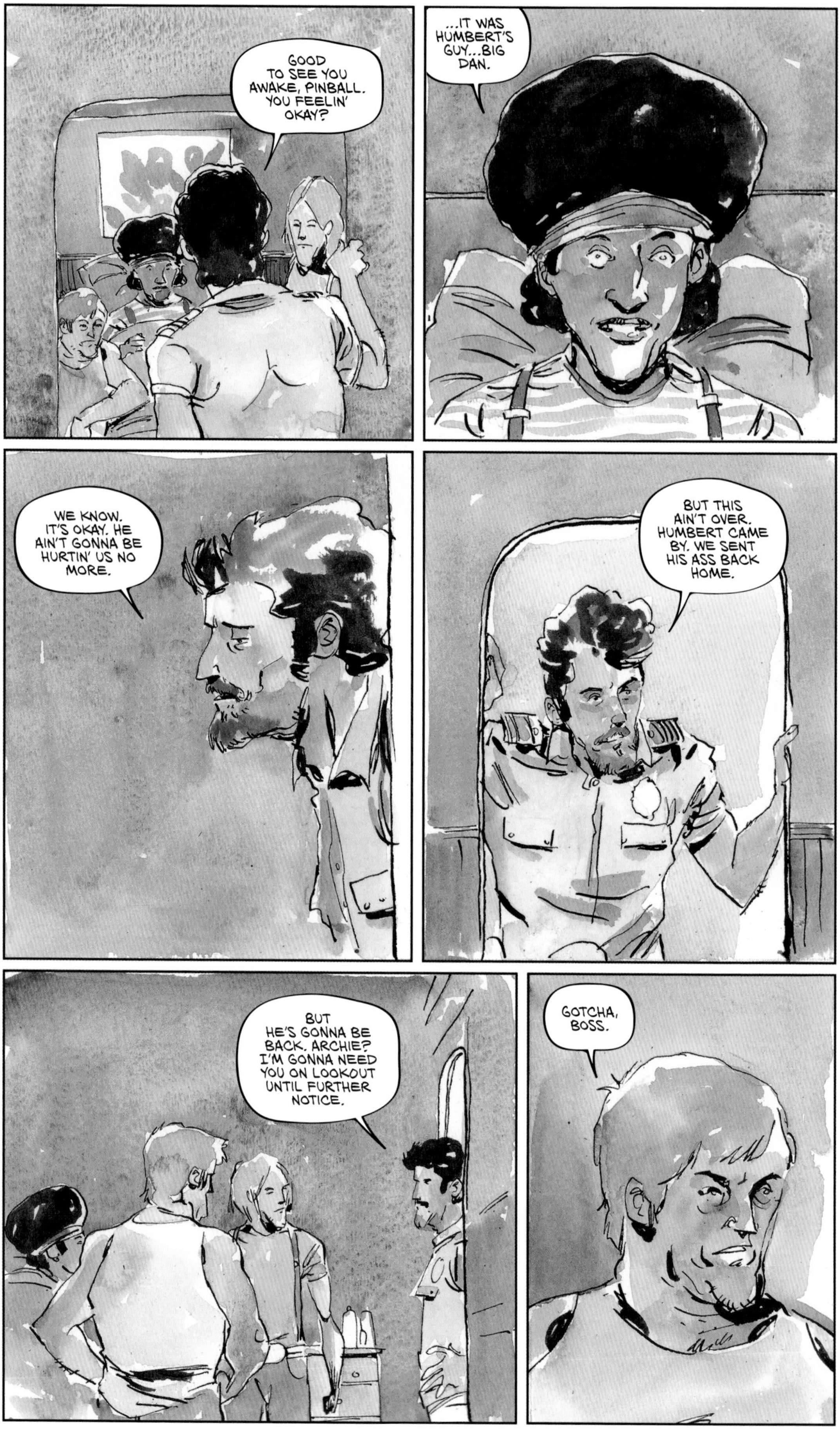
GOOD TO SEE YOU AWAKE, PINBALL. YOU FEELIN' OKAY?
...IT WAS HUMBERT'S GUY...BIG DAN.
WE KNOW. IT'S OKAY. HE AIN'T GONNA BE HURTIN' US NO MORE.
BUT THIS AIN'T OVER. HUMBERT CAME BY. WE SENT HIS ASS BACK HOME.
BUT HE'S GONNA BE BACK. ARCHIE? I'M GONNA NEED YOU ON LOOKOUT UNTIL FURTHER NOTICE.
GOTCHA, BOSS.

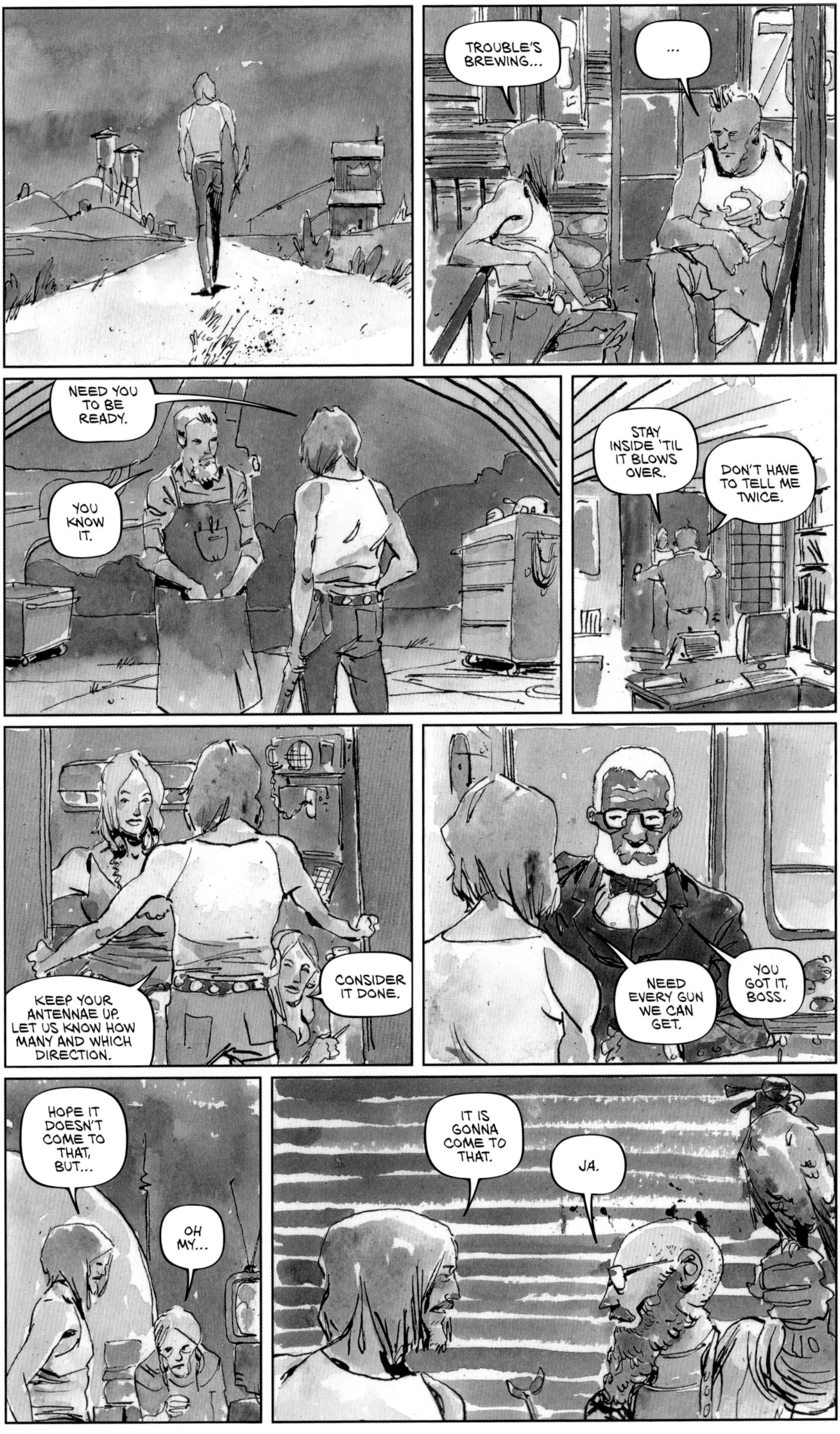
TROUBLE'S BREWING...
...
NEED YOU TO BE READY.
YOU KNOW IT.
STAY INSIDE 'TIL IT BLOWS OVER.
DON'T HAVE TO TELL ME TWICE.
KEEP YOUR ANTENNAE UP. LET US KNOW HOW MANY AND WHICH DIRECTION.
CONSIDER IT DONE.
NEED EVERY GUN WE CAN GET.
YOU GOT IT, BOSS.
HOPE IT DOESN'T COME TO THAT, BUT...
OH MY...
IT IS GONNA COME TO THAT.
JA.

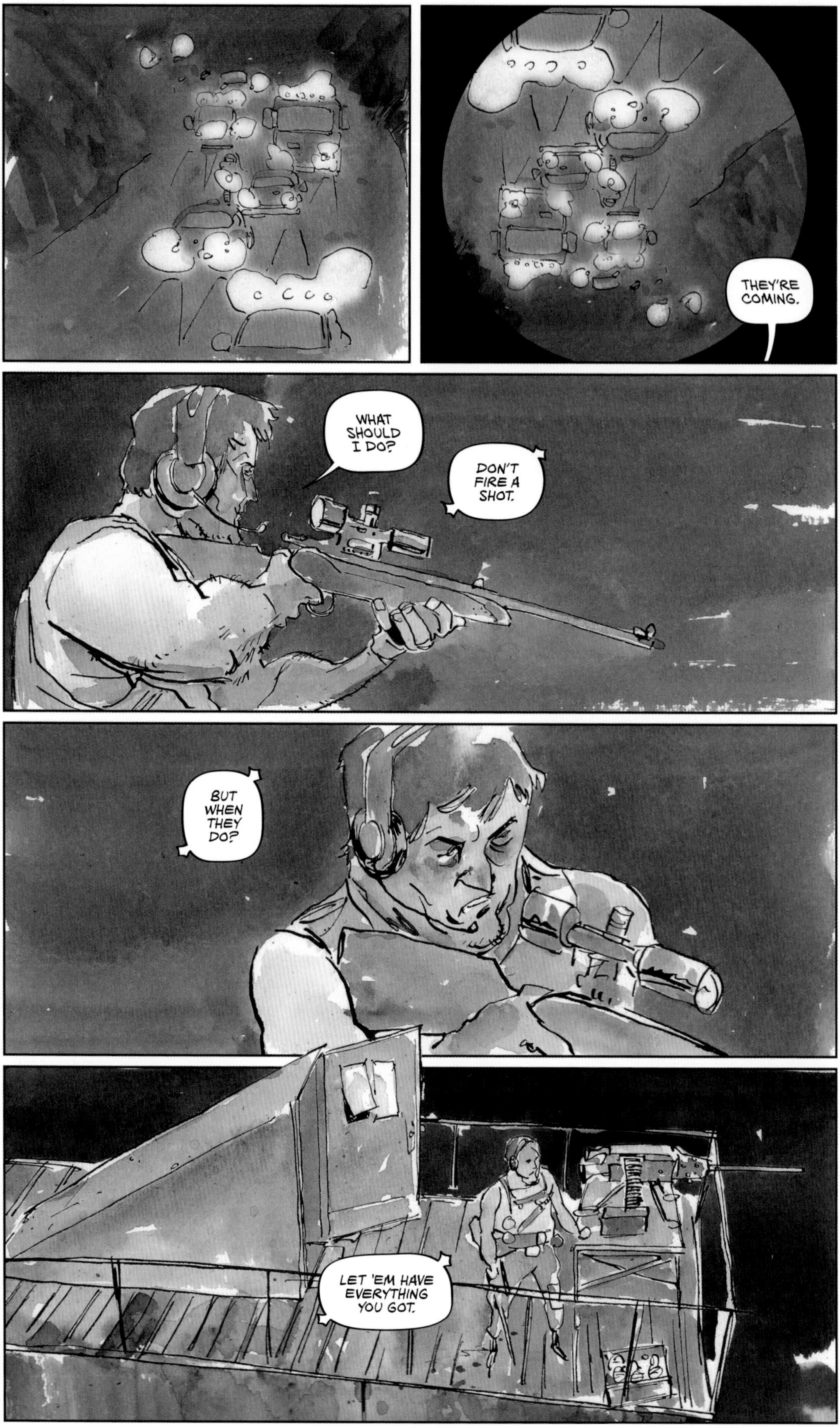
THEY'RE COMING.
WHAT SHOULD I DO?
DON'T FIRE A SHOT.
BUT WHEN THEY DO?
LET 'EM HAVE EVERYTHING YOU GOT.

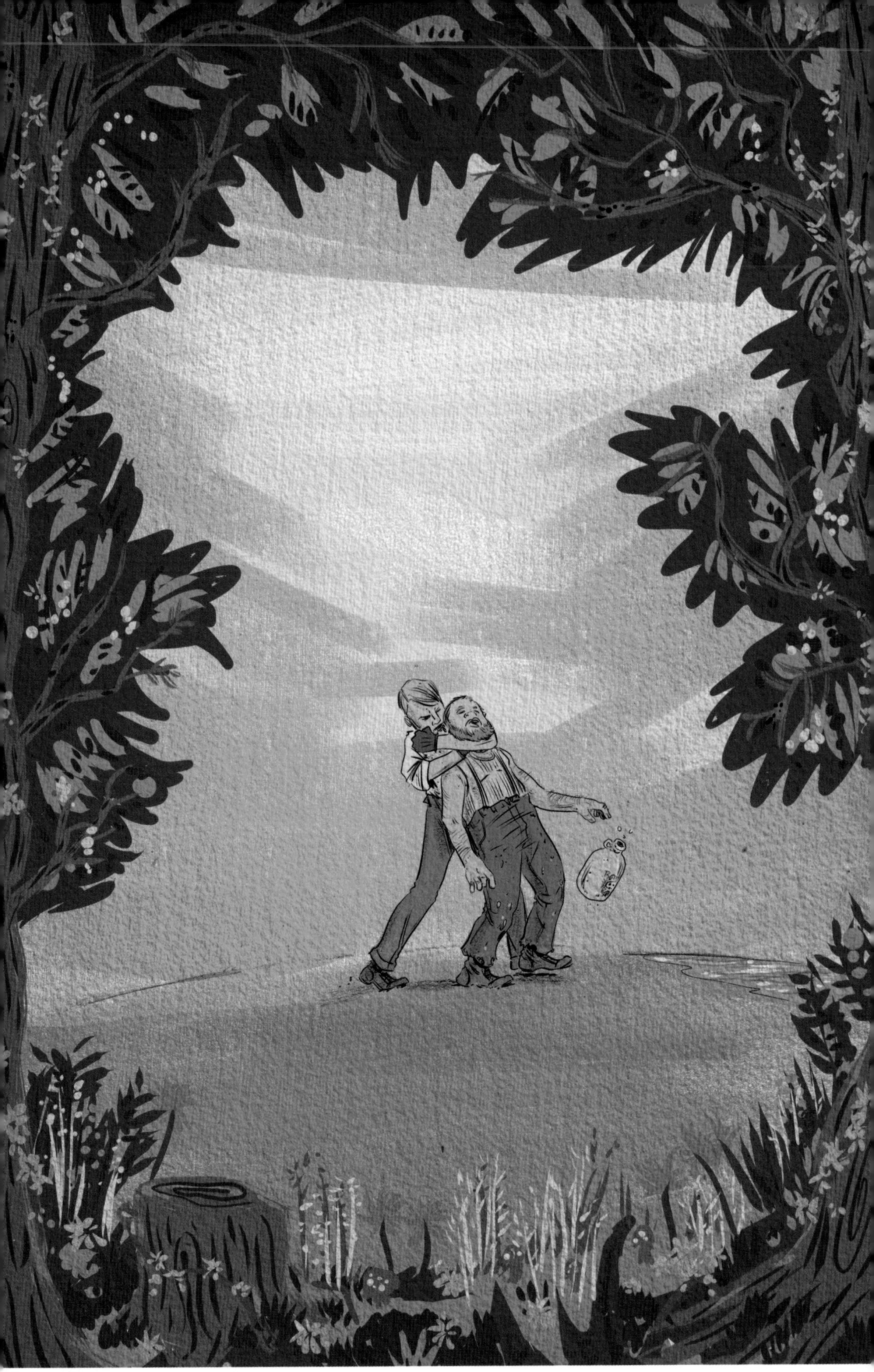

issue #4 cover by matt kindt

# chapter five

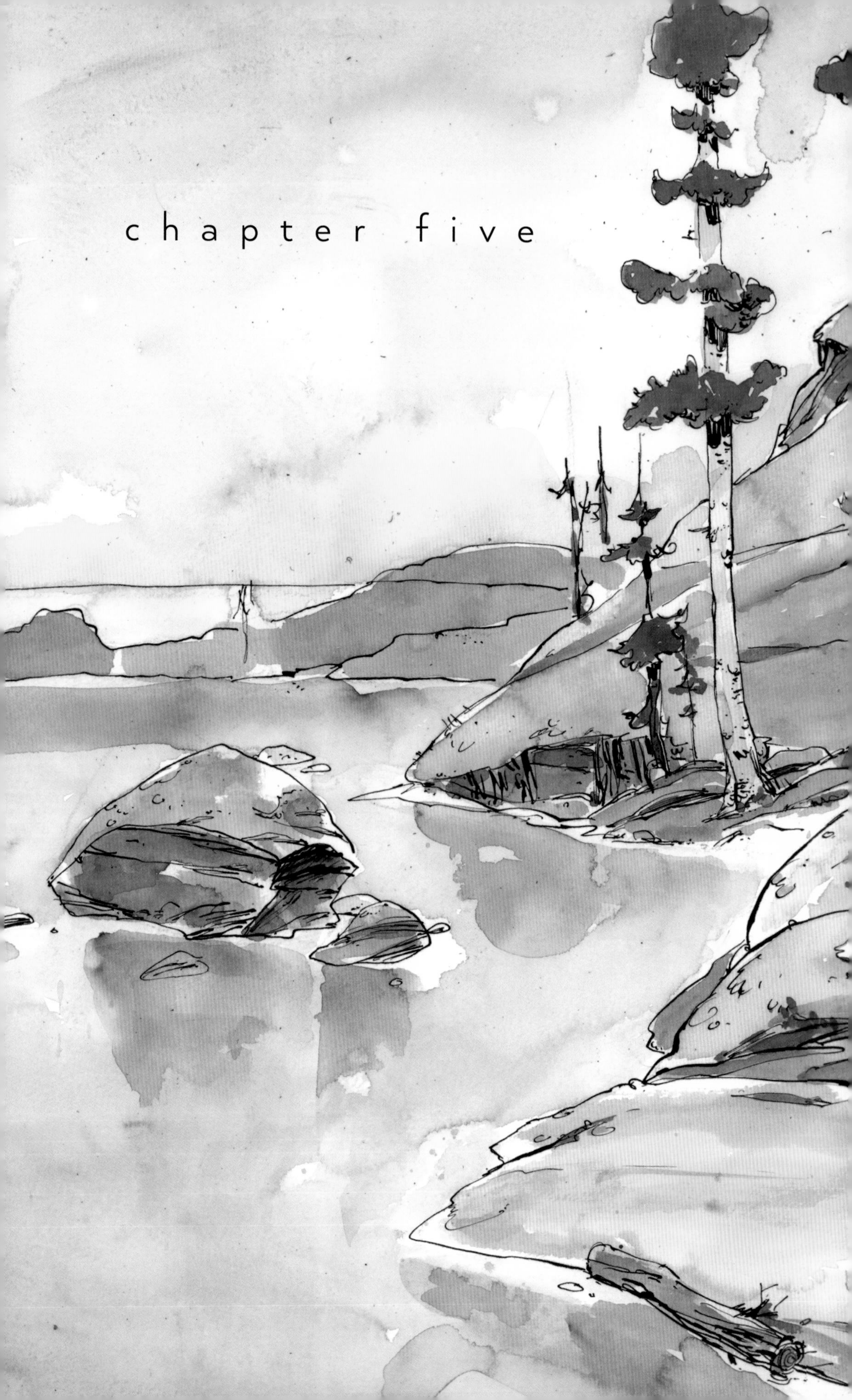

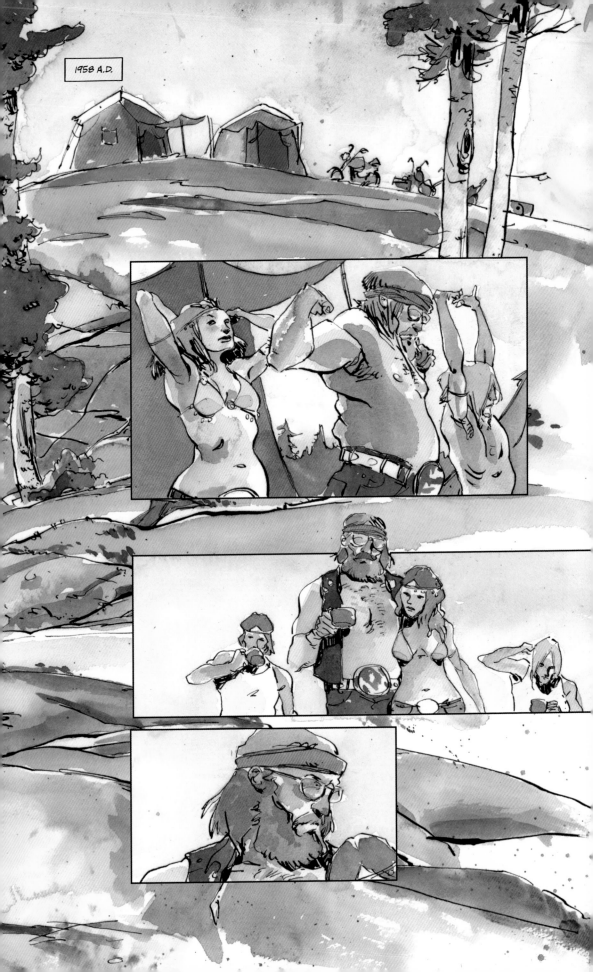

1958 A.D.

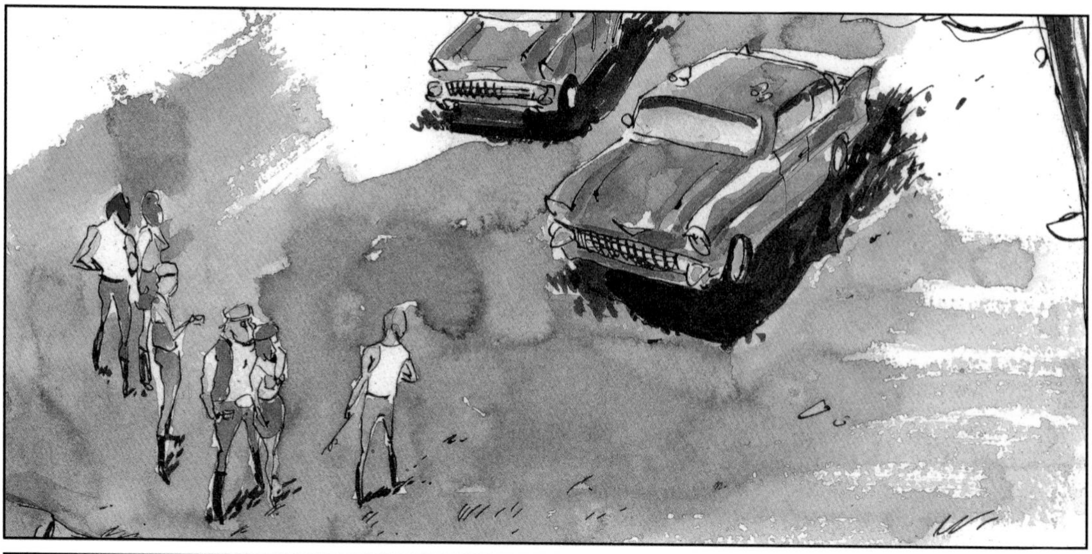

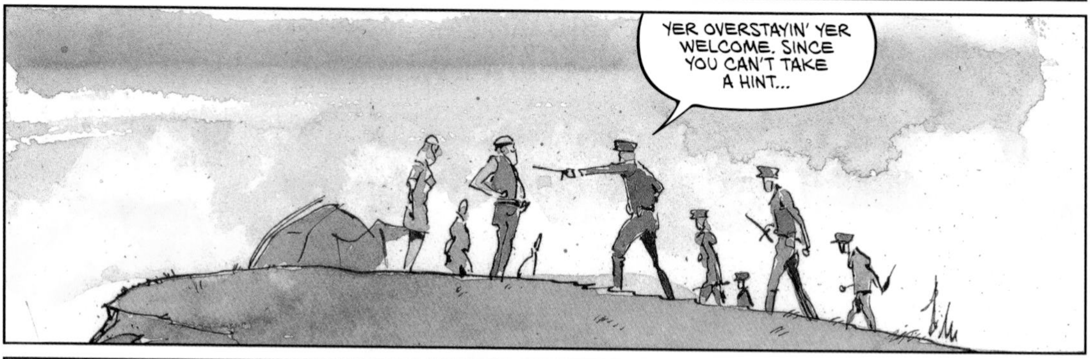
YER OVERSTAYIN' YER WELCOME. SINCE YOU CAN'T TAKE A HINT...

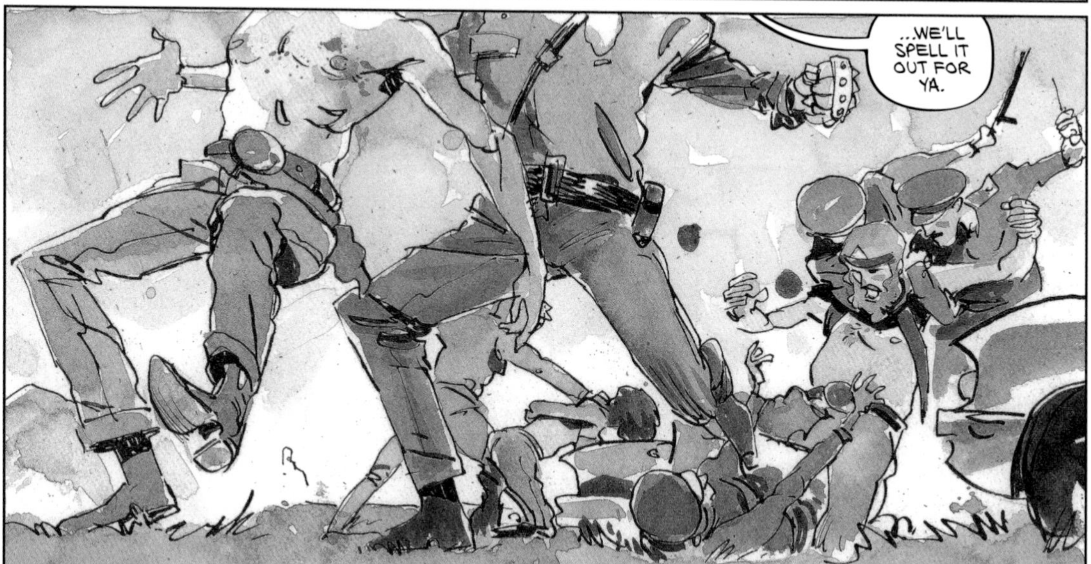
...WE'LL SPELL IT OUT FOR YA.

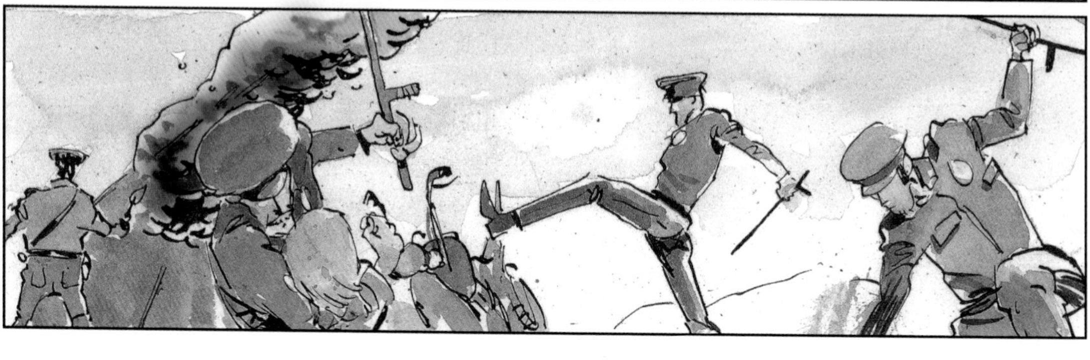

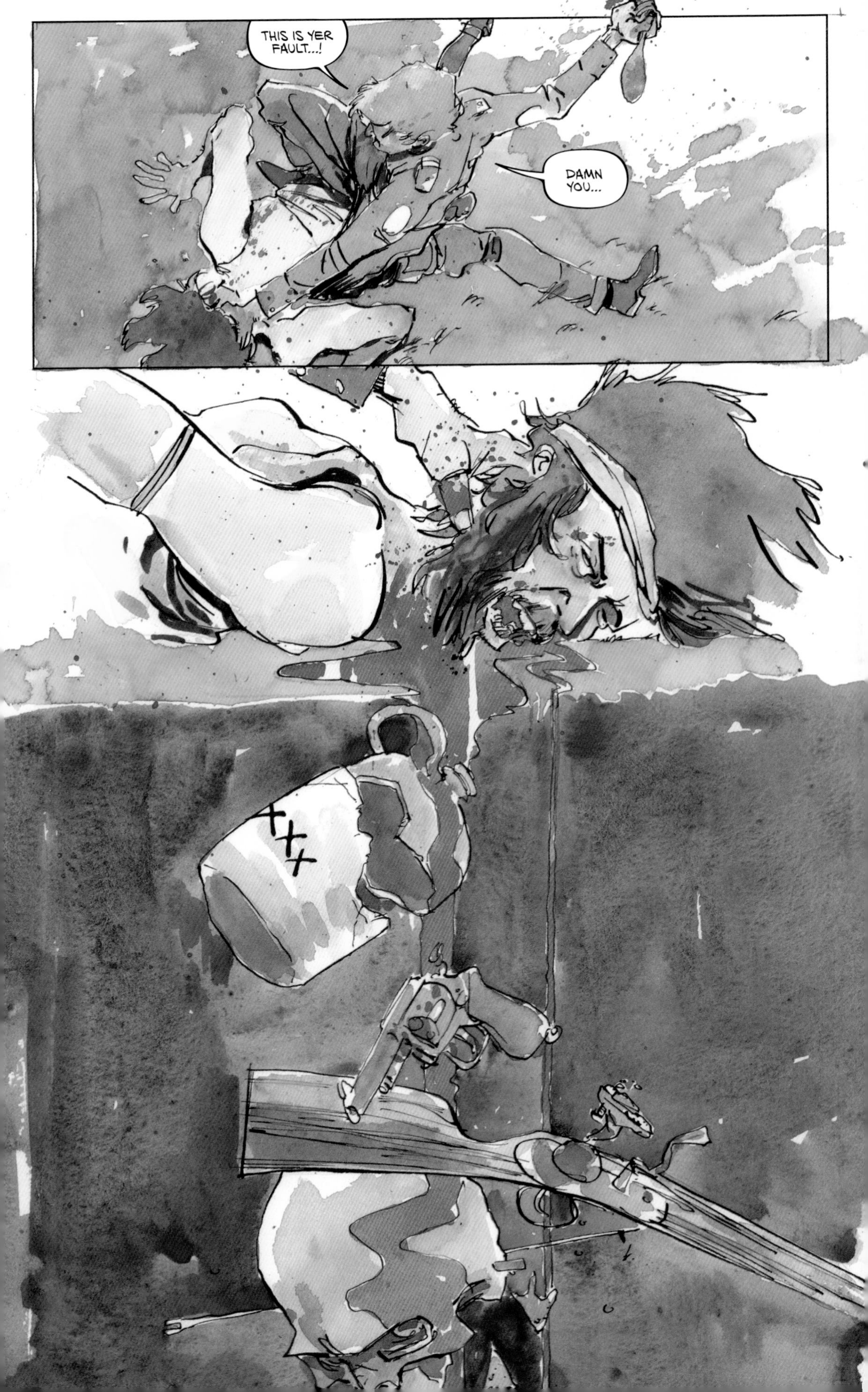
THIS IS YER FAULT...!
DAMN YOU...

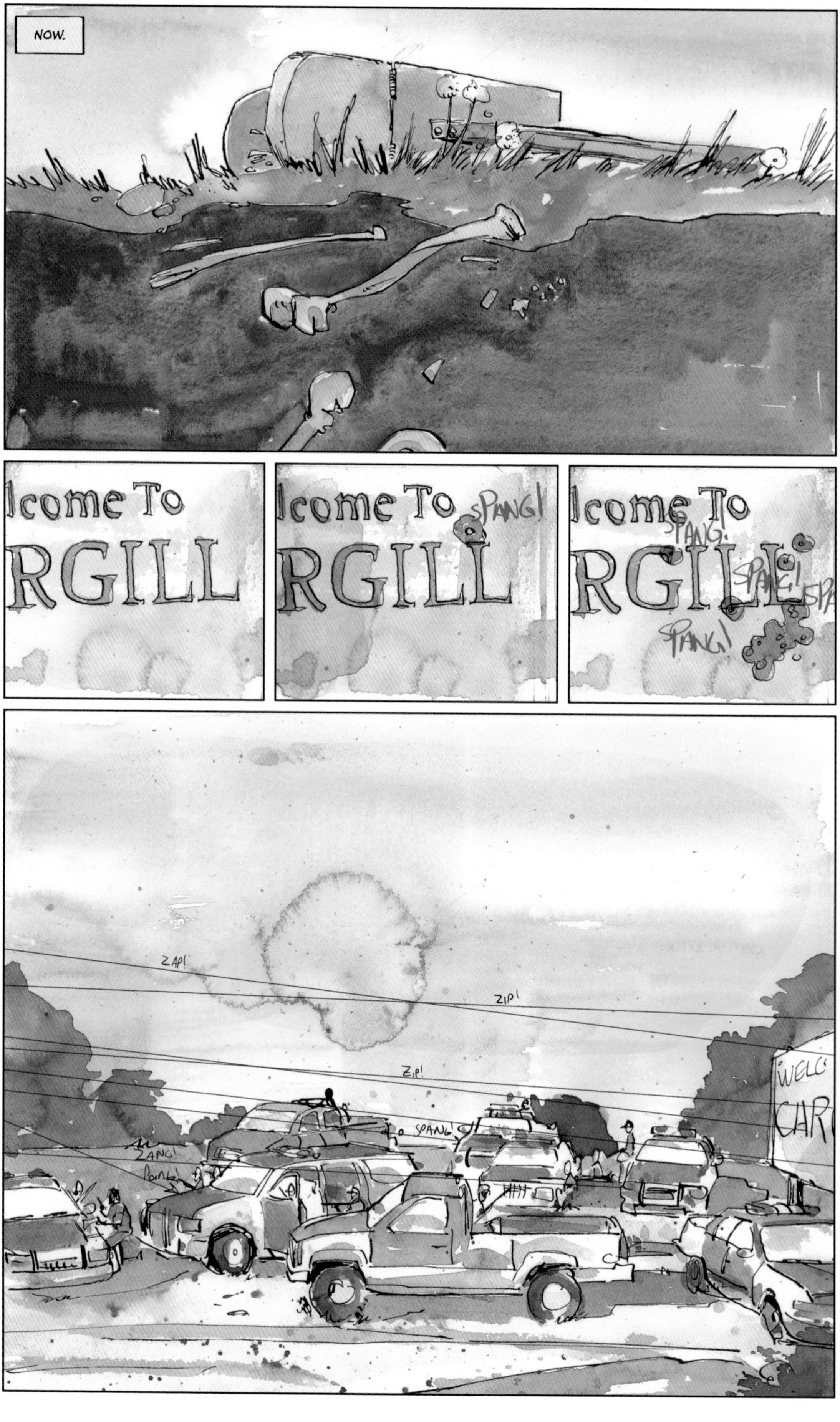
NOW.
lcome To
RGILL
lcome To
SPANG!
RGILL
lcome To
SPANG!
RGILL
SPANG!
SPANG!
ZAP!
ZIP!
ZIP!
SPANG!
ZANG!
WELC
CAR

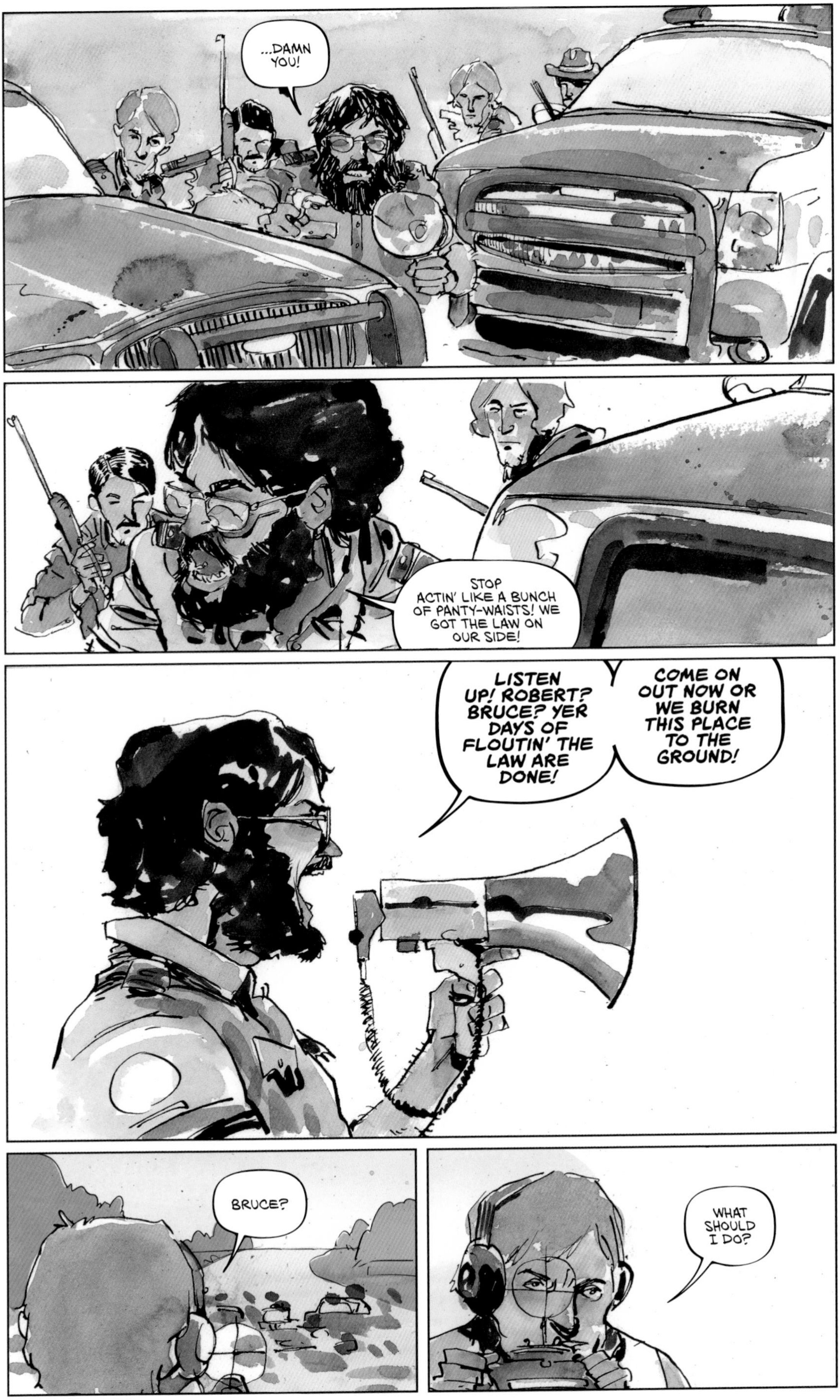
...DAMN YOU!
STOP ACTIN' LIKE A BUNCH OF PANTY-WAISTS! WE GOT THE LAW ON OUR SIDE!
LISTEN UP! ROBERT? BRUCE? YER DAYS OF FLOUTIN' THE LAW ARE DONE!
COME ON OUT NOW OR WE BURN THIS PLACE TO THE GROUND!
BRUCE?
WHAT SHOULD I DO?

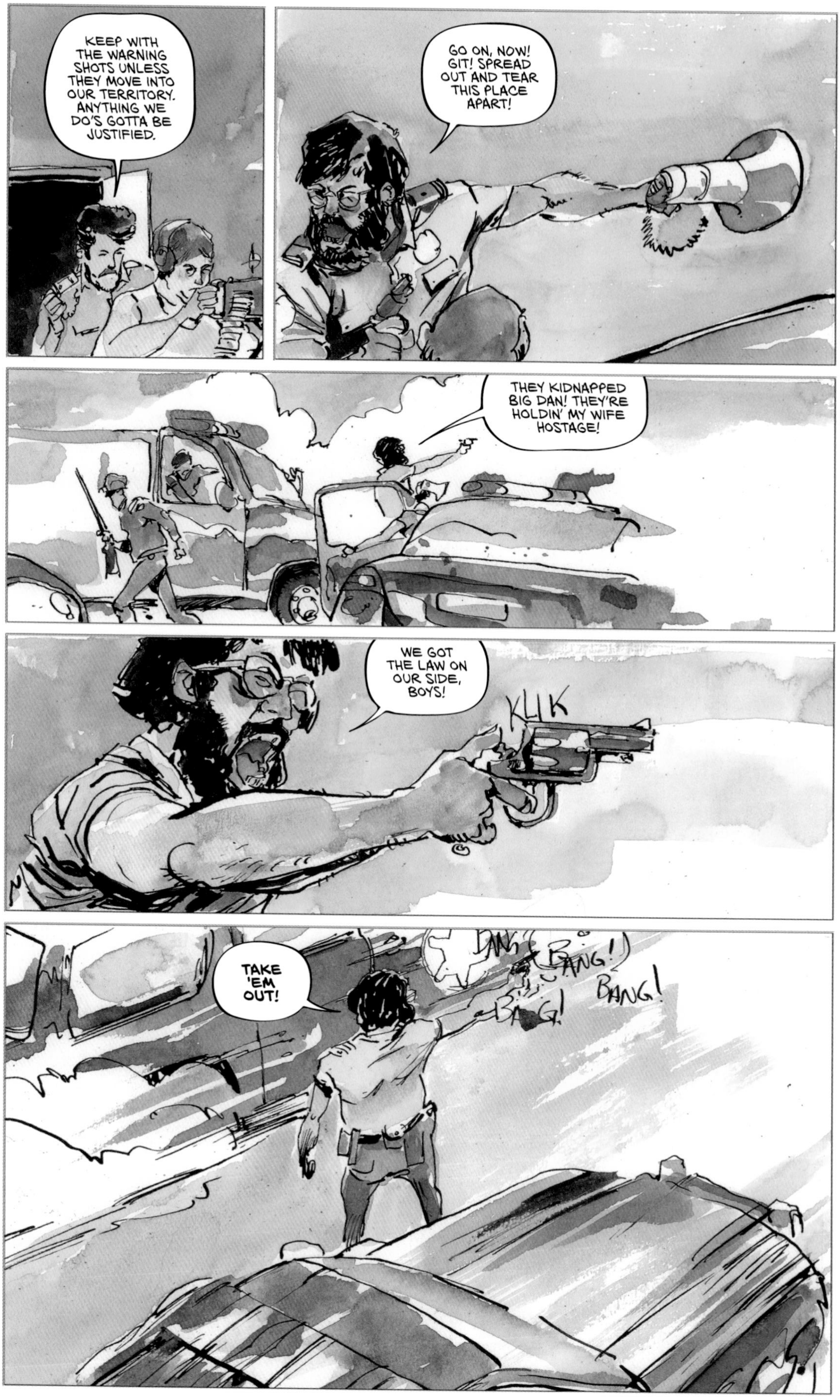
KEEP WITH THE WARNING SHOTS UNLESS THEY MOVE INTO OUR TERRITORY. ANYTHING WE DO'S GOTTA BE JUSTIFIED.
GO ON, NOW! GIT! SPREAD OUT AND TEAR THIS PLACE APART!
THEY KIDNAPPED BIG DAN! THEY'RE HOLDIN' MY WIFE HOSTAGE!
WE GOT THE LAW ON OUR SIDE, BOYS!
KLIK
TAKE 'EM OUT!
BANG! BANG! BANG! BANG!

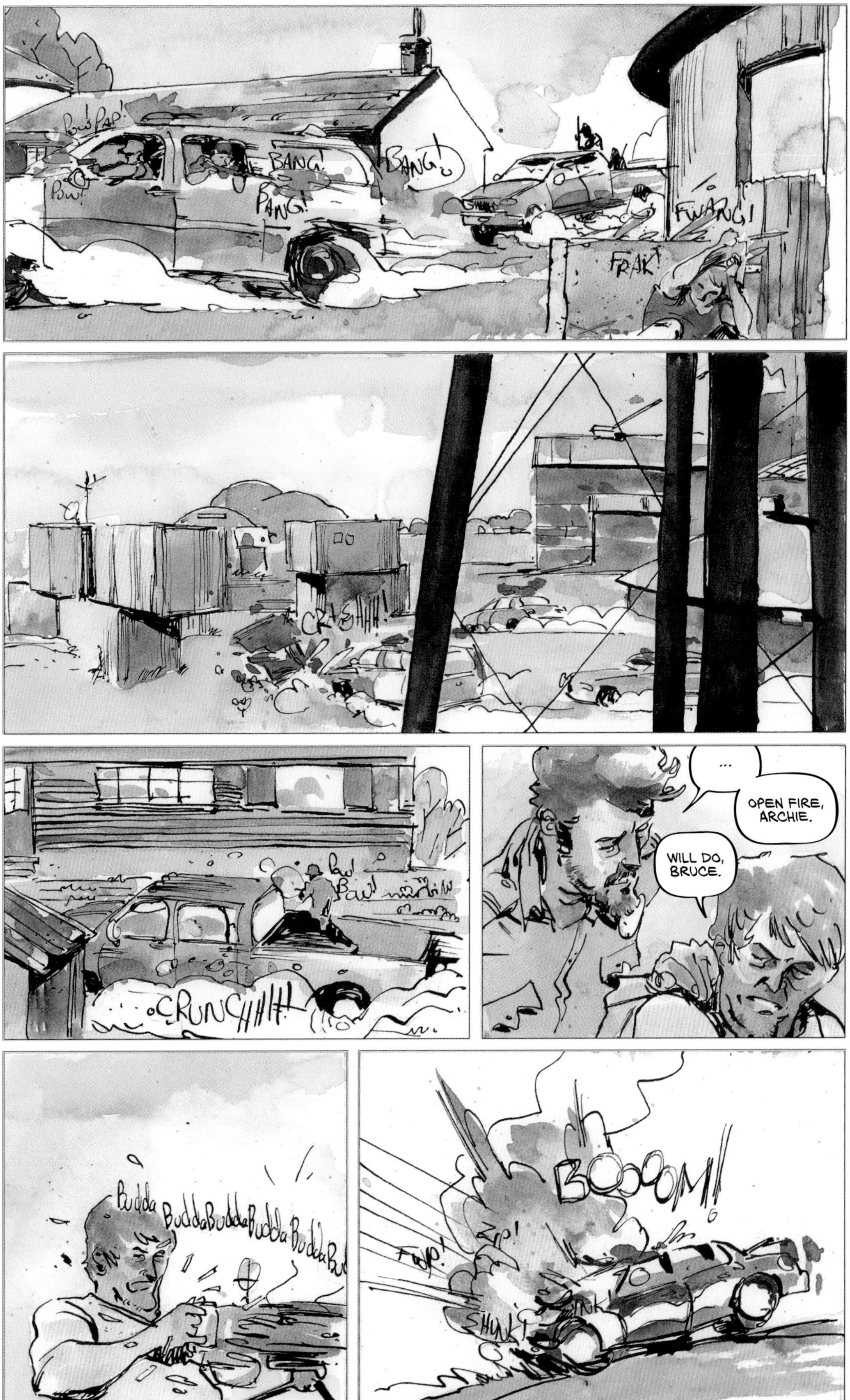
BANG!
BANG!
PANG!
POW!
FWANG!
FRAK!
CRASHHH!
CRUNCHHH!
...
OPEN FIRE, ARCHIE.
WILL DO, BRUCE.
BOOOOM!
ZIP!
SHUNK!

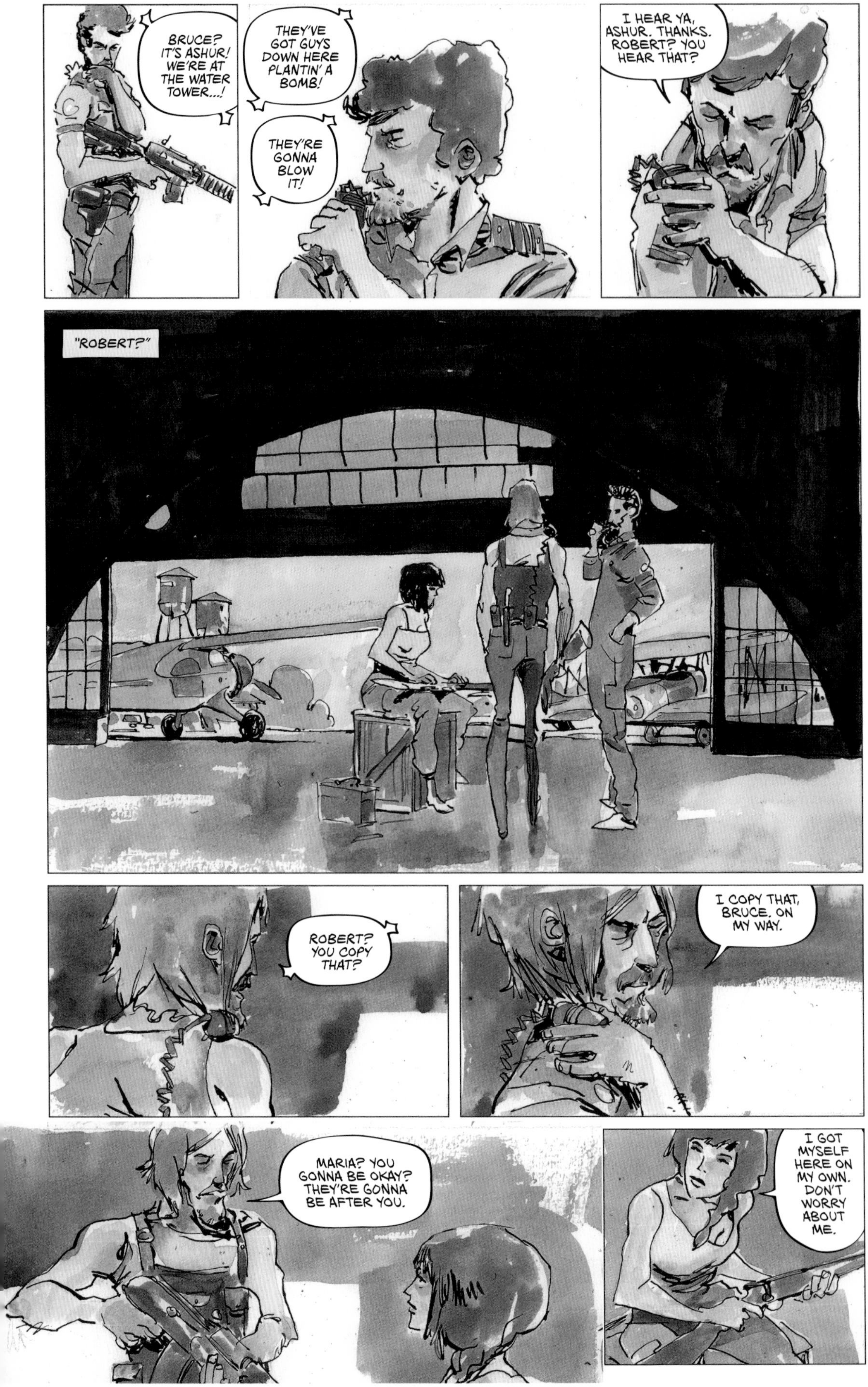

BRUCE? IT'S ASHUR! WE'RE AT THE WATER TOWER...!
THEY'VE GOT GUYS DOWN HERE PLANTIN' A BOMB!
THEY'RE GONNA BLOW IT!
I HEAR YA, ASHUR. THANKS. ROBERT? YOU HEAR THAT?
"ROBERT?"
ROBERT? YOU COPY THAT?
I COPY THAT, BRUCE. ON MY WAY.
MARIA? YOU GONNA BE OKAY? THEY'RE GONNA BE AFTER YOU.
I GOT MYSELF HERE ON MY OWN. DON'T WORRY ABOUT ME.

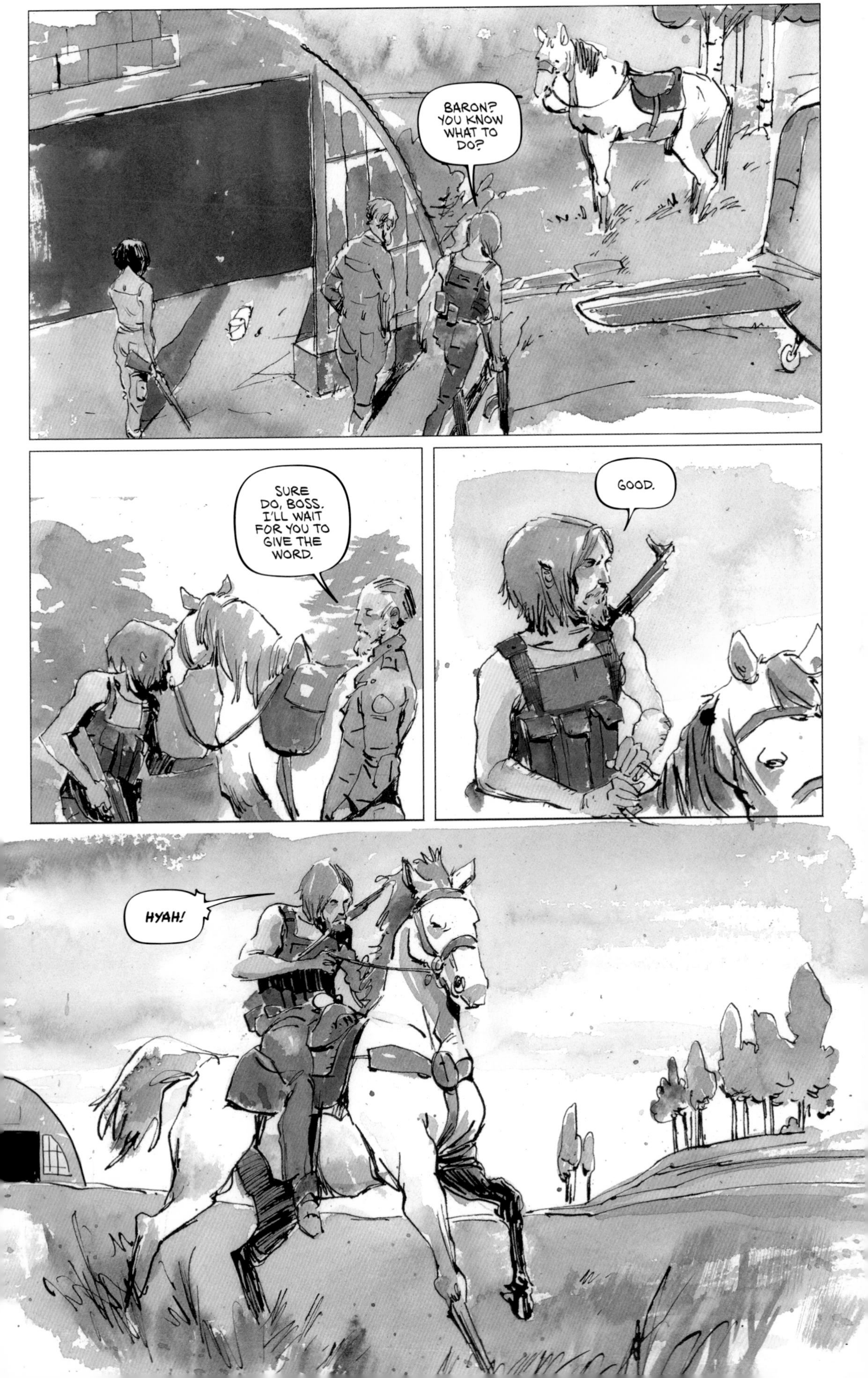
BARON? YOU KNOW WHAT TO DO?
SURE DO, BOSS. I'LL WAIT FOR YOU TO GIVE THE WORD.
GOOD.
HYAH!

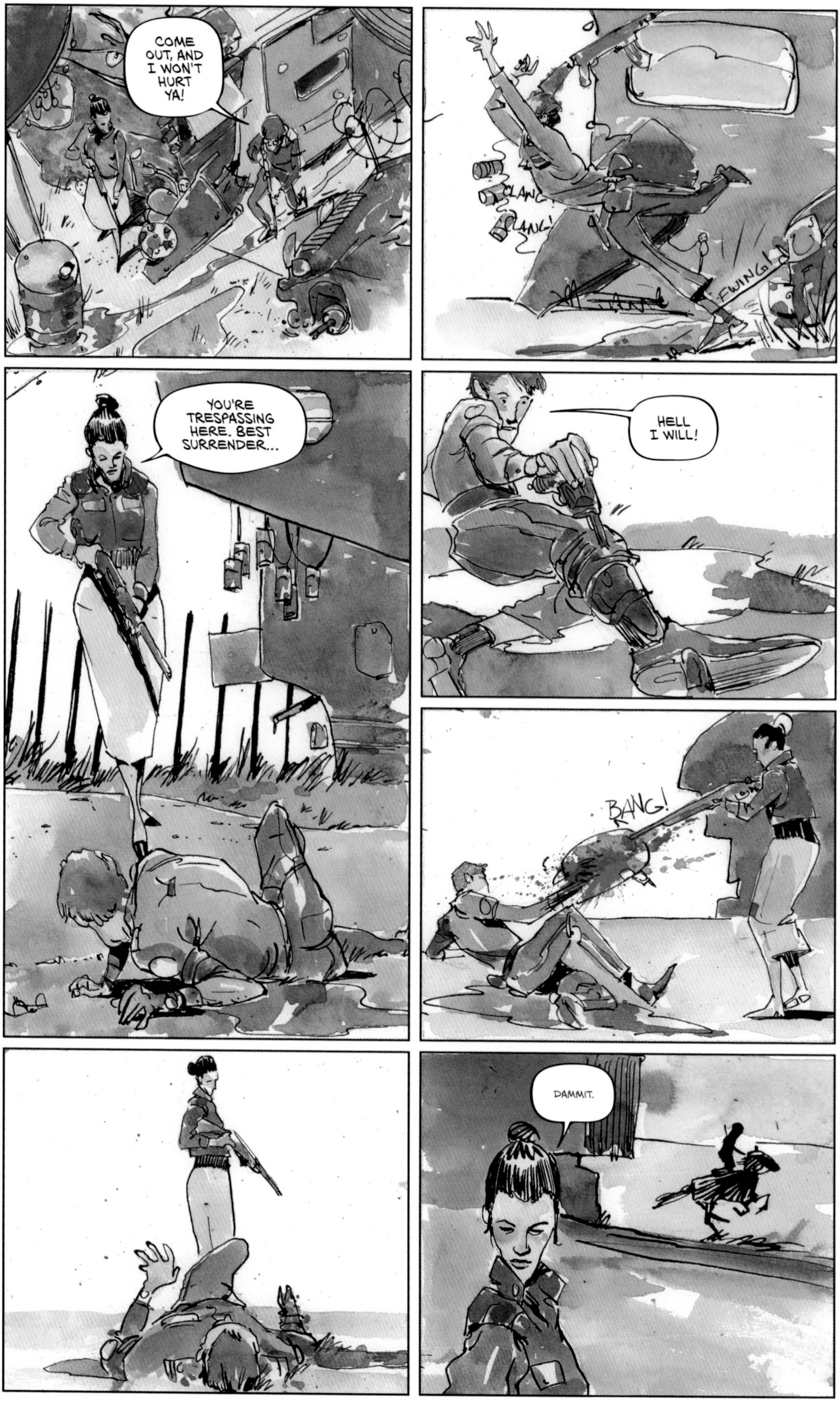
COME OUT, AND I WON'T HURT YA!
CLANG!
CLANG!
FWING!
YOU'RE TRESPASSING HERE. BEST SURRENDER...
HELL I WILL!
BANG!
DAMMIT.

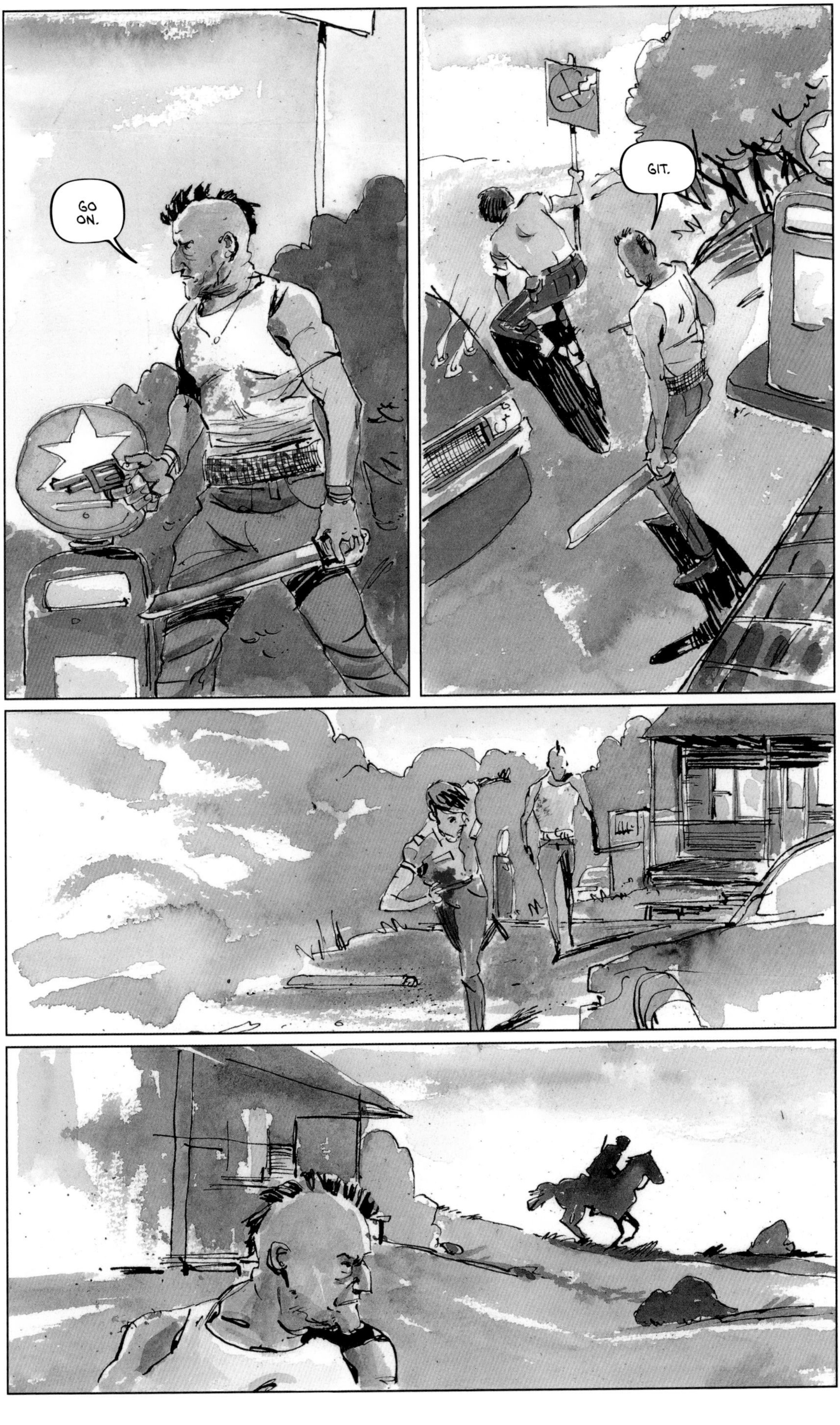
GO ON.
GIT.

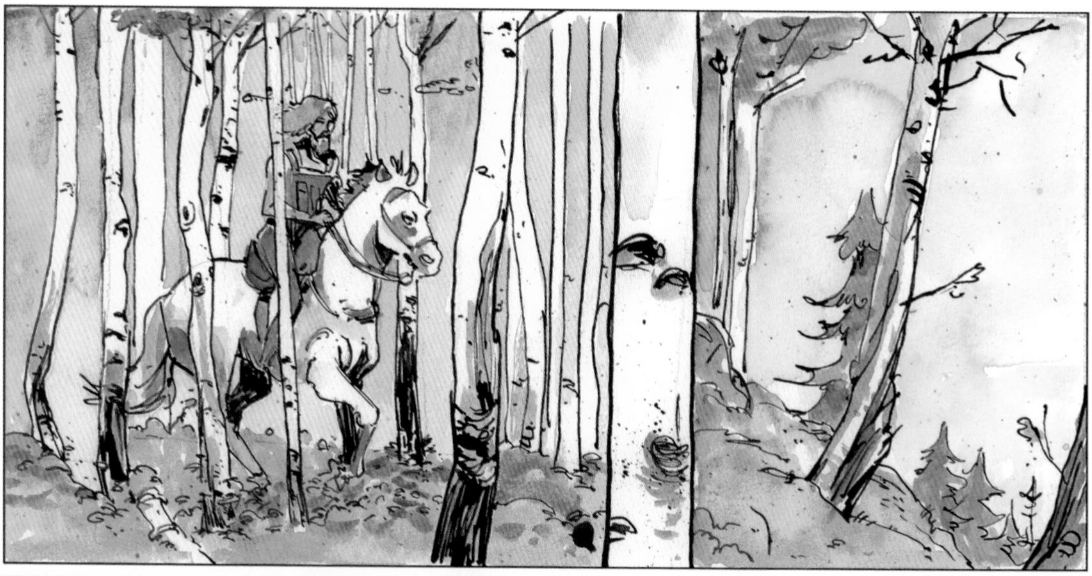

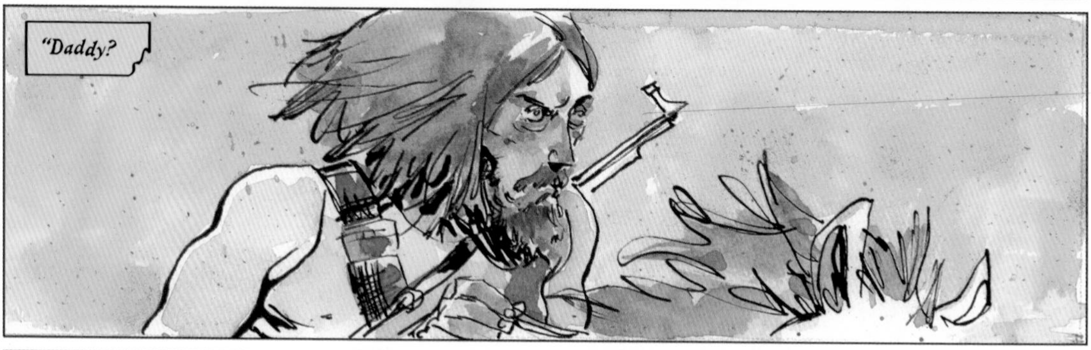
"Daddy?"

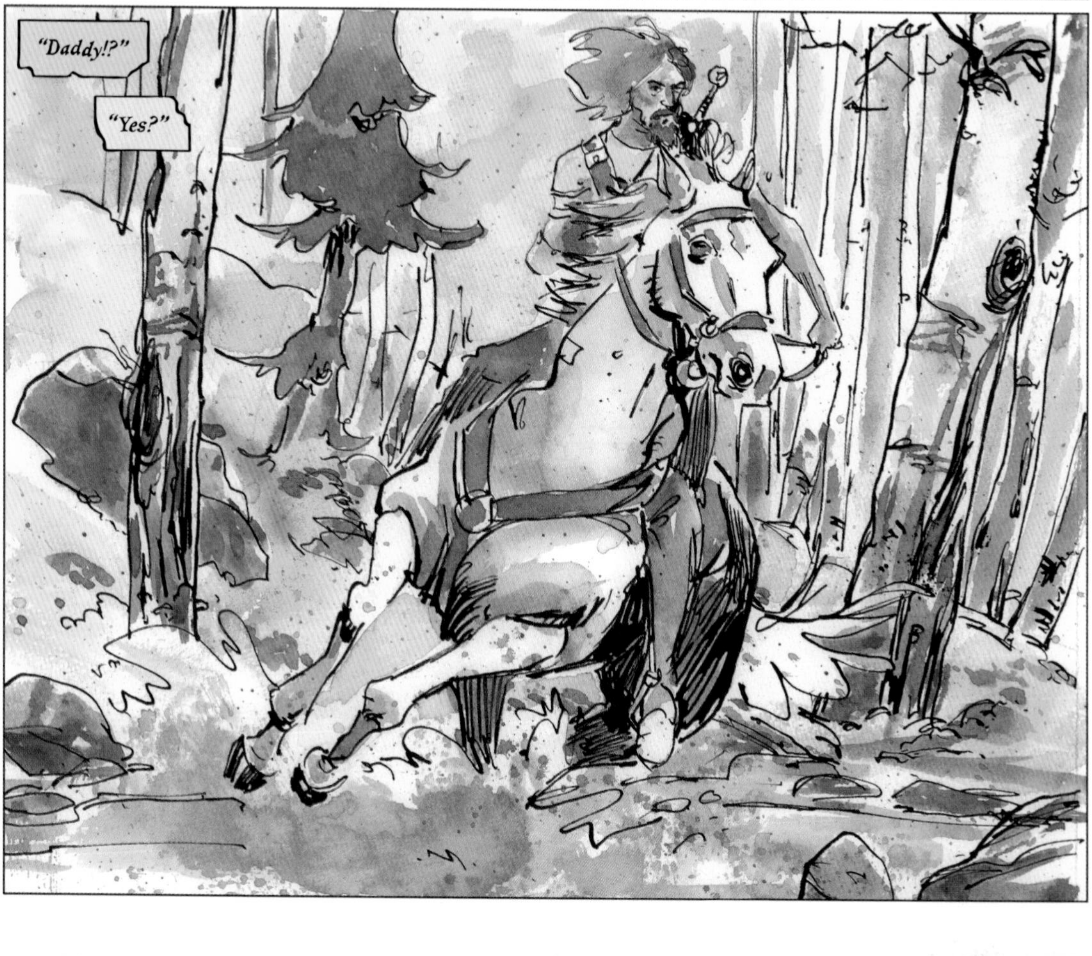
"Daddy!?"
"Yes?"

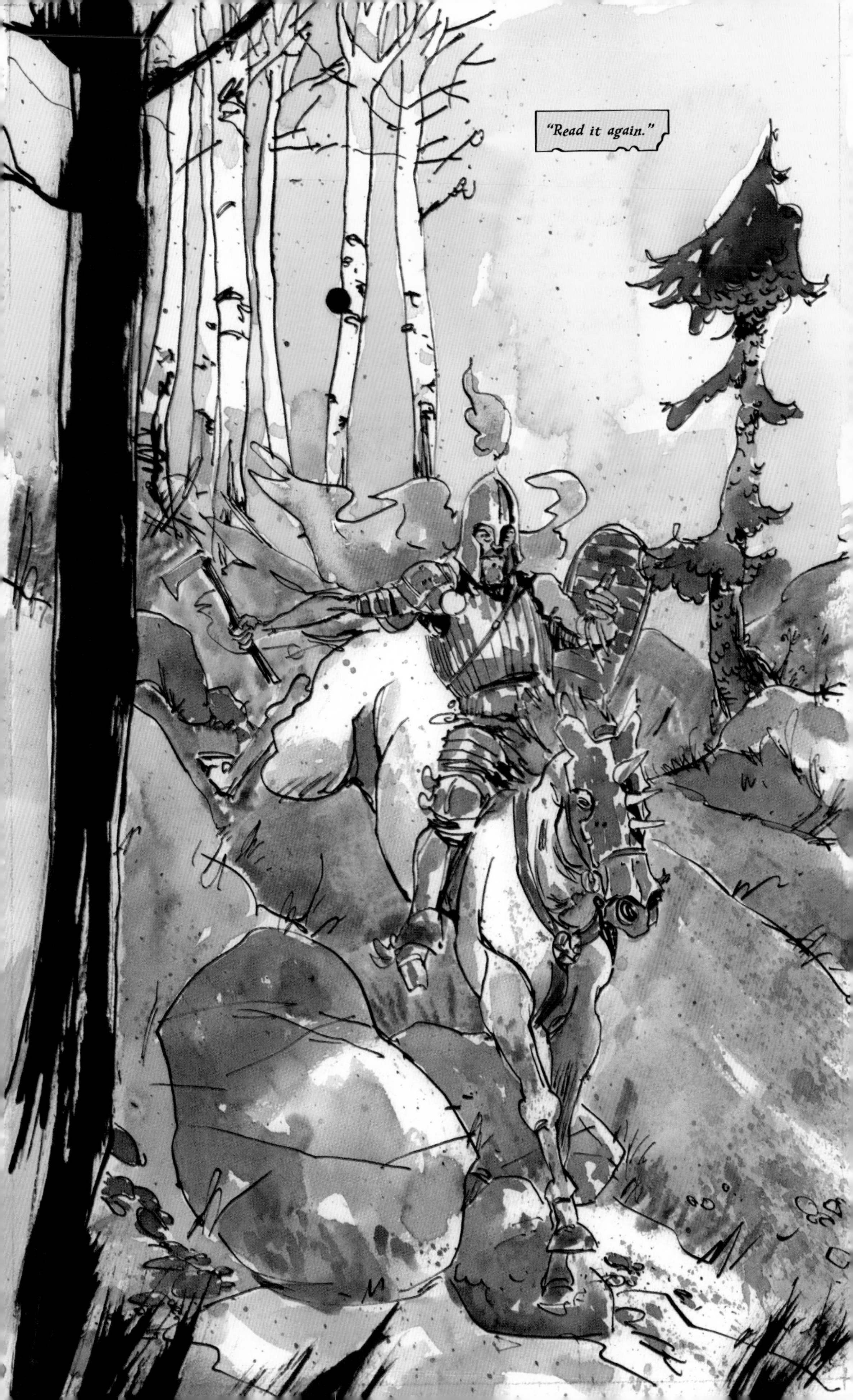
"Read it again."

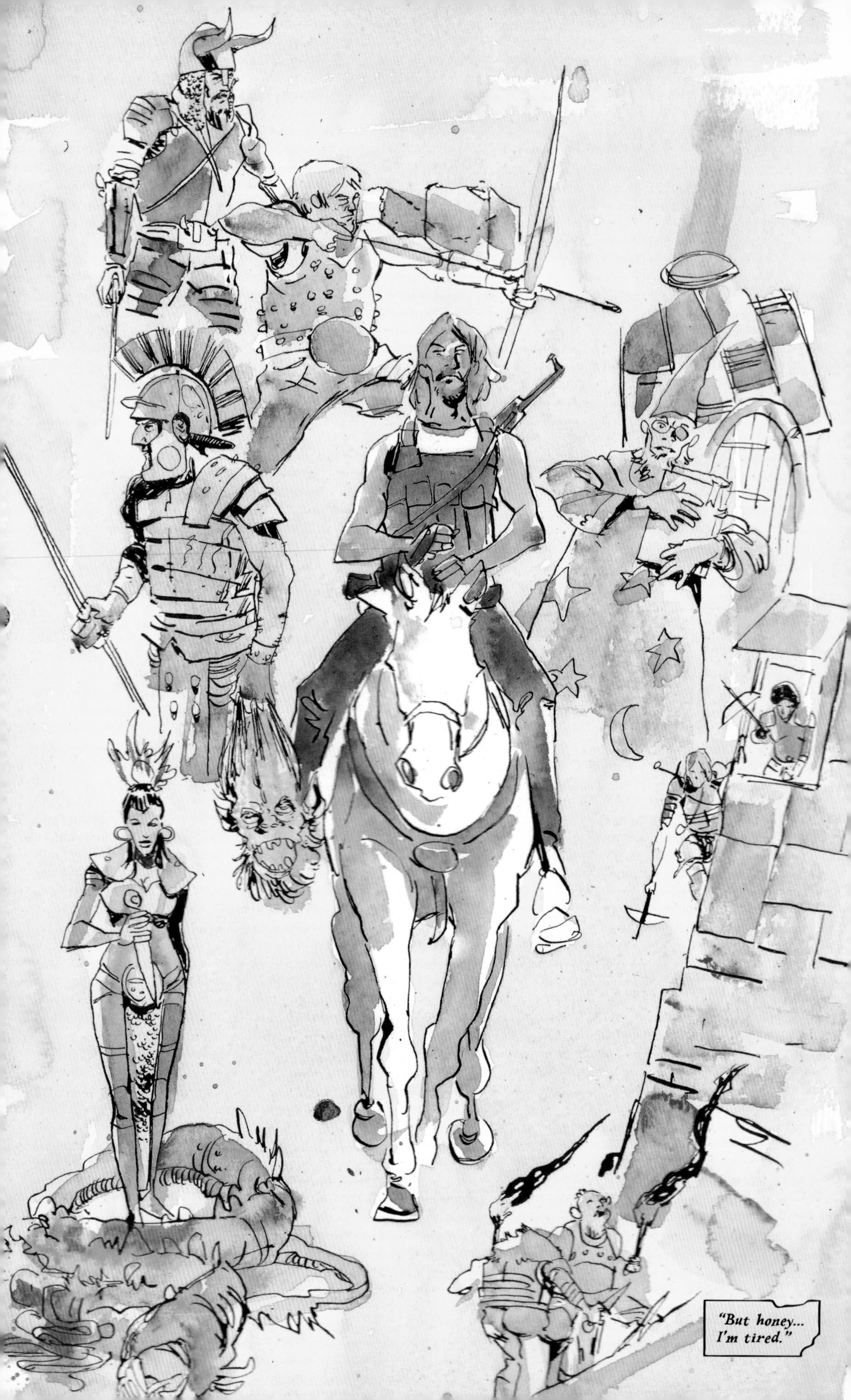
"But honey...
I'm tired."

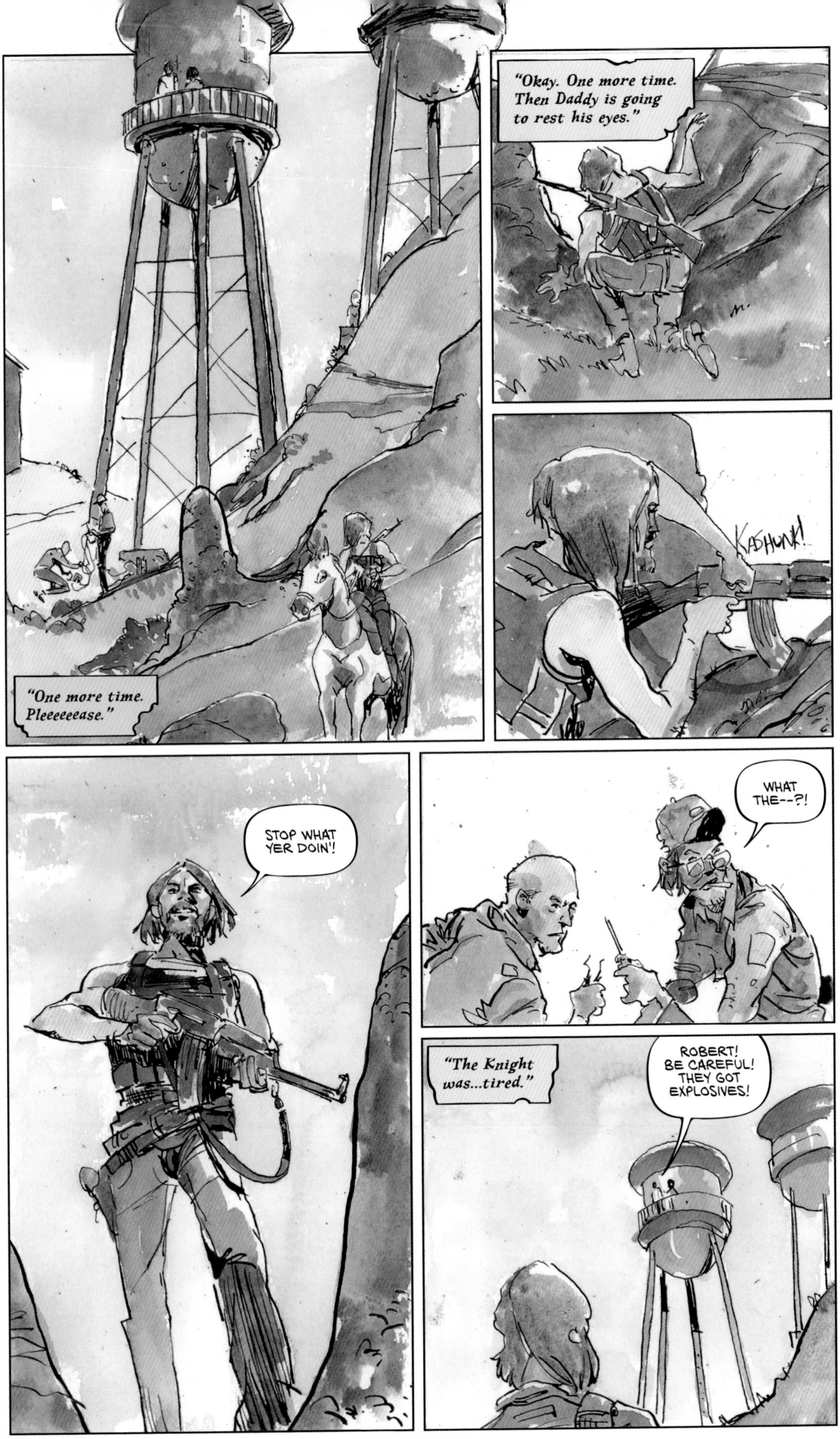
"One more time. Pleeeeeease."
"Okay. One more time. Then Daddy is going to rest his eyes."
KASHUNK!
STOP WHAT YER DOIN'!
WHAT THE--?!
"The Knight was...tired."
ROBERT! BE CAREFUL! THEY GOT EXPLOSIVES!

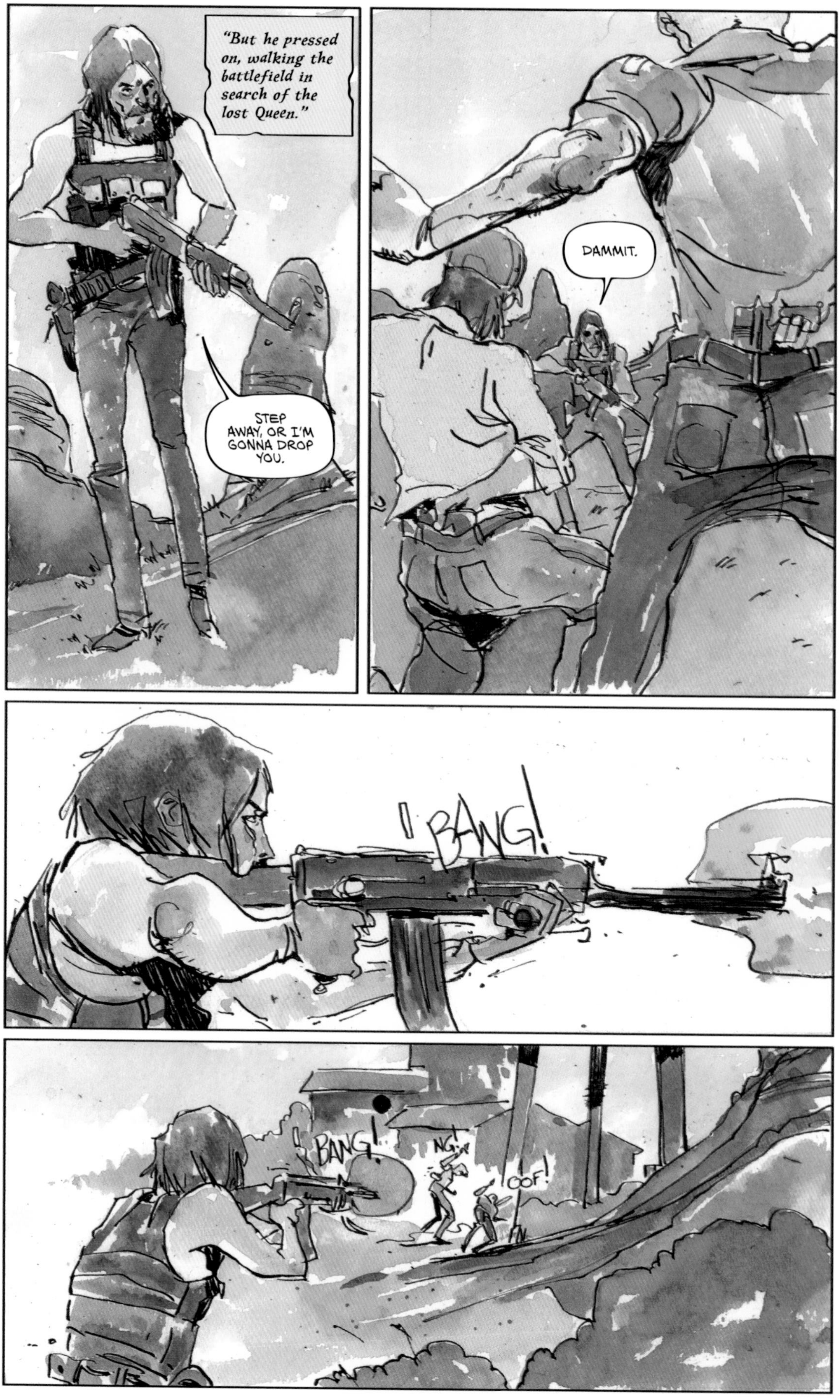
"But he pressed on, walking the battlefield in search of the lost Queen."
STEP AWAY, OR I'M GONNA DROP YOU.
DAMMIT.
BANG!
BANG!
NG!
OOF!

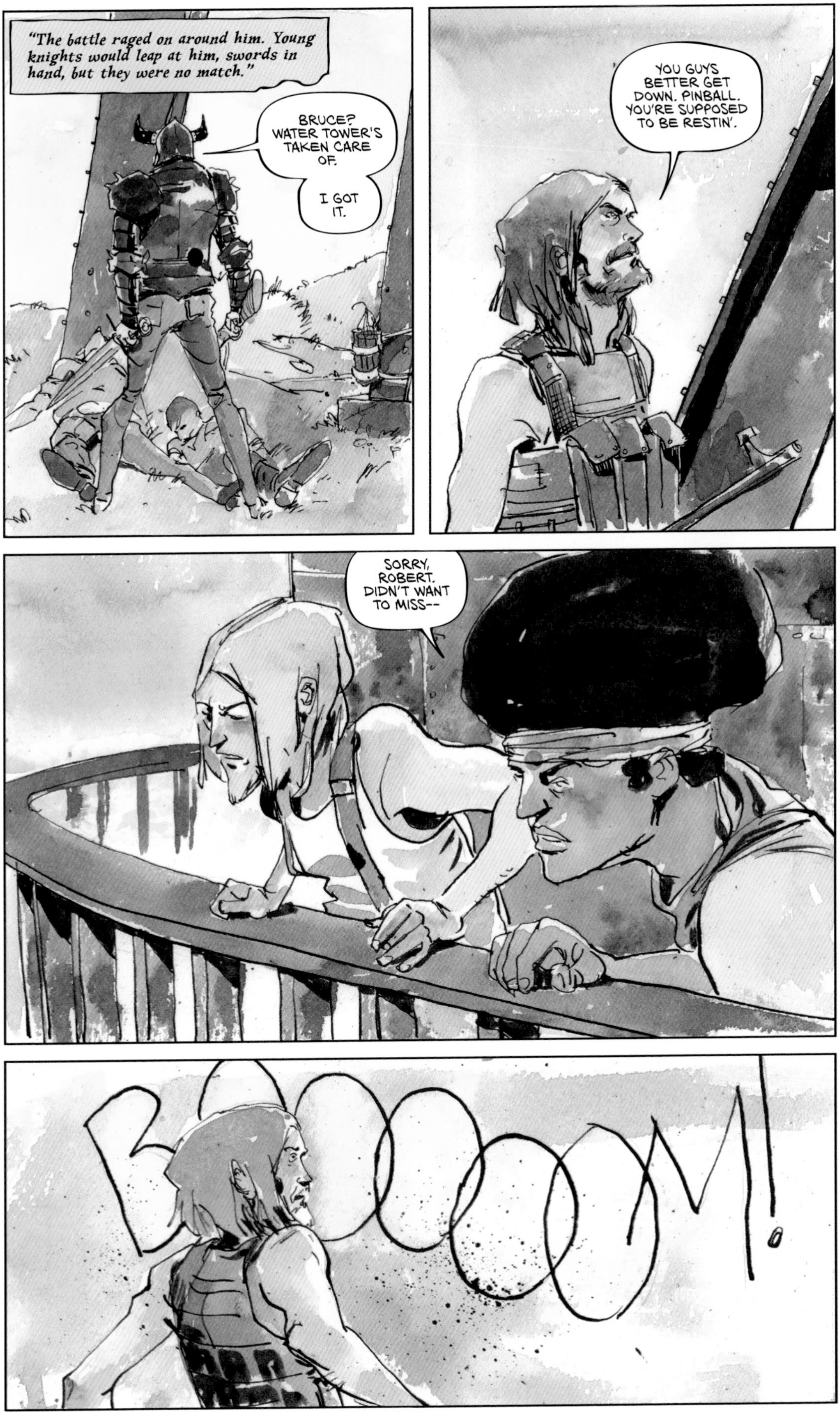
"The battle raged on around him. Young knights would leap at him, swords in hand, but they were no match."
BRUCE? WATER TOWER'S TAKEN CARE OF.
I GOT IT.
YOU GUYS BETTER GET DOWN. PINBALL. YOU'RE SUPPOSED TO BE RESTIN'.
SORRY, ROBERT. DIDN'T WANT TO MISS--
BOOOOOM!

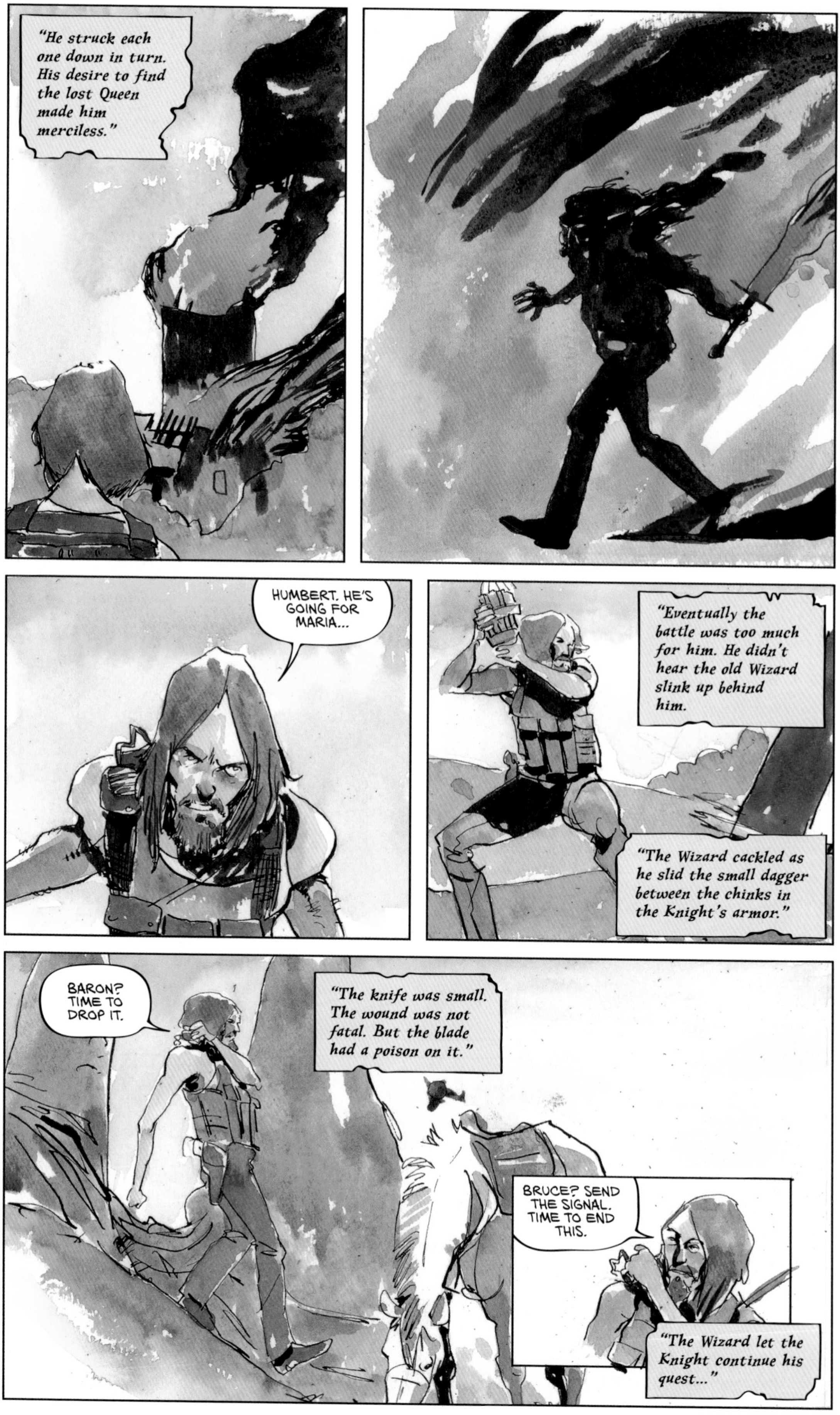
"He struck each one down in turn. His desire to find the lost Queen made him merciless."
HUMBERT. HE'S GOING FOR MARIA...
"Eventually the battle was too much for him. He didn't hear the old Wizard slink up behind him.
"The Wizard cackled as he slid the small dagger between the chinks in the Knight's armor."
BARON? TIME TO DROP IT.
"The knife was small. The wound was not fatal. But the blade had a poison on it."
BRUCE? SEND THE SIGNAL. TIME TO END THIS.
"The Wizard let the Knight continue his quest..."

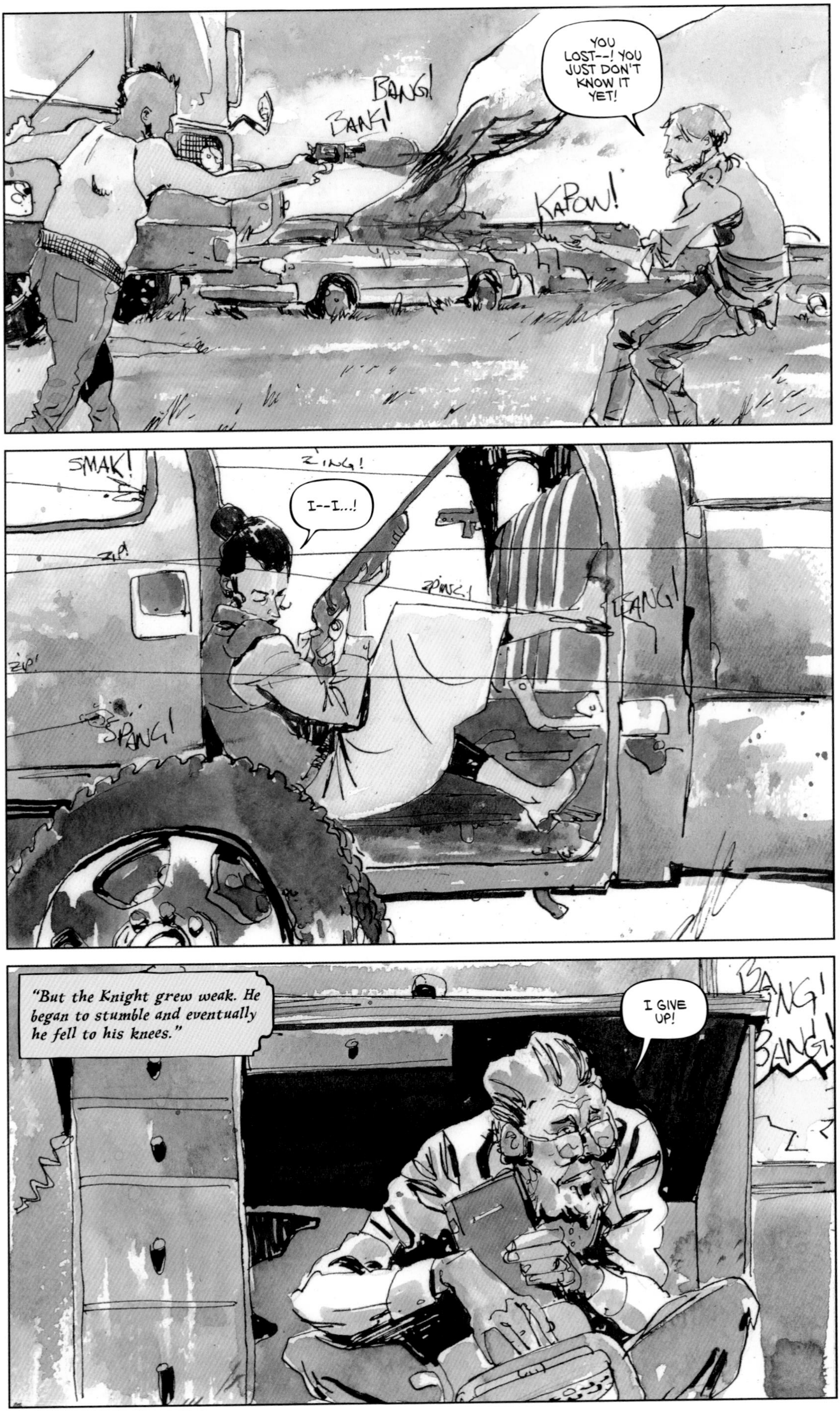
BANG!
BANG!
YOU LOST--! YOU JUST DON'T KNOW IT YET!
KAPOW!
SMAK!
ZING!
I--I...!
ZIP!
ZPING!
BANG!
ZIP!
SPANG!
"But the Knight grew weak. He began to stumble and eventually he fell to his knees."
I GIVE UP!
BANG!
BANG!

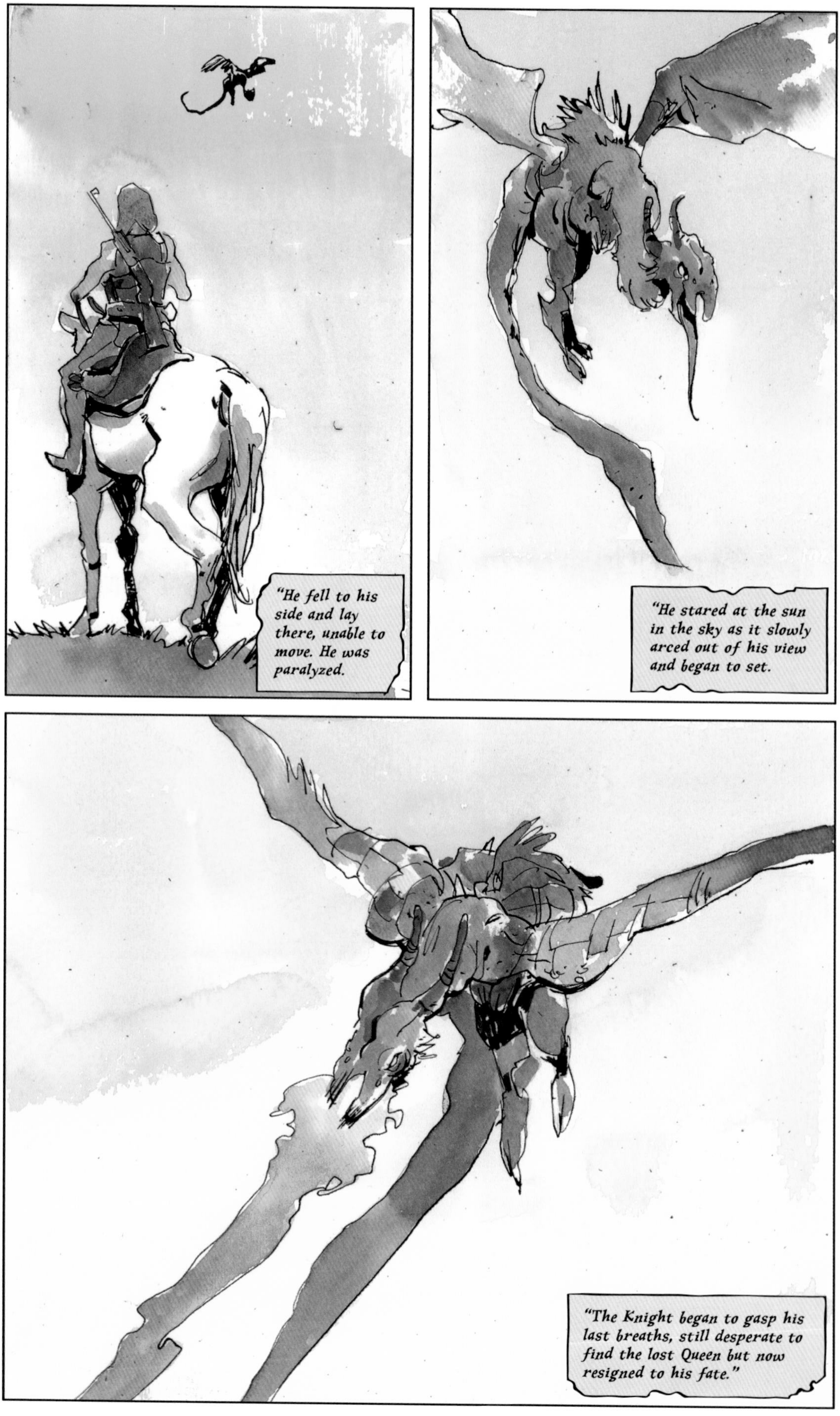
"He fell to his side and lay there, unable to move. He was paralyzed.
"He stared at the sun in the sky as it slowly arced out of his view and began to set.
"The Knight began to gasp his last breaths, still desperate to find the lost Queen but now resigned to his fate."

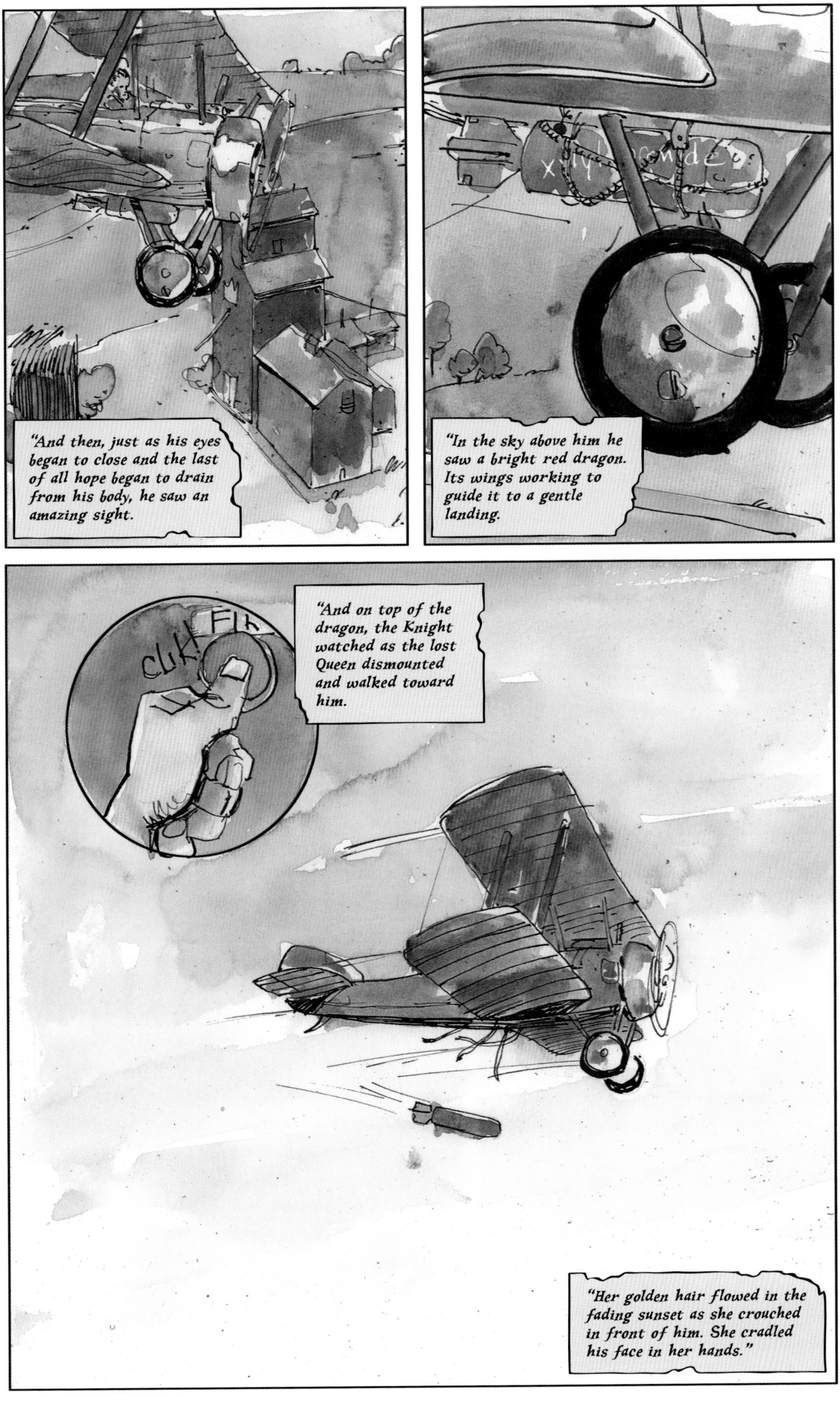
"And then, just as his eyes began to close and the last of all hope began to drain from his body, he saw an amazing sight.
"In the sky above him he saw a bright red dragon. Its wings working to guide it to a gentle landing.
CLIK!
"And on top of the dragon, the Knight watched as the lost Queen dismounted and walked toward him.
"Her golden hair flowed in the fading sunset as she crouched in front of him. She cradled his face in her hands."

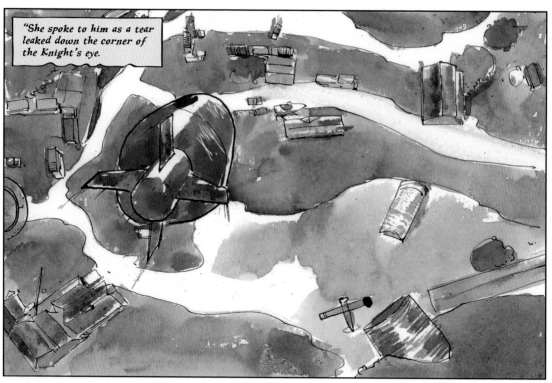

"She spoke to him as a tear leaked down the corner of the Knight's eye."

"'You fool,' she said. 'The Wizard wanted you to waste your life trying to find me...and now he has truly succeeded. You let him kill you.'

"'And now I will truly be the lost Queen...forever beyond your reach.'"

FWABOOOOM!

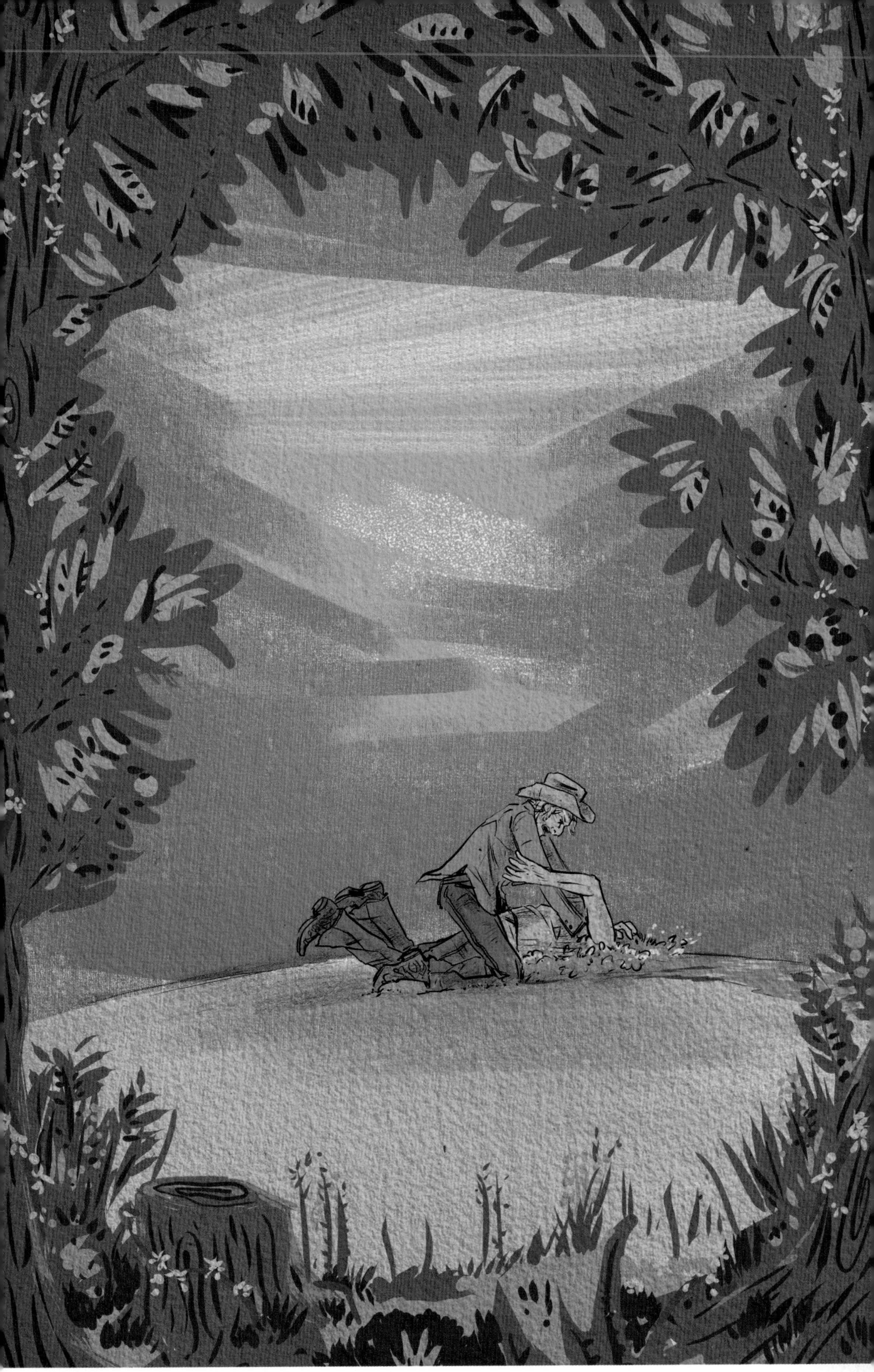

issue #5 cover by matt kindt

# chapter six

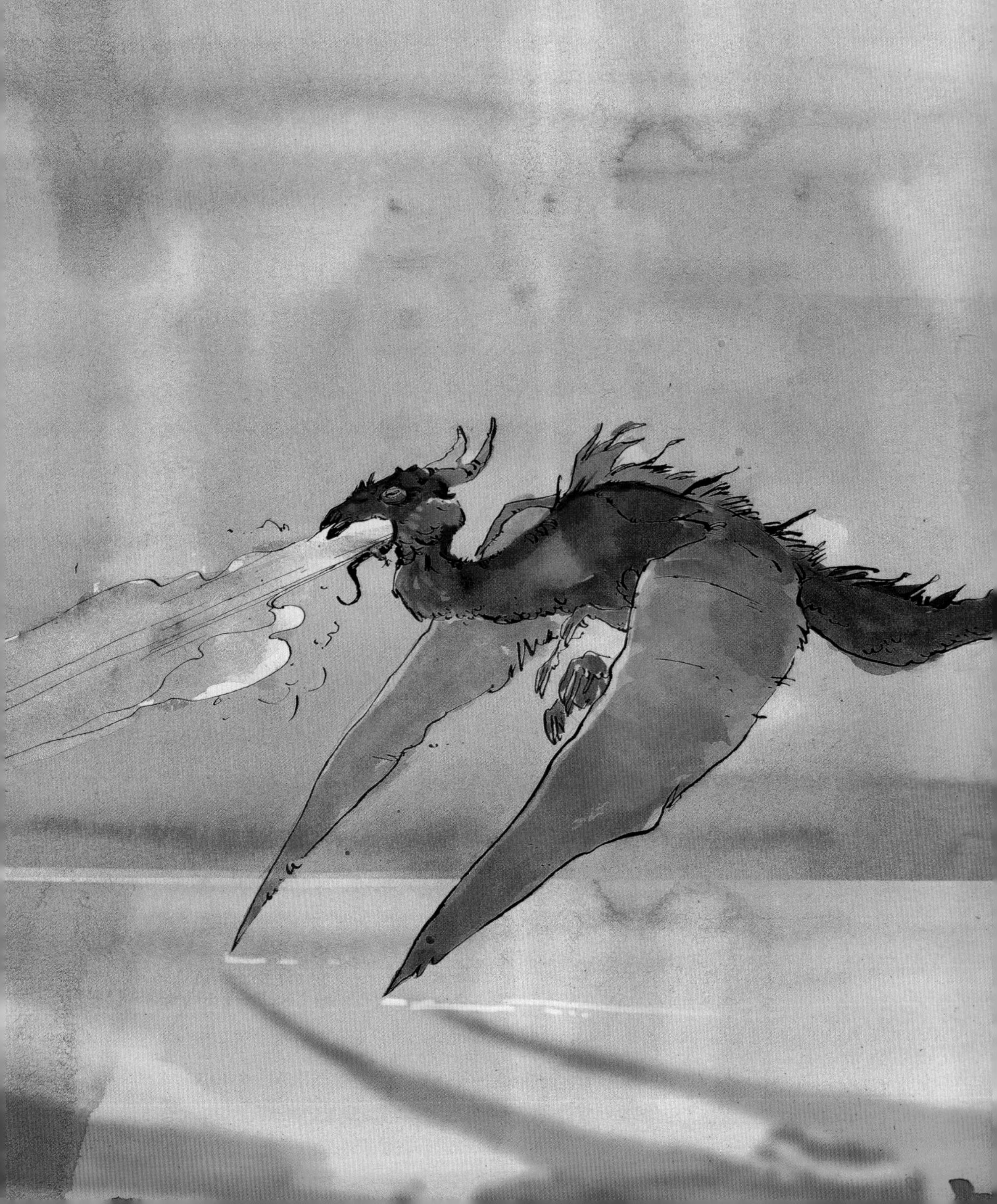

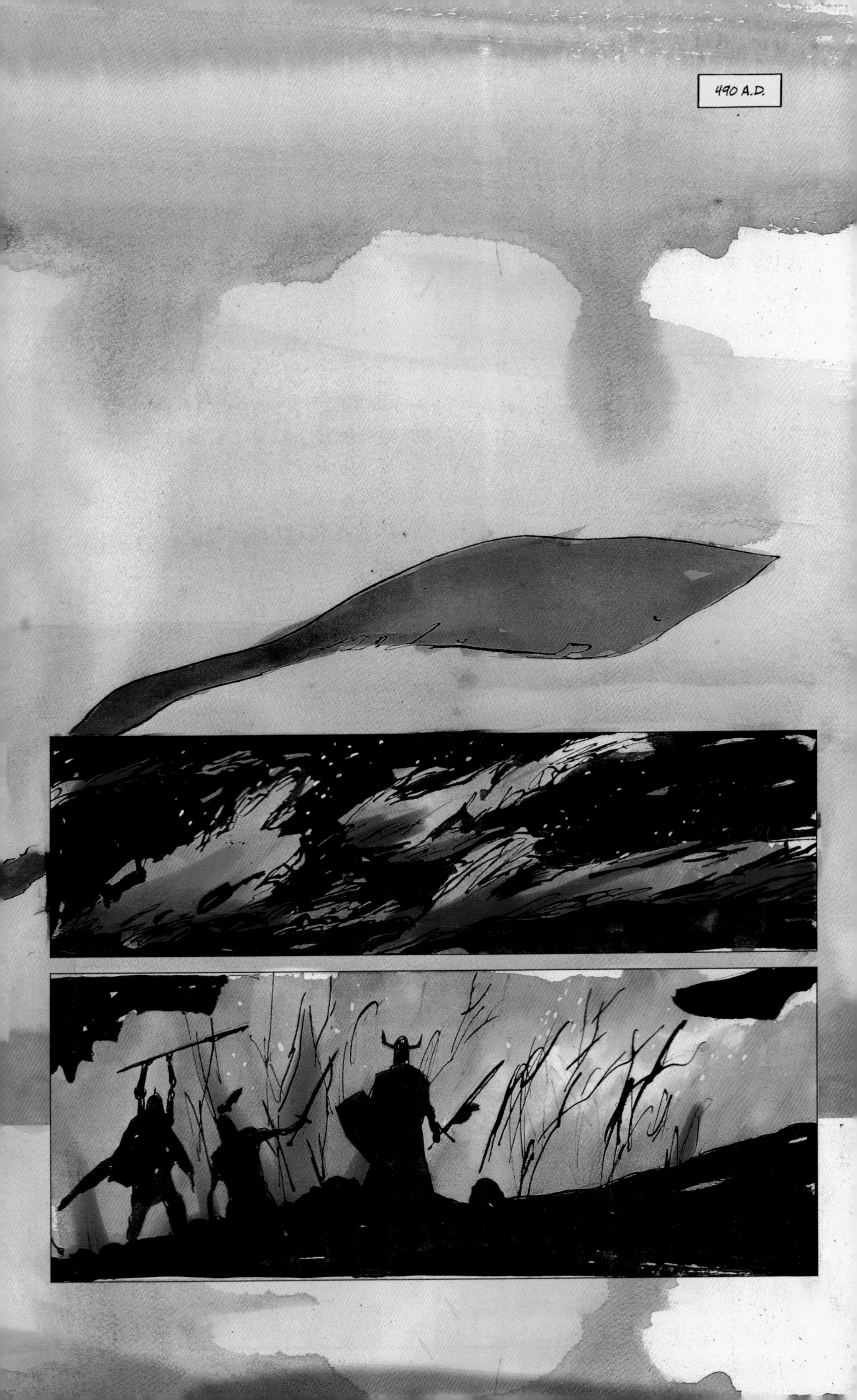
490 A.D.

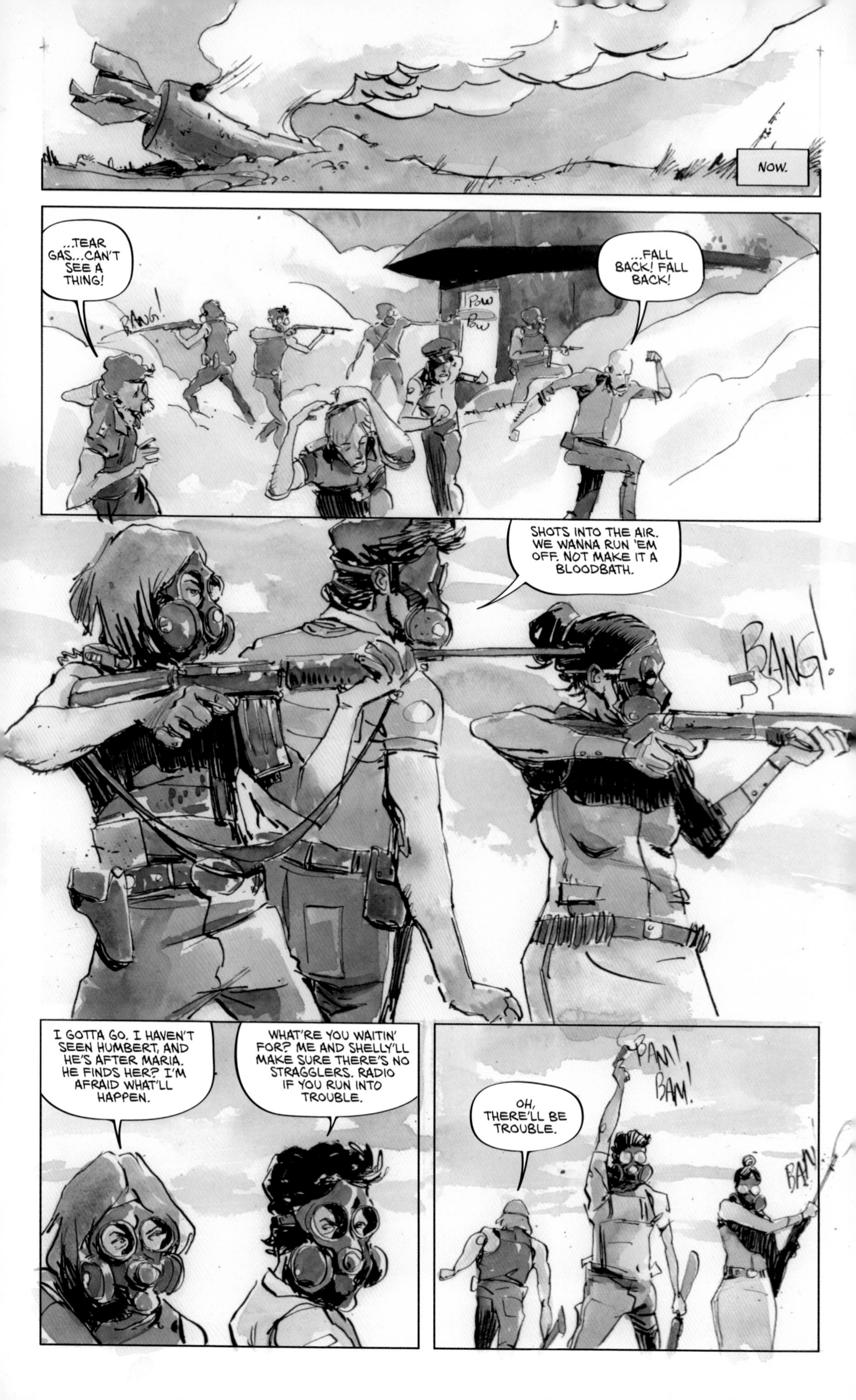

NOW.
...TEAR GAS...CAN'T SEE A THING!
BANG!
POW
POW
...FALL BACK! FALL BACK!
SHOTS INTO THE AIR. WE WANNA RUN 'EM OFF. NOT MAKE IT A BLOODBATH.
BANG!
I GOTTA GO. I HAVEN'T SEEN HUMBERT, AND HE'S AFTER MARIA. HE FINDS HER? I'M AFRAID WHAT'LL HAPPEN.
WHAT'RE YOU WAITIN' FOR? ME AND SHELLY'LL MAKE SURE THERE'S NO STRAGGLERS. RADIO IF YOU RUN INTO TROUBLE.
OH, THERE'LL BE TROUBLE.
BAM!
BAM!
BAM

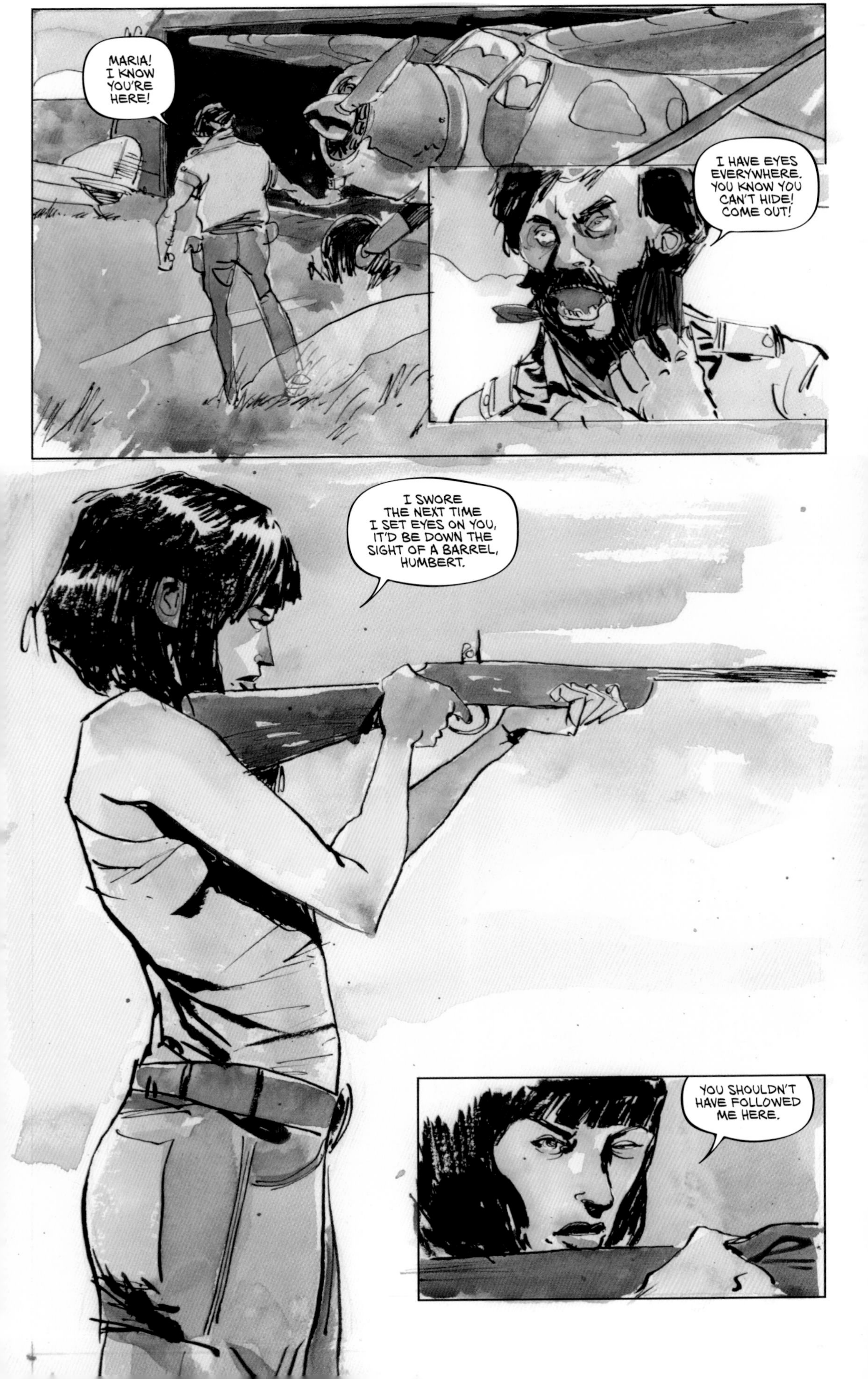
MARIA! I KNOW YOU'RE HERE!
I HAVE EYES EVERYWHERE. YOU KNOW YOU CAN'T HIDE! COME OUT!
I SWORE THE NEXT TIME I SET EYES ON YOU, IT'D BE DOWN THE SIGHT OF A BARREL, HUMBERT.
YOU SHOULDN'T HAVE FOLLOWED ME HERE.

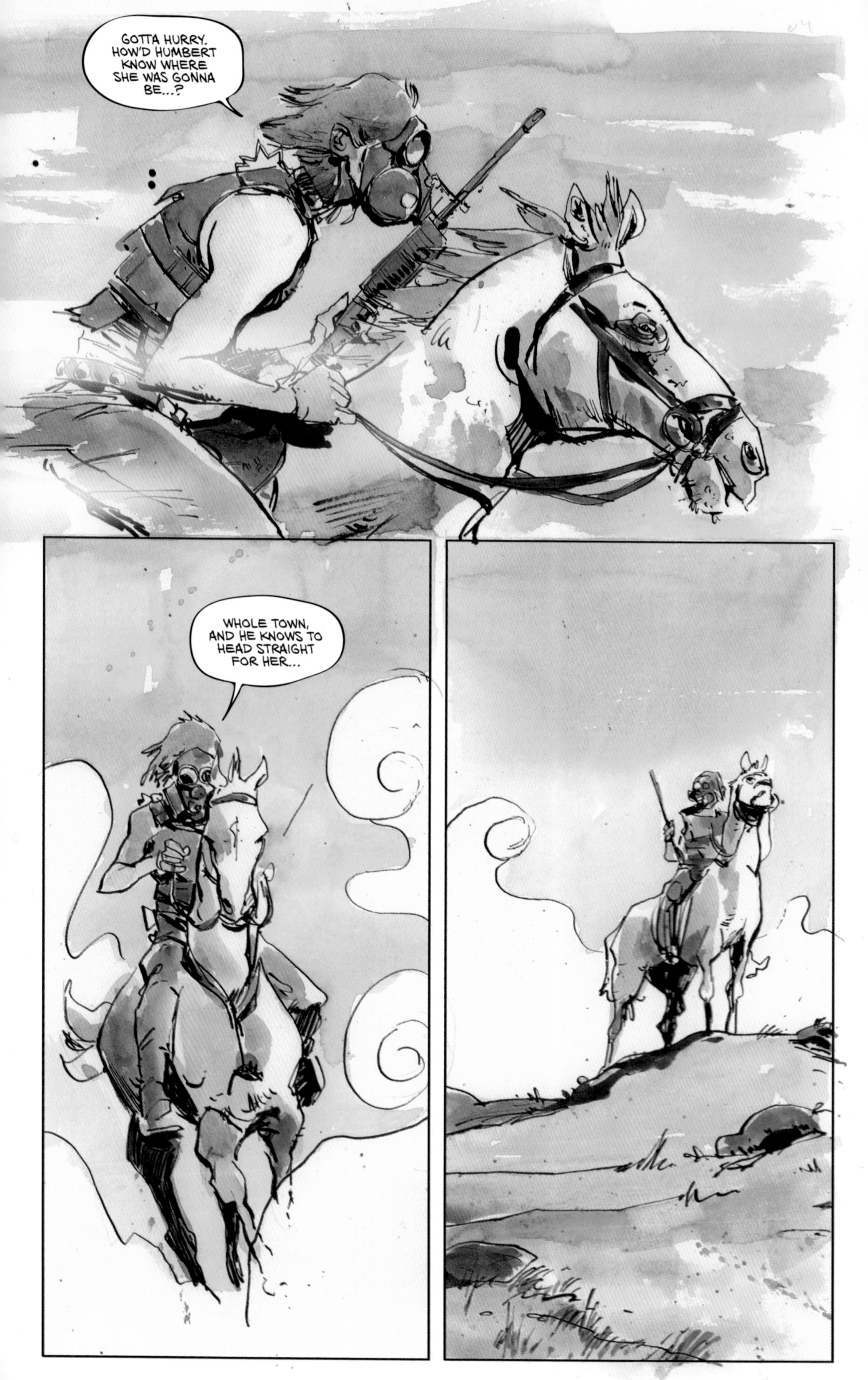
GOTTA HURRY. HOW'D HUMBERT KNOW WHERE SHE WAS GONNA BE...?
WHOLE TOWN, AND HE KNOWS TO HEAD STRAIGHT FOR HER...

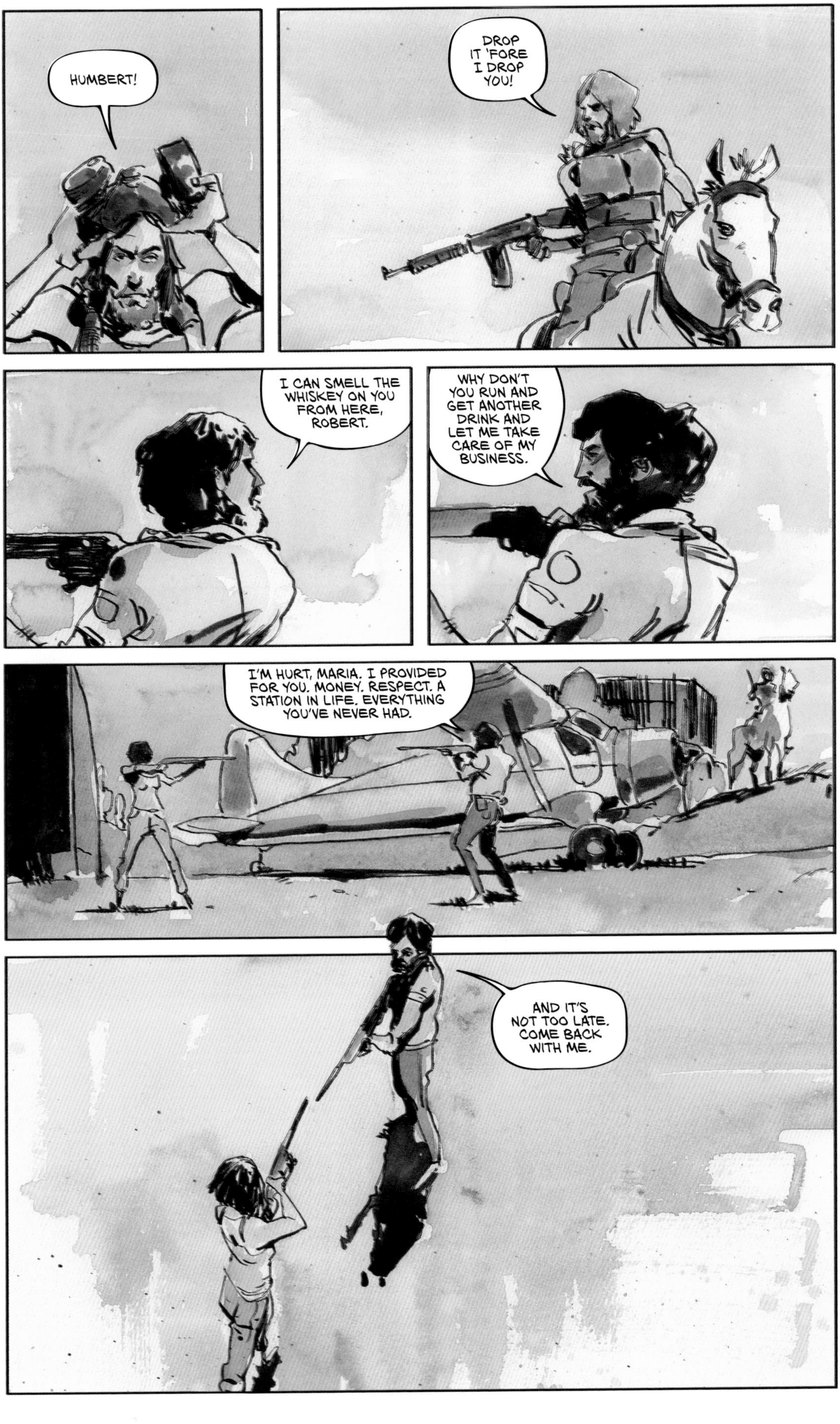

HUMBERT!
DROP IT 'FORE I DROP YOU!
I CAN SMELL THE WHISKEY ON YOU FROM HERE, ROBERT.
WHY DON'T YOU RUN AND GET ANOTHER DRINK AND LET ME TAKE CARE OF MY BUSINESS.
I'M HURT, MARIA. I PROVIDED FOR YOU. MONEY. RESPECT. A STATION IN LIFE. EVERYTHING YOU'VE NEVER HAD.
AND IT'S NOT TOO LATE. COME BACK WITH ME.

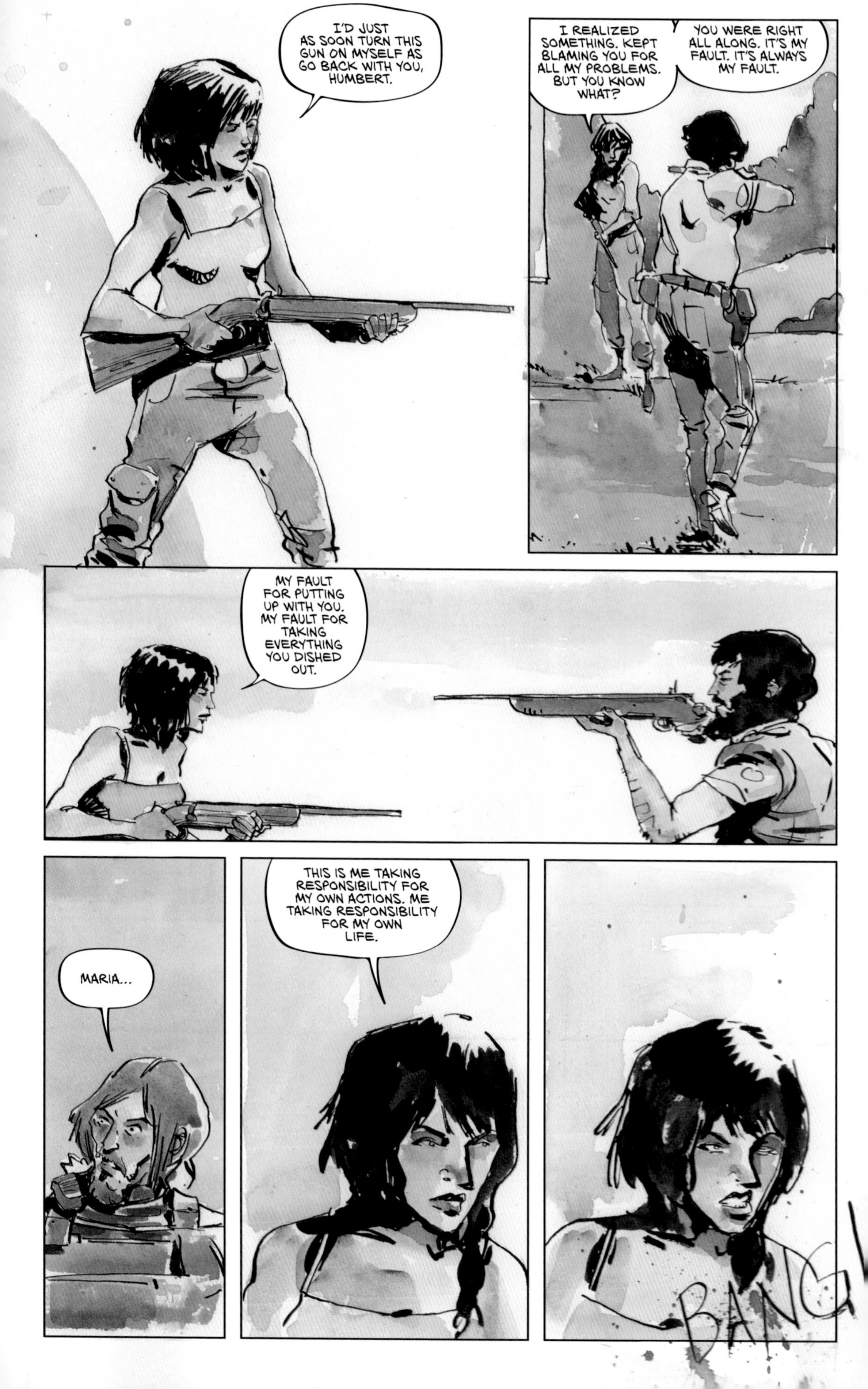
I'D JUST AS SOON TURN THIS GUN ON MYSELF AS GO BACK WITH YOU, HUMBERT.
I REALIZED SOMETHING. KEPT BLAMING YOU FOR ALL MY PROBLEMS. BUT YOU KNOW WHAT?
YOU WERE RIGHT ALL ALONG. IT'S MY FAULT. IT'S ALWAYS MY FAULT.
MY FAULT FOR PUTTING UP WITH YOU. MY FAULT FOR TAKING EVERYTHING YOU DISHED OUT.
MARIA...
THIS IS ME TAKING RESPONSIBILITY FOR MY OWN ACTIONS. ME TAKING RESPONSIBILITY FOR MY OWN LIFE.
BANG!

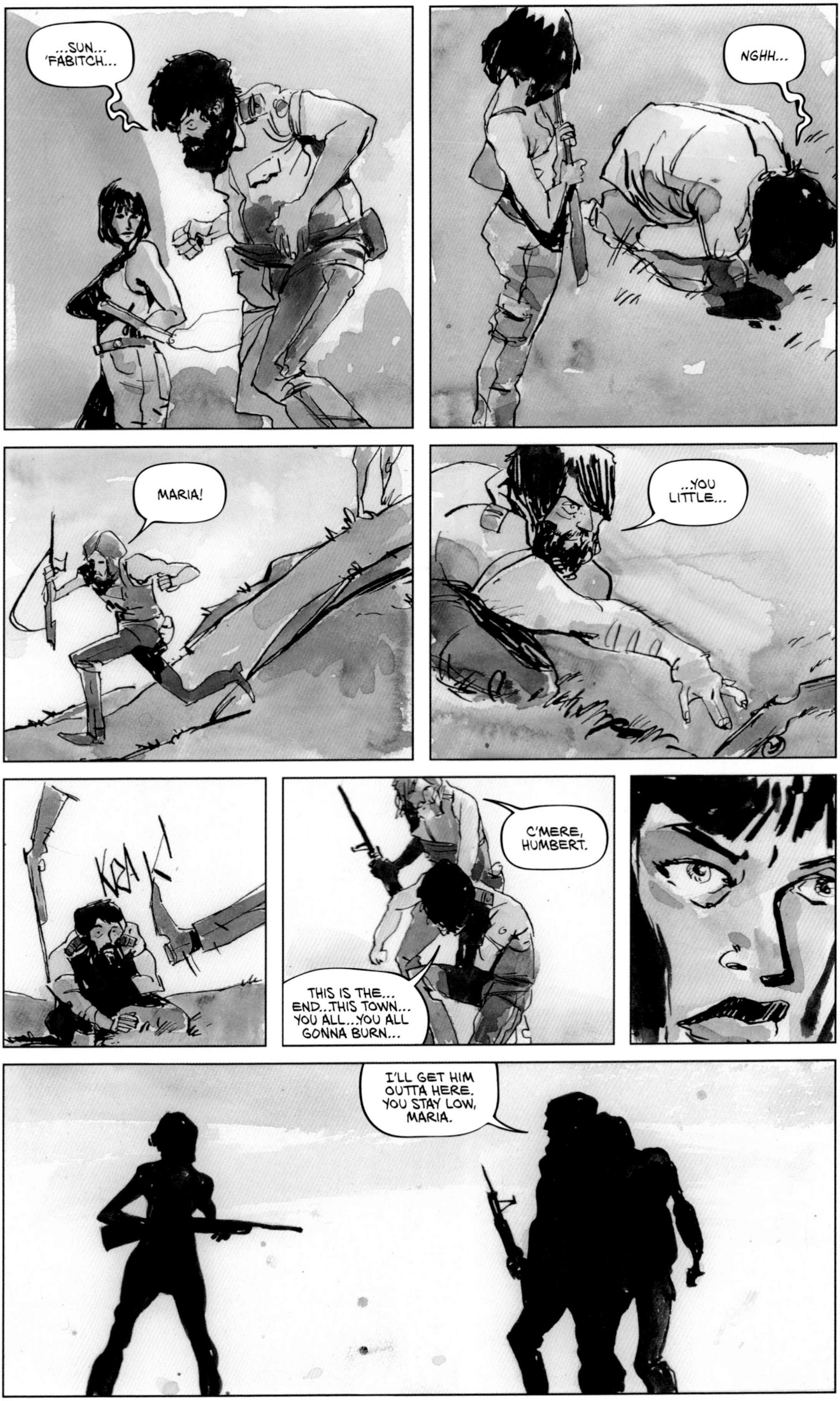
...SUN... 'FABITCH...
NGHH...
MARIA!
...YOU LITTLE...
C'MERE, HUMBERT.
THIS IS THE... END...THIS TOWN... YOU ALL...YOU ALL GONNA BURN...
I'LL GET HIM OUTTA HERE. YOU STAY LOW, MARIA.

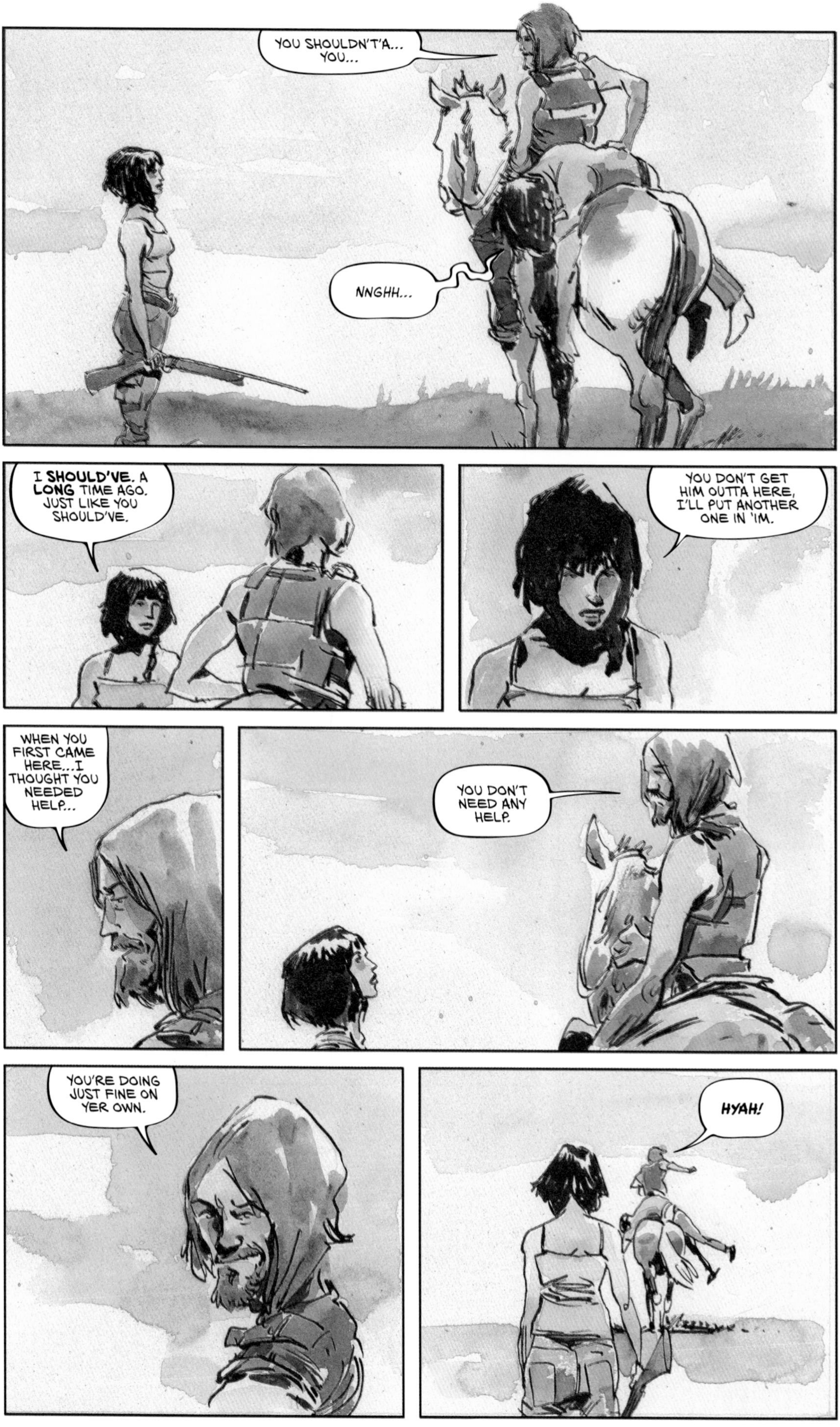
YOU SHOULDN'T'A... YOU...
NNGHH...
I **SHOULD'VE.** A **LONG** TIME AGO. JUST LIKE YOU SHOULD'VE.
YOU DON'T GET HIM OUTTA HERE, I'LL PUT ANOTHER ONE IN 'IM.
WHEN YOU FIRST CAME HERE...I THOUGHT YOU NEEDED HELP...
YOU DON'T NEED ANY HELP.
YOU'RE DOING JUST FINE ON YER OWN.
HYAH!

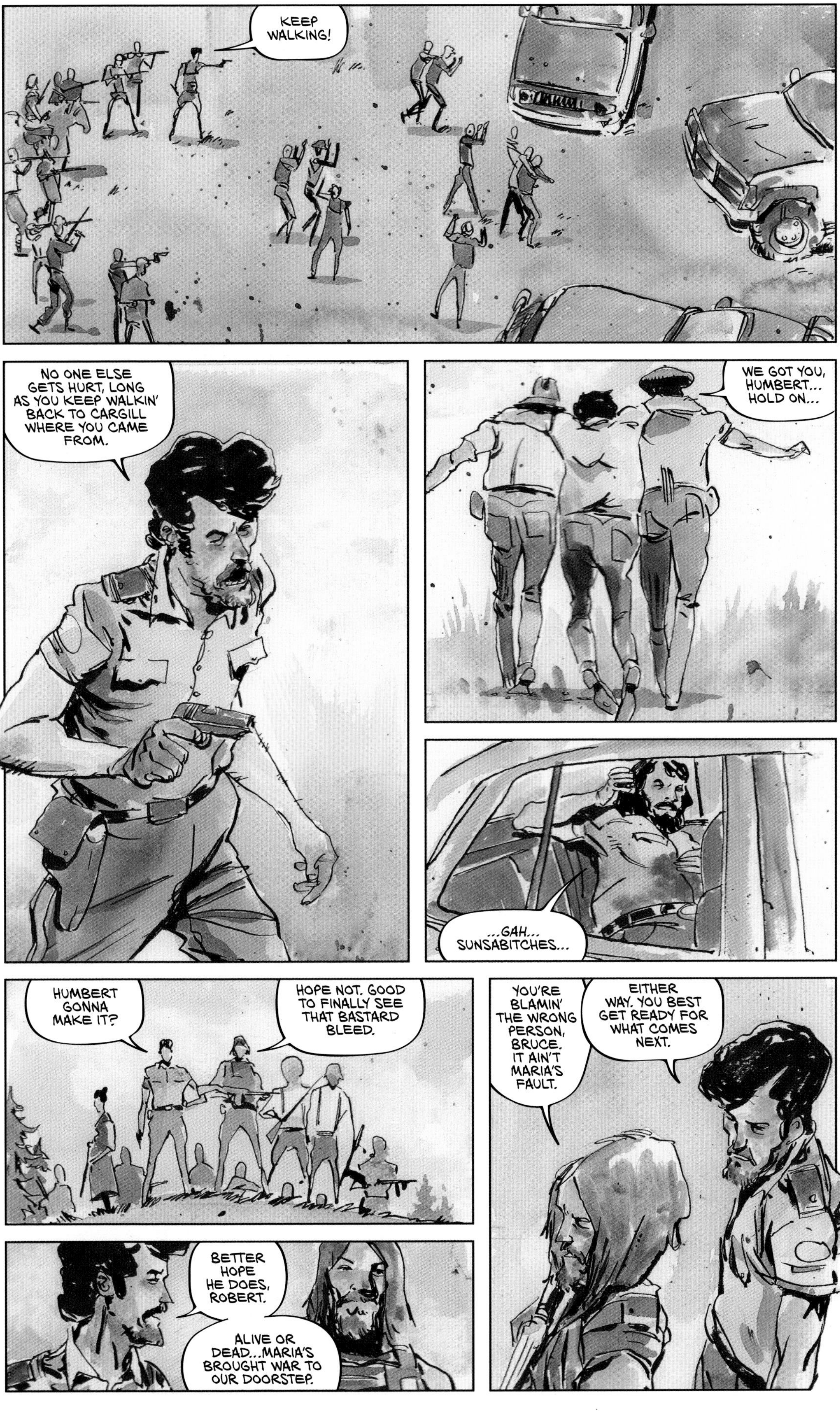
KEEP WALKING!
NO ONE ELSE GETS HURT, LONG AS YOU KEEP WALKIN' BACK TO CARGILL WHERE YOU CAME FROM.
WE GOT YOU, HUMBERT... HOLD ON...
...GAH... SUNSABITCHES...
HUMBERT GONNA MAKE IT?
HOPE NOT. GOOD TO FINALLY SEE THAT BASTARD BLEED.
BETTER HOPE HE DOES, ROBERT.
ALIVE OR DEAD...MARIA'S BROUGHT WAR TO OUR DOORSTEP.
YOU'RE BLAMIN' THE WRONG PERSON, BRUCE. IT AIN'T MARIA'S FAULT.
EITHER WAY. YOU BEST GET READY FOR WHAT COMES NEXT.

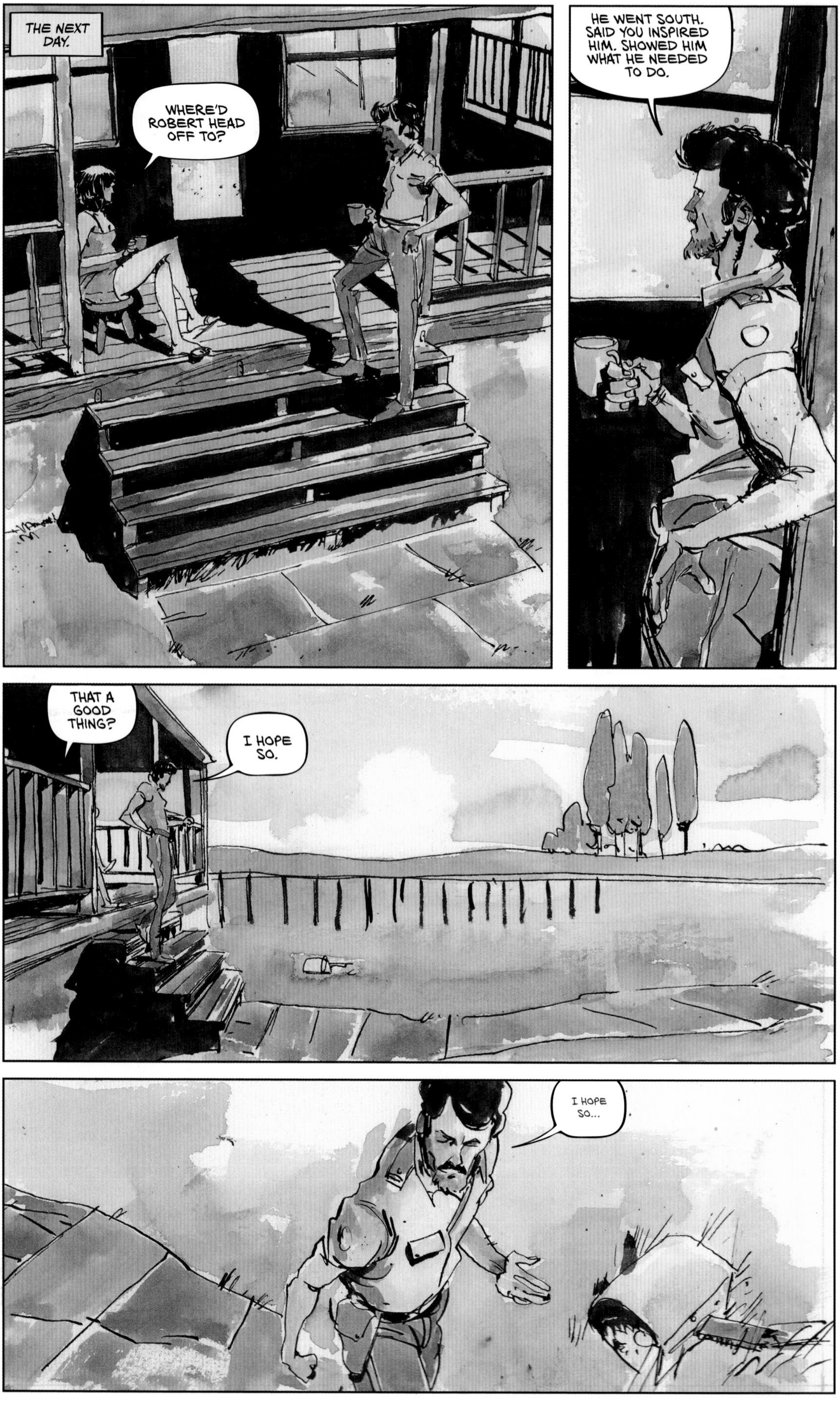
THE NEXT DAY.
WHERE'D ROBERT HEAD OFF TO?
HE WENT SOUTH. SAID YOU INSPIRED HIM. SHOWED HIM WHAT HE NEEDED TO DO.
THAT A GOOD THING?
I HOPE SO.
I HOPE SO...

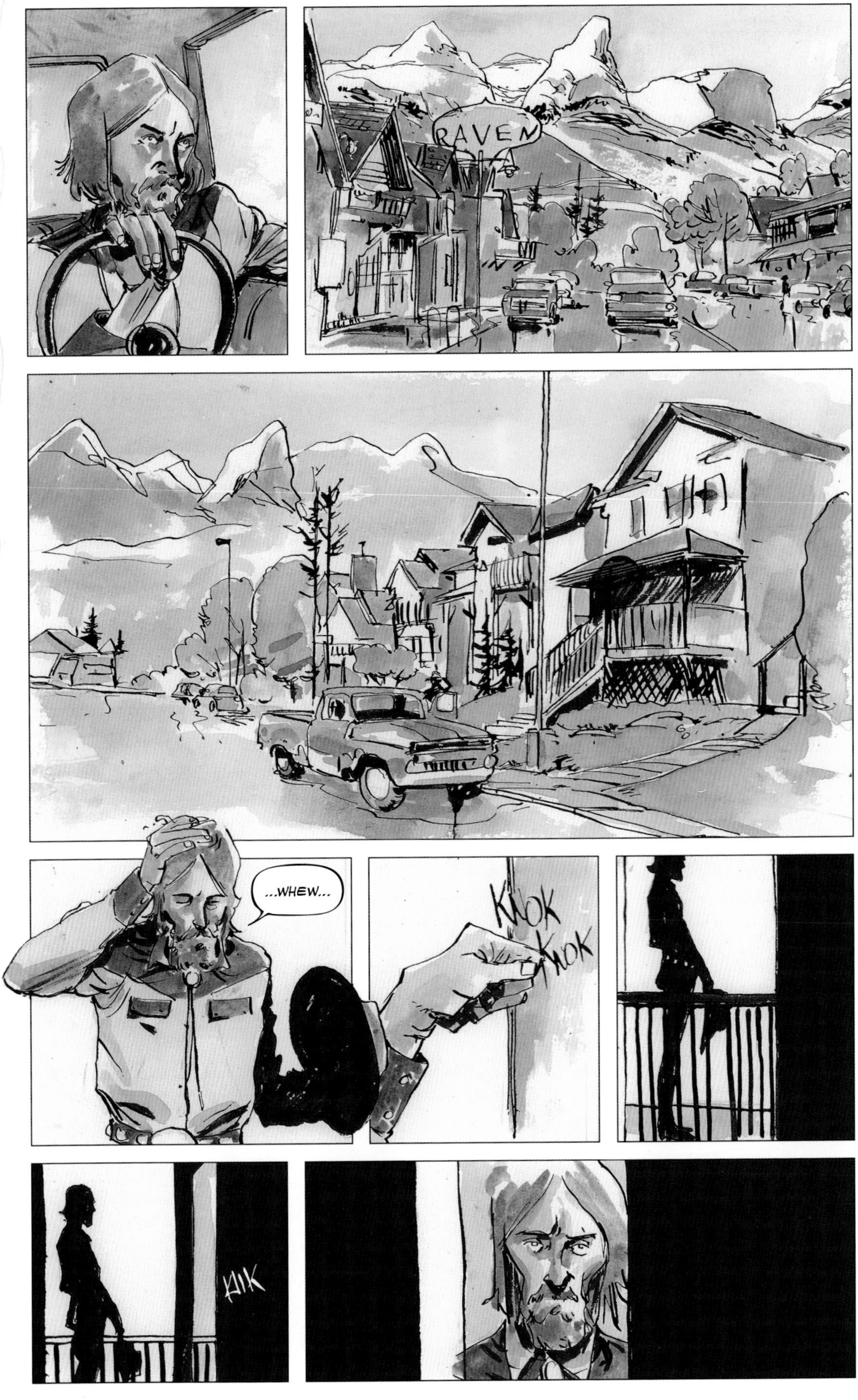
RAVEN
...WHEW...
KNOK KNOK
KLIK

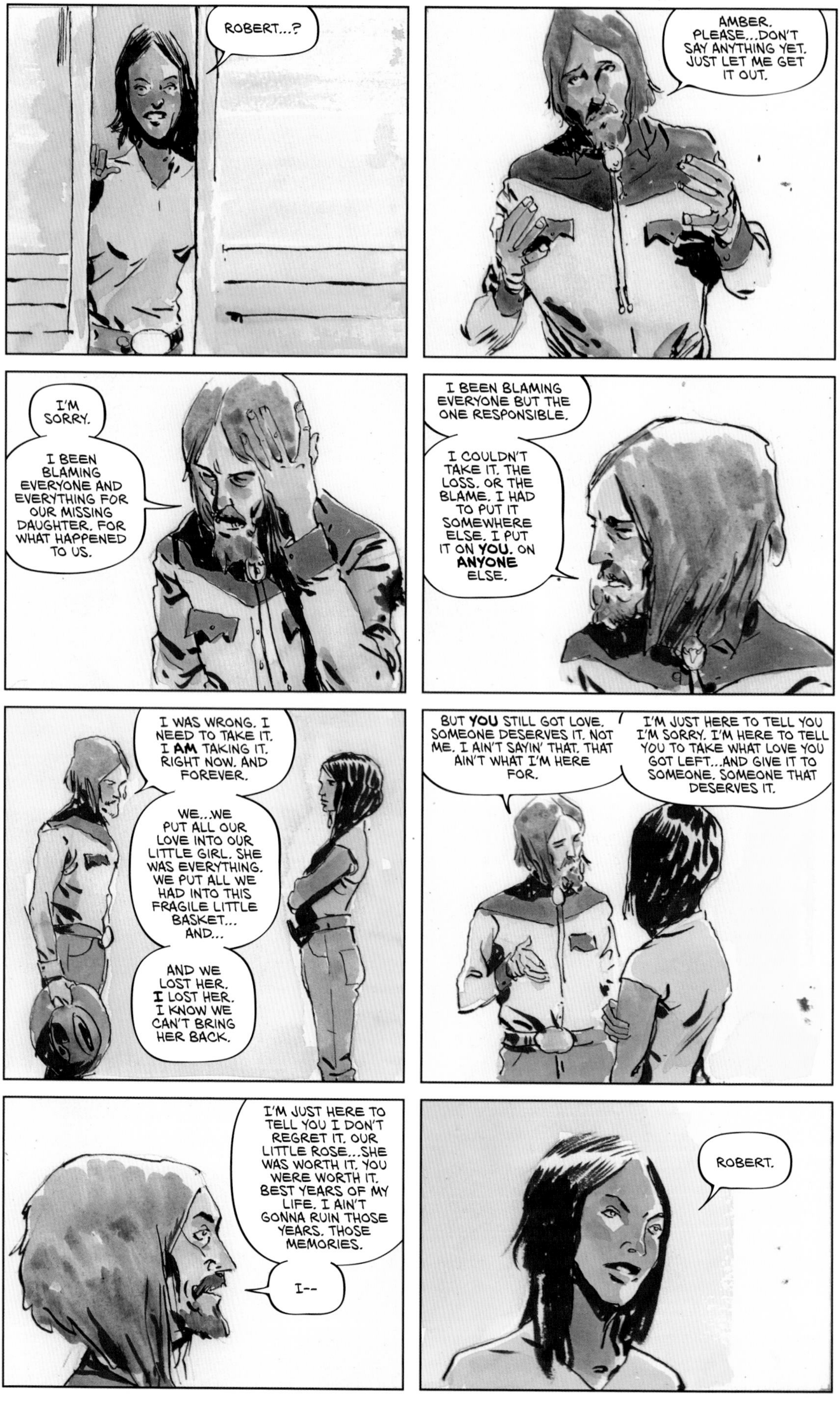
ROBERT...?
AMBER. PLEASE...DON'T SAY ANYTHING YET. JUST LET ME GET IT OUT.
I'M SORRY.
I BEEN BLAMING EVERYONE AND EVERYTHING FOR OUR MISSING DAUGHTER. FOR WHAT HAPPENED TO US.
I BEEN BLAMING EVERYONE BUT THE ONE RESPONSIBLE.
I COULDN'T TAKE IT. THE LOSS. OR THE BLAME. I HAD TO PUT IT SOMEWHERE ELSE. I PUT IT ON **YOU.** ON **ANYONE** ELSE.
I WAS WRONG. I NEED TO TAKE IT. I **AM** TAKING IT. RIGHT NOW. AND FOREVER.
WE...WE PUT ALL OUR LOVE INTO OUR LITTLE GIRL. SHE WAS EVERYTHING. WE PUT ALL WE HAD INTO THIS FRAGILE LITTLE BASKET... AND...
AND WE LOST HER. **I** LOST HER. I KNOW WE CAN'T BRING HER BACK.
BUT **YOU** STILL GOT LOVE. SOMEONE DESERVES IT. NOT ME. I AIN'T SAYIN' THAT. THAT AIN'T WHAT I'M HERE FOR.
I'M JUST HERE TO TELL YOU I'M SORRY. I'M HERE TO TELL YOU TO TAKE WHAT LOVE YOU GOT LEFT...AND GIVE IT TO SOMEONE. SOMEONE THAT DESERVES IT.
I'M JUST HERE TO TELL YOU I DON'T REGRET IT. OUR LITTLE ROSE...SHE WAS WORTH IT. YOU WERE WORTH IT. BEST YEARS OF MY LIFE. I AIN'T GONNA RUIN THOSE YEARS. THOSE MEMORIES.
I--
ROBERT.

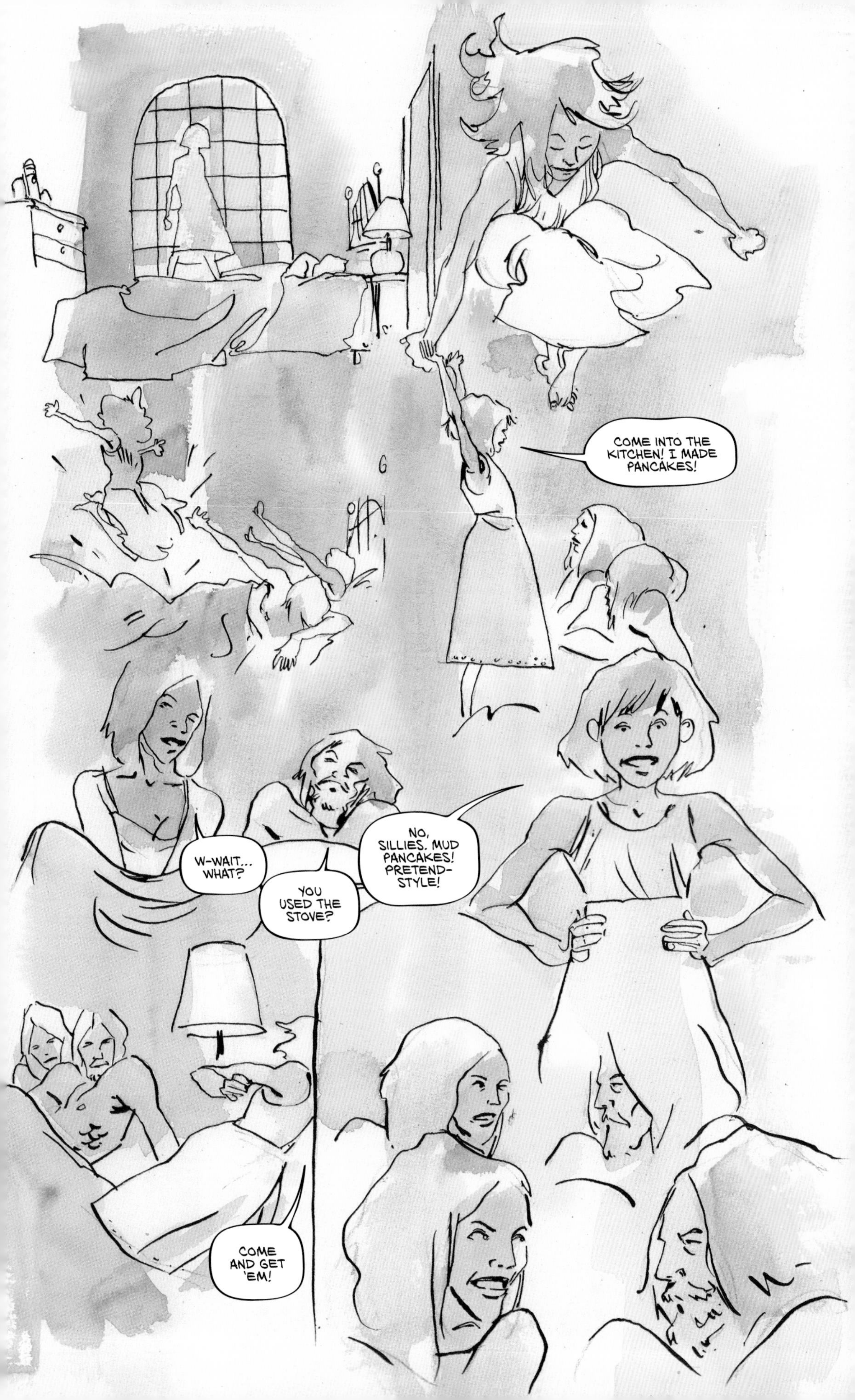
COME INTO THE KITCHEN! I MADE PANCAKES!
W-WAIT... WHAT?
YOU USED THE STOVE?
NO, SILLIES. MUD PANCAKES! PRETEND-STYLE!
COME AND GET 'EM!

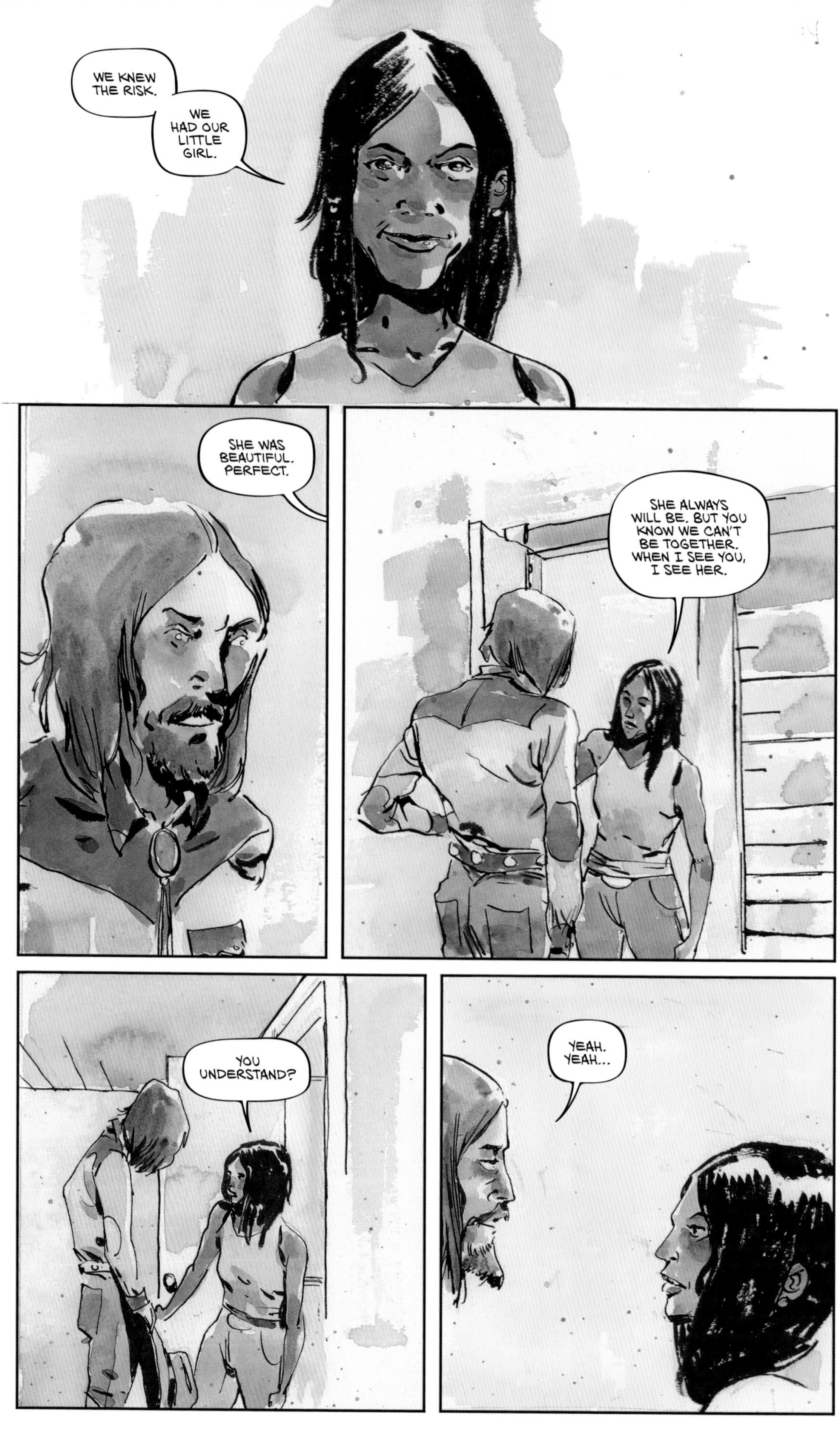
WE KNEW THE RISK.
WE HAD OUR LITTLE GIRL.
SHE WAS BEAUTIFUL. PERFECT.
SHE ALWAYS WILL BE. BUT YOU KNOW WE CAN'T BE TOGETHER. WHEN I SEE YOU, I SEE HER.
YOU UNDERSTAND?
YEAH. YEAH...

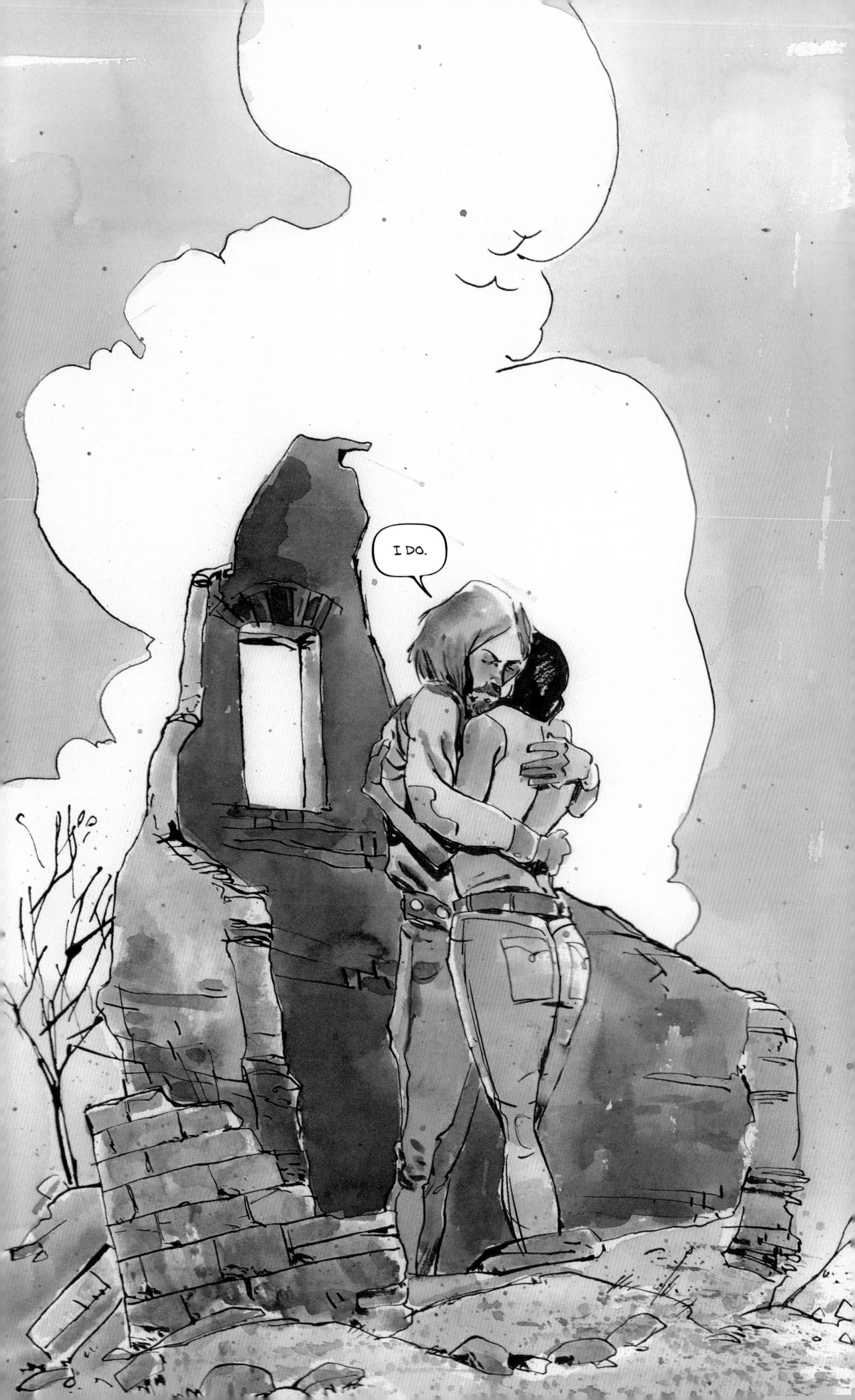
I DO.

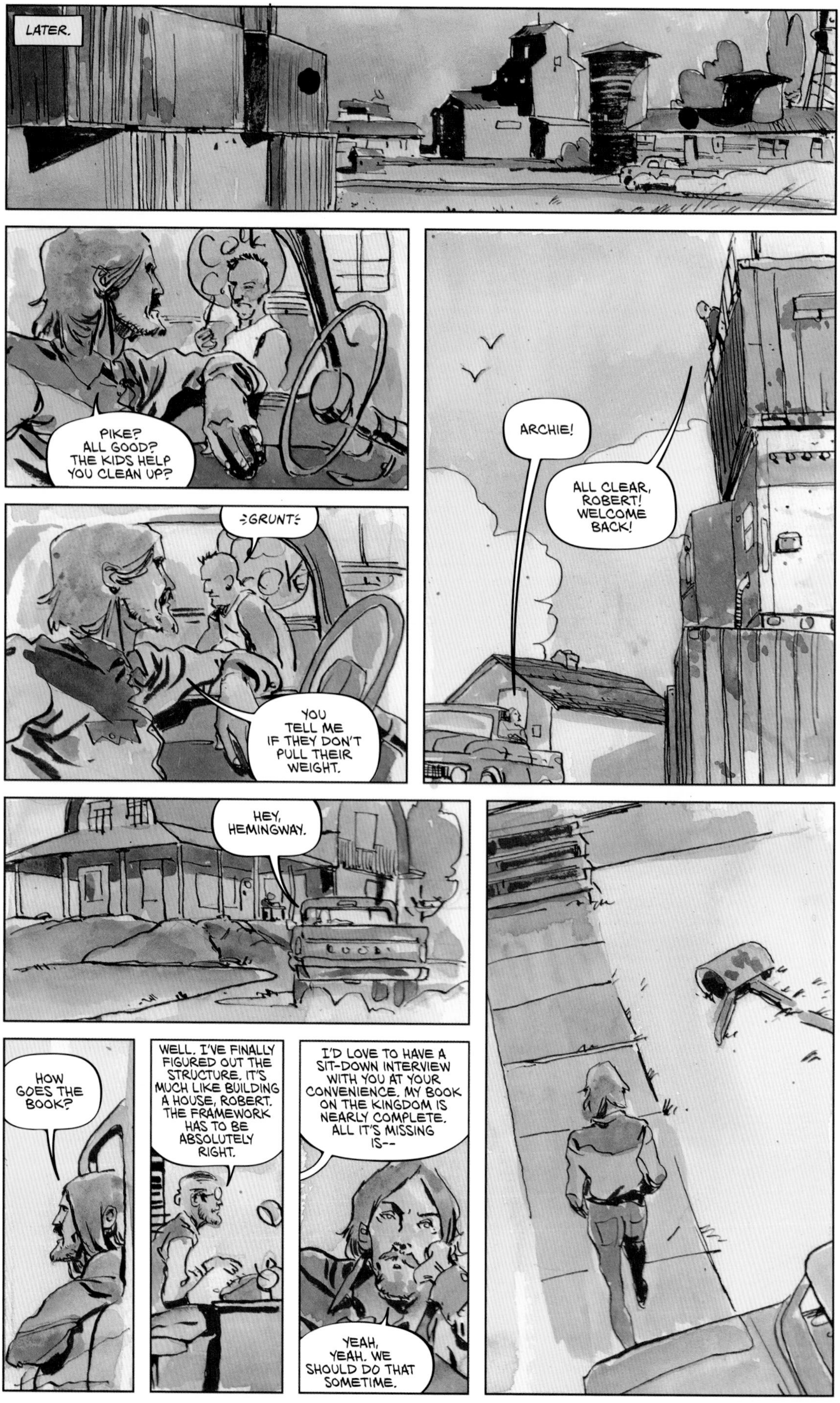
LATER.
PIKE? ALL GOOD? THE KIDS HELP YOU CLEAN UP?
≈GRUNT≈
YOU TELL ME IF THEY DON'T PULL THEIR WEIGHT.
ARCHIE!
ALL CLEAR, ROBERT! WELCOME BACK!
HEY, HEMINGWAY.
HOW GOES THE BOOK?
WELL, I'VE FINALLY FIGURED OUT THE STRUCTURE. IT'S MUCH LIKE BUILDING A HOUSE, ROBERT. THE FRAMEWORK HAS TO BE ABSOLUTELY RIGHT.
I'D LOVE TO HAVE A SIT-DOWN INTERVIEW WITH YOU AT YOUR CONVENIENCE. MY BOOK ON THE KINGDOM IS NEARLY COMPLETE. ALL IT'S MISSING IS--
YEAH, YEAH. WE SHOULD DO THAT SOMETIME.

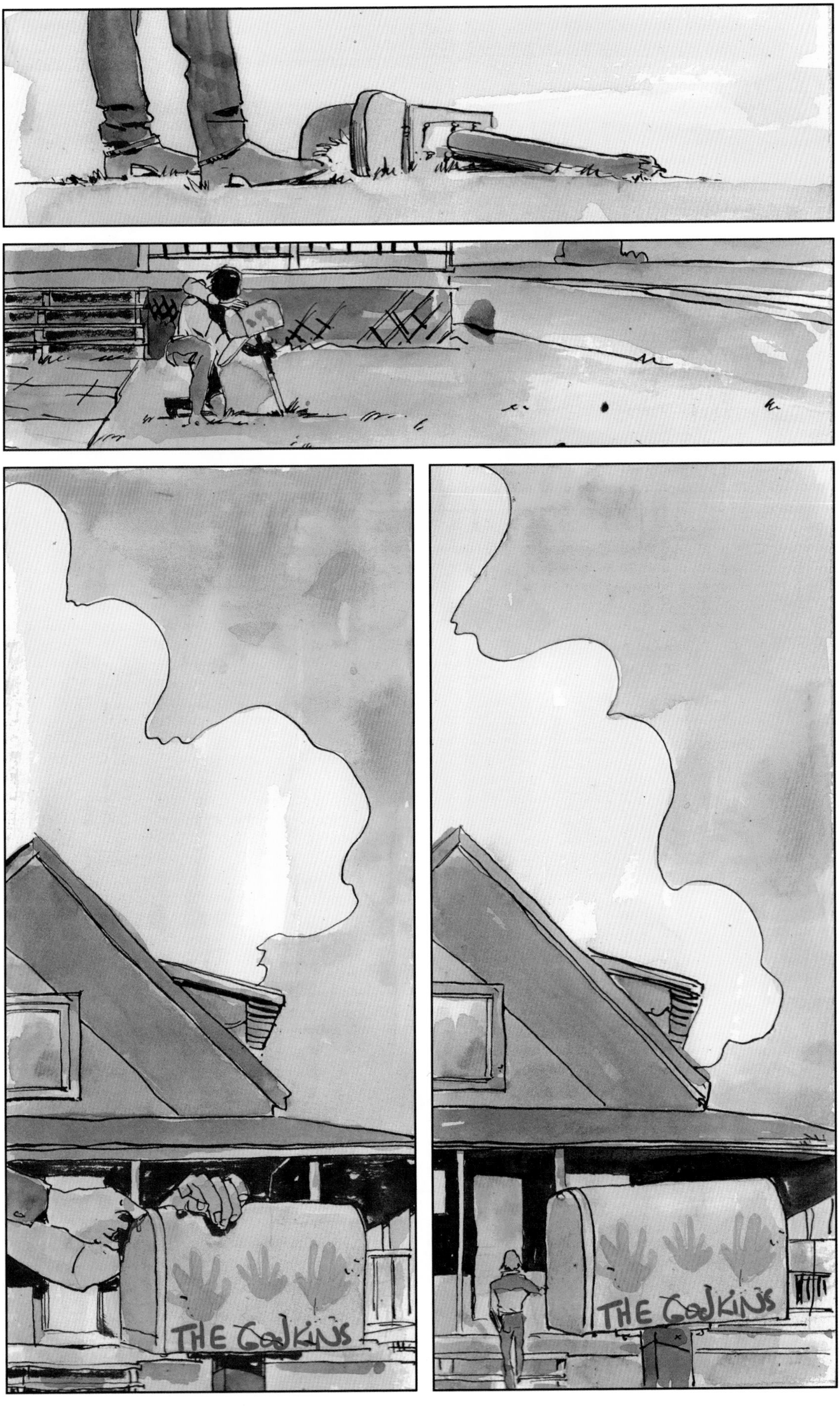
THE GODKINS
THE GODKINS

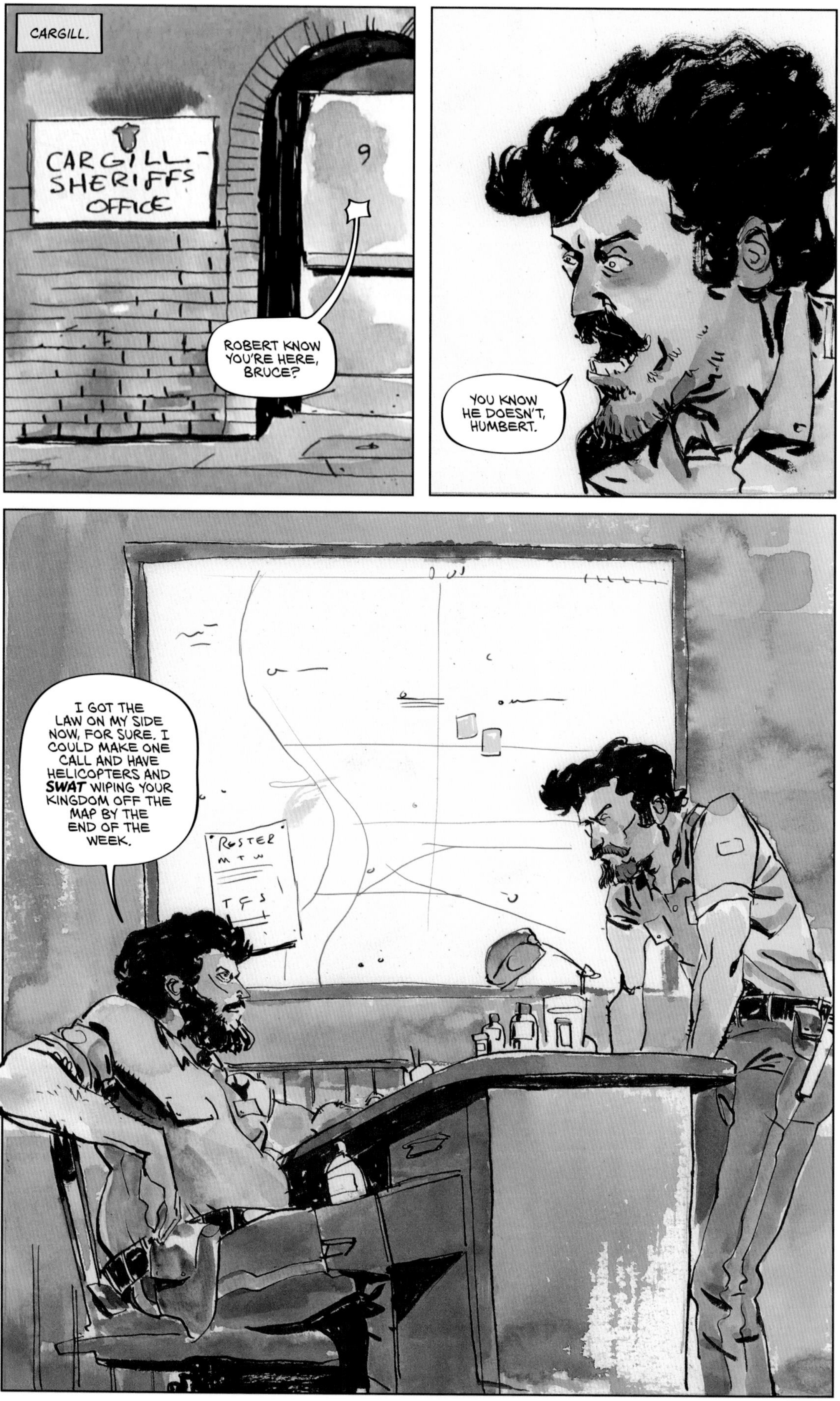
CARGILL.
CARGILL- SHERIFFS OFFICE
ROBERT KNOW YOU'RE HERE, BRUCE?
YOU KNOW HE DOESN'T, HUMBERT.
I GOT THE LAW ON MY SIDE NOW, FOR SURE. I COULD MAKE ONE CALL AND HAVE HELICOPTERS AND **SWAT** WIPING YOUR KINGDOM OFF THE MAP BY THE END OF THE WEEK.
ROSTER

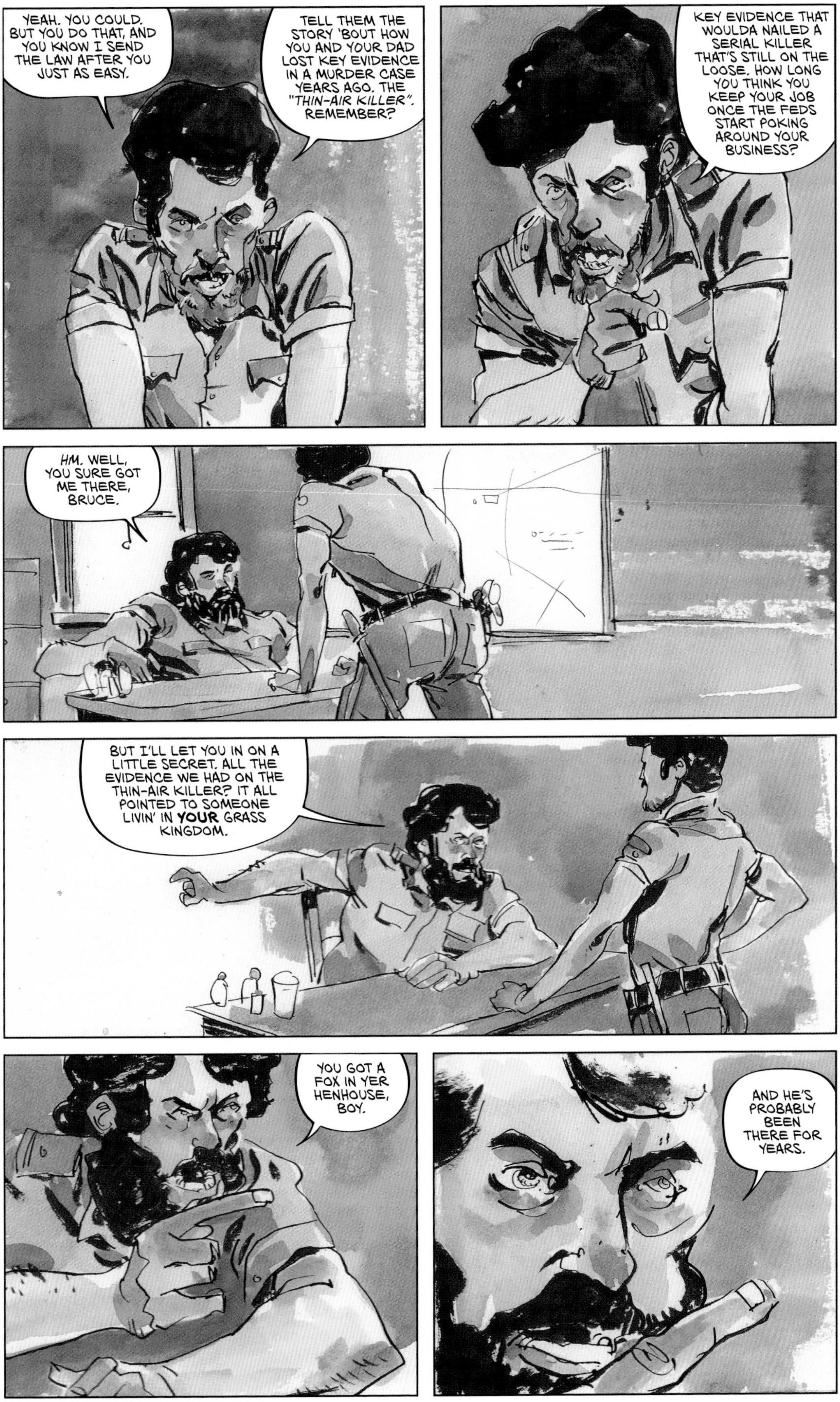
YEAH. YOU COULD. BUT YOU DO THAT, AND YOU KNOW I SEND THE LAW AFTER YOU JUST AS EASY.
TELL THEM THE STORY 'BOUT HOW YOU AND YOUR DAD LOST KEY EVIDENCE IN A MURDER CASE YEARS AGO. THE "THIN-AIR KILLER". REMEMBER?
KEY EVIDENCE THAT WOULDA NAILED A SERIAL KILLER THAT'S STILL ON THE LOOSE. HOW LONG YOU THINK YOU KEEP YOUR JOB ONCE THE FEDS START POKING AROUND YOUR BUSINESS?
HM. WELL, YOU SURE GOT ME THERE, BRUCE.
BUT I'LL LET YOU IN ON A LITTLE SECRET. ALL THE EVIDENCE WE HAD ON THE THIN-AIR KILLER? IT ALL POINTED TO SOMEONE LIVIN' IN YOUR GRASS KINGDOM.
YOU GOT A FOX IN YER HENHOUSE, BOY.
AND HE'S PROBABLY BEEN THERE FOR YEARS.

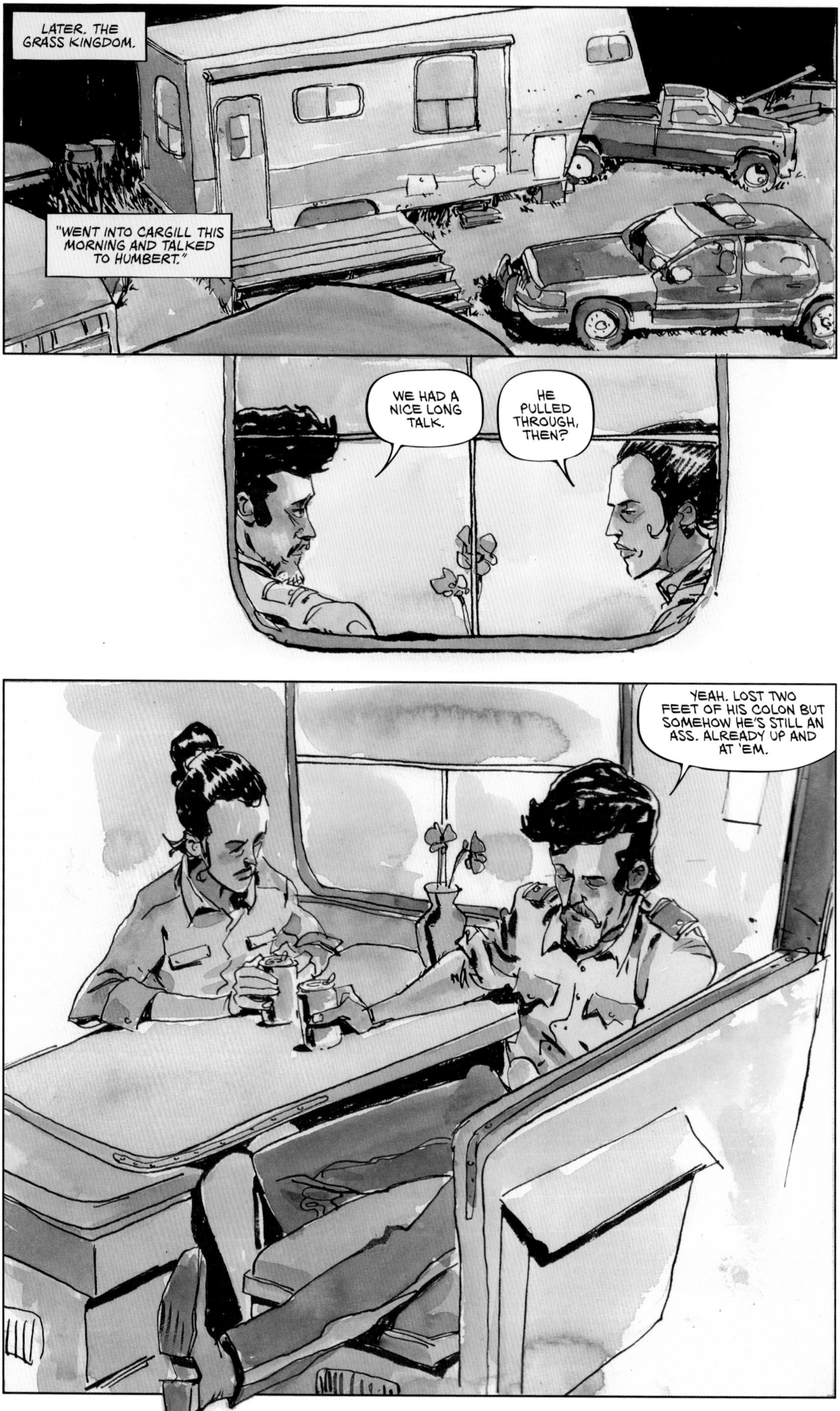
LATER. THE GRASS KINGDOM.
"WENT INTO CARGILL THIS MORNING AND TALKED TO HUMBERT."
WE HAD A NICE LONG TALK.
HE PULLED THROUGH, THEN?
YEAH. LOST TWO FEET OF HIS COLON BUT SOMEHOW HE'S STILL AN ASS. ALREADY UP AND AT 'EM.

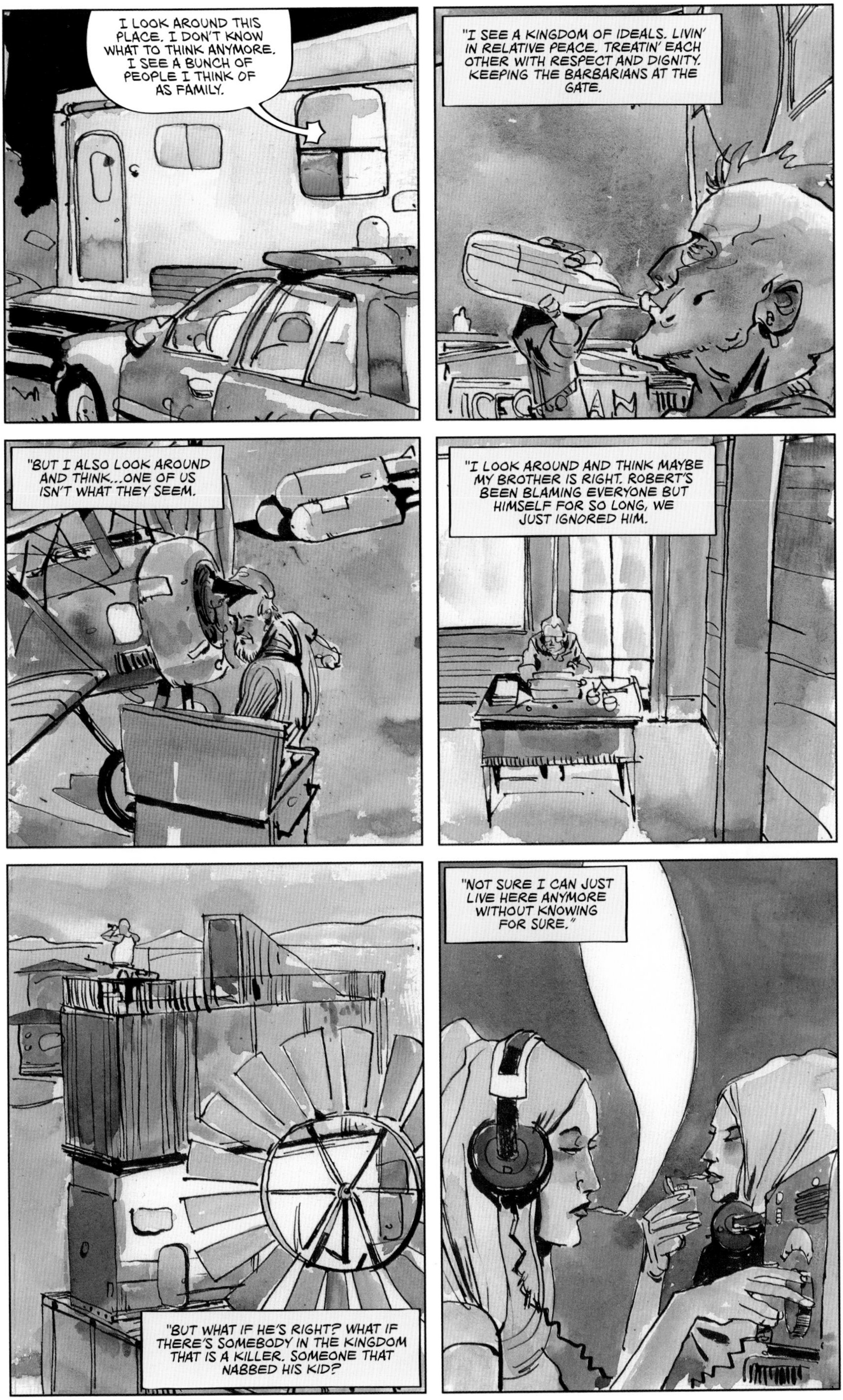
I LOOK AROUND THIS PLACE. I DON'T KNOW WHAT TO THINK ANYMORE. I SEE A BUNCH OF PEOPLE I THINK OF AS FAMILY.
"I SEE A KINGDOM OF IDEALS. LIVIN' IN RELATIVE PEACE. TREATIN' EACH OTHER WITH RESPECT AND DIGNITY. KEEPING THE BARBARIANS AT THE GATE.
"BUT I ALSO LOOK AROUND AND THINK...ONE OF US ISN'T WHAT THEY SEEM.
"I LOOK AROUND AND THINK MAYBE MY BROTHER IS RIGHT. ROBERT'S BEEN BLAMING EVERYONE BUT HIMSELF FOR SO LONG, WE JUST IGNORED HIM.
"BUT WHAT IF HE'S RIGHT? WHAT IF THERE'S SOMEBODY IN THE KINGDOM THAT IS A KILLER. SOMEONE THAT NABBED HIS KID?
"NOT SURE I CAN JUST LIVE HERE ANYMORE WITHOUT KNOWING FOR SURE."

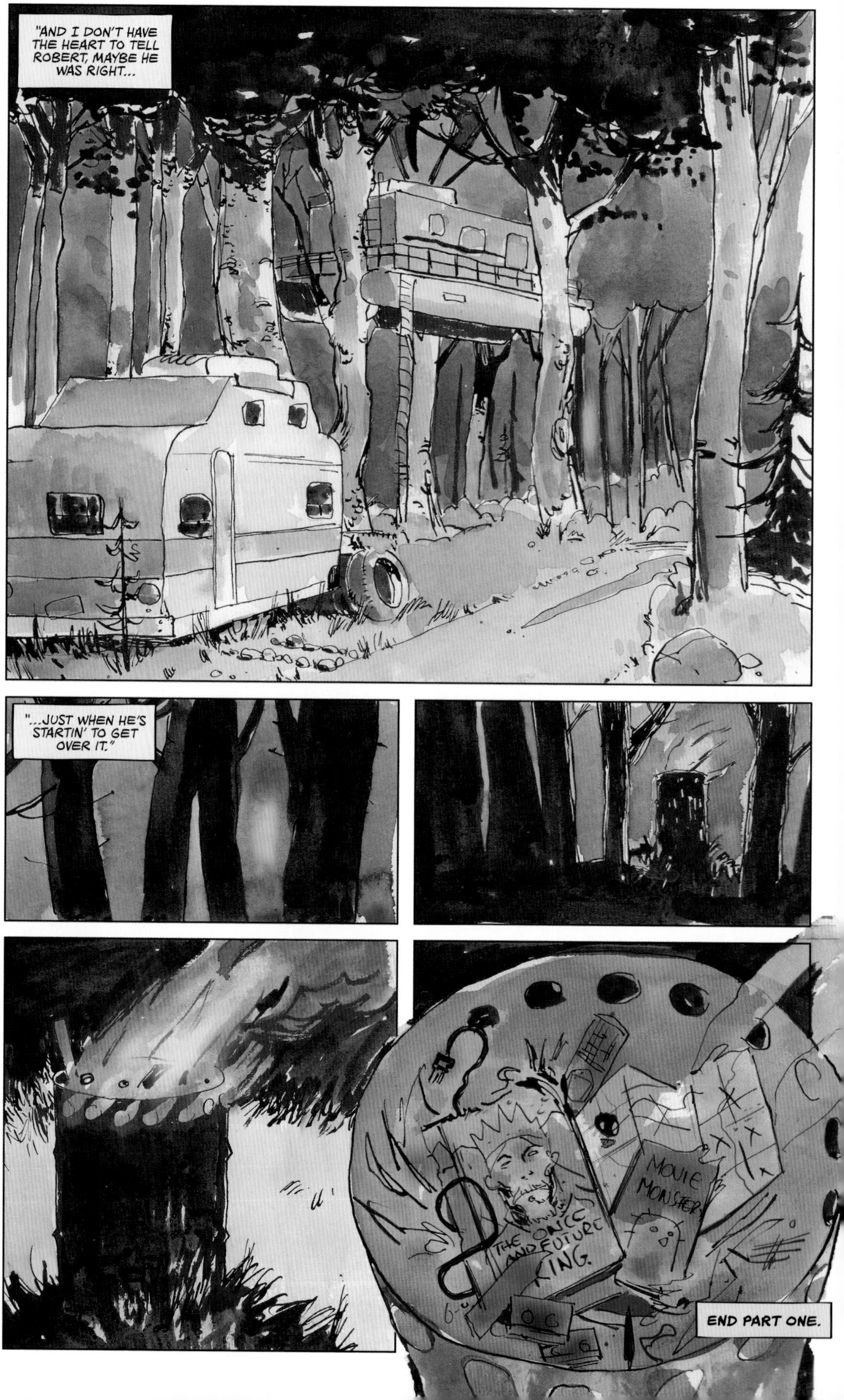
"AND I DON'T HAVE THE HEART TO TELL ROBERT, MAYBE HE WAS RIGHT...
"...JUST WHEN HE'S STARTIN' TO GET OVER IT."
MOVIE MONSTERS
THE ONCE AND FUTURE KING.
END PART ONE.

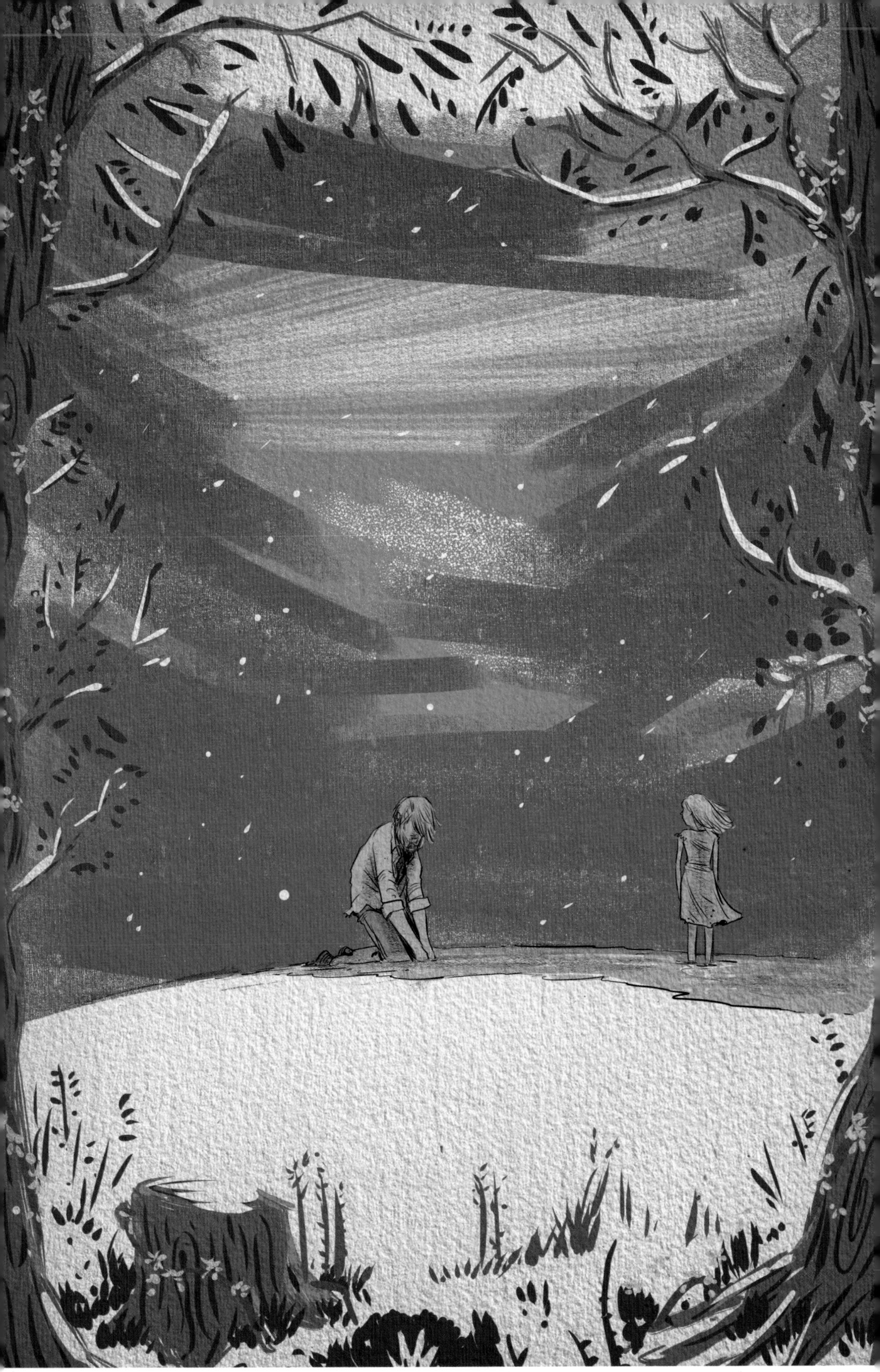

issue #6 cover by matt kindt

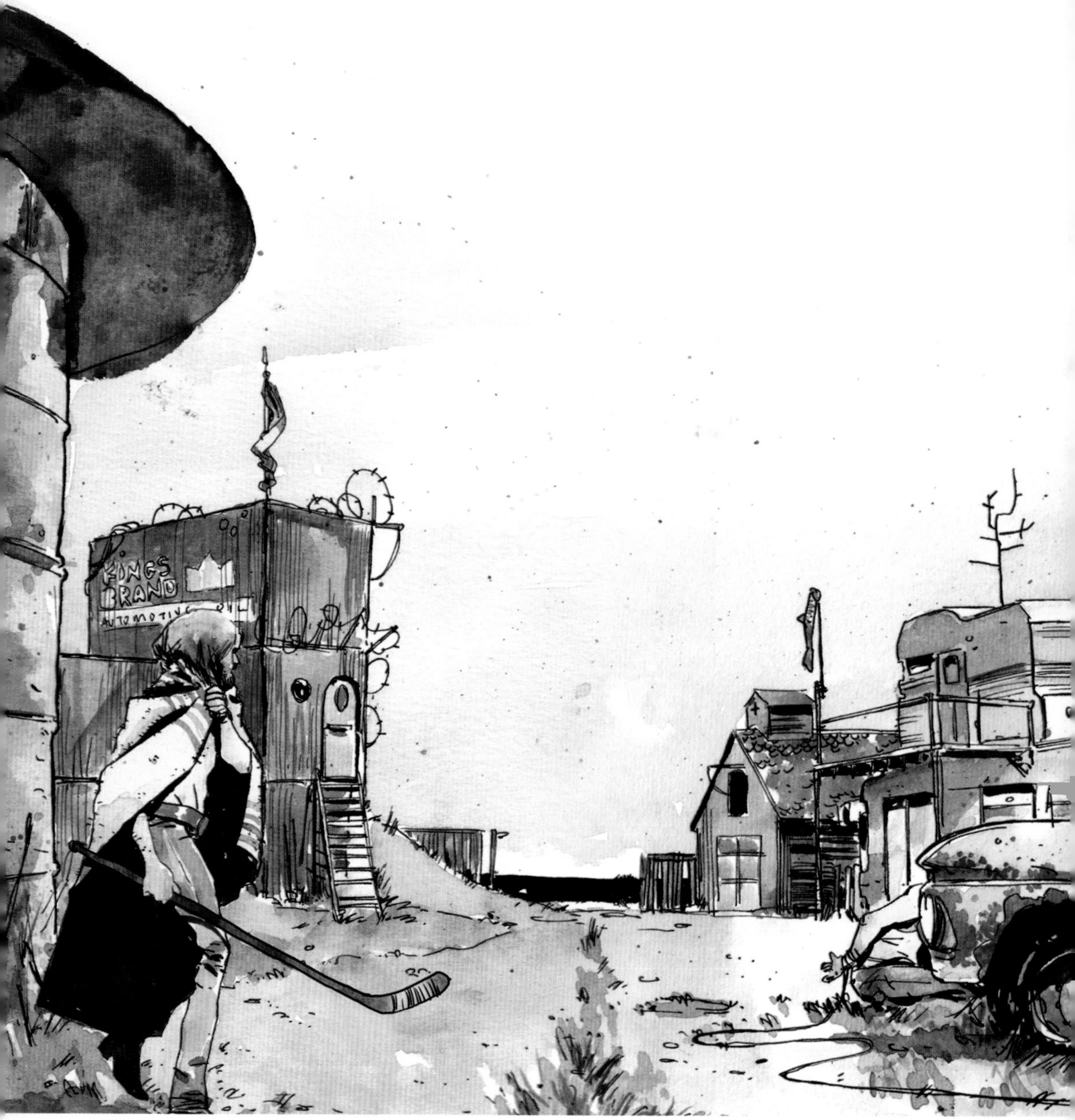
KINGS
BRAND

issue #1 cover by tyler jenkins

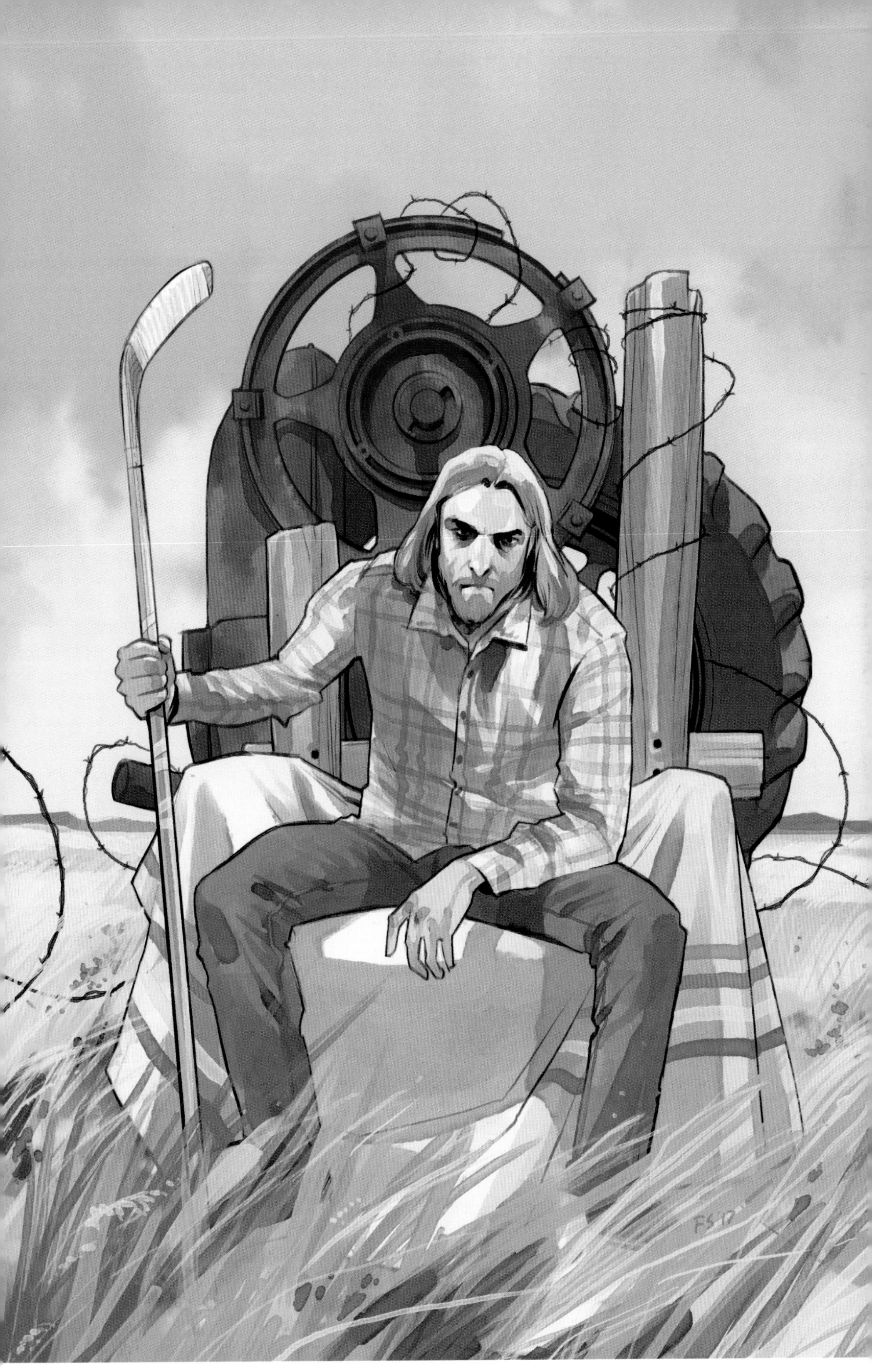

issue #1 unlocked retailer variant cover by fiona staples

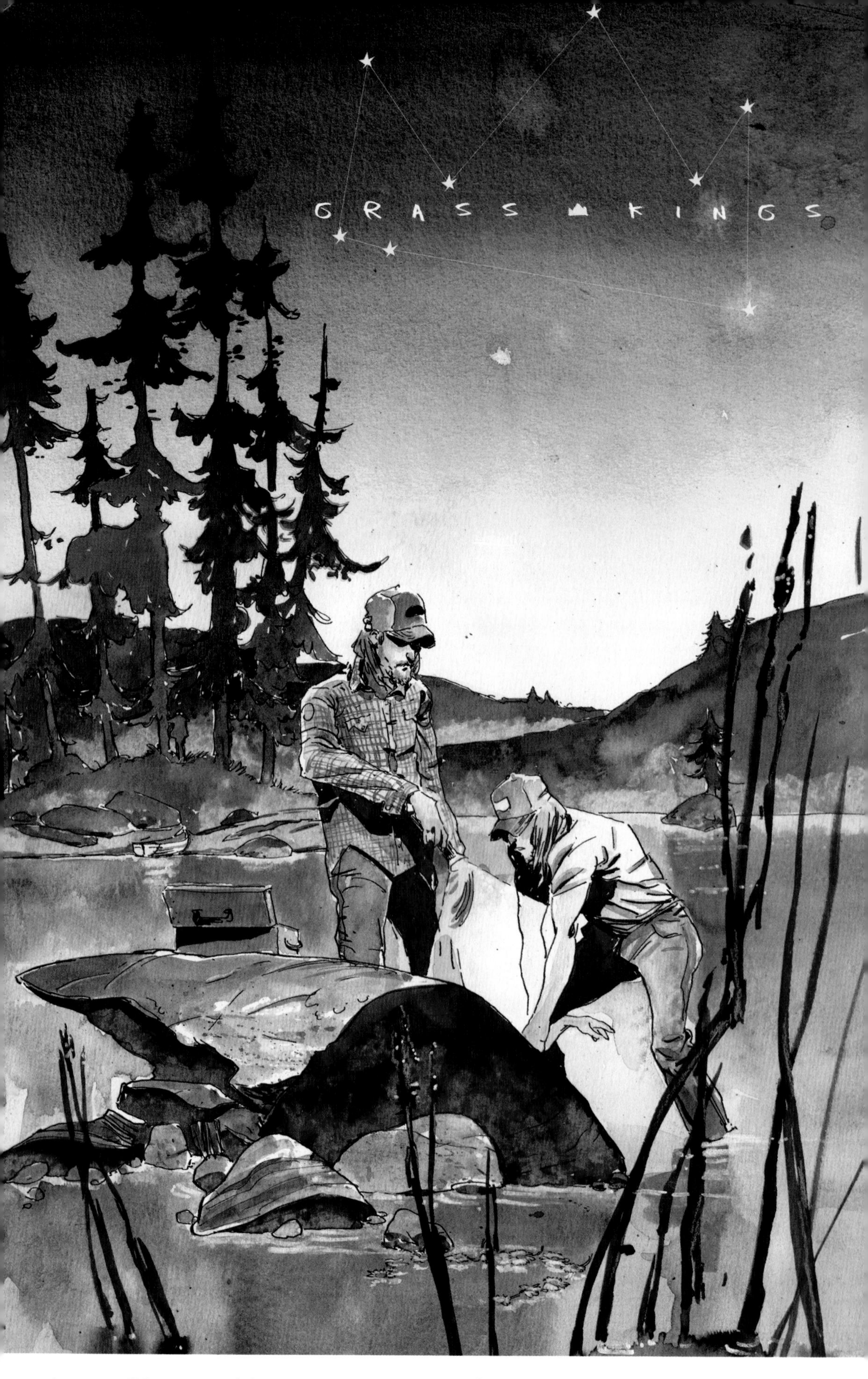
GRASS KINGS

issue #1 emerald city comicon exclusive cover by tyler jenkins

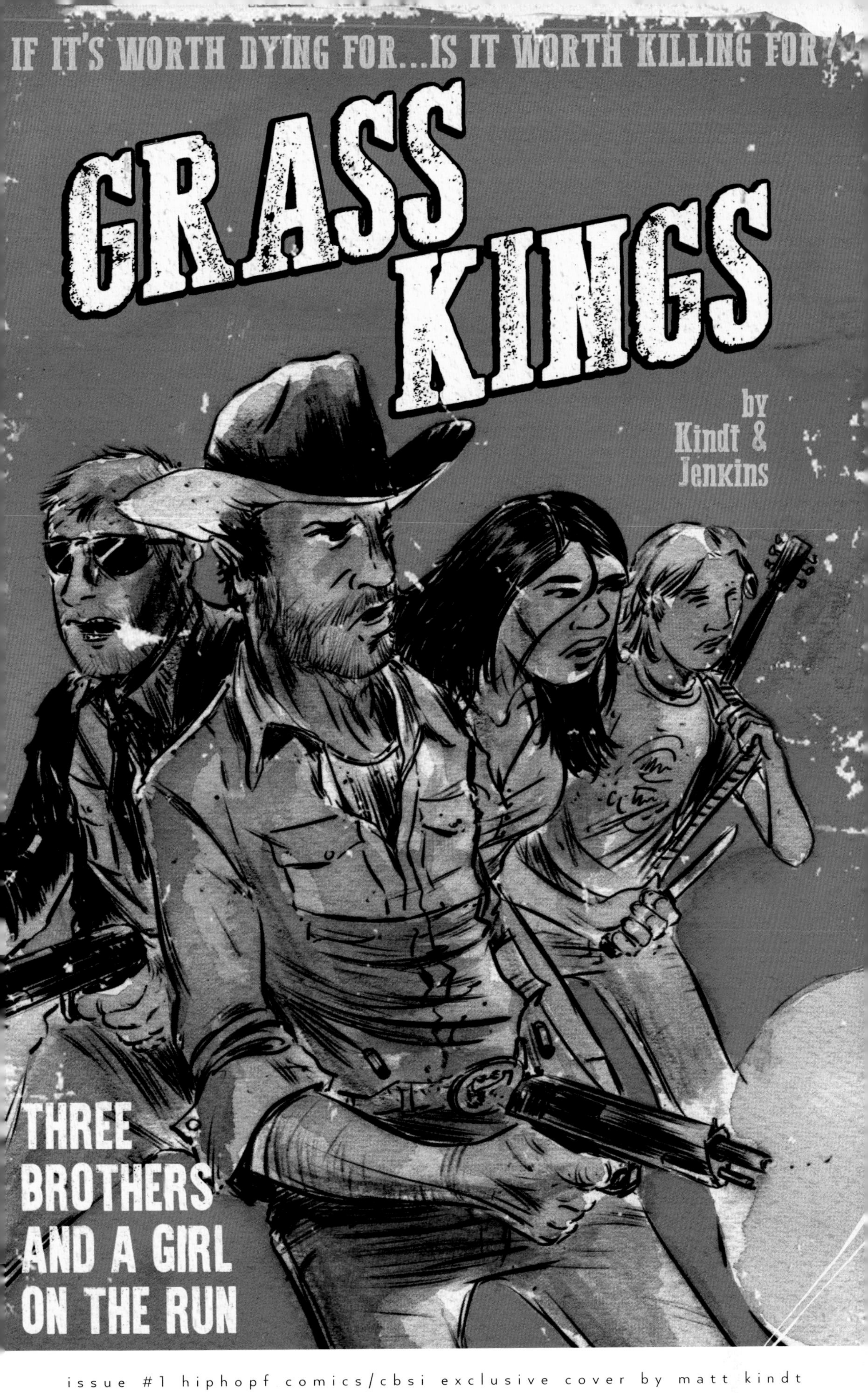


issue #1 hiphopf comics/cbsi exclusive cover by matt kindt

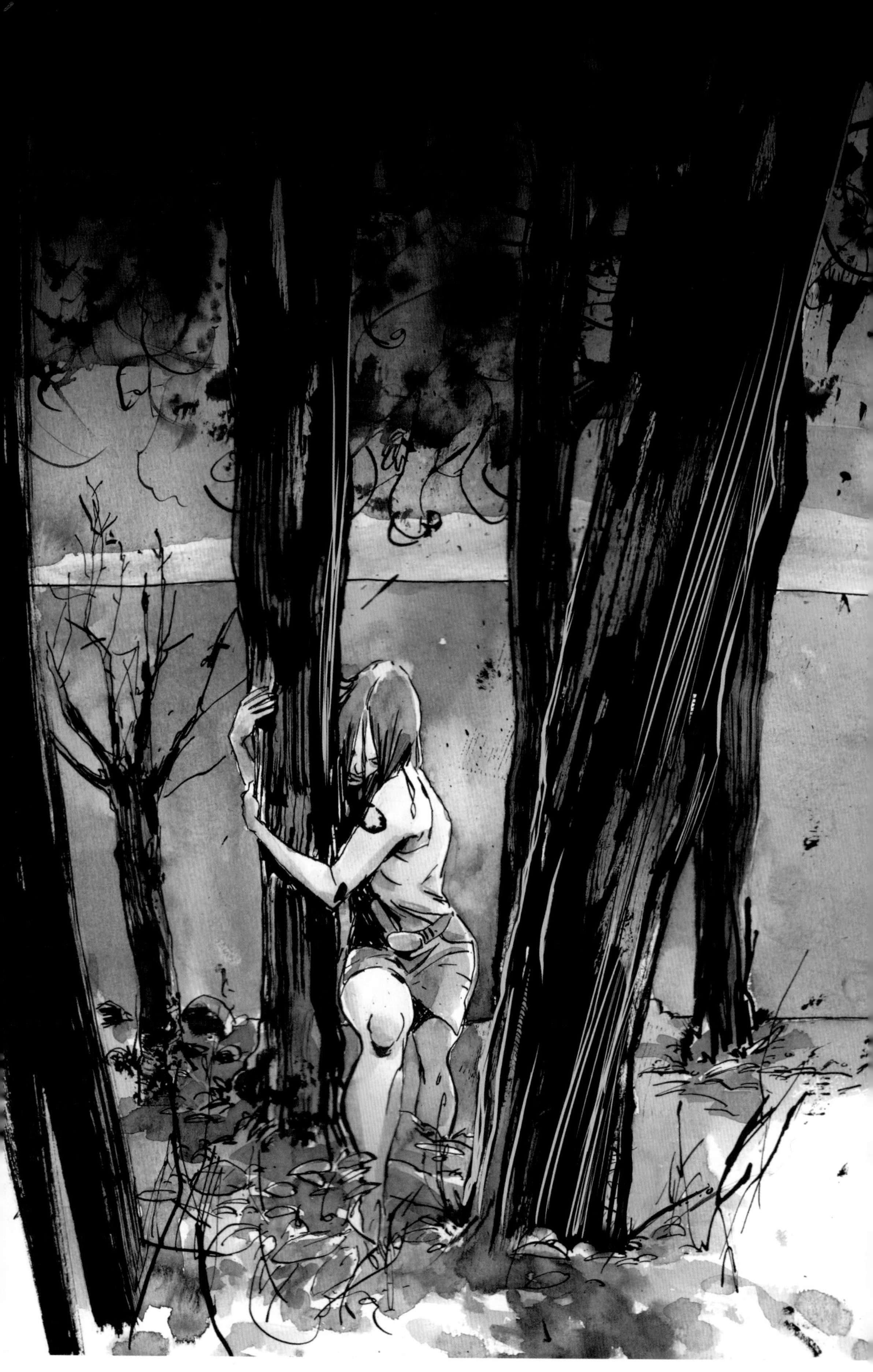

issue #2 cover by tyler jenkins

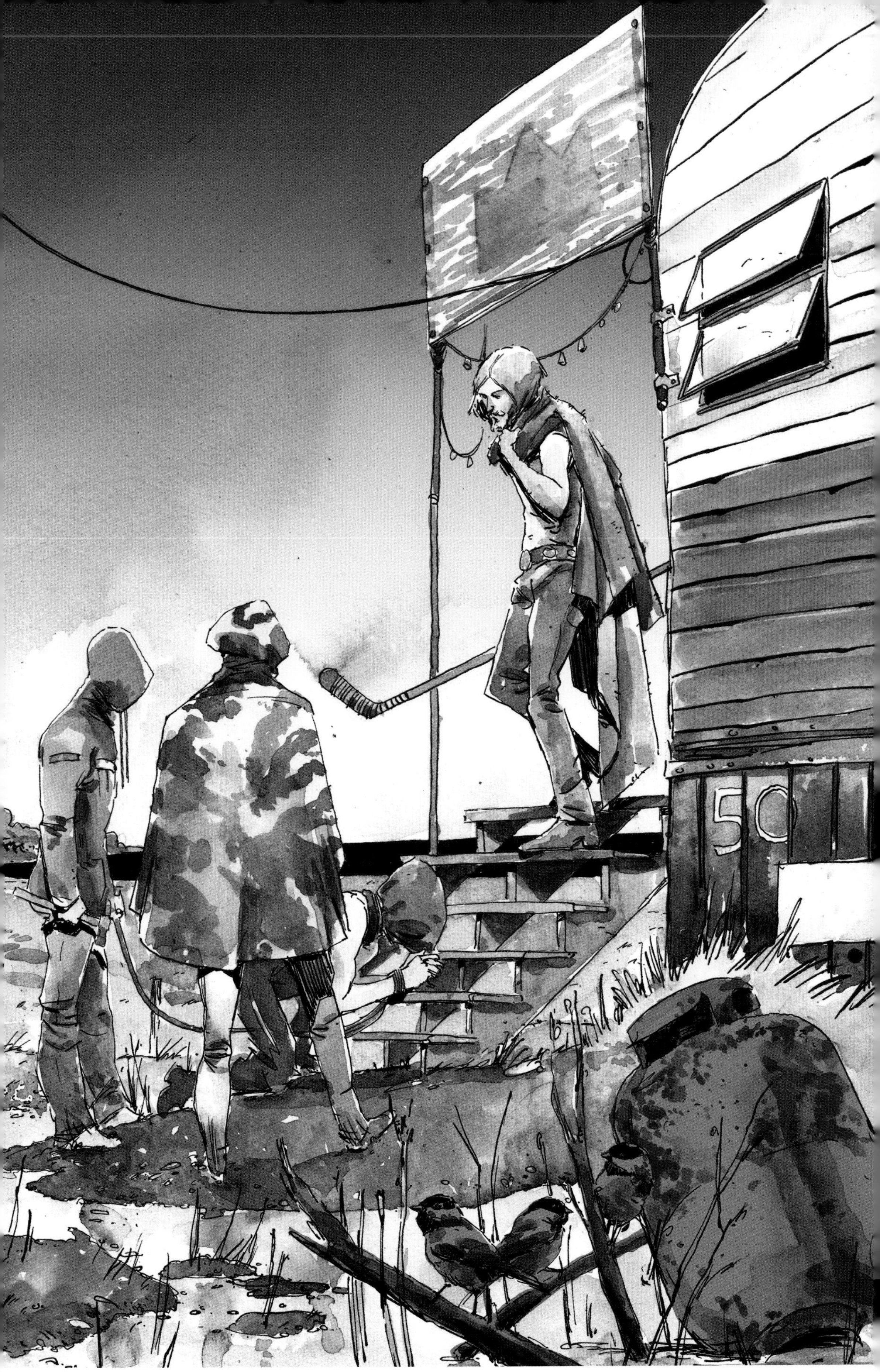
50

issue #2 unlocked retailer variant cover by tyler jenkins

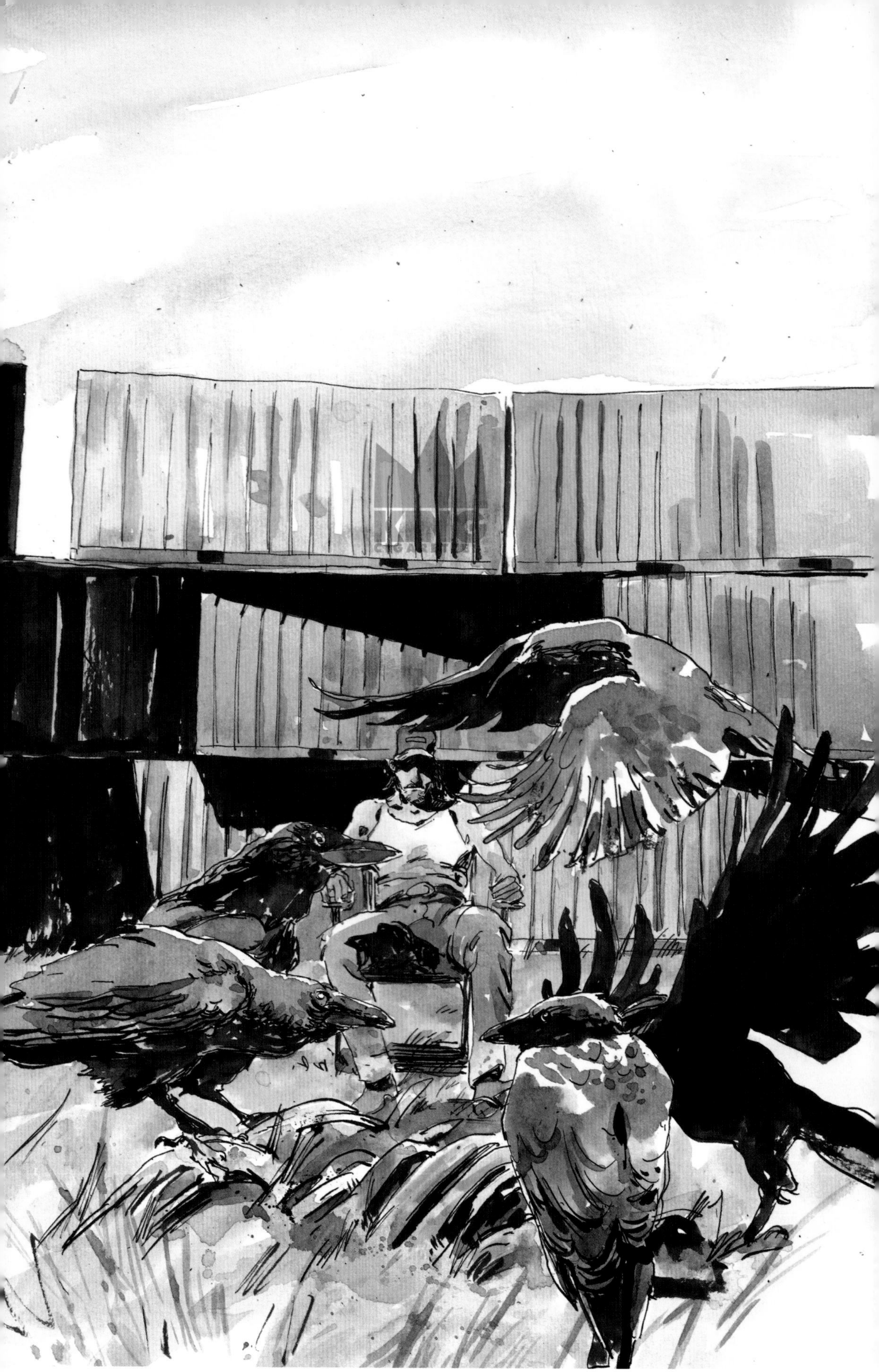

issue #3 cover by tyler jenkins

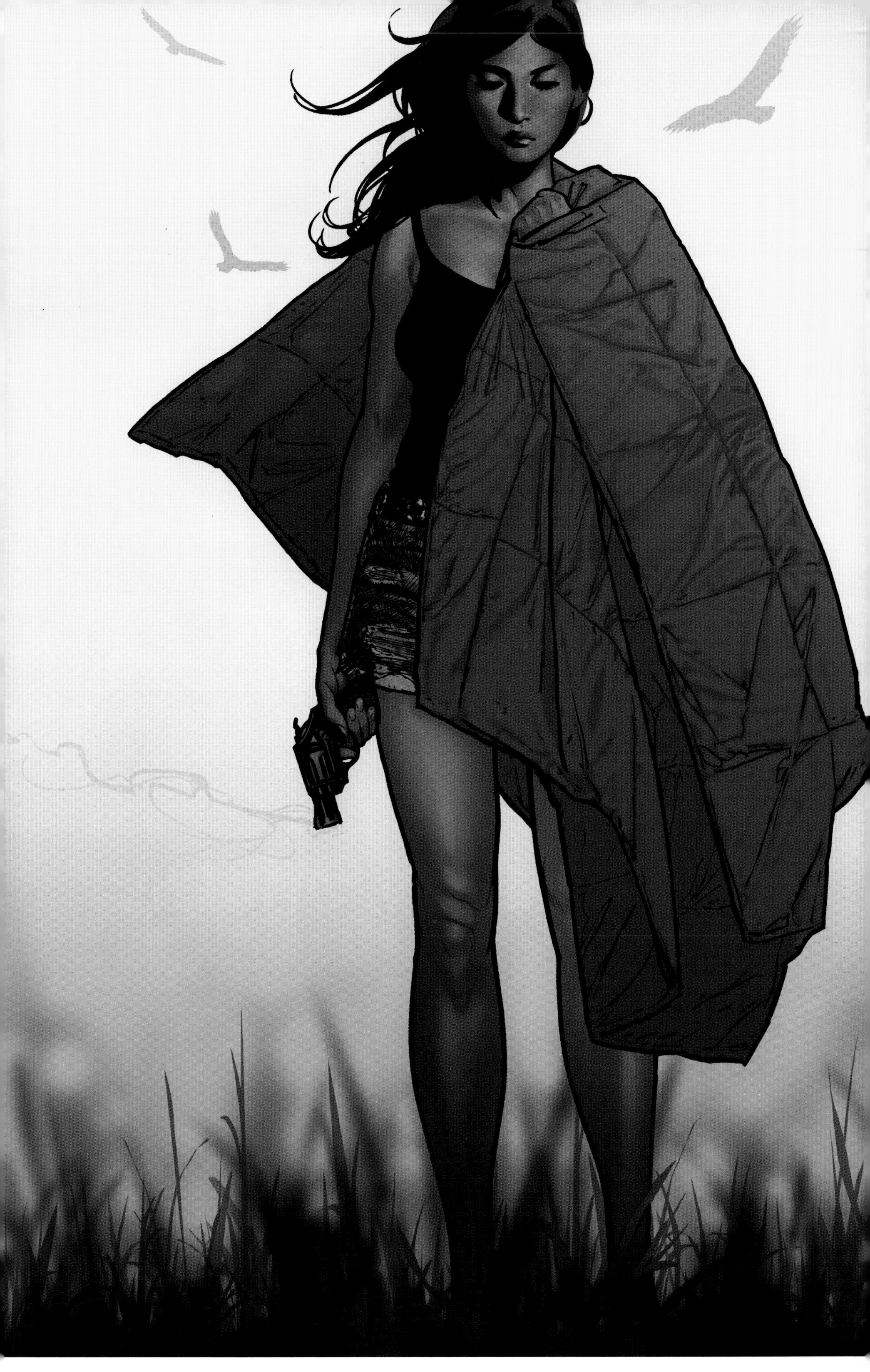

issue #3 unlocked retailer variant cover by ryan sook

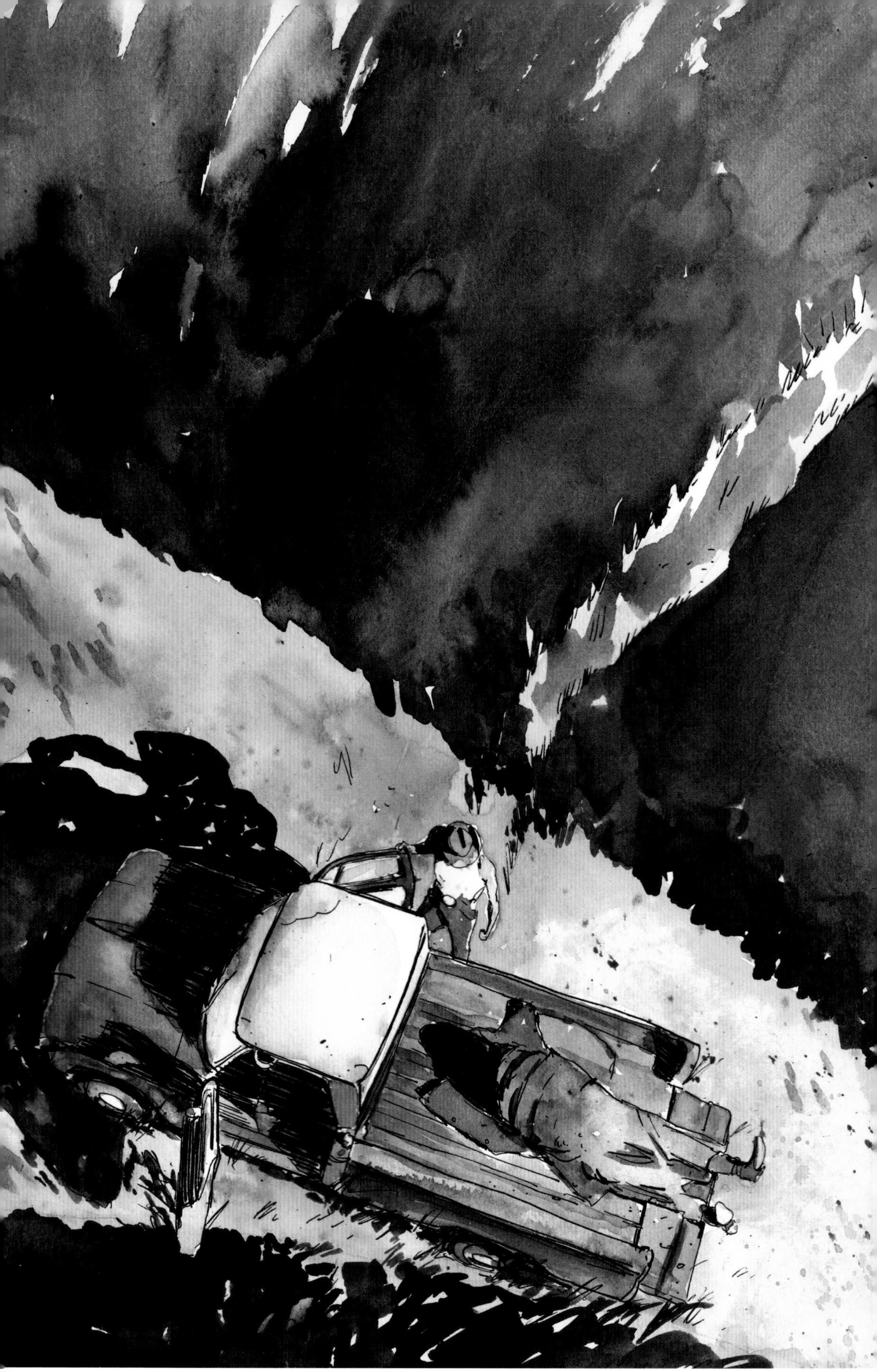

issue #4 cover by tyler jenkins

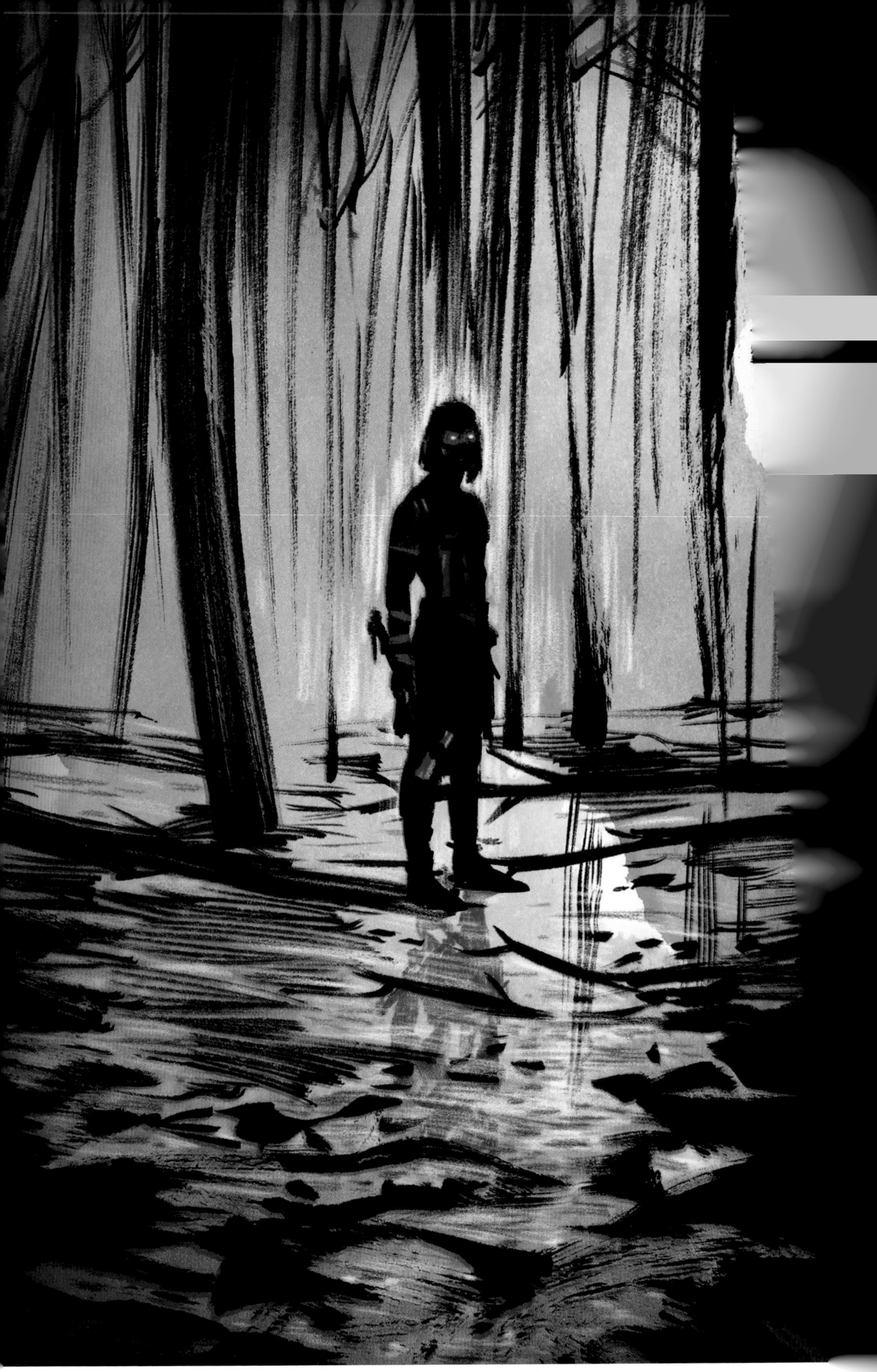

issue #4 unlocked retailer variant cover by tula lotay

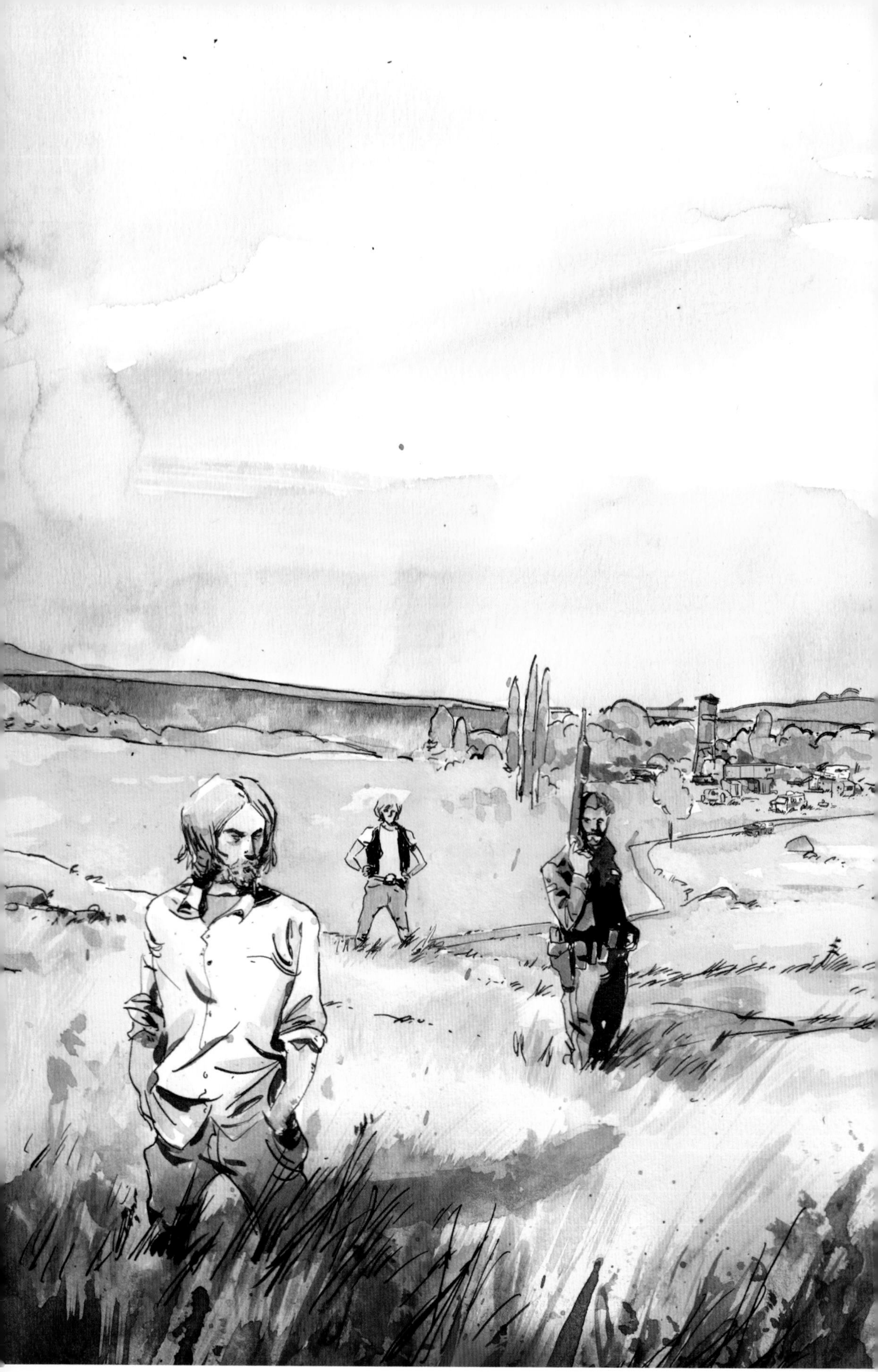

issue #5 cover by tyler jenkins

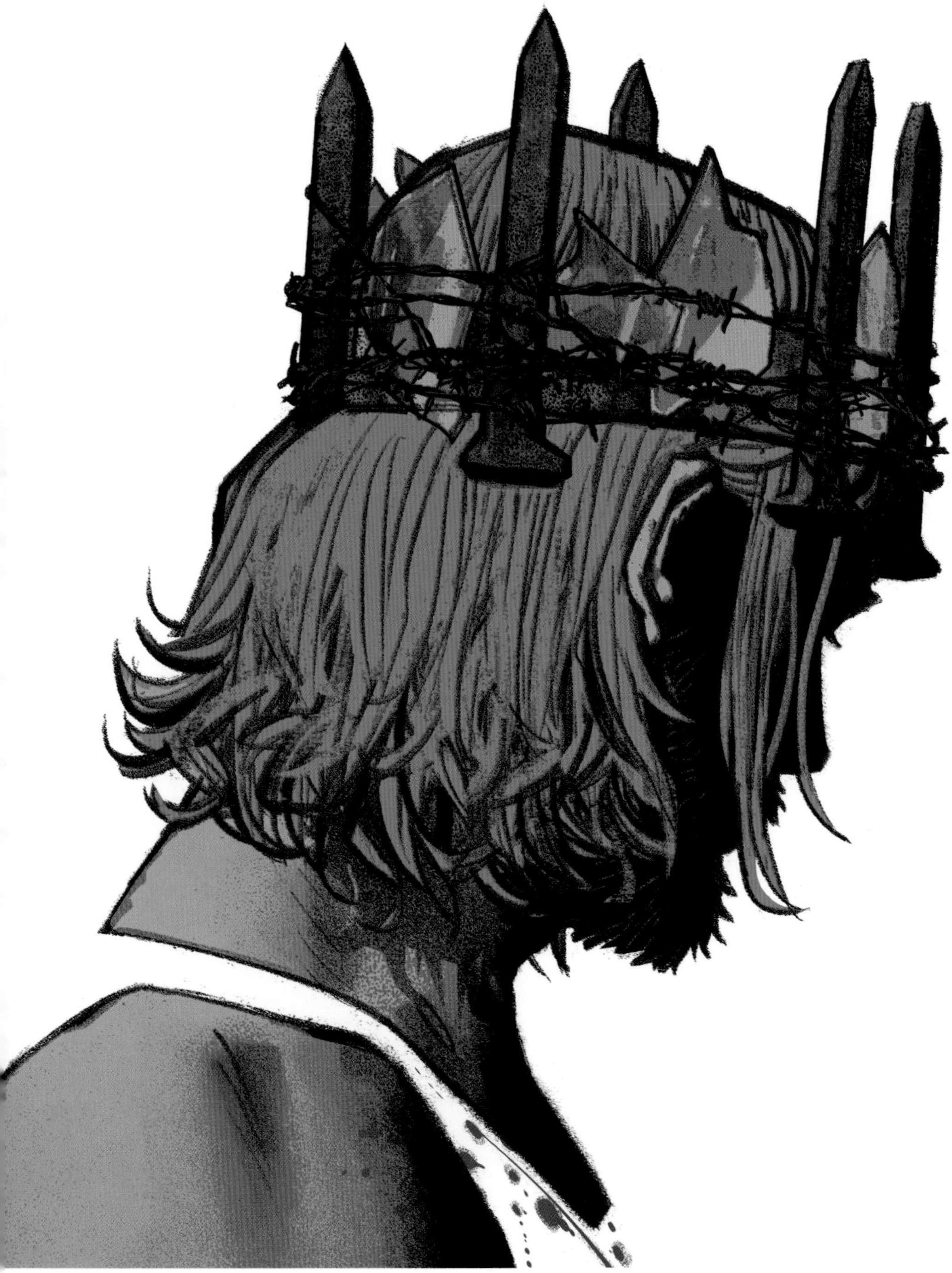

issue #5 unlocked retailer variant cover by greg smallwood

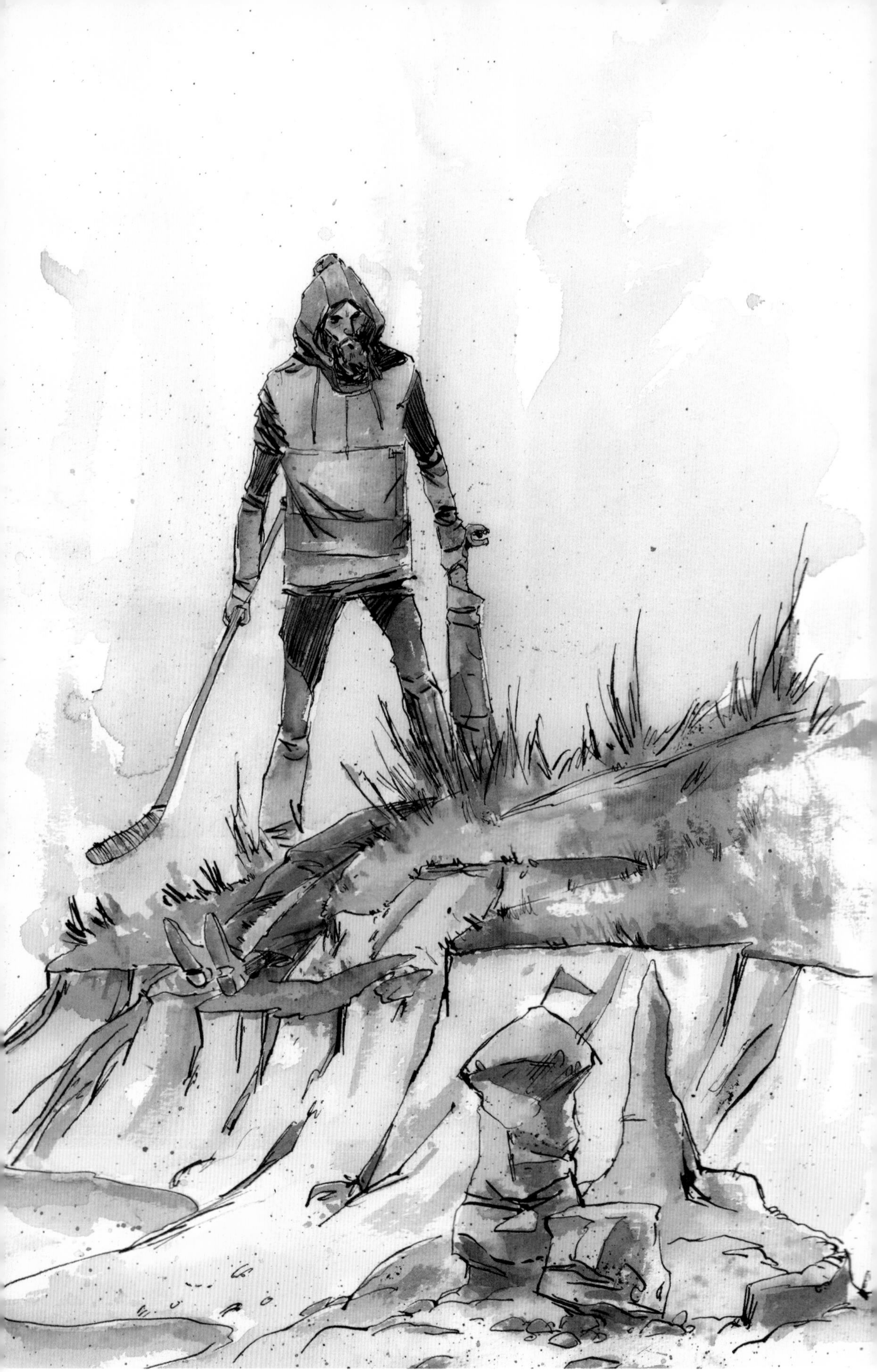

issue #6 cover by tyler jenkins

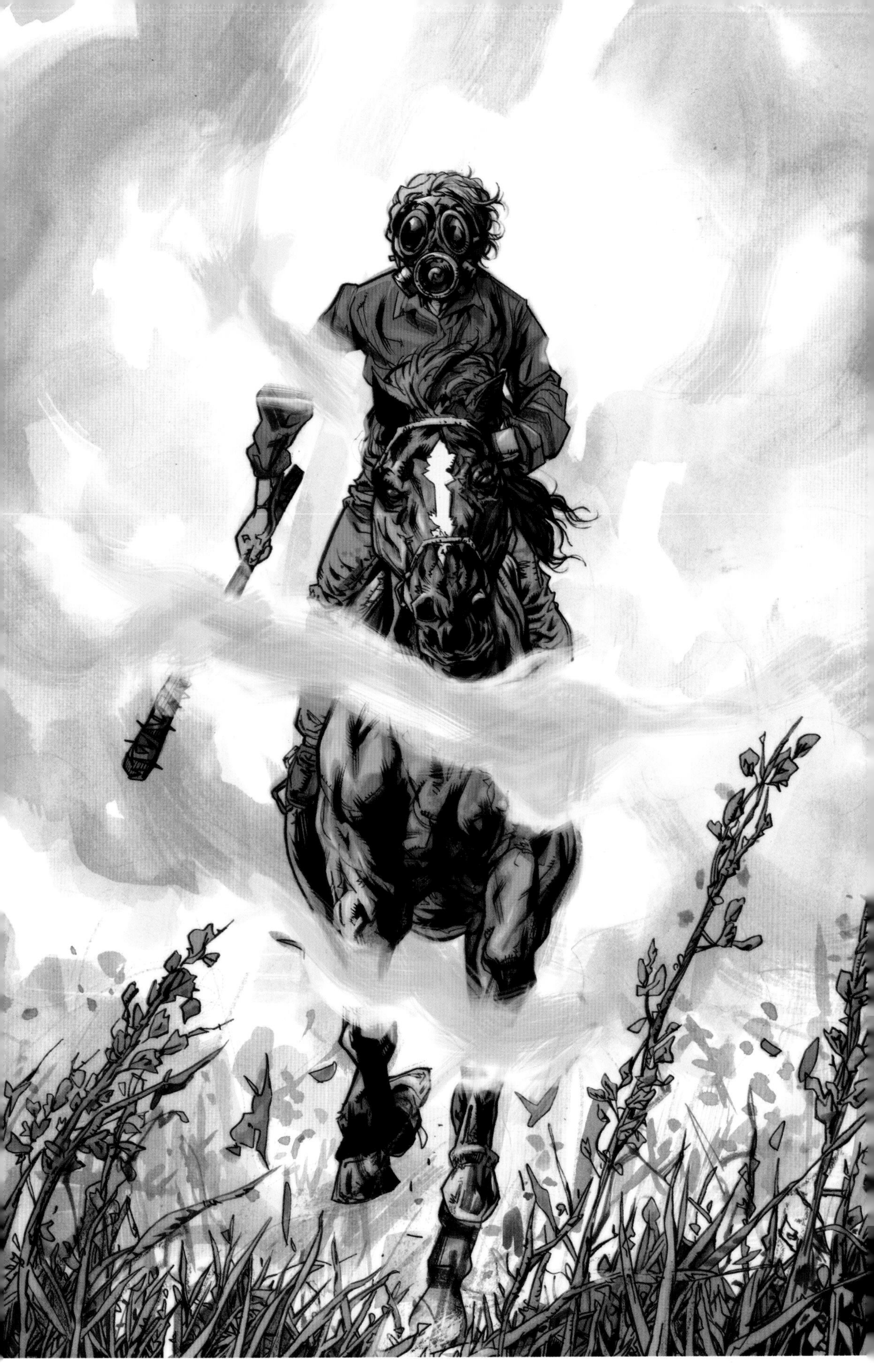

issue #6 unlocked retailer variant cover by ryan kelly

additional artwork by tyler jenkins

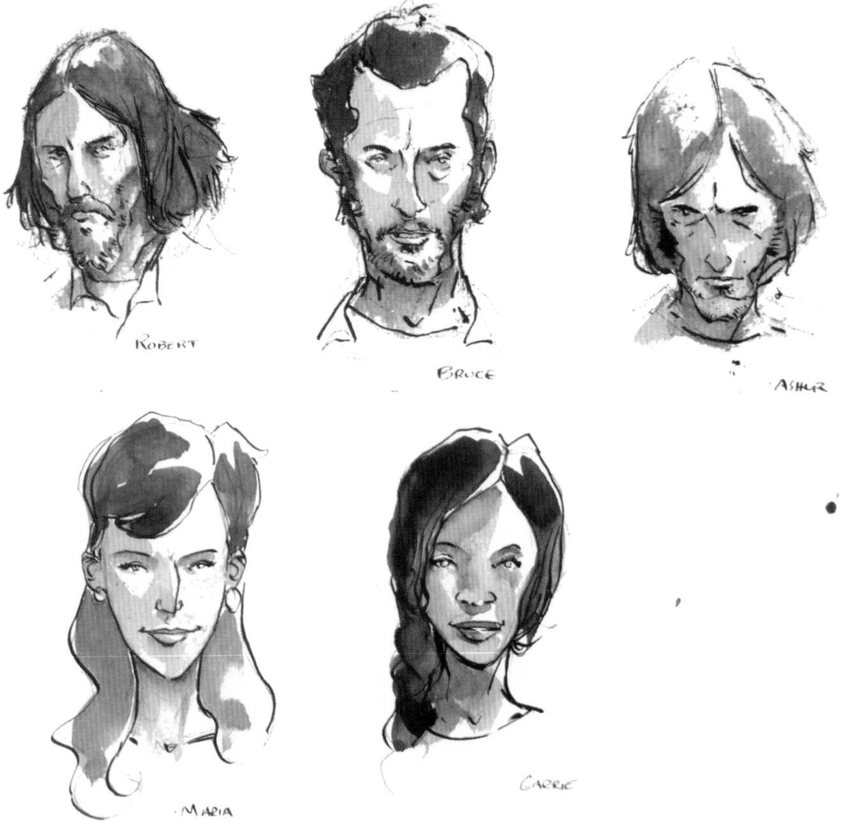
ROBERT
BRUCE
ASHUR
MARIA
CARRIE

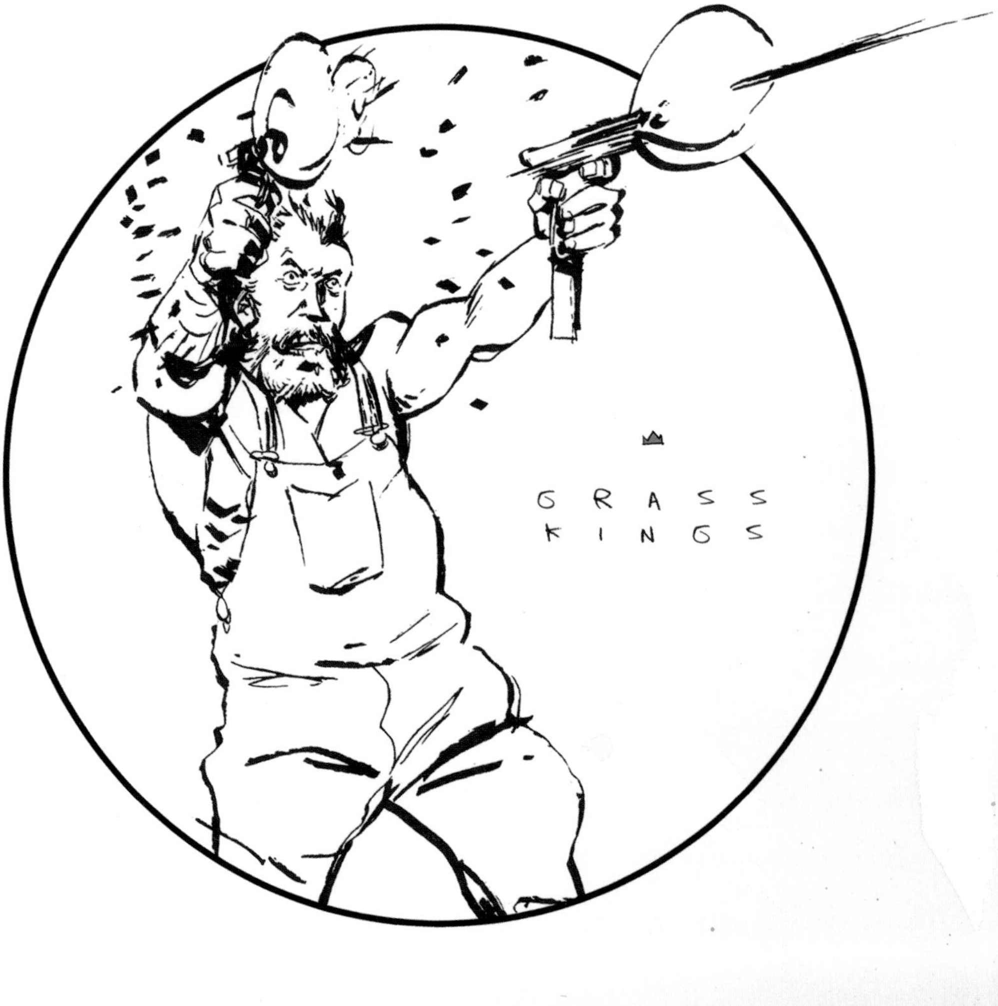
GRASS
KINGS

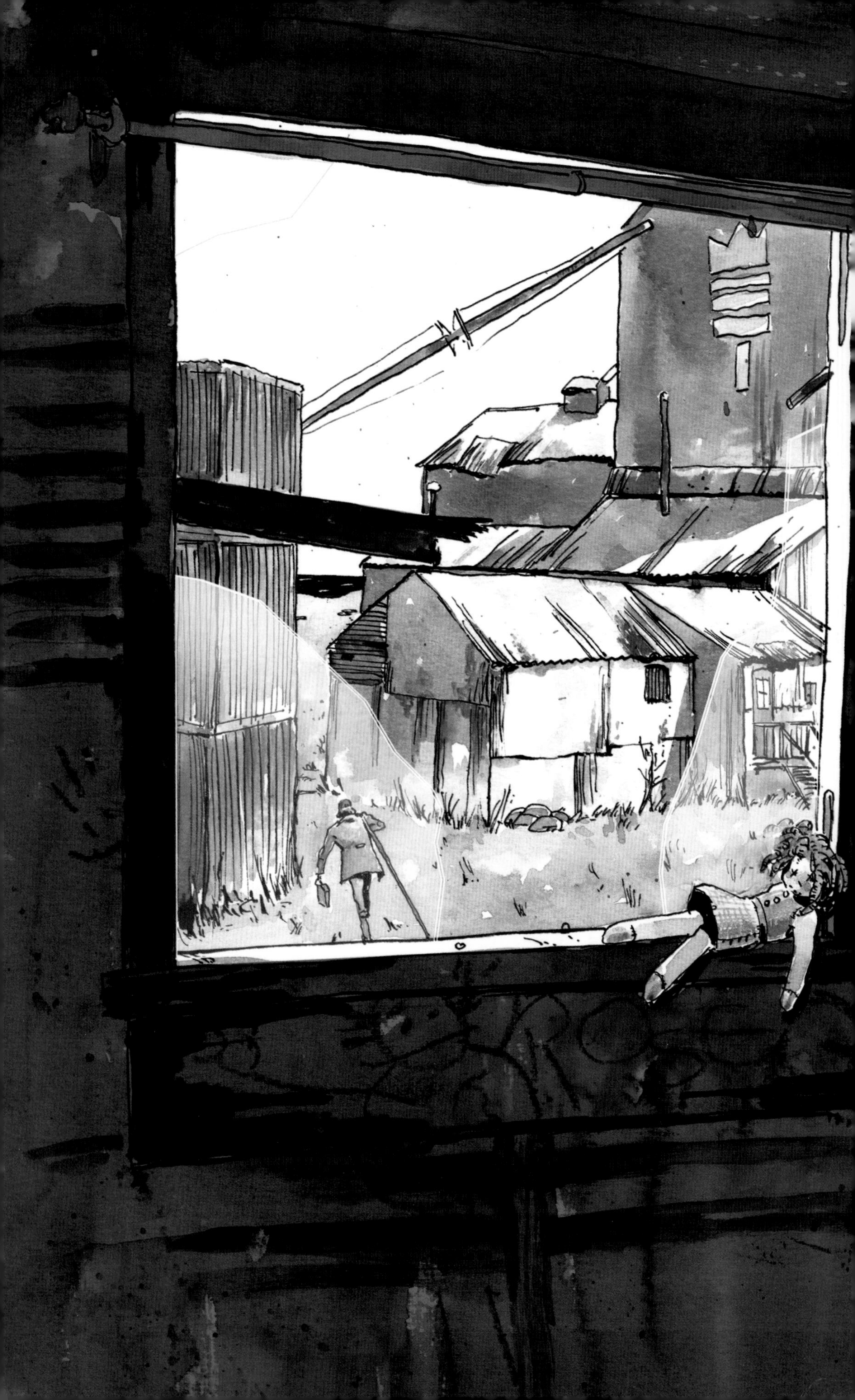

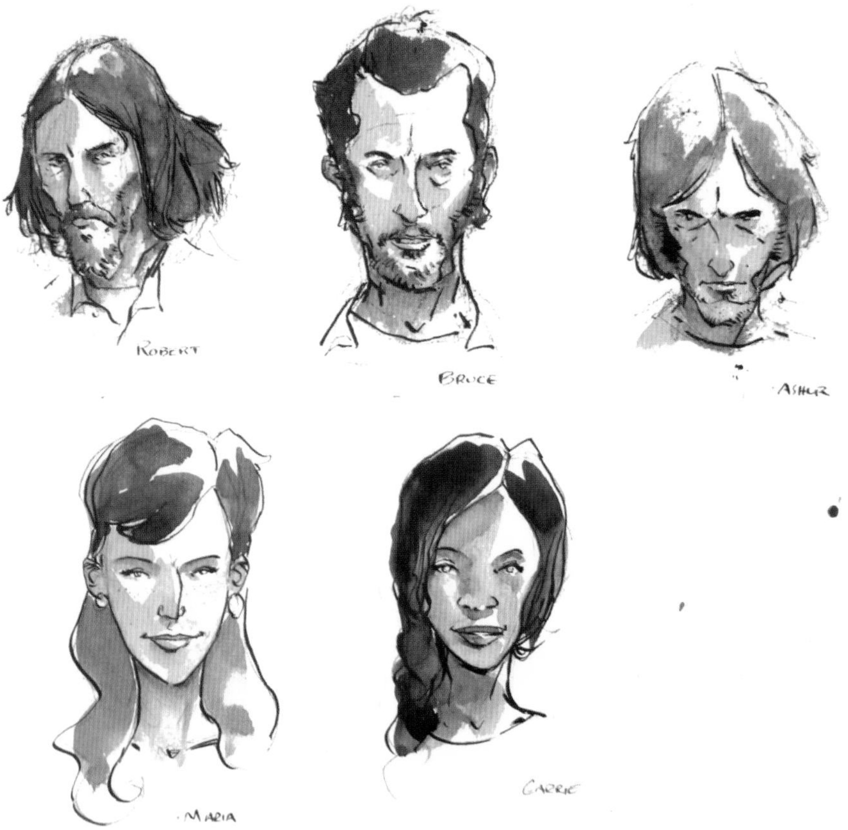
ROBERT
BRUCE
ASHER
MARIA
CARRIE

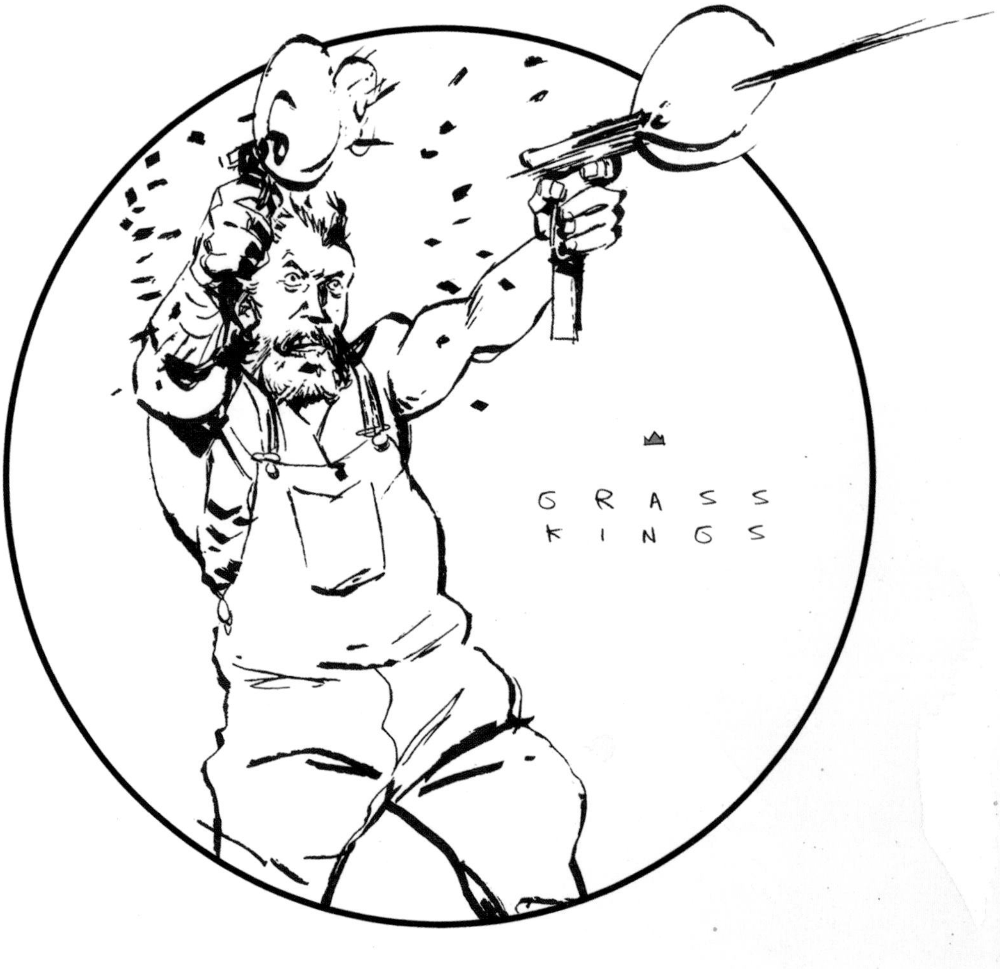
GRASS
KINGS

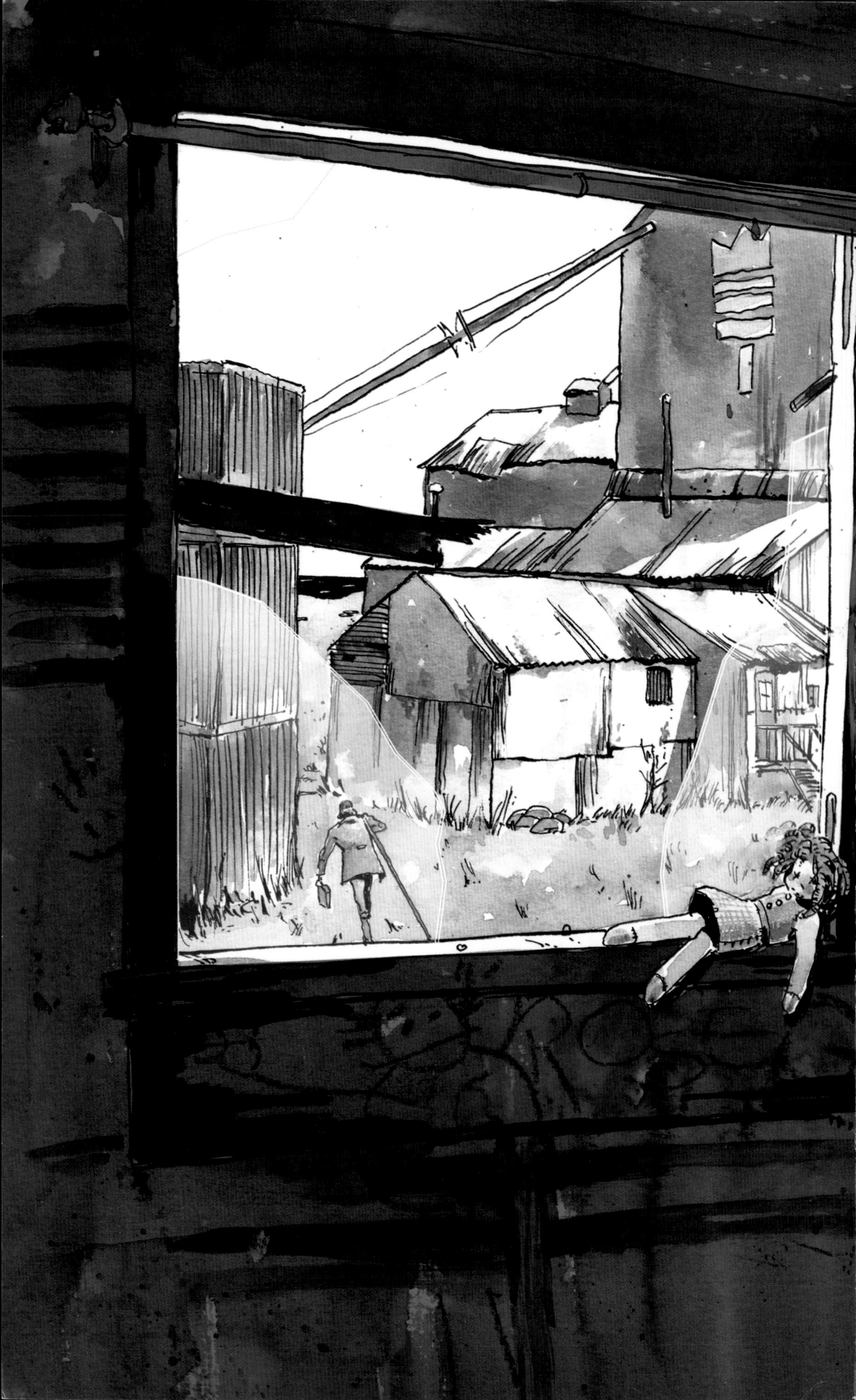

## about the authors

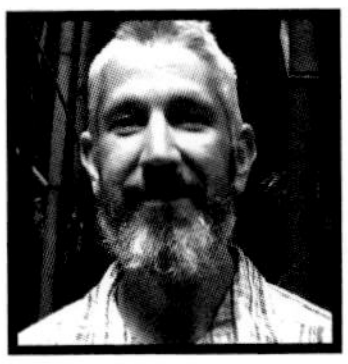

**Matt Kindt** is the *New York Times* best-selling writer and artist of the comics and graphic novels *Dept. H, Mind MGMT, Revolver, 3 Story, Super Spy, 2 Sisters,* and *Pistolwhip,* as well as the writer of *Grass Kings, Ether, Justice League of America* (DC), *Spider-Man* (Marvel), *Unity, Ninjak, Rai,* and *Divinity* (Valiant). He has been nominated for six Eisner and six Harvey Awards (and won once). His work has been published in French, Spanish, Italian, German and Korean.

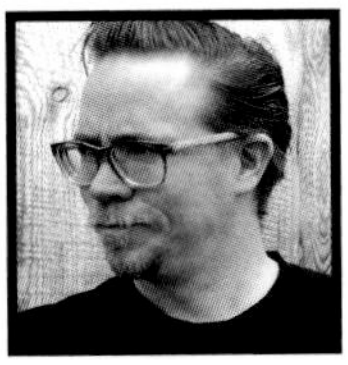

**Tyler Jenkins** is a dude who draws comics, makes art and music, and on occasion barbecues a mean back of ribs. Notable accomplishments this year include, primarily, launching the series *Grass Kings* with Matt Kindt and BOOM! Studios. Tyler is best known for creating *Peter Panzerfaust* with Kurtis Wiebe and handling art duties on *Snow Blind* with Ollie Masters and *Neverboy* with Shaun Simon. Tyler lives in rural Alberta, Canada, with his wife, 3 small child-like creatures, and more gophers than you can shove in a tin pail. Find him at tylerjenkinsprojects on Instagram.

Espionage and action from the
Eisner Award-nominated team
behind *Grass Kings*

MATT KINDT
and
TYLER JENKINS

ALWAYS BE
PREPARED